The United States, Norway and the Cold War, 1954–60

Mats R. Berdal
Research Fellow
International Institute for Strategic Studies
London

Foreword by Olav Riste

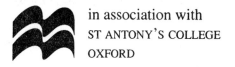

in association with
ST ANTONY'S COLLEGE
OXFORD

First published in Great Britain 1997 by
MACMILLAN PRESS LTD
Houndmills, Basingstoke, Hampshire RG21 6XS and London
Companies and representatives throughout the world

A catalogue record for this book is available from the British Library.

ISBN 0–333–60700–7

 First published in the United States of America 1997 by
ST. MARTIN'S PRESS, INC.,
Scholarly and Reference Division,
175 Fifth Avenue, New York, N.Y. 10010

ISBN 0–312–16281–2

Library of Congress Cataloging-in-Publication Data
Berdal, Mats R., 1965–
The United States, Norway and the Cold War, 1954–60 / Mats R.
Berdal ; foreword by Olav Riste.
p.   cm. —(St. Antony's series)
Includes bibliographical references and index.
ISBN 0–312–16281–2
1. United States—Foreign relations—Norway.   2. Norway—Foreign
relations—United States.   3. Cold War.   I. Title.   II. Series.
E183.8.N6B47   1996
327.730481—dc20   96–22554
                                                              CIP

This book is printed on paper suitable for recycling and made from fully managed and sustained forest sources.

10   9   8   7   6   5   4   3   2   1
06   05   04   03   02   01   00   99   98   97

Printed in Great Britain by
The Ipswich Book Company Ltd
Ipswich, Suffolk

Contents

Abbreviations

The following abbreviations appear regularly in footnotes and in the text:

AFNORTH	-	Allied Forces Northern Europe
AFOIN	-	Air Force Office of Intelligence (US)
BJSM	-	British Joint Services Mission, Washington, DC
CINCLANT	-	Commander in Chief, Atlantic (US)
CINCNORTH	-	Commander in Chief, Allied Forces Northern Europe
CNO	-	Chief of Naval Operations
CONUS	-	Continental United States
COS	-	British Chiefs of Staff
DDEL	-	Dwight D. Eisenhower Library, Abilene, Kansas
DOD	-	Department of Defence (Pentagon)
EDP	-	Emergency Defence Plan
FD	-	Det Kgl. Forsvarsdepartement (The Norwegian Ministry of Defence)
IAC	-	Intelligence Advisory Committee (US)
JCS	-	Joint Chiefs of Staff (US)
JIC	-	Joint Intelligence Committee (US)
JLPC	-	Joint Logistics Plans Committee (US)
JSPC	-	Joint Strategic Plans Committee (US)
MAAG	-	Military Assistance Advisory Group (US)
MDAP	-	Mutual Defence Assistance Programme (US)
NID	-	Naval Intelligence Division of the Admiralty Staff
NIE	-	National Intelligence Estimate (US)
NEC	-	Northern European Command (NATO)
NHC	-	US Navy Operational Archives Branch, Naval Historical Center, Washington, DC
NARA	-	National Archives and Records Administration, Washington, DC
OCB	-	Operations Coordinating Board of the NSC
ONI	-	Office of Naval Intelligence (US)
OPNAV	-	Office of the Chief of Naval Operations (US)
RNAF	-	Royal Norwegian Air Force
SAC	-	Strategic Air Command
SNIE	-	Special National Intelligence Estimate (US)

SSB	-	Ballistic Missile Submarine
SSB(N)	-	Ballistic Missile Submarine, Nuclear Powered
SSN	-	Nuclear-fuelled Submarine
TACAN	-	Tactical Air Navigation
UD	-	Det Kgl. Utenriksdepartementet (The Norwegian Ministry of Foreign Affairs)
USNIP	-	United States Naval Institute Proceedings
WHO	-	White House Office

Acknowledgements

In preparing this book I have benefited greatly from the support and encouragement of numerous individuals in Great Britain, the United States and Norway. At Oxford, Professor Robert O'Neill very effectively supervised and guided my research for three years. I would also like to record a special debt of gratitude to Dr Eric Grove who kindly offered his advice and comments on those aspects of my work relating to British and US naval policy. My thanks are due also to Captain Gordon Wilson and Caroline Llewellyn at the Royal Naval College at Greenwich, both of whom helped me in every possible way during the course of my study.

In the United States I am particularly grateful to Mrs Kathy Lloyd at the US Navy Operational Archives Branch in Washington D.C. who spent so much time ensuring that I found the relevant files and records. The library staff at the Dwight D. Eisenhower Library in Abilene, Kansas, also gave generously of their time during my stay at the library.

In Norway I am much indebted to Professor Olav Riste and Professor Rolf Tamnes at the Norwegian Institute for Defence Studies. They encouraged me to focus on this particular period of the Cold War and provided important advice and valuable comments as the study progressed. Finally, I thank Dominique Jacquin for her constant support and encouragement.

Foreword

With the progressive release of official records under the thirty years' rule, now gradually becoming the standard in the western countries, historical studies of the Cold War have multiplied. Already it is possible to identify certain "waves" in the flood of books and articles: First, an American wave, due to the United States being for a long time in the forefront in the release of documents; then a European wave, as Britain and then France, albeit with many restrictions, instituted their thirty-year rule. We are now entering what will hopefully turn out to be a Russian wave as the archives of the former Soviet Union become available for research.

However, as so often before the international history of the Cold War has tended to be described almost exclusively in great-power terms and based on the documents of the great powers. With the two superpowers standing head and shoulder above all the other players, it is hardly surprising that US policy, and US–Soviet relations, have been the dominant concern of cold war historians. Yet the middle and minor powers have clearly played more important roles in the half century after the Second World War than in any earlier period of international history. For that reason alone it has been gratifying to note an increasing number of important studies of the Cold War being contributed by historians of countries other than the great powers. Not only do they bring different perspectives to bear on the East-West confrontation, they also represent a tradition of multi-archival and multi-lingual research which has not been a notable feature of American, British, or French scholarship.

In order to make an impact on the international historiography of the Cold War it is of course necessary for the historians of those middle or minor countries to write or at least publish in English. It is therefore not surprising that the majority of such contributions to the literature has come from smaller countries in which English is a close second to the native language – particularly the Netherlands, Denmark, and Norway (although Danish historians are still handicapped by restricted access to their own archives). Authors' names that readily come to mind include Cees Wiebes and Bert Seeman from the Netherlands, Nikolai Petersen from Denmark, and Geir Lundestad and Rolf Tamnes from Norway.

It is in this tradition that this book by Mats Berdal finds its place. It epitomises the best characteristics of the research now coming from the smaller countries: new perspectives wherein the viewpoints and policies of the minor powers do not replace but complement the traditional great power *optique*. As the author stresses, this book is not about Norwegian security policy *per se*. By concentrating instead on Norway's place in American thinking and strategy, and by focusing on the operational level of policy making, he gives us new insight into an alliance relationship which superficially would seem to be just another example of the relations between a protector and his client. By highlighting the perspective of NATO as a superstructure or legitimising framework for bilateral cooperation Dr Berdal has in fact opened up important new avenues for research into the history of the Atlantic Alliance.

Through his wide-ranging research the author has also brought a wealth of hitherto unused sources to bear on Norway's role as a function of its geographic proximity to the Soviet Union, with particular emphasis on intelligence gathering for early warning and route planning for strategic bombing, and later for keeping an eye on an area of intensive build-up of Soviet naval strength. By focusing on naval strategy he furthermore sheds important new light on Britain's – albeit declining – maritime role in the North Atlantic. In the political sphere he shows how the US State Department's perception of Norway's role as in many ways the linchpin of NATO's northern flank tempered the Defense Department's occasional impatience with Norway's cautious approach to allied activities that might be construed as provocative by the Soviets.

Olav Riste

Introduction

AMERICAN STRATEGIC POLICY, NORWAY AND THE COLD WAR IN THE 1950S

This book examines the role and position of Norway in the strategic policies of the American government between 1954 and 1960. By strategic policy I refer broadly to the set of policies conceived and pursued by the American administration with a view to containing the political and military threat posed by the Soviet Union. Strategic policy, therefore, seeks to integrate both *military* and *political* dimensions in support of a given strategic objective which, in this case, was to prevent "the Soviet Union from using the power and position it won as a result [of World War II] to reshape the post-war international order."[1] The meaning of *strategy* in this context corresponds closely to Edward Mead Earle's definition of the term as "the art of controlling and utilizing the resources of a nation or a coalition of nations – including its armed forces, to the end that its vital interests shall be effectively promoted and secured against enemies, actual, potential or merely presumed."[2]

The changes in "basic national security policy" announced by the Eisenhower administration in late 1953 and enshrined in NSC 162/2, provide a natural point of departure for this study.[3] Whereas NSC 68 under President Truman had sought to avoid excessive reliance on nuclear weapons, recommending instead a substantial build-up across the board of military capabilities, Eisenhower's "New Look" promised just the opposite: explicit reliance on the deterrent effect of American nuclear forces. Strategic weapons would threaten the Soviet and the Chinese homelands; tactical weapons would be employed for traditional battlefield purposes in order to offset Soviet advantages in geography and manpower, especially in Europe.[4] By stressing the ubiquitous role of nuclear weapons, Eisenhower hoped to reconcile the requirements of defence on the one hand, with maintaining service economies and a balanced budget on the other. In the words of John Lewis Gaddis, "central to the strategy was the idea of regaining the initiative while simultaneously lowering costs".[5] It represented a new set of budgetary and strategic priorities to which Norway and other allies had to adjust.

Examining Norway's specific place in American policy, however, requires more specific questions to be asked. Underlying and informing this study are three basic questions:

(1) In which areas of American strategic policy did Norway make its principal contribution towards the overall containment strategy adopted by the Eisenhower administration? The question requires an assessment of the nature of Norway's role in relation to American *intelligence* efforts, as well as to American *air* and *maritime* strategy. But it also raises the issue of Norway's value as a *political ally* during a phase of the Cold War which was characterised by intense ideological hostility, rapid technological change and deeply entrenched fear within the American political and defence establishment of surprise attack as the opening move of any future war.

(2) What were the main factors which *determined* Norway's relative importance as an ally in American eyes? The copious literature on alliances indicate a range of possible factors that may influence the importance of one ally to the other.[6] Among the elements that need to be considered are: Norway's geographic proximity to the Soviet Union; the impact of rapid changes in weapons technology; American assessments of Soviet capabilities and intentions in north-west Russia; and Norway's *own* perceptions and policies.

(3) Finally, in light of Norway's strong emphasis on keeping confrontation with the Soviet Union at a low level, the question arises as to the degree of understanding shown by the American administration towards the constituent elements of Norway's "low tension policy" (*lavspenningspolitikk*) in Northern Europe. This issue involves a closer look at administration attitudes towards Norway's self-imposed restrictions with respect to foreign bases, nuclear weapons and allied military activity in Norway in peacetime.

SOURCES AND LITERATURE: THE NEED TO DISTINGUISH BETWEEN DECLARATORY AND OPERATIONAL POLICY

In his much-acclaimed book *America, Scandinavia and the Cold War, 1945–49*, the Norwegian historian Geir Lundestad notes how "very little, if anything, is written about the role of Scandinavia and the policies of the United States toward this part of Europe."[7] Lundestad was concerned about the role of Scandinavia during the intensification of East-West rivalry in the years 1945 to 1949. Yet, with one important exception, his observation also holds true for the role of the Scandinavian countries in the policies of the United States after 1949. A survey of the literature shows that the policies and strategies of great powers towards Norway after 1955 in particular, have not been examined in sufficient depth.[8] The exception is provided by a pioneering study in which Rolf Tamnes offers the first comprehensive treatment of "the Cold War in the High North," covering the period from 1943 to the late 1980s.[9] While Tamnes' work provides an important point of reference for this study, there are two areas where this book differs in its emphasis. First, it devotes more attention to the maritime dimension of American interests in Norway and its contiguous sea areas. Specifically, it explores what these interests entailed in terms of *actual* preparations for war; how they were related to the diminishing role of Britain and the Royal Navy in the North Atlantic, especially after 1957, and the extent to which US naval activity complicated Norway's pursuit of a "low tension policy" in the region. Second, the present book examines Norway's role as a political ally of the US by focusing specifically on Norway's mediating role in US–Icelandic relations in the 1950s. The paucity of primary sources has until recently complicated the study of Iceland's special role in relation to US defence plans in the late 1940s and 1950s. Yet, as will be seen, throughout the fifties Iceland was viewed as a critically important link in US strategic and defence planning.

The comparative neglect of Scandinavia in much of the literature on the Cold War owes much to the fact that, whereas the broad strategic significance of the region, and especially Norway, came to be recognised by the United States during the course of the Second World War, in the period between 1945 and 1960 the affairs of the region were rarely of direct, personal and sustained interest to the President and his immediate circle of advisers. There are, of course, important exceptions to this pattern of limited presidential and top-level involvement with respect to Scandinavia. Between 1947 and 1949 high-level American interest in the region as a whole increased, culminating in Foreign Minister Halvard Lange's visit to Washington in February 1949. Then, "for a few days, Truman, the top military leadership, and the State Department were all actively involved in discussions about Scandinavia's relationship with the Western powers."[10] During the Eisenhower presidency Norway appeared on the presidential agenda in connection with the U-2 high-altitude aerial reconnaissance programme and the American Arctic inspection zone proposal of April 1958.[11] President Eisenhower also took special, if disapproving, note of Norway's persistent refusal to countenance Spanish membership of NATO and her early recognition of the People's Republic of China[12]. In addition to such specific issues, during the Eisenhower period the Planning Board of the National Security Council (NSC) undertook periodic policy reviews, co-ordinated by the Special Assistant for National Security Affairs, in order to clarify and update high-level policy guidance with respect to both geographic regions and functional issues. Policy review processes involved a re-examination of basic policy objectives and relied on input from relevant agencies such as the Joint Chiefs of Staff (JCS), the Central Intelligence Agency (CIA) and the Office of Civil Defence and Mobilisation (ODM).[13] Two such review processes were undertaken with respect to Scandinavia in the 1950s. On these occasions the President became directly involved in the issues concerning countries in the region.[14] Under Eisenhower, Norway's place in American strategic calculations was also considered *indirectly* by the NSC and its Operations Coordinating Board (OCB) when policies towards Finland and Iceland were reviewed. Finally, individual reports commissioned by the President outside the formal NSC machinery – those concerned with US Overseas Bases, Continental Defence and the Mutual Defence Assistance Programme – contained sections on Norway which touched, directly or indirectly, upon the issue of the country's strategic importance to the US.[15]

On the whole, however, the pattern described above of limited high-level policy attention to Norway was the norm. This is well illustrated by the opening paragraph of a State Department memorandum for the President in November 1954 regarding a forthcoming visit by the Norwegian Prime Minister:

> Prime Minister Torp of Norway requested to see you privately on matters concerning Norwegian defence but this was not practical. In view of the importance he attaches to speaking to you briefly on this, we believe it would be useful if you could speak to him privately for a few moments before or after the luncheon.[16]

However, as will be argued, the fact that Norway was seldom a subject of high-level policy deliberations within the NSC proper, the Planning Board or the Operations Coordinating Board (OCB), does not reflect its real and evolving significance in American strategic policies during the period. This is because any attempt to assess the importance accorded to Norway by the American "administration" requires an appreciation of the different *levels* at which US national security policy was conducted, and of the various institutional *actors* – agencies, armed services and specified commands – whose interests led to a focus on the Northern region. It follows from this that a more complete picture of Norway's importance to the US necessitates a focus on the intermediate layer of government and the *operational* level of policy.

The distinction between declaratory and operational policy was first alluded to by Paul Nitze in 1956.[17] Nitze used the term "action" rather than "operational" policy, defining it as "the general guidelines which we believe should and will in fact govern our actions in various contingencies." By contrast, declaratory policy he defined as "policy statements which have as their aim political and psychological effects."[18] Paul Nitze was a contemporary critic of administration policies, and the declassification of primary sources has made it possible to explore in far greater depth the relationship to which he alluded. David A. Rosenberg, in particular, has shed important new light on the "reality" of US nuclear policy in the early post-war period by disclosing the degree of divergence between declaratory and operational aspects of policy.[19] According to Rosenberg, "massive preemption" encapsulates the essence of US nuclear strategy in the 1950s far better than does the declaratory emphasis on "massive retaliation".[20] Similarly, in Martin Navias's authoritative study of British strategic planning between 1955 and 1958, the distinction drawn between declaratory and deployment policy is used to illustrate how service departments pursued policies that diverged from a declaratory emphasis on massive retaliation between 1952 and 1957.[21] In both these cases, the availability of hitherto classified primary sources has meant that the notion of operational policy has been applied more restrictively, not merely referring to "general guidelines" as Nitze put it in his 1956 article. A more precise definition is also adopted for the purposes of this study. Specifically, by operational policy is understood: planning, exercises and service programmes carried out in peacetime in order to maximise military effectiveness and support specific missions in the event of war.

The distinction between operational and declaratory policy is central to a more complete understanding of Norway's place in American strategy for two reasons. In the first place, and most obviously, it allows for a more accurate assessment to be made of the extent and nature of cooperation between the two countries in key areas such as intelligence, strategic air operations and naval strategy. Norway's specific contribution to the US in all three of these areas resulted from the interaction of several factors of which Norway's geographic location, advances in military technologies and US perceptions of Soviet threats emanating from submarine and air bases in north-west Russia, were among the most important. While this study, like previous studies, highlights Norway's position in relation to American intelligence efforts and air strategy, it draws particular attention to Norway's evolving importance in American maritime strategy. Furthermore, Norway was also seen by the State Department as having an important political role to play within the Nordic region, especially with regard to Denmark and Iceland. This aspect of Norway's role in

US strategy clearly demonstrates that the character of an alliance relationship is "never governed solely by quantitative or objective factors."[22] It is also shaped by less tangible and non-material factors which do not easily form the basis for general propositions about alliance behaviour.

As indicated above, however, there is a second and more subtle issue which a clearer understanding of operational activities highlights. In an early study, George Liska, a pioneer in the study of alliances, explored the inherent relationship between the "efficacy of alliances" on the one hand, and the degree of integration or non-integration among their members on the other.[23] Liska noted that while "technical possibilities may permit a measure of non-integration and domestic political necessities may require it," there are "relatively distinct areas of activity" where integration among allies is needed to ensure that "parties cannot act separately without crippling dislocation."[24] One of these areas, Liska argued, "encompasses command over forces in the field, backed by governmental consultation in the sphere of political, economic and military policy planning and strategy."[25] A second key area "encompasses facilities for communications, transport and supply of all sorts."[26] As will be seen, the degree of integration between the US and Norway at the operational level – in areas designed to avoid "crippling dislocation" of activity in the event of war – increased steadily and assumed more regularised forms throughout the 1950s. Yet, at the same time, Norway also placed explicit limits on the degree of integration which it was prepared to accept within the alliance. This was done through the adoption of a "non-nuclear policy" and the other self-imposed limitations in the realm of military policy.[27] These *declared* limits served important domestic and external political purposes, yet the exact relationship between declaratory and operational policy has always been more difficult to ascertain. It is a relationship which raises a number of interesting questions, a key one of which was formulated by Nitze himself, namely, at what point does declaratory policy become ineffective in its political consequences if it deviates too far from operational policy.[28] A greater understanding of this relationship is now possible owing to the growing availability of American, British and Norwegian sources from the period, including the highly sensitive areas of intelligence and military planning. This book, which is based on extensive work in American, British and Norwegian archives should be seen as a contribution towards the effort to obtain a more thorough understanding of the various dimensions of, as well as the strength of the ties that shaped, the US–Norwegian alliance.

STRUCTURE OF THE BOOK

To explore the issues outlined above, the book has been divided into four parts. Part I provides the historical context to the period between 1954 and 1960. It focuses on the process whereby the United States gradually succeeded Britain after the Second World War as the main power to which Norway looked for assistance in the security sphere. It also briefly examines the background to Norwegian membership of NATO and the emergence of specific US service and agency interests in Norway before 1954. Part II explores Norway's importance to the US in terms of its ability to provide intelligence on and early warning of Soviet military developments in north-west Russia. Subsumed under this is an assessment of Norway's role in American strategic air operations. Particular attention is devoted in this section to the development of Soviet naval power in the High North on the grounds that it was the American response to this which increasingly came to influence Norway's place in US strategy during the Eisenhower period. In light of this, Part III explores the evolution of US naval interests in the Atlantic and Norway's precise contribution towards American forward maritime strategy in the latter half of the decade. This section also considers, albeit briefly, growing Soviet concerns about developments in the Arctic after 1957. These were generated, above all, by the prospective US deployment of Polaris-type submarines and the forward operations of fast carrier task forces in northern waters. The final part of the book considers the political context of US–Norwegian security cooperation. This involves a look both at Norway's value as a political ally and attitudes of the American administration towards Norway's unilateral policies of restraint.

It is important to stress that this study is not about Norwegian security policy *per se*, nor is it concerned about the crystallisation in the 1950s of what was later to be described as "the Nordic security pattern."[29] While an appraisal of Norwegian policy is clearly important, especially with respect to the issues examined in part IV, the book is primarily concerned with Norway's place in American thinking and strategy. For this reason, the build-up of the Norwegian armed forces and Norwegian concerns about securing allied reinforcements in the event of war between 1954 and 1960 have not been examined in detail. Similarly, the internal Norwegian debates between 1957 and 1960 about the possible contribution of tactical nuclear weapons to the defence of Norway and the limited preparations that were taken with a view to accepting such weapons, have not been the subject of detailed study.[30]

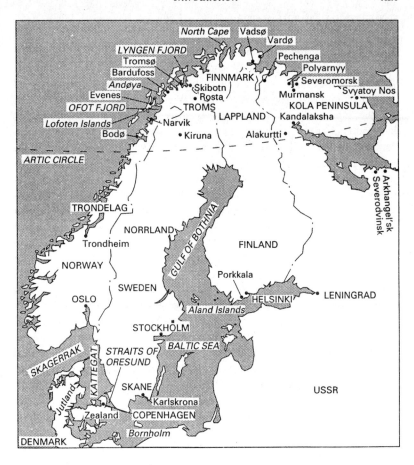

SCANDINAVIA

Part I: The Historical Setting

Both the US and Norway have enjoyed a long background of neutrality and relative isolation from European conflicts. Both have undergone parallel foreign policy revolutions of relatively recent origin as the result of German aggression in the last war and the existing threat of Soviet expansion which has for the first time during peace made relations between the two countries a matter of vital concern to both.[1]

US State Department, 1950

1 Anglo-American Strategic Policy and Norway, 1945–54

I THE POLITICAL CONTEXT: BRITAIN, AMERICA, AND THE CHANGING ASSUMPTIONS OF NORWEGIAN STRATEGIC THINKING, 1945–1949

The British Guarantee and Norway's Rejection of Isolationism

Throughout the Second World War, Norway was recognised by all three members of the Grand Alliance as belonging to the British and American sphere of military responsibility. Moreover, the country was also assumed to be an area of special interest to Britain. This was a reflection both of the development of extensive functional ties during the war and historically close Anglo-Norwegian political and economic links. This "closeness" encompassed and was reinforced by mutual security interests pre-dating their common struggle against German hegemonic aspirations in Europe. More specifically, both Norway and Britain had shared a long-standing concern about the vulnerability of Norway's northernmost province of Finnmark to possible Russian attempts to extend its short ice-free coastline to the Atlantic seaboard.[2] While Britain viewed Norway as belonging to its sphere of interest, Norway for its part came to rely on an "implicit" British security guarantee. As the work of Olav Riste has shown, underlying Norwegian security policy after 1905 was the "unspoken assumption ... that Great Britain with her sea power could be relied upon to prevent, in her own interest, any attempt by other powers to gain a foothold on the Norwegian coast."[3]

However, neither the perceived protection afforded by geographical remoteness, another cornerstone of pre-war Norwegian foreign policy, nor the "presumed protective shield of British naval supremacy in the North Sea" could prevent Norway from becoming involved in the Second World War.[4] Even so, Anglo–Norwegian diplomatic and military co-operation flourished during the years of conflict and occupation, and the functional ties created in the course of the war persisted into the early post-war years.

The reassessment of Norwegian security policy conducted by the government in exile after the debacle of the Norwegian campaign in 1940 led to a recasting of the basic assumptions that guided Norwegian strategic thinking before the war. The clearest expression of this came in May 1942, when the Norwegian Government officially proposed the establishment after the war of a North Atlantic mutual security system embracing both the United States and north-western Europe.[5] The Government's "Atlantic Policy," however, reflected above all a concern with the recrudescence of German militarism and was motivated by a strong desire to reject decisively the pre-war tenets of neutrality.[6] Though this ambitious scheme was gradually abandoned in 1944 and 1945, the new policy of "bridge-building", based on universal co-operation within the framework of the United Nations, did not signify a renunciation of the strategic assumptions upon which the "Atlantic policy" had been based. The Second World War had demonstrated that Norway could no longer be viewed as a strategic periphery, and that with its small and scattered population, it could not hope to defend on its own the longest stretch of coastline on the European continent.[7] In particular, the Norwegian government recognised that Norway's geostrategic importance in the "air age" made it vulnerable to pre-emptive assault in a Great Power conflict.[8] Thus while Norway adopted a neutral bridge-building policy after the war, believing that it "could usefully serve as a conduit of Great Power collaboration," there was never a question of a return to the *status quo ante*.[9] Indeed, according to Riste, the policy of bridge-building was "hardly more than hope against hope for the re-establishment of tacit Great-power understanding about Scandinavia as a sanctuary from the threatening Cold War."[10]

The recognition of new post-war realities was also evident in the assumptions underlying the first programme to rebuild the Norwegian armed forces after the war. In the *Three-Year Plan* for the reconstruction of Norwegian Defence, presented to the Storting in September 1945, it was argued that the "reconstruction of Norwegian defence" would proceed on the assumption that "Norway's armed forces must be able to hold on alone until we get effective assistance from *those who might become our allies*."[11] In practice, this meant that the declaratory emphasis on "bridge-building" between 1945 and late 1947 was accompanied by an attempt to strengthen military co-operation with Britain. Indeed, as far as the Norwegian Government was concerned, post-war Anglo-Norwegian co-operation was not merely a question of functional ties in a narrow military-technical sense. The notion of "semi-alliance" encapsulates more accurately the Norwegian conception of the character of these ties.[12] In this respect, as Olav Riste points out, the unspoken assumption of British assistance in the event of war persisted into the post-war period, though the Norwegian Government was now no longer prepared to take the British guarantee "for granted as being sufficiently motivated by Britain's own interests alone."[13] Norway had, in the first place, to build up its own armed forces to a level sufficient to withstand an attack until effective assistance could be obtained. Later, as the Cold War intensified and it became quite clear that British defence priorities lay elsewhere, the Norwegian political and military leadership turned to the US for assistance in the security sphere rather than opt for a "neutral" Scandinavian Defence Union as promoted by Sweden in 1948–1949.

Yet, the process whereby the US came to replace Britain as the chief guarantor of Norwegian security was a gradual and uneven one. As will be shown, until late 1957, British seapower continued to be a critical element in the balance of external influences bearing on the Nordic region as a whole.

Early Limitations of American Policy

The view that Norway belonged to a British sphere of interest was not seriously challenged by either the Soviet Union or the US at the close of the war. Stalin explicitly recognised British influence as early as December 1941 when, in a conversation with Foreign Secretary Anthony Eden in Moscow, he remarked that the "Soviet Union would not object ... to Britain establishing bases in Denmark and Norway."[14] Although a growing sense of uncertainty within Norwegian government circles about Soviet policies towards Norway is evident in 1944–45, there is "no indication that Stalin at any time during the war aimed at annexing any part of Norway proper or strove for exclusive political control in the country after the war."[15] Soviet political pressure was felt more keenly in bilateral dealings between the Norwegian and Soviet governments, thus foreshadowing a pattern very much in evidence in the period between 1954 and 1960. Norway responded to this in the closing stages of the war by seeking to improve relations and to clarify long-term Soviet aims in the region.[16] The impression which Soviet authorities left with the two other members of the war-time alliance, however, was that Norway was clearly within the Western sphere of influence.[17]

Under the war-time administration of President Roosevelt the United States was anxious publicly to distance itself from any spheres-of-influence approach to the post-war security order.[18] Between 1945 and 1948 the State Department nonetheless accepted that "Scandinavia was a part of Western Europe where Britain's strategic, political and economic interests were considerably greater than those of the United States."[19] As a result, both the State Department and the Joint Chiefs of Staff (JCS) were prepared to leave the initiative in matters relating to Scandinavia to their British counterparts, the Foreign Office and the Chiefs of Staff (COS). This was reflected in practical matters such as the supply of military equipment to Scandinavian countries after the war, as well as in more substantive issues such as the international legal status of the entrances to the Baltic Sea.[20] For all this, in the period of transition from war to peace, neither the US nor Britain gave any consideration to concrete measures aimed at limiting Soviet influence in the region. Once the Soviet Union withdrew its forces from Finnmark in September 1945, and later from the Danish Baltic island of Bornholm in March–April 1946, high level interest in this part of Western Europe largely disappeared.

NATO Membership and the Origins of Norwegian Base Policy

It was after the collapse of the Council of Foreign Ministers meeting in December 1947, Ernest Bevin's Western Union speech on 22 January 1948, and, most significantly, the events in Czechoslovakia and Finland in February 1948, that the domestic debate about the nature of Norway's external alignments began in earnest. Meanwhile, in March 1948, Norway's diplomatic and military vulnerability also became a source of concern at senior levels of government in London and Washington.[21] Growing American high-level appreciation of Scandinavia's importance at the nexus of East-West strategic interests crystallised in September 1948, when President Truman approved the first NSC policy paper on the "position of the United States with respect to Scandinavia."[22] According to this document the Scandinavian countries were

> strategically important to the United States and the USSR. They lie astride the great circle air route between North America and the strategic heart of Western Russia, are midway on the air route between London and Moscow, and are in a position to control the exits from the Baltic and Barents seas. Domination of Scandinavia would provide the Soviets with advanced air, guided-missile and submarine bases, thus enabling them to advance their bomb line to the west, to threaten allied operations in the North Atlantic, and to form a protective shield against allied sea or air attack from the Northwest. Control either of Sweden or Norway would also increase the industrial potential of the USSR. The extensive oil shale and kolm deposits in Sweden are potential sources of uranium.

The policy paper also noted that

> The chief threat to the Scandinavian nations arises from the possibility of direct Soviet action against one or more of them in the form of severe diplomatic pressure or outright attack.[23]

NSC 28/1 notwithstanding, membership of NATO in April 1949 did not immediately ease Norway's strategic predicament which the deterioration in East-West relations since early 1948 had accentuated. The reason for this was simply that until the cumulative impact of the Soviet nuclear test explosion in August 1949, the "loss of China" shortly thereafter, and, finally, the outbreak of the Korean War in June 1950, the "North Atlantic Treaty was concerned less with the manner of America's commitment than with the fact of its existence."[24] Initial Allied acceptance of Norway's unilateral policy of restraint with respect to the stationing of foreign armed forces on its territory must be seen against this background.

The Norwegian "base policy", as it came to be known, constituted a self-denying ordinance banning the stationing of foreign troops on Norwegian territory "as long as Norway [was] not attacked or *subjected to threat of attack.*"[25] When the policy was first enunciated on 1 February 1949, in response to a Soviet note demanding to know whether the Norwegian Government would be "undertaking any obligation to the Atlantic Alliance regarding the establishment of air or naval bases on Norwegian territory,"[26] there was no American or British pressure for the construction of Allied bases on Norwegian territory.[27] Both the US and Britain assumed that Norwegian membership of the alliance would, by itself, serve as a deterrent to possible Soviet aggression. Plans for closer allied military integration following the outbreak of the Korean War and the Soviet accusation that Norway was allowing its territory to be used by the armed forces of the "aggressive North Atlantic bloc" prompted the Norwegian government to issue a further clarification of its base policy.[28] This was done by Defence Minister Jens Christian Hauge before the Storting on 21 February 1951, though he was careful not to provide an inclusive interpretation of the policy, emphasising instead the contingent nature of Norway's self-imposed restrictions in the realm of military policy. It is useful in the present context to quote *in extenso* that part of Hauge's statement which indicated the scope of permissible allied activity:

> The Norwegian base policy does not prevent Norway from making bases available to Allied armed forces in the event of an armed attack on the North Atlantic area, or at a time when the Norwegian authorities consider themselves exposed to threat of attack and summon Allied armed forces to the country.

Nor does Norwegian base policy prevent Norway in prescribed constitutional forms from entering into conditional agreements with our allies, having a situation of this kind in mind.

Our base policy cannot prevent Norway from developing her military installations according to a pattern which will make them capable of receiving and effectively maintaining Allied armed forces transferred to Norway in order to assist in the defence of the country.

Our base policy cannot prevent Norway from participating in joint Allied exercises or being visited for short periods by the naval and air forces of our allies even in peacetime.[29]

Also in January 1951, Orders in Council were made which limited the operation of Allied aircraft over Norway and naval vessels in Norwegian territorial waters to the area east of the twenty-fourth meridian. The number of allied units visiting Norway at any one time was also regulated, as was the need for prior clearance for all flights over Norwegian territory.

The foundations of the Norwegian base policy were partly historical. The country had been only fully independent since 1905 and the "tradition of neutrality" and the isolationist impulse persisted into the postwar period.[30] There were other and related domestic considerations as well. The Labour government of Einar Gerhardsen was anxious to preserve cross-party consensus on matters of foreign and defence policy, while also placating the relatively small but vocal section within the Labour Party which opposed closer military integration with the West. The declaration on bases therefore was partly designed to ensure domestic political acceptance of the change in Norwegian security policy which NATO membership signified. In the 1950s Norwegian government officials also frequently asserted that the original decision not to allow foreign armed forces on Norwegian territory in peacetime had reflected a genuine concern about both Sweden's position of neutrality and the delicate balance of Soviet–Finnish relations.[31] Far more important than this in 1949, however, was the desire on the part of the Norwegian government to *reassure* the Soviet Union about the defensive character of the alliance.

To sum up, the aforementioned considerations support the argument that although NATO membership represented a dramatic change in Norwegian security policy at the *declaratory* level, "in a long-term perspective ... it can be seen as merely the formalisation of an existing but until then implicit assurance that the control of Norwegian territory by a hostile great power would be intolerable to the West."[32]

From the US and British perspective the single most important factor influencing policies towards Norway was the perceived need to prevent

Soviet control of any part of Norwegian territory. In so far as it is possible to talk of a high-level strategy with respect to Scandinavia in general and Norway in particular, the concept of *denial* was the central criterion which shaped Anglo-American strategic interests in the region.[33] This was even more evident further down in the government and service hierarchies, especially at the level of defence planning and threat assessment.

II BRITISH POSTWAR STRATEGY AND NORWAY, 1945–54

The British Chiefs of Staff and Scandinavia

If "bridge-building" can be described as a "hope against hope" policy on the part of the Norwegian government, the expectation of British military assistance to Norway in the event of war was equally unrealistic. In the period 1945–50, the British Chiefs of Staff, having to base their global planning on much diminished post-war resources, made no provision for and attached no priority to the defence of Norway. COS planning, especially in 1945–48, focused primarily on the Middle East which was deemed more important even than the defence of Western Europe.[34] Field Marshal Lord Montgomery, the Chief of the Imperial General Staff, was one of a few senior officers who regarded the direct defence of Western Europe to be as important as "the maintenance of a firm hold on the Middle East."[35] Yet, even his proposals centred on a "continental commitment" and defence along the Rhine, with no mention made of the flanks.[36] As for the Royal Navy – a service traditionally conscious of the interdependence of British and Norwegian security concerns – it is true that the First Sea Lord, Admiral Sir John Cunningham, made a much-publicised visit to Norway on 5 June 1947. Yet, on 17 March 1948, at an important COS meeting convened to discuss future strategy, Admiral Cunningham expressed his agreement with Lord Montgomery, who had bluntly stated that "Scandinavia could not be considered vital to us."[37] As if to underline the importance of the Mediterranean, the First Sea Lord also made it clear that he considered the defence of Italy and Greece more important than measures of support to Norway.

This is not to suggest that the British military did not appreciate the strategic importance of Norway in relation to the defence of both the British Isles and the sea lines of communication across the Atlantic. A study by the Joint Planning Staff in June 1947 on the "strategic considerations involved in the question of a common arrangement by Norway,

Denmark and Sweden for the defence of Scandinavia" did stress the "great strategic importance" of Scandinavia to the Western Powers and Russia in the event of a future conflict.[38] The Joint Planning Staff "regarded the integrity of Scandinavia in the event of war as almost as important as the integrity of France, Holland and Belgium."[39] On the crucial question of British backing for a possible "Scandinavian defence bloc", however, the report stated that while the idea of such a bloc ought not to be discouraged, "we cannot on any grounds give any sort of guarantee or promise of military aid."[40] In March 1948 the Joint Planning Staff again considered the problem of Scandinavian defence, this time in response to a detailed questionnaire by the Norwegian Minister of Defence, Jens Chr. Hauge.[41] While Scandinavia's "great strategic importance in relation both to the protection of sea communications and air warfare" was again acknowledged, the Joint Planning Staff felt unable to commit itself "at this stage on the major questions of strategy" raised by the Norwegians.[42] The report did, however, stress the advantages of a Scandinavian bloc consisting of Norway, Sweden and Denmark, describing it as a matter "of great importance that the three countries should adopt a policy of combined defence."[43]

The priorities of the COS, specifically the importance attached to the defence of the Middle East as a staging area for the strategic bombing offensive against the Soviet Union, was reaffirmed in the first joint Anglo-American emergency war plan agreed in October 1948, known as 'Doublequick' to the British and 'Fleetwood' to the Americans.[44] In a new joint plan agreed in October 1949 a change of emphasis was evident, following US Army pressure in favour of an allied build-up in French North Africa in the event of war with the Soviet Union.[45] Still, planners on both sides of the Atlantic expressed their pessimism about the possibility of holding "even a bridgehead" on the European continent.[46] As for Scandinavia, 'Galloper', the British version of the plan, argued in typically convoluted language that there was perhaps:

> a reasonable chance that the Scandinavian countries together might become strong enough to provide at least a deterrent sufficient to make the Russians hesitate from embarking on a campaign against them whilst engaged in Western Europe.

In the far north Galloper envisaged that defence should at the outset be "based on the line Lyngen Fjord/Finno-Swedish Frontier." It went on to state that "a withdrawal of up to 300 miles to a general line covering Trondheim-Sundsvall could, however, be accepted." Yet, as far as direct assistance by Anglo-American forces was concerned, this "would be limited to keeping open one sea route from the United Kingdom."[47] Consequently, only one British fleet carrier was allocated to the North Atlantic.

Plan Galloper, then, was consistent with the established pattern of limited British commitments to the defence of northern Europe, a pattern which Norway's accession to NATO had not altered. Initial British reluctance, first to join the North European Regional Planning Group (NERPG) and later to assume direct responsibilities in the North European Command, activated in April 1951, were further indications of the same trend.[48] Similarly, the negotiating record of the final and revised version of NATO's first defence plan – the Medium Term Defence Plan (MTDP) approved by the Council in December 1950 – was also symptomatic of British attitudes.[49]

Briefly, the plan assumed that Norway would be attacked in the first stage of a war, the main thrust of the assault coming from the south, though operations in Scandinavia would still be secondary to operations on the continent.[50] There was disagreement between the British and the Norwegians within the NERPG about the likely direction and nature of a Soviet attack, the British stressing an overland attack and the Norwegians emphasising the need to prepare for a maritime assault. British emphasis on the overland scenario assumed that Sweden would become involved. This, in turn, would have slowed down the Soviet advance and hence reduced the need for immediate British assistance to the region. Nonetheless, the final version of the Medium-Term Defence Plan was less gloomy than earlier pre-Korean War plans about the prospects of holding parts of Norway. In the wake of the outbreak of the Korean War the plan rather ambitiously envisaged a defensive stand in North Norway along the Skibotn line, including the holding of Tromsø, Bodø and Narvik.[51] As far as ground force contributions were concerned, however, the plan itself did not involve direct allied commitments. And, while Britain agreed to provide a contingent from the British Army on the Rhine to assist a Danish-Norwegian covering force in North Germany, it made no further *ground* commitment in the North.

In the first post-war decade, the overall place of Norway in British defence priorities was always influenced, not only by prior strategic commitments and limited resources, but also by extremely pessimistic assessments about the possibilities of defending the country.[52] It has been argued, for example, that in the spring of 1951 Field Marshal Montgomery was favouring an Allied strategy which envisaged that "every effort" should be made to hold "the Southern and Northern Flanks – including Norway and Denmark – to ensure that the West retained a foothold in

Europe and to provide air bases."[53] However, by March 1952, Montgomery, who was then serving as Deputy SACEUR in Paris, appears to have rejected firmly the feasibility of implementing a "flank concept". Commenting upon General Eisenhower's proposed Annual Report, Montgomery expressed views very much in line with the aforementioned approach taken by the COS:

> He [Montgomery] objected to the inference that we conceive of two strong "fortresses", one on either flank. He said our known weaknesses in Italy are bad enough, but when we look at the North Flank we see almost no strength there and very little in prospect. Talk of a Northern "bulwark" is rubbish.[54]

Most revealing of British priorities, however, were the early drafts of the Emergency Defence Plans for the Northern European Command area (EDPNE), submitted to Norwegian authorities by CINCNORTH for comment and approval.[55] As opposed to medium-term plans, emergency defence plans prescribed the allocation of *existing resources* at D-Day. By their nature, therefore, they gave the clearest indication of strategic priorities. To the frustration of Norwegian officials CINCNORTH's early EDPs all emphasised the defence only of a limited part of south-west Norway, the area around Stavanger.[56] During discussions between Sivert Nielsen, Major General Vaage and representatives of CINCNORTH's Plans Division in January 1954, the central subject, as it had been since 1951, was the "Defence Area in Norway."[57] Again, Norwegian authorities did not accept the concept embodied in the draft version of CINCNORTH's EDP and discussions about the "defence area in Norway" continued for another five months.[58] Norwegian officials regarded the early EDPs as reflecting primarily British defence interests as defined by the COS.[59]

It is clear, then, that while British officials were willing to reaffirm the "closeness" of political ties, and to acknowledge the strategic value of Norway in general terms,[60] specific commitments were more difficult to elicit.[61] The British Defence Minister's views, conveyed to the First Sea Lord, Admiral Sir Rhoderick McGrigor, by the Commander, Allied Naval Forces Northern Europe in 1954, are typical in this respect:

> I gained the impression that he is alive to the strategical importance of Scandinavia to the United Kingdom, but that his real concern is with the added warning which Scandinavia could give of air attack on the United Kingdom.[62]

Lord Alexander during this visit also publicly reiterated the centrality of the central front in Allied strategy, saying there was no need for Allied bases in Norway.[63]

When the COS in 1952 embraced Sir John Slessor's view that NATO defence policy should be based on the "nuclear bomber" as the "Great Deterrent" and the only effective "counter-threat to the vast armies and tactical air forces of our potential enemy," Norway's role in British defence plans diminished further, except for the early warning role to which Lord Alexander alluded in 1954.[64] For all this, the Royal Navy, as will be discussed in chapter five, did provide an important exception to the pattern of limited interest outlined above, particularly after the establishment of an integrated command structure for NATO in 1951–52.

III   NORWAY IN AMERICAN POST-WAR STRATEGY: WAR PLANS AND SERVICE VIEWS, 1945–54

American Joint Plans and Scandinavia

Shortly before the British Joint Planning Staff presented its report on Scandinavia in June 1947, its American counterpart, the Joint War Plans Committee (JWPC), had completed a "strategic study of Western and Northern Europe."[65] It was the first American joint plan to examine in some detail the significance of Scandinavia's strategic location and its potential role in a future conflict with the Soviet Union. The study – as with other war plans in the Pincher series – did not seriously consider the impact of nuclear weapons on future operations.[66] Although too much should therefore not be read into this early study, it nonetheless revealed early concerns with regard to Scandinavia, and particularly Norway, which the "nuclear revolution" of the 1950s only served to intensify. Control of Norway and Sweden by the Soviet Union, the report stated, would permit the establishment of "bases for air and naval operations in the Atlantic and against the British Isles." From bases in Norway, submarines would be able to operate against Allied sea lines of communications to the UK and other parts of Western and Northern Europe.[67] The JWPC report, however, also recognised the potential advantages which access to Norwegian territory held for the US. In view of the subsequent development of US–Norwegian military co-operation, it is particularly interesting to note that the JWPC emphasised that

Soviet ships using the sea route from Murmansk (or Archangel) passing through the Arctic Ocean to the Atlantic Ocean would ... be extremely vulnerable to an attack from Allied bases in the Scandinavian countries, particularly in Northern Norway.[68]

It was against the background of these kinds of considerations that a joint report in November 1948 by the USAF Directorate of Intelligence and the Office of Naval Intelligence, referred to Norway as being "the key to the entire northern Europe and may be termed a gigantic Gibraltar."[69]

The US Air Force, the Arctic and the Question of Bases

The US Army Air Force first registered its interest in Norway in May 1945 when the JCS forwarded a proposal to the State-War-Navy Coordinating Committee (SWNCC), suggesting that eight bases – each consisting of one heavy bomber group, one depot group and one fighter squadron – be established in France, Italy, Denmark and Norway.[70] The Norwegian base was to be located in the Stavanger area and, as with the bases in Denmark, Italy and France, the basic motivation behind the proposed JCS plan was to ensure German compliance with the terms of surrender. Although the SWNCC accepted the JCS basing plan, Acting Secretary of State Joseph C. Grew was concerned lest American demands on Norway and Denmark would precipitate Soviet countermoves. Fearing that the Soviet Union might make similar requests, Grew urged a military re-evaluation.[71] The eventual outcome of this process was that the JCS in October 1945 accepted General Eisenhower's view that US bases in France and Italy would suffice for the purpose of policing Germany and maintaining peace in Europe.[72]

The one area where it was conceivable that the Soviet Union would ask for reciprocal base rights was in the Spitsbergen Archipelago. Along with Bear Island, this Arctic archipelago had been granted to Norway under international treaty in 1920, subject to certain restrictions.[73] Soviet interest in Norway's Arctic possessions was most dramatically revealed in November 1944 when Vyacheslav Molotov presented the Norwegian Foreign Minister Trygve Lie with a Soviet demand for revision of the Spitsbergen Treaty and the outright secession of Bear Island. The reasons given by Molotov for presenting his demands were twofold. First, the Soviet Union had been excluded from the original treaty negotiations in 1920. Second, and more ominously from a Norwegian perspective, Soviet security requirements necessitated that a change be made in the status of Norway's Arctic possessions. The initial American reaction to the Soviet proposal was far more accommodating than Norwegian authorities would have desired.[74] Although the State Department and the service departments involved urged opposition to Soviet proposals as a matter of principle, if Soviet demands were pressed, the US was willing to go as far as considering the possibility of exchanging base rights on Greenland and Iceland with Soviet rights on Spitsbergen. In the event, Molotov's November initiative was not pursued and the issue only resurfaced in 1947 by which time the American position, notably within the military, had stiffened considerably.[75] Although NSC 28/1 noted that "several sites exist for runways for very heavy bombers" on the Archipelago, the principal aim of US policy was to secure Norwegian sovereignty over the islands and thus deny "their military use by a hostile power."[76]

USAF interests in base rights in Norway re-emerged after the events of February and March 1948, when General Carl Spaatz ordered a "special study of bomber bases in Norway and Greenland in particular."[77] The outcome of this particular study is not known.[78] The JCS did, however, address the issue of SAC bases in Norway when, in February 1948, it responded to a series of "questions regarding possibilities and probable character of American assistance to Norway in case of war" raised by Defence Minister Hauge in conversation with the US Naval and Air Force attachés in Oslo.[79] This meeting, held on the 17 February, was the clearest sign yet of the Norwegian government's drift in the direction of greater reliance on the US as an extra-regional security guarantor. The American Embassy report accurately spelled out the nature of Norwegian concerns at the time. According to the report, the Norwegian Defence Minister:

> specifically asked what place Norway might have in American air strategy, what aid might be expected in the early stages of war, and whether, where, and at what stages in such emergency the US would want to establish air, sea and land bases in Norway. He placed considerable emphasis on Norway's role in guided missile warfare. Hauge gave the definite impression he hoped to obtain some form of American commitment to aid Norway should war occur.[80]

The JCS response, although accepting that Norwegian territory was of potential use against enemy shipping in the Baltic (and as staging area for SAC escort fighters), emphasised that the proximity of Norwegian territory to Soviet air bases militated against the construction of heavy bomber bases in Norway, the establishment of which might provoke a preemptive Soviet attack against Norway.

Still, in the late 1940s and early 1950s the strategic significance of Norway was seen by Norwegian and American authorities alike as deriving primarily from its role in air warfare, specifically the planned strategic air offensive. And the USAF continued to explore the possibilities which Norway's location appeared to offer in relation to critical target complexes in the USSR–Moscow, the Donbass region (Kharkov), the Urals and the Volga Bridges. In early October 1950, Colonel Bernt Balchen, Special Assistant on Arctic Affairs to the Secretary of the Air Force in 1951–52, reported that Sola airport in the Stavanger area was capable of handling very heavy bombers (VHB) and had "more than adequate" logistics capabilities.[81] According to Balchen, Sola's potential as a operational heavy bomber base for strikes against targets in the Soviet Union was ideal, at a distance of only 1100 nautical miles to Moscow, 1585 miles to Stalingrad, and 1880 miles to Magnitogorsk.[82]

In October 1952, after prolonged negotiations, a secret "arrangement" was concluded whereby SAC was allowed to use the airfields of Sola and Gardermoen near Oslo.[83] The agreement involved the stockpiling of "reasonable quantities of supplies, technical equipment and ammunition" at the airfields for use during hostilities.[84] Furthermore, it involved the construction of technical facilities to support emergency landings as well as pre- and post-strike operations of fighter escorts. In the case of Gardermoen, provisions were to be made for "emergency post-strike staging of approximately 60 medium bombers per month."[85] But it did not involve the peacetime stationing of bombers or escort fighters on either airfield.[86] Apart from Norway's base policy, the question of permanent stationing was ruled out by the aforementioned problem of close-target vulnerability. Although the actual need for forward bases gradually diminished with the improvement of inflight refuelling techniques and the introduction of the B-36 and later the B-52 bombers, by 1954 the vulnerability of forward bases was in itself accepted as a factor militating against construction of main operating bases along the Soviet periphery. The chief conclusion of an influential RAND report in April 1954 which examined "the critical factors in strategic-base selection," was that an air-base system "consisting of US operating bases and overseas refuelling bases [was] markedly superior" to a system where "bombers [are] based on advanced overseas operating bases in time of war."[87] Unlike Greenland and Iceland, Norway was not listed as an operating base in the basing plan proposed by the RAND report. Similarly, the *Killian Report* on the threat of surprise attack, presented to the President in February 1955, argued that SAC was already "unacceptably vulnerable to even a small scale surprise air attack."[88] It should nonetheless be noted that while Norwegian territory was not deemed suitable for the location of SAC "Main Operating

Bases"(MOB) it continued to perform an important, albeit more *indirect*, function in relation to SAC war plans.[89]

A further indication of growing American involvement and reduced British commitment with respect to Norway in the early 1950s can be found in the discussions about the outside provision of *tactical* air power to the region. In 1952 plans were considered for the stationing of one American fighter wing in Norway (75 aircraft at Torp in South Norway) and two, possibly three, in Denmark (150 aircraft at Tirstrup and Vandel on Jutland). Both deployments were specifically intended to enhance the credibility of NATO's Medium-Term Defence Plan. General Eisenhower, in talks with Norwegian officials, "stated that actually he would have preferred to have British units up here but they are not available at this time."[90] Although members of the Norwegian cabinet were prepared to reconsider the base policy, in the end, the political costs involved in altering it were deemed to be too high. Instead, an alternative arrangement was agreed, whereby both Norway and Denmark would receive "visiting airplanes for short periods of time, which would not be interpreted as permanent stationing."[91]

The US Navy: The Ascendancy of the Carrier and the Early Interest in the "Northern Seas"

In February 1945 James Forrestal, in one of his many commissioned studies on the role of the Soviet Union after the war, turned his attention to Scandinavia.[92] Although the Soviet Union was not believed to harbour aggressive intentions with respect to any part of Scandinavia, the study noted that:

> the acquisition of a common frontier with that country [Norway] in the Far North and the proximity of Norwegian territory to Murmansk, Russia's only ice-free port opening directly on the high sea, give Norway a very special place in Russian eyes.[93]

The report concluded on a pessimistic note:

> it appears quite possible that the Russians will seek a pact with Norway which will provide for joint Norwegian-Soviet defence of northern Norway against any third power.

The importance which Forrestal evidently attached to this particular report – he included the entire report in his diary – must partly have reflected the significance of its conclusions for the future roles and missions of the US Navy, whose cause he was busy championing at the time. Preparing for the coming "unification struggle" with the other services and conscious of the widespread support for air power, James Forrestal had redefined the future mission of the Navy in terms of "sea-air power."[94] Briefly, this held that fast self-contained carrier groups would form the centrepiece of the modern navy. Meanwhile, operational planning would emphasise the role and development of carrier-based aviation at the expense of the traditional battleship.[95] The importance of carrier offensive capabilities became a persistent theme in naval planning from 1945 onwards and it acquired a new dimension when the navy in 1947 began to position itself for a role in the strategic air offensive.[96] Given Forrestal's belief that "sea-air power would give the navy a key role in war with the Soviet Union", it is not surprising that he showed such interest in the report on Scandinavia. In early 1946 Forrestal sanctioned *Operation Frostbite*, a "special series of experimental missions into the Arctic Ocean to learn how efficiently carriers and aircraft could operate in snowy weather, icy sea and low visibility."[97]

For all this, once the Navy did redirect its focus from the Pacific to Europe in early 1946 it was, as with the British COS, the Mediterranean, specifically its eastern parts, which became the principal theatre of American interest and operational activity. In the autumn of 1946 the United States made a permanent commitment of naval forces to the Mediterranean, with the establishment of the Mediterranean Fleet (soon to be renamed the Sixth Fleet).[98]

In an important statement on naval strategic thinking, presented to the President on 1 January 1947, Admiral Forrest P. Sherman, then Head of the Strategic Plans Division (OP-30), stressed the vital importance of dominating "the Mediterranean sea line of communications."[99] Although "retarding Soviet advances into Norway, Spain, Italy, Greece and Turkey" was listed as a naval task in the event of war, the importance of the Arctic regions was assessed primarily in light of their future role in American strategy:

> With the passage of time and the expected development of airborne missiles, the importance of the northern approaches to the United States will increase. We anticipate that naval forces will be called on to operate in Arctic regions to seize and support bases for our air forces, and to prevent the use of the Arctic regions as bases for attack against us. For that reason we are grasping every opportunity to increase our skill in cold weather operations and to improve our material for such service.[100]

Sherman's presentation also formulated the basic tenets of the Navy's strategic concept, as it had crystallised since the end of the war. The two central and related elements were: the importance of forward offensive operations against land targets (subsumed under the notion of "attack at source") and the centrality of the *carrier task force* as the key to accomplishing a range of Navy missions, including amphibious operations, anti-submarine warfare (ASW) and air strikes against targets on land. Sherman was, however, still thinking in terms of conventional operations.

The American commitment to defend Western Europe against the putative threat of the Soviet Union, symbolised by the establishment of NATO in April 1949, necessarily meant that the US Navy had to reconsider its post-war focus on the Mediterranean as the principal theatre of operations in European waters. The outbreak of the Korean war in June 1950 not only provided a powerful impetus for a rapid expansion of the US Navy, but also accelerated the trend whereby the earlier exclusive emphasis on the Mediterranean shifted towards the direct defence of Western Europe. With agreement on a Strategic Concept and the creation of an integrated command structure, a more sustained focus on the problems of defending Europe could be conducted. Two developments in 1951–52 reflected a growing US naval interest in Northern Europe. The first of these was the creation in April 1952 of an integrated Atlantic Command (ACLANT) under a US Supreme Commander (SACLANT). The second was SACEUR's own strategic conception for the defence of Europe which, under General Eisenhower, strongly emphasised the provision of naval support to NATO's northern and southern flanks in the event of war with the Soviet Union.

When ACLANT was set up in 1952 it was divided into two major geographical command areas: the Western Atlantic Area (WESTLANT), commanded by a US officer, and the Eastern Atlantic Area (EASTLANT) under joint command of a British naval Commander-in-Chief and British air Commander-in-Chief. In addition to this, the Strike Fleet Atlantic was established as a functional rather than geographical command, directly subordinate to SACLANT regardless of the particular area in which it might be operating.[101] Organised around two Carrier Groups, it consisted of attack carriers, heavy surface ships and supporting vessels, making it the Alliance's "battle fleet". In September 1952 the Strike Fleet came into operation for the first time when SACLANT, responding to a hypothetical attack on Norway and Denmark, provided outside carrier forces in support of the land battle in North Norway and Denmark. This occurred as part of a large scale exercise known as Mainbrace. It was an exercise specifically designed to put into practice Eisenhower's "flank-concept".[102]

Central to Eisenhower's thinking was the emphasis he placed on a very heavy concentration of sea and air assets on the flanks to compensate for weaknesses on the central front. In a meeting held with President Truman in late January 1951, Eisenhower elaborated on his concept and described how, having assembled "a great combination of air and sea power in the North Sea", he would, "if the Russians tried to make a move ahead in the center ... hit them awfully hard from both flanks."[103] Two months later, in March 1951, Eisenhower was asked by the Standing Group to submit his estimated force requirements for the defence of Western Europe based on D-Day of July 1954. In his reply, Eisenhower requested four carriers to be available on each flank at D-Day. Moreover, at D+15 a third carrier task group would reinforce the "weaker flank according to SACEUR's decision" and a fourth carrier task group would reinforce the other flank at D+30.[104] In other words, a total of sixteen attack carriers – eight on each flank with "atomic capabilities" – would be on station 30 days after D-Day.[105]

In June 1951, SACEUR's flank concept was succinctly summarised by his Chief of Staff, General Alfred Gruenther:

Under this concept, General Eisenhower has in mind that the two flank commands, Northern Europe and Southern Europe, are going to be primarily naval and air commands. At this stage in the development of forces, there are not sufficient ground forces in either of these areas to constitute a strong defence. General Eisenhower's concept of the strategy is that by the use of air and naval power on these flanks he then forces the decision in the Central area. As a matter of fact, this area becomes the cork that closes in and shuts up the bottle.[106]

Importantly, from Norway's point of view, Eisenhower would use the carriers principally in support of the defence of Norway and Denmark.[107] As he wrote to Admiral Bruce Fraser, the First Sea Lord, in September 1951:

it is beyond my comprehension to envisage the defence of Norway and Denmark, vulnerable as they are to seaborne attack and dependent as our meagre land and air forces will be for support by the sea, unless adequate naval forces are ready to operate...

Norway and Denmark alone cannot provide the naval forces that will be needed. It is obvious that carrier, heavy support, and amphibious units must be provided in the area by other NATO nations, chiefly by the British and the United States.[108]

As indicated above, the concept was put to the test during the Mainbrace exercise. An Anglo-American carrier task force – four US and two British carriers – sailed from the Firth of Clyde to North Norway where aircraft delivered interdiction and close support strikes to "stabilise the front" for the NATO defending force. At the same time, a convoy was run between the UK and Bergen while the task force itself engaged in offensive ASW operations.[109]

It is important to stress here that the growth of US Navy interests in Northern Europe in the early 1950s should not be seen merely as a function of SACEUR's operational requirements. The US Navy was developing an interest in the "northern seas" *independently* of SACEUR's plans for the defence of Western Europe. As a result, although Eisenhower's defence concept and the very ambitious NATO force goals upon which the flank concept was predicated were ultimately shelved, this *did not* lead to a corresponding diminution of naval interest in the region.

Not surprisingly, the section within the Navy which first began to pay greater attention to Northern Europe was the Office of Naval Intelligence (ONI) which was charged with the task of monitoring and estimating Soviet naval activity and capabilities. Later, the Strategic Plans Division, responsible for long-term strategic planning in the Navy, also began to show increasing interest in the High North.[110] In September 1949 the ONI presented a report on the modernisation of ship repair and dry docking facilities in the Kola Inlet (Kol'skiy Zaliv), within which lay the port of Murmansk and the naval operating bases of Vayenga (Severomorsk) and Polyarnyy.[111] In addition to these two main bases, the ONI briefly referred to "minor naval facilities" at Pala Bay, Olenya Bay and Tyuva Bay, which functioned as an auxiliary to the main submarine base at Polyarnyy. The Rosta Naval Dockyard was listed as the site of the "major" repair and dry-docking facilities in Northern Russia and was reported to be under further construction. The ONI report concluded that a "strong naval base in the Kola Inlet can be a threat to North Atlantic shipping routes or can support an invasion of the Norwegian coast."[112]

In January 1951 the ONI had drawn up a "recommended" list of five targets in the "Barents Sea area" whose destruction "would make a contribution towards reducing the Soviet capability to conduct submarine warfare." These were: Rosta Naval Base and shipyard Sevmorput; Pechenga submarine pens; Polyarnyy Naval Base; Iokanga Naval Base and Vayenga Naval Base.[113] Both these intelligence reports, however, were primarily concerned with the then unexplored potential of naval and air bases on this Arctic peninsula.

In March 1953 the strategic importance of the area from a naval point of view, as well as the need to make fast attack carriers available for operations along the Norwegian coast and in "the Murmansk area", were openly discussed in hearings before the Subcommittee on Appropriations for the Navy.[114] During the hearings it was pointed out how the operation of carrier forces in the Murmansk area in the early days of World War II might "have done a great deal" to reduce "the terrific loss of ships" in the area. With carriers in the North Atlantic, the Assistant Secretary of the Navy (Air) told Committee members, "we could have hit those aircraft [German aircraft operating against Allied convoys] on the ground and destroyed them before they ever got off to destroy our ships or aircraft."[115] In contrast to the immediate post-war years, Navy spokesmen during these hearings also confidently asserted that fast-carrier operations in the Murmansk area could be conducted "year around" since "it is ice-free."[116] The impression which the Navy spokesmen sought to leave with the Committee was that the carrier task forces, "for which there is no substitute", were ideal against both tactical and strategic targets in the Northern region.

An even clearer indication of the Navy's growing concern about developments in the High North came in October 1953 when Admiral Arleigh Burke described the "Northern Seas" (defined as the Northeast Atlantic–Norwegian–Barents Sea area) as an area whose importance to the security of the US was now as great as the Mediterranean.[117] A comprehensive study by the Strategic Plans Division, prepared in order to "develop a recommended Attack Carrier Force Level for a prolonged period of Cold War," concluded that ten attack carriers would be required in the Atlantic Fleet. In the event of conflict four of these would constitute a "task group" for the Norwegian Sea–Barents Sea. It would "cover the northern approaches to Europe" and among its primary task would be the destruction of "submarine and air bases in the Barents Sea area."[118]

Conclusion

In a long-term historical perspective the years between 1945 and 1949 emerge as the period in which Norway's position in the international system shifted from being an exposed flank in an extended Anglo-German conflict to one where it occupied a new and vulnerable position at the nexus of East–West strategic interests. It was only in 1951, however, following the general rearmament programme in the US and the establishment of an integrated command structure in Europe and the Atlantic, that the question of external support for the Northern Flank became a subject of allied concern.[119] The British inability and, indeed, unwillingness to make firm commitments, except in the maritime sphere, made it increasingly obvious that only the US could possibly bridge the gap between the aspirations of NATO's first Medium Term Defence Plan and the capabilities available to defend the region. From 1950 onwards a noticeable expansion of US activity in Northern Europe took place and was reflected in the inflow of aid through the Mutual Defence Assistance Programme (MDAP) and the activities of the Military Assistance Advisory Group (MAAG).[120]

By 1954 three partly overlapping perspectives concerning the place of Norway and its Arctic possessions in US strategy had manifested themselves. First, the area represented a *tactical flank* in relation to the central European front. In 1951–52, while Eisenhower's strategic concept for the defence of Europe influenced NATO planning, this was the dominant perspective. Second, the area's potential importance as a springboard for *offensive* operations was reflected in the agreement between SAC and the Norwegian Air Force in 1952 concerning the wartime use of Sola and Gardermoen. Third, as the Soviet Union improved its air and sub-surface long-range delivery capabilities, Norway and the contiguous sea areas became ever more important for the Arctic and sub-Arctic *defence belt* of the continental United States (CONUS).

In the period between 1954 and 1960, Norway's role as a tactical flank in relation to the central front receded into the background. The other two perspectives, however, continued to influence Norway's place in US strategy. The US Air Force, although not as active as in the late 1940s and early 1950s, retained a strong residual interest in Norway, not least from the point of view of intelligence gathering and early warning. The interests of the US Navy in the region continued to increase, as did the interests of the American intelligence community more generally. In all this, it was Norway's proximity to the north-western parts of the Soviet Union, to the Nordic neutrals of Finland and Sweden and to NATO's reluctant ally, Iceland, which brought Norway to the centre of American strategy.

Part II: Norway in American Threat Assessments, 1954–60

A war situation now exists between the Soviet Bloc and the group of Western nations under the leadership of the United States ... If general war does not develop, this situation will almost certainly continue, possibly increasing in intensity, throughout the period of this estimate.[1]

US Intelligence Advisory Committee, 1953

For no defence, based only on our own shores, has any hope of success in the age of foreshortened geography. With the increase in speed and range of new weapons and the shrinking of the map, the "outpost line" – the line to give US warning of attack – must be pushed out farther and farther from our shores if any sort of defensive tactics and defensive implements are to have even moderate success.[2]

Hanson W. Baldwin, 1953

INTRODUCTION

The importance which the Eisenhower administration attached to strengthening ties with Norway was, in large part, the result of Norway's place in US early warning and intelligence programmes. Given the assumptions about the character of the conflict with the Soviet Union embodied in the 1953 estimate of the Intelligence Advisory Committee, it was hardly surprising that the US sought to elicit Norwegian co-operation in its efforts to obtain detailed knowledge about military and scientific developments inside the Soviet Union. Part II explores the extent and nature of Norway's contribution towards this effort. It also examines how this contribution in turn shaped US perceptions of the nature of the Soviet threat in the 1950s. Specifically, it details how American maritime interests in the high north between 1954 and 1960 evolved in response to the build-up of Soviet submarine and naval air forces on the Kola Peninsula. The political issues and complications arising out of US – Norwegian collaboration in the intelligence sphere is examined in greater detail in the chapter eight.

2 Intelligence and Air Strategies in the Arctic, 1954–60

I ESTABLISHING ESTIMATES: INTELLIGENCE OBJECTIVES AND RESOURCES IN THE FAR NORTH 1954–60

Norway and American Intelligence Requirements, 1954–60

Between 1954 and 1960 Norwegian territory afforded a unique location from which to collect *strategic* and *tactical* intelligence on the Soviet Union.[3] There were several reasons for this.

The most basic reason was that certain intelligence targets within the Baltic, Leningrad and Northern Military Districts of the Soviet Union were regarded by the US intelligence community and the JCS to be among their "highest intelligence priorities."[4] What, then, were these specific targets bordering the Scandinavian peninsula?

Shortly after the U-2 incident in May 1960 the Director of the CIA, Allen W. Dulles, in secret testimony before the Senate Foreign Relations Committee, sought to place the U-2 project within the broader context of the Agency's collection efforts over the past ten years. The U-2 programme, he said, had been directed against five "critical problems" affecting national security.[5] These were: the Soviet long-range bomber force, the missile programme, the atomic energy programme, the submarine programme, and, finally, the Soviet air defence system. In fact, between 1954 and 1960, these were the *principal* target categories not only of the U-2 project but of the entire US strategic intelligence effort. Moreover, in each of these areas co-operation with allies and "friendly" powers on the Scandinavian peninsula was extremely valuable to the United States. As will be argued, Norway's contribution was most significant in three of the areas listed by Allen Dulles: the monitoring of the Arctic bomber threat between 1953 and 1957, the development of the Soviet air defence system, and growth of the long-range submarine force of the Northern fleet. It is interesting to note in this connection that the National Intelligence Estimate for 1955 concluded that the "most important increase in Soviet capabilities" were estimated to be precisely in the fields of "submarine warfare, long-range aviation and air defence."[6] Before turning to these areas in greater detail, however, it is necessary to consider briefly three other reasons why Norway assumed such an important role in the intelligence sphere.

First, prior to the emergence of earth-satellite reconnaissance systems, Norway's proximity to the north-western part of the Soviet Union was of particular value to the US intelligence community. The first American spy satellite, Corona/Discoverer, was successfully launched on 28 February 1959, though not until January 1961 did it become a fully dependable photo-satellite reconnaissance system.[7] In this pre-satellite era, Norway as a "front-line" state provided support, maintenance and staging facilities for ferret, photo and balloon reconnaissance flights.[8] Furthermore, access to Norwegian territory allowed for visual observation of military activity in the border area as well as for forward placement of SIGINT stations.[9]

Secondly, the relative importance of geographic proximity during this period must be seen in the context of the very limited amount of *basic intelligence* possessed by the US on the Soviet Union.[10] The critical need for information about the Soviet Union was complicated by the fact that major industrial and demographic areas, especially in the interior regions of the Eurasian land mass, had been effectively sealed off to foreigners until Stalin's death in March 1953. In June 1953 the Director of Air Force Intelligence, Lieutenant-General John A. Samford, noted in an internal memorandum that there existed "no accurate up-to-date terrestrial or cultural coverage of the USSR."[11] General Samford, explaining why such coverage was needed, argued that only an extensive programme of pre-hostilities reconnaissance could "provide the USAF with the vital information necessary for the proper developing and conducting of war plans."[12] In late 1953 a memorandum for Director of Plans, USAF, reiterated the

> urgent need for extensive reconnaissance coverage of Russia for the location and identification of industrial areas, military installations, transportation and population centers ... and for preparation of maps, charts and target materials.[13]

As evidence emerged of Soviet progress in the thermo-nuclear and ballistic missile fields in 1954–55, and the "marriage of nuclear warheads and long-range ballistic missiles" became a distinct possibility, the need for intelligence was seen to increase even further.[14] Norway's significance in this context was further heightened when, in the first half of the decade, Soviet Arctic regions were given top priority by air and naval intelligence as an area requiring *continual* monitoring for warning of attack.[15] In

February 1955 the study of the Killian Panel on the threat of surprise attack submitted to the President, specifically recommended that the US

> should at once take steps to develop the special equipment and specialised personnel needed for intelligence operations in the region of the polar pack ice, the largest area contiguous to Russia still accessible to us.[16]

In the summer of 1957 a report by the ONI referred to the continued existence of "broad intelligence gaps" in Arctic Russia and the need to fill them.[17]

The third factor which in the 1950s strongly influenced both the extent and intensity of the American intelligence-gathering effort and Norway's role in it, was the much greater degree of independence exercised by service agencies in the US.[18] Before the *Defence Reorganisation Act* (1958), the establishment of the *Defence Intelligence Agency* (1960) and the *National Reconnaissance Office* (1960), individual service and agency programmes were marked by duplication and intense bureaucratic rivalry.[19] Even the Reorganisation Act of 1958 was only partially successful in remedying the situation, and the defining features of the period remained those of "intelligence permissiveness, with casual direction from the Presidency and almost no meaningful monitoring by Congress."[20] With respect to the Arctic, the Air Force Office of Intelligence (AFOIN) and the ONI each carried out major, but separate, collection programmes. The documentary records available, though admittedly of a fragmentary nature, suggest that these programmes were principally tailored to the interests of individual services and their missions in war and were conducted with a minimum of service co-ordination.[21]

The Soviet Nuclear Test and Ballistic Missile Programmes

The documentary material concerning Norway's *precise* role in monitoring the early stages of Soviet Union's nuclear and missile programmes is limited. There is, however, sufficient evidence to show that activity associated with long-range missile and nuclear test facilities constructed in the north-western and Arctic regions of Russia was closely monitored from North Norway, with the US providing technical assistance, funding and logistic support.[22]

Between 1955 and 1960 a series of tests were conducted on a nuclear testing ground "in the area of the Barents Sea," and on the island of Novaya Zemlya.[23] The third in a series of five nuclear detonations detected by the US in 1955 was an underwater burst in the Barents Sea.[24] An indication of continued Soviet test activity in 1956 is found in a précis prepared for Anthony Eden's bilateral talks with Prime Minister Gerhardsen in October of that year. The brief anticipated that the "Norwegian Government's concern at increasing radioactivity over Norway" would be raised, and that Norway might take up the issue at the UN General Assembly.[25] In January 1958 British naval intelligence reported that a "considerable area" around Novaya Zemlya had been closed to shipping the previous autumn while nuclear weapon tests were being conducted.[26] Norway's proximity to Soviet testing grounds meant that the distribution of by-products generated by nuclear explosions could be investigated from Norway. In the mid-1950s the US Air Force Technical Command and the Norwegian Defence Intelligence Staff initiated work on two electronic observation posts in east Finnmark, at Høybuktmoen and Karasjok (referred to as Operation "Crockpot").[27] The technical equipment involved as well as the construction costs were provided bilaterally through the auspices of the USAF.[28] In the 1960s the first Large Aperture Seismic Array (LASA) outside the US was constructed in Norway.[29]

In addition to these ground stations North Norwegian airfields were utilised in connection with the so-called High-Altitude Sampling Programme (HASP), whereby aircraft collected radioactive gases and particles from the upper atmosphere in order to analyse Soviet test explosions.[30] This did not normally involve any violation of Soviet air space. In October 1958, shortly after the resumption of Soviet nuclear testing, a U-2 aircraft from Detachment 10/10 in Adana in Turkey – temporarily deployed to Operating Location at Bodø – conducted one such high altitude sampling flight in the vicinity of Novaya Zemlya.[31] This flight took place during a particularly intense period of US and Soviet nuclear testing.[32] According to Jay Miller, it "proved very successful and gave the US intelligence community its best insight to date into the Soviet nuclear weapons programme."[33]

With respect to the missile programme, Erik Himle, State Secretary at the Norwegian Ministry of Defence between 1958 and 1961, has noted that ground-based telemetry interception from Norway was of "considerable" value to the US intelligence community in its attempt to chart the progress of the Soviet ICBM programme.[34] The only facility to which Himle could have referred was located at *Plesetsk,* the Soviet Union's first operational ICBM site some 200 kilometres south of Arkhangelsk.[35] According to Colonel Stan W. Beerli, commander of Detachment 10–10 at Adana, the need to cover the suspected site at Plesetsk was also the specific purpose of the single most extensive and long-running U-2 deployment to Bodø.[36] It appears, however, that it was in early 1960 that the US intelligence community first became seriously preoccupied with developments at Plesetsk. In early April, information based in part on ground-based SIGINT stations in Finnmark intercepting radio and tele-graphic transmission from the launch area in the preparatory phase, indi-cated that an ICBM site had been constructed.[37] This information seems to provide, at least, part of the answer as to why Eisenhower sanctioned Gary Powers's ill-fated mission in early May, an overflight whose northerly leg would have covered Plesetsk, Arkhangelsk, Kandalksha and Murmansk before landing at Bodø.[38] According to Richard Bissell, the architect of and the CIA officer operationally responsible for the U-2 project, the "most vital target" for the May flight was indeed Plesetsk.[39] Michael Beschloss suggests that a U-2 flight on 9 April had found evidence of an ICBM site at Plesetsk, and that this "and other sources" had led to the decision to go ahead with the May flight. It is highly unlikely, however, that the 9 April flight uncovered anything about Plesetsk; it had begun in Adana to cover the ABM test facility at Saryshagan in Kazakhstan.[40] The April evidence about Plesetsk, which prompted Bissell to insist on a flight so close to the Paris summit, must therefore have come largely from Norwegian SIGINT sources.

In addition to the information derived from ground-based stations, in December 1959 Britain and the United States approached the Norwegian authorities with a request for a significant increase in the number of "reconnaissance flights" (ELINT) from Norwegian airfields. The request was justified by reference to the importance of acquiring details about the Soviet ICBM developments in Northern Russia.[41] Although the proposal was rejected by the Norwegians on political grounds, the allied request indicates that a key function of those ELINT operations that did take place was to monitor Soviet missile developments.[42]

In spite of the evidence that does exist about Norway's role in monitor-ing Soviet atomic and missile programmes, its contribution in these fields should not be exaggerated. Norwegian sources, perhaps with the exception of Plesetsk in 1960, appear to have been most valuable as "confirmatory data."[43] All of the more important test sites were located in Soviet Central Asia, including Semipalatinsk in Kazakhstan, Tyuratam Tam east of the Aral Sea, Alma-Ata and, as we have seen, Saryshagan, also in Kazakhstan.[44] As Rolf Tamnes has shown, Northern Russia was never "a major target of the U-2 flights."[45] Instead, the U-2 efforts to obtain pre-burn-out telemetry of ICBM launchings and to sample the atmosphere for radioactive fall-out, were concentrated in the southern sector.[46] Here, Turkey, the only other NATO ally apart from Norway to share a common border with the

Soviet Union, provided bases for overflights and peripheral ELINT operations, as well as for missile detection and performance monitoring equipment. A further indication of the preeminent importance of the southern sector with respect to these two target categories, is that the principal US long-range tracking radar for missile detection during this period – designated as FPS-17 and developed by *General Electric* – was deployed near Samsun in Turkey in 1955, but does not appear to have been operated from Norway.[47] It is necessary, therefore, to turn to the other areas in which, as indicated above, Norway's contribution was highly significant.

II NORWAY AND US AIR STRATEGY

The New Look and the Polar Concept

Under the *New Look*, the name given to the set of defence policies adopted by the administration in late 1953, the *strategic air offensive* became the principal instrument through which the US would seek to compensate for Soviet advantages in geography and manpower.[48] By this time, the Polar Concept had become firmly established as a central element in US strategic planning.[49] In March 1952 the significance of this "concept" was spelled out by General Kepner, Commander-in-Chief Alaskan Command, in a lecture delivered at the National War College on the subject of the "Strategic Importance of the Arctic."[50] According to Kepner, the Polar concept embodied:

> possible contacts between eight great industrial areas bordering in general on the Arctic ocean and capable of supporting a modern war; and it incorporates the finding that the straight line routes or variations thereof connecting these areas pass through Arctic regions ... briefly, then, this concept simply states that the shortest path between two distant points of the Polar Cap in the Eastern and Western Hemisphere will follow a great circle route.[51]

Immediate post-war plans listing US air base requirements overseas – notably the plans revised by the JCS in the fall of 1945[52] – had also pointed to the importance of America's new "air frontier" in the Arctic. In the early post-war years leading air power enthusiasts and wartime heroes such as Henry Arnold, Commanding General of the USAAF during the war, George Kenny, the first Commander of SAC, and James Doolittle, Commander of the Eighth Air Force in the later stages of the war, all stressed the importance of the "polar perspective" as the key to an understanding of America's geostrategic predicament. As Michael Sherry makes clear, this interest in the Arctic did represent a "new awareness of the Soviet Union, its capacity to develop strategic air power, and the probable paths of attack in the air age."[53] Yet, until the late 1940s, the "polar strategy" does not appear to have had a *decisive* impact either on base or operational requirements of the USAF.[54] It was, above all, after the outbreak of the Korean War and the subsequent implementation of NSC-68 that the influence of the Polar Concept began to exert a more determining influence on the logistic and operational activities of the USAF.

In October 1950 the JCS activated the United States Northeast Command with the Northeast Air Command as its major component.[55] According to its first Commanding Officer, Lt-General Charles Myers, its creation reflected a "revised strategic concept" since the northeastern area had become "a frontline, a point of departure and a buffer between industrial centers of conflicting world powers."[56] The Greenland base agreement, signed on 27 April 1951, the subsequent construction of the strategic air base at Thule in north-west Greenland, and the US–Icelandic base agreement concluded in May 1951 (with additional rights granted to the US by a "supplementary understanding" in May 1954), were all expressions of the same trend.[57] In 1955 the Thule Air Base – constructed with unprecedented speed in 1951–52 following the recommendation of the Glober Committee of the USAF – was described by two influential commentators as "the most essential" of all of America's forward bases.[58] The importance of the polar routes in US strategic war plans, if anything, increased throughout the decade, as is indicated by a memorandum in February 1959 forwarded to General Twining, Chairman of the Joint Chiefs, by General Thomas Power, Commander of SAC. In the memorandum General Power stressed the urgent need for improvements in communications in the "Northern Area" since "approximately 90 percent of our alert force strike via a route traversing Alaska, Canada and Greenland."[59] How, then, as one writer put it, did this "budding awareness everywhere of the North, and the world-wide push into the Big Frontier," influence Norway's position in American strategy?[60]

Norway in American Air Strategy: Direct and Indirect Roles

Following the series of RAND studies in 1952–54 on the vulnerability of US strategic forces, SAC's deployment policy evolved from the principle of forward basing of whole bomber units to a greater emphasis on operations conducted from the continental United States[61] In 1955 SAC introduced "rotational training", whereby combat wings and air refuelling squadrons were deployed overseas for short periods of time.[62] These changes in SAC's concept of operations meant that Norway's role became primarily *indirect*, stemming from what Colonel Balchen described as a "double function" of the Arctic regions in relation to American air strategy.[63] First, Norway's central location in relation to the "minimum penetration paths" for American bombers *en route* to targets in the Soviet Union made it an important "route for missions."[64] As a result, Norway acquired a key role in monitoring *passive* and *active* Soviet air defences. Of particular importance in this respect was the radar order of battle and the extension of Soviet early warning (EW) and ground control intercept (GCI) radars along the northern Arctic approaches to the Eurasian land mass and along the Soviet-Finnish border.[65] Secondly, Balchen stressed the value of Norwegian territory as an outpost from which to obtain early warning of an attack against the US.[66] As an embassy report noted in 1957, Norway's strategic importance to the US derived, above all, from the fact that it provided "the most forward areas for early radar warning of possible attack on the continental United States, Canada and the UK."[67]

Before examining these functions in greater detail, however, it should be emphasised that even Norway's *direct* contribution to SAC's strategic bombing offensive did not disappear altogether.[68] There are three considerations here. In the first place, the arrangements that had been agreed between SAC and the Norwegian Air Force (RNAF) in 1952 concerning the use of Sola and Gardermoen for escort and post-strike staging of SAC units, remained in place. Secondly, in addition to the Main Operating Bases, American strategic air bases overseas fell into several distinct categories. And the use of these by American aircraft was, as the Secretary of Defense, Charles Wilson, told Eisenhower in 1953, governed both by "formal and informal understandings."[69] In a report by the British Joint Planning Staff prepared for the Prime Minister's visit to Moscow in 1959, Norway was listed as having eight "additional airfields" from which "fully laden B-47s of Strategic Air Command could operate if dispersed there in emergency."[70] The wording suggests that "informal" arrangements or "understandings" did govern the *wartime status* of Norwegian airfields other than Sola and Gardermoen.[71] Thirdly, in 1955, further service level agreements between the United States Air Force in Europe (USAFE) and the RNAF resulted in basing rights being granted for three GLOBECOM high-frequency radio communication stations in Norway to serve SAC requirements. One of these was at Bodø, the other two close to Gardermoen and Sola.[72] The GLOBECOM stations formed part of SAC's world-wide, point-to-point and air-ground communications system which was being rapidly expanded under Curtis LeMay's tenure as Commander of SAC. The relay stations were to "provide the link to pass tactical, strategic and traffic-control information and instructions between command posts, operational bases, air-traffic control centres and air-craft."[73] It would seem, however, that the Norwegian stations were of marginal importance to SAC plans throughout this period; the station at Sola was deactivated in the fifties and the facility at Bodø, manned by three US technicians in peacetime, was only activated in the late 1950s.[74] Shortly after the U-2 and RB-47 incidents in 1960, operations both at Gardermoen and Bodø were suspended.[75]

Norway's indirect role, however, only grew in importance after 1954. And, as indicated above, it was increasingly tied to two closely related functions: early warning of air attack against Continental United States and intelligence gathering about the Soviet radar order of battle and other components of the Soviet air defence system.

Mapping Soviet Air Defences in Northwest Russia

By 1953 the USAF was flying regular ELINT flights out of Norway and Britain directed against Soviet electronic capabilities. These "ferret" operations were designed to provide information about the technical characteristics, location and functions of Soviet radars by analysing a range of detectable variables. These included radio frequency, pulse width and pulse recurrence frequency, horizontal/vertical antenna pattern, antenna rotation and polarisation. Information about these variables made it possible to determine both the type of radar installations and their location along the Arctic coast. Starting in 1953 the US Air Force, in addition to airborne ELINT operations, also sponsored a programme of airborne platform intercept of VHF and UHF transmission of military activity on the Kola Peninsula. This was to be an "interim capability," the aim being to obtain "technical continuity on Soviet units which had ceased HF operations and are beyond the capability of ground-based intercept."[76]

In late 1953 the "minimum requirement" established for RB-50 ferret missions in Europe was nineteen missions during each three month period. The routes covered by these aircraft included one flight every ninety days to Franz Josef Land, known as *Route Victor*, and six flights each ninety days covering *Route Whisky*, the Barents Sea – Murmansk area.[77] In early 1954 the Director of Operations, USAF, requested that the Office of Intelligence, starting on 31 May 1954, provide *weekly* reconnaissance flight reports for the RB-50G ELINT flights in Europe.[78] In 1955 the RB-47H and RB-47K Stratojet began to replace the vulnerable RB-50s, RB-36s and modified B-29s in the ELINT role.[79] Between 1953 and 1955 the USAF had also taken delivery of another version of the aircraft, the RB-47E, which was equipped with advanced cameras for night and day photography. These various versions of the RB-47 became the backbone of the US strategic reconnaissance effort well into the 1960s and operated regularly in the far north.[80]

The US Navy carried out their own programme of airborne peripheral operations using "transport-type aircraft" and converted maritime patrol aircraft (Consolidated PB4Y Privateer and P4M-1Q Mercator) designed to obtain both electronic and communications intelligence.[81] Most peripheral ELINT flights along the Arctic coast were launched from bases in Britain, principally Lakenheath, Sculthorpe, Brize Norton and Mildenhall, but from 1956 onwards an increasing number of flights were also launched from North Norway, principally from the new airfield at Bodø. Even when flights were direct from Britain, the route chosen would follow the North Norwegian coast, utilising traffic control information provided by the Norwegian air force and, occasionally, emergency landings on Norwegian airfields would be required.[82] As seen in Chapter One, Norwegian authorities insisted that prior clearance be obtained through the Norwegian Foreign Ministry for any operation overflying Norwegian territory, and no flying of allied aircraft over Norwegian territory was permitted east of 24 degrees east. When prior clearance was not obtained, as in December 1952 when a KB-29 and a RB-45 reconnaissance aircraft from Lakenheath violated Norwegian air space at several points along the coast, formal protests were issued.[83]

What, then, did these operations reveal about the Soviet radar developments in the far north? Before 1955 the radar signals intercepted by RB-50G ferrets were primarily of two kinds, the Rus Dumbo-type radar and the Token radar signals.[84] The principal conclusion of these ferret operations was that the Soviet early warning system suffered from very limited range and height finding capabilities. An "especially significant shortcoming of Soviet air defences" was the lack of airborne interception radar for night and all-weather operations.[85] In order to overcome these weaknesses in the far north, a "significant effort" on the part of the Soviet Union was initiated in the latter part of the decade to "close the Arctic gap."[86]

In 1952 Soviet Arctic radar sites had been limited to a chain in the Murmansk area, capable of providing only very limited early warning and Ground Control Intercept (GCI) coverage. In the Western areas the growth of Soviet radars began in 1953 when a radar was established at Belushya Guba on Novaya Zemlya. By 1955, as much as sixty per cent of the Northern coast of the Soviet Union was provided with Aircraft Control and Warning (AC&W) cover, though "the Kola Peninsula was the only area along the Soviet Arctic Coast with what could be considered adequate radar coverage."[87] In 1956 a series of new radar sites was established along the Northern Arctic coast as well as on various Arctic islands scattered along the northern approaches to the Soviet Union. Further radars were constructed on Novaya Zemlya. And, between 1955 and 1958, a radar chain was gradually established eastward from the Severnaya Zemlya Islands to the Western coast of the Chukotski Peninsula. In October 1957 radars were also established on Franz Josef Land, on Wrangel Island and on some drift stations in the Arctic. By 1958 the ONI reckoned that the "Arctic gap" had effectively been closed. Soviet radar coverage was now estimated to extend from the Norwegian border to the Chukotski Peninsula, providing early warning coverage of 100 to 125 nautical miles.[88] The Norwegian Defence Intelligence Staff in June 1957 estimated that the Soviet Union had about 60 "control and warning" radars between the Norwegian border and the Urals north of the Arctic circle.[89]

In addition to the Russian Arctic coast line the Norwegian Defence Intelligence Staff also provided the US with detailed information about the location of Soviet air defence radars along the Soviet–Finnish border. This information showed that the Soviet radars were located well inside Soviet territory, a feature which formed the basis for what Norwegian intelligence representatives came to refer to as the "wedge-theory."[90] This simply held that the shortest distance for US bombers *en route* to Moscow, with minimum warning for Soviet air defences, would be through the Finnish wedge, over Finnish air space down to the central Baltic, and then east towards Moscow.[91] The "wedge theory" was presented to the members of the Standing Group intelligence committee in 1954 in an attempt to draw attention to the importance of the Northern flank.[92]

Norway as an Early Warning Outpost for CONUS

In September 1957, the American ambassador to Oslo, Frances Willis, in a meeting with her fellow Chiefs of Mission in Europe, stressed the

> close relationship between the security of North America and Norway since a Soviet air attack by the shortest route would pass over Norwegian territory. Norway thus takes on importance as a part of the early warning system.[93]

The importance which the US attached to this function in the latter half of the decade is evident in the provision of early warning equipment – long-range radars, heightfinders and tropospheric scatter communication systems – provided principally through bilateral channels in the form of grant aid.

Between June 1955 and the first half of 1956 a series of national radar stations (designated Combat Reporting Centres), equipped with American early warning radars provided bilaterally to Norway through the MDAP, became operational and underwent calibration flights. Most of these stations were at first equipped with two types of radar. The FPS-8, produced by General Electric, was a long-band long-range search radar with moving target indicator (MTI).[94] The other system, designated TPS-10D was produced by Radio Corporation of America, and was a heightfinder with a range of 220 kilometres designed to provide a basic ground controlled intercept capability. In 1955 these became operational at Måkerøy and Kongsvinger (July), Bodø (August) and Randaberg and Gråkallen (October). In January 1956 a TPS-10D installed at Kautokeino became operational, and in April 1956 the Combat Reporting Centre at Andenes began technical tests.[95] Simultaneously, following the decision in 1955 by SACEUR, General Gruenther, to establish an integrated early warning system along the approaches to Allied Command Europe, efforts were made to integrate the Norwegian stations into a continuous chain of radars.[96] On 21 June 1956 the stations in the NEC area went into 24-hours operation, with stations reporting to regional air centres which in turn reported to SHAPE and SAC. In May 1957, when additional stations in Bodø, Kautokeino and Vardø became operational, the chain of national stations covering the line of approach to Allied Command Europe was further extended.[97] By 30 September 1957 Phase I of SHAPE's Early Warning Plan, with six stations in Norway and five in Denmark, all operating on a 24-hour basis, was completed.[98] When discussions were held at SHAPE, in November and December 1955, about the integration of early warning systems in Western Europe, it was also decided that five high-power stations should be built in Norway in addition to existing ones. As Ambassador Willis pointed out in a despatch in June 1957, the early warning heavy radar chain in Norway would, when completed, cover as much as one-third of the NATO line.[99]

The northernmost stations in the early warning chain, such as the one at Vardø close to the Soviet border, also provided SHAPE with important "intelligence data."[100] Indeed, it is difficult to separate the early warning from the intelligence function, although certain stations were clearly geared more exclusively towards the intelligence function.[101] According to John Prados, seven COMINT stations were built in Norway in the latter part of the 1950s, although his source is not specified.[102] What is known is that in March 1955 General Samford forwarded a memorandum to the

Director of Plans, USAF, concerning the selection of sites for "several high-powered long range radar installations" in areas adjacent to the Soviet Union. Samford stated that "in light of general technical considerations such as range of equipment and the need for dispersion of units," the most suitable countries for these installations were Norway, Sweden, Greece, Iran and Afghanistan.[103] Half a year later, a memorandum for the newly appointed Secretary of the Air Force, Donald Quarles, shows not only that negotiations with Norway were progressing satisfactorily, but also that the Swedish Air Force was not adverse to co-operation with the US in the intelligence sphere. Responding to an earlier enquiry from Quarles whether "there had been any development in our requirement for detection stations in Sweden," General Samford, following a meeting with General Ljungdahl, Chief of the Swedish Air Force, wrote:

> I find that negotiations appear to be developing satisfactorily with Norway and that the requirement for a Swedish site does not presently appear to exist. We have found, however, that the Swedish representatives appear eager to assist in many ways, and in the event a detection site is required in Sweden, negotiations could be opened.[104]

It is worth noting in this context that the Commission on Neutrality Policy, established by the Swedish Government in July 1992, concluded in its final report that "permanent tele-communications links" between Sweden, Norway and Denmark were established in the 1950s.[105] These were ostensibly set up to support search-and-rescue operations. Although the links (initially only two voice channels) did not amount to a fully integrated air defence system for Scandinavia, they "facilitated communications between Swedish and Norwegian command and control centres and airbases". Moreover, the "main body" of those interviewed by the Commission about the project, was "of the opinion that these (links) also created scope for other types of co-operation (with Norway and Denmark; and, by further connection, also with other Western states)."[106]

Another project which the US considered particularly important was the establishment in Norway, initially on a test basis, of forward scatter communications lines. Forward ionospheric or tropospheric scatter techniques were not only more reliable than existing forms of communications, but were also required in the North and the Arctic because of the difficulties encountered with high or low frequency techniques in those regions.[107] On 7 December 1955 the requirement for a NATO-wide forward scatter system, to form the backbone of all NATO communications, was recommended by SHAPE to the Standing Group.[108] Following this recommendation, an initial pilot project for a four-station tropospheric scatter system from Oslo to Bodø was carried out under the auspices of SHAPE. This project, known as "Hot Line", was to be constructed on a top priority basis for the purpose of technical tests and operational evaluation. The priority for allocation of circuits was: (1) early warning, (2) "atomic strike co-ordination and control" and (3) command and alert.[109] Gruenther's Chief of Staff, General Schuyler, attached "the greatest significance to the accomplishment" of this project and the case provides a very good indication of Norway's direct importance to the US over and above their link through NATO.[110] Clearly, neither Schuyler nor his superior, General Gruenther, were merely thinking of the importance of early warning for NATO's Northern Flank. In fact, it is clear that the "additional warning" which a scatter system would give for an attack on North America by way of the polar basin was uppermost in their minds. In a signal from Gruenther in December 1957, approval of US funding for the project was urged on US Secretary of Defense Charles Wilson on the grounds that the system not only was vital for air operations in the North European theatre, but would also "contribute to our ability to provide early warning of possible air attack directed toward continental North America."[111] On 24 January the US government did approve payment of the Oslo-Bodø scatter line on a "test" basis, and in March the Norwegian Government accepted the proposals for the project.[112] By late 1957, four scatter lines had been planned for the NEC area: (1) a tropospheric scatter from Oslo via Trondheim and Mosjøen to Bodø and northwards to Vardø; (2) a tropospheric scatter from Oslo via Stavanger, thence to Paris via the Shetland Islands, Scotland and England, (3) a spur off the main system from Shetland to Iceland, and finally, an ionospheric link from Oslo to Denmark. The entire system was paid for by the US and used only for military purposes. It was completed in 1958.[113]

The relative scale of Norway's contribution in the field of electronic intelligence, communications and early warning is seen in the fact that in the latter half of the decade the US authorities became increasingly concerned about Norway's inability to man all the systems. In June 1958 Ambassador Willis noted that the "greatest manpower problem for the Norwegian military establishment is obtaining and retaining personnel trained in electronics ... [as] all new military as well as intelligence developments in Norway require this skill."[114] In 1960 the head of SHAPE's signals division told journalists that Norway simply had "too large electronic communications and early warning facilities compared with what the population can provide of qualified personnel."[115]

Having explored the practical steps taken to monitor the development of Soviet air defences and to obtain added warning through co-operation with

Norwegian authorities, it is necessary to look closer at US concern about the long-range bomber threat emanating from the Kola area.

III THE AIR THREAT FROM THE KOLA PENINSULA TO CONTINENTAL UNITED STATES, 1953–57

In the period between 1953 and late 1957 USAF intelligence focused its attention on the only areas from which Soviet Long Range Aviation (*Dalnaya Aviatsiya*) could – given limitations in aircraft design and inflight refuelling techniques – conceivably mount an attack on the North American continent: from forward bases in the Arctic and sub-Arctic regions of the Soviet Union. Three areas – the Chukotsky Peninsula, Kamchatka and the Kola Peninsula – were "deemed particularly advantageous as forward bases for surprise attack" since they were closest to the great circle routes to the US and would initially avoid overflight of "friendly" territory.[116] Yet the most important of these was clearly the Kola Peninsula, whose logistic location, though far from ideal, was more suitable than Far Eastern areas and northeastern Siberia.[117] In addition to the 277 kilometres-long Baltic–White Sea Canal (only open six months a year), there was one rail-line between Leningrad and Murmansk and one between Moscow and Arkhangelsk. By comparison, transportation facilities into Chukotski were in 1954 thought to be "limited to non-existent."[118]

In June 1952 the ONI presented a report on air facilities on the Kola Peninsula, stressing their *potential* threat against naval forces in the Barents Sea and as "bases for strategic bombing missions of long range."[119] By this time no aircraft of heavy or medium bomber class had operated in the area, nor were there any airfields capable of handling sustained operations of these types with the possible exception of Alakurtti, built by the Finns and used as a fighter base by the Germans in 1944, and Murmansk/Vayenga, used by both the Air Force and Naval Aviation. Although a number of smaller airfields and seaplane stations, mostly built by the Germans, were listed, the report concluded by stating that no "firm indications" suggested that heavy bomber airfields were being built. Instead, the construction programme in progress seemed to be "aimed at providing jet interceptor bases and improving facilities at fighter bases rather than improving Soviet offensive capabilities."[120]

In 1953, however, growing concern about the construction of airfields and support facilities on the Kola is evident. As a result, both the Air Force and the Navy began to take a more active interest in developments on the Peninsula. In late January the *New York Times* reported the existence of five Soviet airfields, all less than thirty-one miles from the Norwegian border.[121] Some of these were reported to have runways of more than 2000 yards. In September the AFOIN requested JCS approval for a photographic reconnaissance mission overflying the Kola Peninsula. The justification for violating Soviet air space was spelled out in a detailed memorandum.

> In order to assess properly a portion of the Soviet Air Force capability to launch strategic attacks against the continental United States, a critical requirement exists to obtain aerial photographs of certain specific areas on the Kola Peninsula.... Since the Kola Peninsula is one of the most favourably situated forward base areas for launching long range air attacks against the United States, accurate information on air base status and military and logistical activities for support of such operations represents one of the highest intelligence priorities.[122]

In late May 1954 the Director of Naval Intelligence, Admiral Carl Espe, in a letter to John Samford, his counterpart in the Air Force, requested that photography from two missions over "Murmansk–Kola Inlet Area ... completed with radarscope photography being obtained on the first mission and visual photography obtained on the second mission" be forwarded to his office.[123]

In addition to these reconnaissance missions, visual observation of Soviet air and ground traffic, radar installations and missile firing sites (from the Norwegian side of the border or by actual penetration of Soviet territory), was an important source of information about the Soviet build-up on the Kola Peninsula.[124] While there is little documentary evidence available on HUMINT operations in the border areas, the papers of Colonel Balchen – the Pentagon's foremost specialist on Scandinavian and Arctic affairs between 1948 and 1956 – do contain a detailed report on a "reconnaissance trip" along the Soviet-Norwegian border made between 29 September and 28 October, 1953.[125] While the report is admittedly an isolated one, it does provide an indication of the tactical intelligence targets in the area, as well as the American concern about activities of indigenous communists. The specific object of the trip was to establish the presence of air and radar installations in the Salmijärvi and Pehala area, a guided missile firing site near Kivitunturi–Petsamo–King Oscar Chapel, and "contact centers" between Norwegian communists and Soviet contacts. Heavy traffic, mostly military and including air-patrols straying over Norwegian territory, was recorded, and one local "rumour" suggested that as many as 45,000 Soviet troops were based in the area adjacent to the Norwegian border.

Although American concerns about the development of bomber bases on the Kola grew after 1953, Soviet capabilities remained limited. A Special National Intelligence Estimate in September 1954 calculated that 300 aircraft could be launched from bases in the Kola, Kamchatka and Chukotski areas, but that this could not be done on short notice, thus reducing the degree of surprise that could be achieved.[126] The estimate did stress, however, that by 1957 bases and equipment of Soviet long-range aviation "could" have improved to the point where only minimum preparation and therefore warning would be given prior to attack. By the end of 1954, then, the US intelligence community was still primarily concerned about the future potential of Arctic bases as staging areas for strategic bombing missions against Continental United States but was now expecting a major Soviet effort to be launched in order to realise this potential. In 1954 necessary preparations required for an attack to be launched from the Arctic were thought by the US intelligence community to give 15 to 30 days warning time. By 1957 it was *estimated* that this would have been reduced to a minimum of 24 hours for an attack of 1000 planes.[127] The National Intelligence Estimate of 1955 proceeded on the assumption that the "USSR is devoting a major aircraft production effort to the development of a massive intercontinental air attack capability."[128]

This conclusion was based on the emergence of three new bomber aircraft within the space of less than two years: the "Bison" (Type 37), a four-engine jet heavy bomber, first observed near Ramenskoye airfield in July 1953[129]; the "Badger" (Type 39), a twin-jet medium bomber first seen during the 1954 May Day rehearsals, and, finally, the "Bear", a four-engine turboprop heavy bomber which appeared on the scene in early 1955. With the "Bear" entering service, the Soviet Union achieved for the first time "the basic capability for two-way unrefuelled missions against practically all targets in the continental United States from bases in the USSR."[130] In late 1955 it was estimated that by 1959–60 the Soviet Union would have produced six to eight hundred "Bisons" alone. As a reflection of this growing concern about Soviet intentions in the long-range bomber field, a special Senate Subcommittee on Airpower, chaired by Senator Stuart Symington of Missouri, began hearings in April 1956. During these hearings the Air Force representatives stressed the unparalleled size of the Soviet effort to build up a long-range air force and the threat to the US over the Polar basin.

Already by late 1956, however, the Air Force case was increasingly being questioned by other services as well as by the President and Secretary of Defence. Revisions of the long-range Soviet bomber threat began in December 1956, and throughout 1957 previous alarmist estimates were significantly revised.[131] Much improved intelligence about air developments in the Kola, resulting from close collaboration with Norwegian authorities, made this revision possible.

The "bomber gap" controversy has been dealt with in detail elsewhere and need not be recounted here.[132] What is of interest, however, is that in spite of the gradual recognition that the long-range bomber threat had been overestimated, the Norwegian Defence Intelligence Staff, backed by the Norwegian Ministry of Defence, was clearly anxious to impress upon the US the continued importance of air developments on the Kola Peninsula.[133] There were three basic reasons for this, all of which shed an interesting light upon Norway's position in US and allied planning.

First, documents indicate that until 1957 there was genuine disagreement between Norwegian estimates of developments on the Kola Peninsula and those of the Standing Group of the North Atlantic Military Committee. This can be seen clearly in the comments forwarded by the Norwegian Defence Intelligence Staff in February 1956 to the Norwegian representative in Washington, Admiral Storheil, in connection with the preparation of the Standing Group intelligence estimate for that year.[134] Even in the revised version of the estimate there were still areas of disagreement about the Soviet "air order of battle" and the Norwegian Defence Staff insisted that Storheil make it clear that "with the information which we possess, our aircraft O of B [Order of Battle] is the correct one for the north-westerly area."[135] According to the Norwegian Defence Intelligence Staff, a significant expansion of facilities in the Kola area had taken place since 1945, and "at least fourteen airfields in the Kola area alone had been built to operate modern jet-bombers."[136] Additionally, the Soviet Union had conducted "intense air activity in Kola and other Arctic regions" over the past ten years. Specific disagreements concerned, for example, the construction of the Soviet air base at *Olenya*, which the Norwegians maintained was capable of operating heavy bombers.[137]

The second reason why the Norwegians emphasised the importance of the build-up on the Kola was that by doing so they hoped to highlight the vulnerability of North Norway at a time when NATO planning focused largely on the central front. The dominance of the continental perspective was clearly reflected in NATO's Standing Group intelligence assessments drawn up jointly each year in Washington by French, British and US representatives. The reports were sent to other NATO members for "comments only" and were, at least until 1957, received with dismay by Norwegian authorities.[138] The importance of these estimates to the Norwegians lay in the fact that they provided the basis for operational and logistic plans and therefore also for the allocation of infrastructure funds within NATO. In 1956 Admiral Storheil was instructed specifically to point out the importance of North Norway in the early "intense air war phase" of a war, and the grave consequences for NATO of losing it.[139] Thirdly, whilst the long-range threat to Continental United States turned out to be exaggerated, in 1956–57 a new threat was emerging from airfields on the Kola. At this time, Soviet naval aviation was being upgraded with the introduction of "Badgers" in the Northern Fleet air arm. These aircraft were seen to pose a most serious threat to the forward operations of US fast carrier groups in the North Atlantic.

Conclusion

Although the bilateral agreement which had been reached between Norwegian authorities and SAC in the autumn of 1952 continued to be operative throughout the 1950s, Norway's principal contribution to SAC planning lay in its ability to monitor Soviet air defence systems, especially the radar order of battle along the Arctic coast. The importance of acquiring accurate intelligence in this area was emphasised by the Killian panel which observed that "superior delivery systems... must be able to penetrate the Soviet defences without unacceptable losses."[140]

Apart from demonstrating the importance of Norway to the American intelligence programme, this chapter has also shown that Norway's place in American strategy was not exclusively (or even principally) tied to the formal treaty obligations linking these countries together in NATO. This is seen clearly in connection with the installation of the Forward Scatter communication system in Norway designed to meet requirements for early warning, atomic strike co-ordination and control. Approval of US funding for this project was urged on the US Secretary of Defense by General Gruenther on the grounds that the system was vital for the provision of adequate warning of air attack directed toward the North American conti-nent. In this case, NATO acted as a multilateral framework within which US–Norwegian bilateral issues could be handled. As will be seen, NATO (through SACLANT) performed a similar "legitimising" function during negotiations for pre-D-day construction of facilities and access for US naval patrol bombers to airfields in North Norway. In both cases, the fact that what were largely bilateral arrangements were set in a multilateral framework was also of great importance to Norwegian authorities who were always mindful of the possibility that too close an association with the US might undermine the domestic political consensus on matters of defence and security.

Finally, this chapter has shown that the expected development of a long-range Soviet strategic bombing capability in the Arctic regions of the Soviet Union did not materialise. Instead, the emergence of "Badger" bombers in Naval Aviation units gave added significance to Soviet naval developments in the far north.

3 The United States, Norway and the Soviet Naval Threat in Northern Europe, 1954–60

I THE GROWTH OF THE NORTHERN FLEET AND THE KOLA BASE COMPLEX, 1954–1960

The Baltic Fleet and the Northern Fleet: Shifting American Perceptions of the Naval Threat in Northern Europe after 1954

Until 1955, Anglo-American maritime concerns about Soviet intentions in European waters outside the eastern Mediterranean focused predominantly on the Baltic Sea and the defence of its three natural exits – the Sound, the Great Belt and the Little Belt. At one level, this was hardly surprising. Operating out of bases in Liepaja, Kaliningrad, Baltiijsk, Tallinn, Riga, and Leningrad, the logistic facilities available to the Baltic Fleet (Baltijskij Flot) – including ship repair, dockyard and construction facilities – were clearly superior to those of the other Soviet fleets. Indeed, from 1954 to 1960, the Baltic fleet, measured in terms of the total number of ships and personnel strength, remained the largest of the four Soviet fleets.[1] More important than logistic and gross numerical advantages, however, was the assumption – evident in early joint war plans, in the deliberations of the NAORPG and, later, in the NEC – that the Soviet Union attached the highest priority to securing the Baltic exits in the early stage of a war as part of their central front offensive across the German plain.[2] The corollary of this was the belief that the threat to the Scandinavian peninsula came from the south. Until 1960 this remained a key planning assumption at SHAPE, one consequence of which was that the Supreme Allied Commanders in Europe, and especially their British and, later, West German subordinate commanders, continued to regard the Baltic as strategically the most important fleet area.[3]

In the first half of the 1950s the absence of a West German navy, the weaknesses of Danish and Norwegian naval forces and the perceived importance of safeguarding the exits in support of the land-battle ensured that the US Navy also viewed this as an area of primary strategic interest.[4] In the summer of 1954, the ONI commented on the fact that the heaviest concentration of Soviet naval forces was located in the Baltic.[5] It observed that this was scarcely coincidental and that the importance of the Baltic fleet could not "be attributed merely to the industrial expansion of the Leningrad complex."[6] The Baltic Fleet would also assist in the seizure of all or parts of Scandinavia, since this would provide access to the Atlantic shipping lanes and also "deprive the free world of invaluable Scandinavian bases."[7] A naval intelligence brief a few months later noted that the "militarization of the Baltic States and the Leningrad area continues at a fast tempo" with a total of 76 known airfields that could be utilised by naval aviation drawn from the Leningrad, Baltic and Northern military districts.[8]

By the middle of the decade, however, the threat perceptions of the US Navy were beginning to change.[9] As was observed in Chapter One, signs that the US Navy was readjusting its priorities to a "northern strategy" after the early emphasis on the Mediterranean are evident well before 1955. These early indications of a growing interest in the high north had not, however, been translated into specific commitments nor had they detracted from the primary importance accorded to the Baltic area. By late 1954, the knowledge that West Germany would soon be playing an important role in the defence of the Danish straits was clearly a contributing influence on US naval policy. The principal factors, however, which prompted the growth of a *specific* American interest in the high north were, above all, the expansion of the Northern Fleet complex and the accompanying "shift in operating patterns" of the Northern Fleet itself.[10] More specifically, the US Navy was becoming increasingly concerned about the concentration of long-range submarines in the northern area, and by the parallel strengthening of land-based maritime air forces in the region. Both these developments were accompanied by a marked increase in the operational activities of the Northern Fleet beyond coastal waters in the Arctic. The relative shift in US Navy priorities coincided symbolically, in September 1954, with the first large movement of the Northern Fleet into the North Atlantic where it "conducted extended manoeuvres across the top of Scandinavia and down into the Norwegian Sea."[11]

The Development of the "Murmansk Complex," 1954–60

The report on the Kola Inlet produced by the ONI in September 1949 had examined existing naval facilities – the principal operating bases of Vayenga (Severomorsk) and Polyarnyy and the naval station at Guba Tyuva – in terms of their *future potential* as staging bases for attacking

North Atlantic shipping routes and supporting an "invasion of the Norwegian coast."[12] Close to ten years later, in March 1958, a new report about the Kola Inlet was produced. Significantly, this report discussed the base complex in terms of it being "the closest Soviet seaport, naval base, and military air centre" to the American eastern seaboard.[13] The report, which – as will be shown – benefited from both new sources of intelligence and improved co-ordination between US and Norwegian intelligence agencies, was far more detailed with regard to the strategic significance of the Inlet than previous studies.

Unlike other Soviet fleet areas in European waters, the inlet, being comparatively ice-free the year round and only seventy-five miles from the border with Norway, had easy access to Soviet-controlled waters.[14] Moreover, high and hilly land on either side of the Kola Fjord was seen to provide "excellent protection for a fleet of any size."[15] According to the ONI, recent and ongoing developments included: further construction on the principal supply depot and repair base of the Northern Fleet at the Rosta naval base, indications that the area between Murmansk, Chelnopushka, and Severomorsk was under development and contained a network of naval activities, and the continued dispersal of facilities in the hilly terrain around the Inlet to provide protection against nuclear attack.[16] Furthermore, "considerable improvements" had been made to Severomorsk (formerly Vayenga) – the site of the Northern Fleet headquarters and the principal base for surface units of the Northern Fleet – whose facilities now extended to Guba Varlamova (the bay immediately westwards).[17] Other smaller surface units were based at Guba Tyuva, further north on the eastern side of the inlet. Not far from Severomorsk there was also "one of the most important airfields in the Soviet Union" operated by the Air Force and with a concrete runway of 8000 feet. Clearly of greatest interest to US naval intelligence, however, was the continued expansion of Polyarnyy (and auxiliary bases) since this was the principal long-range submarine base of the Northern Fleet. Polyarnyy, originally the only port and administrative centre in the area until the founding of Murmansk in 1915, was located on the Western side of the Inlet. It was concealed from view by vessels entering the Inlet and benefited from "excellent natural protection."[18] It was supported by additional submarine facilities nearby at Guba Olen'ya and Guba Sayda. Both of these latter bases were listed as submarine and patrol craft bases, with the former having a naval storage depot, and Guba Sayda also serving as a destroyer base.[19] A further "major development in the Arctic in recent years" was the completion of a rail line running along the western side of the inlet to Polyarnyy, and from there further west to Pechenga (formerly the Finnish port of Petsamo). The

ONI report of 1958 suggested that Pechenga, described as "very close to the Norwegian border," was also under development as a naval operating base for the submarines. In fact, three years earlier, in July 1955, British naval intelligence had reported that, whilst no confirmation was available, a series of submarine shelters were believed to have been constructed in the Soviet Northern Fleet area.[20] It was thought that shelters had been built in Maatti Inlet, near Pechenga (Petsamo) and in Saida Guba, near Polyarnyy.[21] In addition to the bases in the Kola Inlet, a further report by ONI in April 1959 pointed to the growth of the Arkhangelsk complex in the White Sea area, and the "important" submarine base at Yokanga (Gremikha) on the Barents Sea coast.[22] Close to Arkhangelsk, by the delta of the Dvina river, was also located the important Severodvinsk shipbuilding yard, a major object of US intelligence.[23]

Interfleet Transfers and the Growth of Naval Aviation in the Arctic, 1954–60

From 1955 onwards there was a marked increase in the rate of interfleet transfers benefiting the Northern Fleet at the expense of the Baltic and Black Sea Fleets. Although there had been similar transfers earlier, notably during the Korean War,[24] the process intensified in the middle of the decade when units began to be redeployed in "considerable numbers."[25] In April 1955 the largest known submarine tender, Neva, sailed from the Black Sea to Murmansk.[26] The following month, a Soviet surface force consisting of two Sverdlov-class cruisers and four Kola-class escorts were reported to have moved from the Baltic to the Northern Fleet areas, proceeding through the Great Belt and along the Norwegian coast.[27] In January 1956, the redeployment of two large naval auxiliaries, *Severodonets* and *Leninskaya Kuznitsa*, from the Baltic to the Northern Fleet, was seen by British naval intelligence to be part "of the present policy of increasing the logistic support of the Northern Fleet."[28] In the light of these developments, the US Joint Intelligence Committee, in February 1956, concluded that Northern Fleet inferiority in surface vessels was "gradually being overcome by transfers from the Baltic and the output of the large yard at Molotovsk in the White Sea."[29] In April and May of 1958, another six major surface combatants, including a Kotlin-class destroyer, relocated from the Baltic to the Northern Fleet. And in August and December that same year, another four Riga-class escorts made similar transfers.[30] Although the movement of surface units from the Baltic to the Northern Fleet between 1955 and 1960 had a somewhat uneven pattern (and was occasionally followed by further redeployment to the

Pacific Fleet via the Northern Sea route), the trend was clear. Moreover, it was accompanied by two further developments which the American intelligence community viewed as far more ominous: (1) the growth of Soviet naval aviation in the Arctic, and (2) the concentration of modern long-range submarines in northern bases.

In late 1953, the US Strategic Plans Division listed land-based aircraft as one of the "principal threats" to Allied shipping and control of the seas. At this time, the major challenge was seen to come from an estimated 700 "Bosun" (TU-14) naval attack aircraft, specifically designed and developed for use against shipping, and some 800 to 1000 "Beagle" light-bombers (IL-28), an aircraft originally designed for use against tactical ground targets.[31] The Strategic Plans Division considered the threat from the "Bosun" force to be "critical in the Northeast Atlantic – Norwegian Sea – Barents Sea Area."[32] The term "critical" in the 1953 paper was inserted partly in order to impress senior administration officials about the need for a "desirable" level of attack carriers. From 1954 onwards, however, the emergence and subsequent incorporation into the Northern Fleet Air Force of a new jet-bomber, the "Badger" (TU-16), became a major source of concern to naval planners. A study presented shortly after the very first appearance of the aircraft in early 1954, stated that the capability to attack Allied naval forces had been "considerably enhanced by the recent acquisition of new twin-jet swept-wing bombers."[33] The study concluded that:

> the Type 39 is an ideal aircraft, entirely suited to act in an offensive role against naval forces. Its estimated speed and high-altitude performance coupled with its bomb-carrying capability, gives the Soviets an opportunity for attack against Allied naval forces which they did not previously enjoy.[34]

Once the *potential* of the "Badger" against Western naval forces had been established, particularly close attention was given to any signs indicating that "Badgers" were becoming operational with the Northern Fleet. Close co-ordination with Norwegian military authorities, relying both on visual observation in the border areas and on radar plotting of air activity in the Barents Sea area, was a key source of intelligence for the US.[35] In the spring of 1955, the Soviet Union was reported to be showing increased interest in naval aviation operations under Arctic conditions. According to the ONI:

> reconnaissance of the northern approaches indicates that the Soviet Naval aviation has an interest in the Arctic approaches and has developed some capability for Arctic reconnaissance.[36]

Later in the year the ONI Review devoted a separate article to the development of Soviet air power in the Arctic, and concluded that

The Soviet capability for air operations in the Arctic is steadily on the increase. This increasing capability is a valuable by-product of a well-thought-out, long-range plan of exploitation of the northern areas for economic and military purposes.[37]

Although the continuation of the jet conversion programme in 1955 resulted in a "greatly improved ... capability for defence of seaward areas and shore installations against enemy naval, amphibious or air attacks,"[38] Soviet naval aviation in the far north remained severely handicapped by the preponderance of obsolete aircraft with limited to non-existent all-weather capability.[39]

Related to these developments, in the middle of the decade the US Air Force and Navy also stepped up their efforts to monitor Soviet Arctic activities in *three* other areas. These were: the use of drifting ice floes as landing strips on island groups, the activities of scientific expeditions,[40] and airfield construction and logistic developments in the Arctic.[41]

In 1956 a significant strengthening of the Northern Fleet Air Force was reported when medium bombers, "Badger" and the earlier piston-engined "Bull", were *actually* observed near Murmansk for the first time. This development, while expected, was judged to give the Soviet Union a new and "considerable potential for attacking Allied naval forces and shipping with atomic weapons."[42] Moreover, the "Badger" provided an ideal platform for air-to-surface missiles of the "Komet" type, of which little was known but which was believed by the US Navy to be designed for maritime operations.[43] Also in 1956, intelligence indicated a continuation of development of major air facilities in the Soviet Arctic. The following year the ONI reported a "major increase in jet medium bombers" for the Navy along with additional indications that "Badger" and "Bull" aircraft were "very active" in the Soviet Northern Fleet Air Force. A marked increase in operational flight exercises over international waters and in the Arctic more generally was also reported to have taken place.[44]

In January 1958 the ONI described how "Soviet military authorities," by introducing "Badger" bombers into naval air units, had succeeded in "enhancing considerably the strike capabilities of naval aviation."[45] Carriers launching strikes within the radius of shore-based "Badgers" were now seen to be faced with a "serious defence problem," and later in the year this particular issue was examined in a separate article.[46] Here it was pointed out that:

the principal value of the "Badger" as a maritime aircraft lies in the fact that it can carry a nuclear payload at a jet speed out to 1,500 nautical miles. That distance covers our carrier launch lines, which would normally be a thousand miles out. An integral part of the "Badger" threat is its capability to deliver 55 mile-range "Komet" air-to-surface missile.[47]

In 1958, the number of "Badgers" was estimated to have increased from 165 to 290, with the Northern Fleet as the "chief beneficiary" having received 75 additional aircraft during the course of the year.[48] With a total "Badger" strength of 110 the Northern Fleet had more than any other fleet. This view was shared by Norwegian military intelligence which in early 1960 noted that the Baltic Fleet air force, unlike the Northern Fleet, had not yet been equipped with "Badgers".[49] In SACLANT's Emergency Defence Plan for 1958 the air threat was assumed to have been "considerably increased" with the introduction of the "Badger" bomber to the naval air arm.[50] In May 1959, the Norwegian Defence Intelligence Staff noted that the Northern Fleet Air Force had completed its conversion programme to medium jet bombers and that these would be used, *inter alia*, to counter NATO Strike Fleet operations in the Norwegian Sea.[51] The report also observed that Soviet long-range offensive capabilities had increased in recent years as a result of the construction of a number of bases in the arctic region in the period after 1955.[52] Finally, in 1960, it was reported that the "Badger" had been equipped with the "Komet" air-to-surface missile and that these had now been introduced into air regiments in the Northern Fleet area.[53]

As indicated earlier, once the decision had been taken to bring West Germany into NATO in late 1954, the task of implementing a forward defence in and around the Baltic Approaches appeared less formidable than it had been earlier in the decade. This had the important effect of allowing the US Navy to concentrate more of its operational activity and intelligence efforts in the North Atlantic, leaving the defence of the Baltic exits to British, German and Danish forces. West German naval rearmament, which began in earnest in 1956, did indeed transform, albeit gradually, the unfavourable strategic situation which had prevailed in the Western Baltic in the early part of the decade. The *Bundesmarine* was given the tasks of denying enemy passage through the Danish straits, interrupting communications as far east as possible, and assisting in the defence of the Danish isles and the German Baltic coast near the Kiel Canal.[54] In August and September 1957, the first allied naval exercise in which the German navy took part, known as Spring Double, was held in Danish waters.[55] Shortly after the exercise, the ONI reported that it was now "doubtful" whether a submerged submarine could transit any of the various channels through the Danish isles undetected.[56] At the same time, a paper released by the US Navy officially acknowledged that exiting the Baltic "under wartime conditions ... could be made only with great difficulty."[57] The submarine threat emanating from Russian northern bases posed an altogether different problem.

II   THE EVOLUTION OF THE SOVIET SUBMARINE THREAT

The Soviet Union's Long-Range Submarine Programme

Although in Congressional hearings military representatives occasionally pointed to the growing potential of the Soviet surface fleet in the 1950s, declassified documents show that it was never regarded as a serious challenge to Western *sea control* in the Atlantic.[58] Western preponderance in major and minor warships was simply too large for there to be any credible surface threat outside coastal waters and the protective cover of shore-based aviation. According to JCS estimates in 1956, the US and its allies had 359 major and minor warships in the Atlantic area. The corresponding "Soviet bloc" figure, which included the Baltic fleet, was 137.[59] Moreover, in 1955 Khrushchev finally shelved the post-war Stalinist "big navy" strategy to create a large and balanced surface fleet.[60]

The perceived threat from the growing force of long-range "Whisky" (W) and "Zulu" (Z) class submarines, and the parallel Soviet efforts to develop a sea-based ballistic missile capability, were seen to pose a very different set of challenges. Before turning to a more detailed examination of the impact of these developments on Norway's place in American strategy, it is necessary first to look more closely at the Soviet submarine programme and American perceptions of it. In so doing, it is useful to distinguish between two periods.

The first period, running from 1950–51 through early 1957, was characterised by a rapid growth in the actual number of submarines. The second period, from 1957 through 1960–61, saw a marked reduction in the rate of production and delivery. This did not, however, lead to any corresponding diminution of American concern about what came to be referred to as the "Red sub peril."[61] On the contrary, against the background of Sputnik and of American technological breakthroughs in the field of nuclear propulsion and guided missile technology, apprehension about the submarine threat only intensified. By late 1957 the focus of intelligence acquisition had shifted towards expected *qualitative* improvements, that is, any signs of a

Soviet breakthrough in the field of nuclear propulsion and/or missile-carrying submarines.

Quantitative Expansion and Bias in Favour of the Northern Fleet, 1951–57

According to the Joint Intelligence Committee (US) in January 1956, between 1951 and 1956 the Soviet Union had launched some 180 modern long-range and 13 medium-range submarines.[62] Again, however, it was in the latter half of 1954 that evidence of a "truly dramatic" construction programme emerged.[63] In the spring of 1955, the ONI concluded that "construction of long-range submarines has reached mass production level, with every indication that this level will be maintained for the time being."[64] In the late 1940s, when production of the *W* and *Z* classes began, four *W* class boats were built for each *Z* class. By 1954 the ratio had changed to ten *W* class submarines for each *Z* class.[65] The "Whisky," the first postwar production design, was a 1050-ton derivative of the advanced snorkel-fitted German Type XXI submarine and had an estimated operational radius of 4250 miles.[66] It was assumed that the "Whisky" class would be employed "in force" as torpedo attack units against allied shipping.[67] The *Z* class, referred to as a "large ocean-going type," was an enlarged 1850-ton derivative of the K-I submarine built by the Soviet Union between 1940 and 1947. Given its extended operating radius, the "Zulu" class was thought to be ideally suited for long-range raiding as well as for supporting a large-scale submarine mine laying campaign for which there was a "traditional Russian predilection."[68]

Some 107 *W* and *Z* boats had been completed by the end of 1954.[69] Developments during 1955 confirmed earlier predictions with 75 long-range and 10 short-range submarines (*Q* class) built in that year alone. The ONI noted alarmingly that the "mass production of submarines is now more apparent than ever."[70] It expected that the entire force of prewar boats would be replaced within the next few years. In the winter and spring of 1956, worries within the American intelligence community about the eventual size of the submarine fleet appear to have reached a highpoint. In January, the JIC predicted that on the basis of existing trends another 90 long-range submarines would be built in 1956, and that a further 105 would be completed in 1957.[71] The Soviet building programme was now described as having accelerated to a rate "never before seen in time of peace, exceeded only by the feverish effort of Nazi Germany at the height of their wartime effort."[72] It was feared that "some time" in 1956, the Soviet Union would be able to keep at sea more long-range submarines of postwar design than did Germany at the very peak of their wartime effort.[73] By 1958, the Soviet Navy would be able to keep on patrol as many as 283 long-range and 42 medium-range submarines.

In terms of operational deployment there was a strong bias in favour of the Northern Fleet. Moreover, given the Fleet's comparatively unrestricted access to the Atlantic, it was assumed to be "logical for future dispositions to favour the Northern Fleet."[74] The National Intelligence Estimate for the period 1955 through 1960, provides a very clear indication of the reorientation of US intelligence and strategic concerns towards the northeast Atlantic and the Northern Fleet area.[75] Whereas the number of modern long-range submarines attached to the Baltic Fleet between 1955 and 1960 was estimated to increase from 43 to 83, the corresponding increase in the Northern Fleet was from 60 to 169.[76]

The growing importance of the Northern Fleet also appeared to be confirmed by what the ONI, NID and Norwegian military intelligence saw as a significant increase in the level of submarine tactical training and the extension of peacetime patrol areas far beyond coastal waters. Between 1954 and 1955, there had been a dramatic increase in the number of "unidentified submarine contacts" world-wide (from 157 to 211).[77] The number of "out-of-area contacts" had increased by fifty per cent, with most contacts taking place in the North Atlantic.[78] Although these figures did reflect improved detection capabilities – brought about, not least, by the introduction in 1956 of the long-range sound surveillance system (SOSUS) in the North Atlantic[79] – an intelligence briefing note for Eisenhower in September 1956 did stress the "marked increase in Soviet submarine patrols in areas far removed from Soviet operational waters."[80] In his report on "Russian naval and related matters" for the third quarter of 1955, the British naval attaché in Moscow observed that 1955 had been "notable for the high intensity of training in submarine warfare" and for the emphasis that was being placed on "training under wartime conditions and also severe winter conditions particularly in the Northern Fleet."[81]

Expected Technological Breakthrough and the SSBN Threat, 1957–60

Although the projected production figure for the *W* class in 1956 was 80, in the latter half of the year it was becoming increasingly obvious that the Soviet naval build-up was slowing down significantly.[82] Evidence pointing in this direction included: the Tallin class of large destroyer was apparently limited to one ship with no new destroyer class identified; the Sverdlov cruiser construction programme was suspended (including work on uncompleted ships); and, most significantly, construction of the largest of the post-war long-range submarines, the Z class, had ceased.[83] In 1957, the ONI reckoned that the Z class construction programme had actually ended as early as in 1955, with a total of 18 delivered units. The trend continued in 1957 when production of the W class also came to an end, with an estimated total of 240 boats delivered.[84] In November 1957, Allen Dulles, the CIA Director, told a Senate investigating committee that the "sharply curtailed" construction of long-range conventional submarines "probably" signalled the termination of this programme.[85] About a year later, in October 1958, the ONI reported that submarine construction had "virtually ceased."[86] Thus, the gloomiest predictions of early 1956 did not materialise and the Soviet submarine order of battle stabilised around 450.[87]

The dramatic slow-down in production did nothing, however, to reduce American concerns about the Soviet submarine threat, which intensified in the summer and autumn of 1957. The basic reason for this was the conviction, held not only by the naval establishment but also by the President and the wider scientific community, that the halt in production could only mean that the Soviet Union would "soon adapt missiles and nuclear propulsion to all classes of warships and return to full-scale naval construction geared to the atomic age."[88]

The prospect of a direct sea-based threat to the eastern sea-board of the continental United States had the effect of further shifting the focus of US maritime interest towards the north-east Atlantic and Soviet northern bases. In November 1957, Dr Herbert Scoville, head of the Office of Scientific Intelligence in the CIA, told the Preparedness Investigating Subcommittee of the Senate – convened to discuss the implications of the Sputnik launchings – that his office was "particularly interested in the large concentration of 115 long-range subs in the Northern Fleet area."[89] The reason for this was partly its geographic location and partly the fleet's potential. It possessed a large number of types available for modification or conversion to guided-missile use. In the period between 1957 and 1960, Admiral Jerauld Wright, CINCLANT and overall Commander for Allied forces in the Atlantic, appears to have been particularly concerned about Soviet submarine developments.[90] And in May 1957, the British Joint Planning Staff, commenting on a recent paper by Admiral Wright noted how he was outlining "a new and major role for NATO naval forces, namely the countering of the threat from Soviet submarines armed with guided missiles."[91]

Given what is now known about the Soviet SSBN programme, the American concern about the potential threat of Russian missile-firing submarines operating against the eastern seaboard of the North American continent emerged surprisingly early and stood in sharp contrast to British assessments. In fact, as early as January 1954, Vice-Admiral Hughes Hallet, Chairman of the British Joint Service Mission in Washington, wrote to Admiral McGrigor, the First Sea Lord, pointing out that:

> There are indications that an opinion is gaining strength within some United States and particularly United States Navy circles that the submarine, armed with the guided missile, presents a major threat to the seaboard cities of the United States.[92]

These initial American concerns centred around possible modifications of the Z class, and although the first successful test-firing of a guided missile from a Z class submarine was reported in 1955, the first "unusually configured" "Zulu"class submarine was only observed in 1956. In his letter to McGrigor in 1954, Admiral Hallett stated that "the exaggerated concept of a submarine borne atomic onslaught against the American Continent is potentially dangerous."[93] The Joint Planning Staff in 1957 felt that although a nuclear threat from submarine launched missiles "may eventually materialise," it was not believed that the Soviet Union would be in "possession of sufficient submarines of the type necessary to contribute significantly to the threat of nuclear bombardment until well after 1962."[94] In 1957 and 1958, the British continued to emphasise the lack of evidence suggesting a direct application of missiles in the Soviet Navy, conceding only that a few submarines may have been "fitted to fire flat trajectory missiles, probably for trials."[95]

Quality of US Assessments: Mirror-Imaging and Focus on Capabilities

Jan S. Breemer, in his study of Soviet submarine strategy, found it surprising that the US naval intelligence community, having discussed the prospect of a Soviet SSB threat to the continental United States since the late 1940s, was "reluctant to accept the existence of a Soviet SLBM capability" until 1959.[96] In fact, as indicated above, the failure of the US naval intelligence to do so certainly did not stem from lack of willingness to present the submarine threat as a real and menacing one. On the contrary, it may be argued that even in 1959, one had to search very hard for evidence of an *operational* SLBM capability in the Soviet Navy, let alone one carried on a nuclear-powered submarine. Breemer appears to acknowledge as much by pointing out that the "Zulu Vs" and the "Golfs" (the two classes which enabled the Soviet Union to claim that it had been the first country to deploy a SLBM system), "contributed little "effective" value to its strategic posture."[97] Although the *conventional* submarine threat appeared formidable on paper,[98] the question arises as to why the US displayed such concern for the Soviet SSBN from 1957 onwards.

Four related factors stand out. First, there was the problem of "mirror-imaging", that is, there was a tendency to estimate Soviet advances in the areas of guided missile technology and nuclear propulsion by analogy with developments in the US.[99] Second, there were the actual technological advances made by the Soviet Union in the latter part of the decade; advances brought into sharp relief by the Sputnik launchings in October and November 1957. A third factor which appears to have influenced American perceptions was the repeated emphasis in Soviet statements on the "revolutionary" impact of advances in submarine technology and their determination to exploit this. A fourth and final factor which shaped American assessments of the nature of the Soviet submarine threat in northern waters was the perceived "gaps in Atlantic naval defences that the reductions in British naval strength [following Sandys's defence review] had opened."[100] This subject will be examined in more detail in chapter five.

Mirror-imaging

Early American concerns about the Soviet Union's ability to launch missiles from submarines corresponded to the US Navy's first tentative experiments with two competing pilotless aircraft for use against targets ashore, the supersonic SSM-N-6 Rigel and the subsonic SSM-N-8 Regulus. Whilst the Rigel was abandoned in 1953, the Regulus was declared operational with nuclear weapons in May 1954, though the first operational deployment appears only to have taken place some two years later.[101] By that time, however, the Fleet Ballistic Missile Programme (Polaris) was under way, having been launched in late 1955 following assurances from the Atomic Energy Commission that a smaller MRBM warhead could be produced to fit a sea-based missile.[102] During the first half of 1957, a series of technological breakthroughs were made during tests with the Polaris missile, an important consequence of which was to influence US intelligence assessments of the future submarine threat once the Soviet Union successfully completed its own programme. In February 1957, the firing of test vehicles in the Polaris programme "successfully evaluated a method for reversing the thrust of a solid propellant missile in flight."[103] The following month, the highest "total impulse ever achieved by a solid fuel rocket in this country" was attained during a Polaris test flight. On the basis of these results, it was decided on 19 April 1957, that the Polaris project should be given the highest priority "which would not interfere with the other missile programs and ... would not be tied to the submarine construction schedule."[104] In June, further technological hurdles were overcome, when solid propellants were used for the first time. The following month, an experimental submarine launcher for the Polaris programme was successfully tested.

Advances in submarine technology, especially improvements in propulsion, had a similar impact on US perceptions about the Soviet Union.[105] The first nuclear-powered submarines, the *USS Nautilus* signalled "underway on nuclear power" on 17 January 1955. The full potential of this "new weapon of war" and its implications for Norway's place in US maritime strategy, became even more apparent in August 1958 when the *Nautilus*, journeying from Hawaii to Iceland, navigated under the North Pole ice cap.[106] This newest achievement of the *Nautilus*, wrote Hanson Baldwin, the *New York Times's* veteran military columnist, had "immense strategic implication."[107] As Baldwin put it, the "missile firing submarine manoeuvring in the Arctic opens a new strategic frontier. The whole vast Arctic coastline of Russia is potentially open to assault."[108] A report prepared by the Underseas Warfare Advisory Panel to a Senate subcommittee was released on "the heels of the exploits of the *Nautilus* and *Skate*" and spoke of a "grossly inadequate" ASW capability to meet the Soviet undersea challenge.[109]

Soviet technological achievements

The tendency towards mirror-imaging and the *capabilities-orientated* approach to intelligence assessment, were reinforced by real evidence of Soviet technological prowess. The launchings of Sputnik I and II in 1957, in particular, seem to have heightened American concerns about an imminent breakthrough in the Soviet submarine-launched missile programme.[110] Although Eisenhower himself does not seem to have been unduly alarmed by the Soviet missile launches the psychological reaction elsewhere showed just how deeply entrenched the belief had become that the American continent was invulnerable to direct external threats.[111] This only reinforced the tendency to impute capabilities and technological achievements on the USSR not warranted by existing intelligence.[112]

Soviet statements on seapower

From 1955 onwards, the expansion of the Soviet submarine fleet was accompanied by repeated statements – official and un-official made at all levels of the Soviet hierarchy – to the effect that the Soviet Navy was now concentrating its efforts on achieving an SLBM capability. Nikita Khrushchev, who had consolidated his power base in 1955, was particularly impressed by the possibilities which the application of guided missiles to submarines appeared to offer.[113] In April 1956, the British Naval Attaché in Moscow, Captain G.M. Bennet, travelled with Khrushchev and Bulganin aboard the Sverdlov-class cruiser *Ordzhonikidze* en route to Portsmouth. In his report, Bennet emphasised how Khrushchev had "made a big point of the importance to the Soviet Union of the submarine fleet."[114] "These, he said, properly armed with guided missiles, would be what they most required and would even be able to attack the United States."[115] In a much-publicised interview with UP correspondent Shapiro on 14 November 1957, Khrushchev told Shapiro in his usual blustering manner that it was possible to keep "all of America's vital centres under fire from submarines and with the help of ballistic missiles, to blockade the United States coast."[116] Soviet military writers, notably from 1957 onwards, also discussed at length the potentiality of submarine-launched missiles against the continental United States.[117]

III NORWAY'S INTELLIGENCE CONTRIBUTION

Norway's geographic location placed it in an ideal position to observe the transfer of units between fleet areas as well as to monitor the increased level of submarine training and the build-up of facilities on the Kola Peninsula. In the first half of the decade, however, co-ordination and reporting mechanisms between US and Norwegian authorities were poorly developed. For example, an intelligence memorandum in the summer of 1952 commenting on the transfer of Soviet cruisers from the Baltic to the Northern Fleet the previous year, observed that Norwegian surveillance on that occasion had been "wholly inadequate."[118]

It was the movement, in the late summer of 1954, of a large Soviet task force out of its northern bases which led directly to an American initiative that sought both to increase intelligence and reconnaissance efforts in the area, and to co-ordinate these more closely with Norwegian military authorities. In November 1954 the Director of Naval Intelligence, Rear Admiral Carl F. Espe, described the recent "operations in the Norwegian Sea, when the entire cruiser strength of the Northern Fleet, accompanied by twelve destroyers, moved out of the restricted area of the Barents Sea for an extended exercise ... as an object lesson of the changes taking place in the Soviet navy."[119] The Soviet exercise had also brought home another lesson: the weaknesses of Western reconnaissance capabilities in the area.

In a letter to Admiral Jerauld Wright (CINCLANT) on 9 November 1954 the Chief of Naval Operations, Admiral Robert Carney, noted that in view of the "lack of adequate reconnaissance ... as evidenced by the recent sortie of Soviet Naval Forces," existing inter-service or bilateral agreements for fleet intelligence gathering in the East Norwegian Sea and North Cape area had to be re-examined.[120] In his response to this query, Admiral Wright noted that "the interest in this problem was engendered ... by the intensification of the threat which could be imposed on the security of the US by the unobserved movement of Soviet naval forces in this part of CINCLANT's area of responsibility."[121] Although Norway in 1951 had assumed joint responsibility for reconnaissance of the East Norwegian Sea and North Cape area, no agreements for continuous reconnaissance in peacetime had been worked out.[122] While Admiral Wright felt that responsibility for reconnaissance of Soviet naval activity in the area should be a "United Kingdom and/or Norwegian task," he gave his qualified approval of a draft plan referred to as "Operation Project Squint".[123] The project, which included the implementation of measures to obtain photographic and electronic countermeasures intelligence in addition to visual reconnaissance and tracking, were indicative of the steadily growing preoccupation in the mid-1950s with developments in and around the Kola peninsula.

Further evidence of this occurred the following year, when the US Navy began to formulate plans for conducting submarine intelligence operations in the high north, a task which had hitherto been entrusted to the Royal Navy. In a letter to the First Sea Lord, Lord Mountbatten, in October 1956, Vice-Admiral R.F. Elkins, the UK Standing Group representative in Washington, reported on recent US submarine activities:

> What has surprised us here has been to discover the scale of these USN submarine intelligence operations. No less than 6 submarines were on patrol between August and October, covering the Siberian end of the Northern Sea Transfer... The USN have been doing this sort of thing with immunity from Russian interference since 1952, and it is evident that at present Soviet A/S measures are such that our submarines might meet little opposition in peace or war.[124]

Not long after this report, the US Navy instituted similar operations covering the Murmansk coast and the Barents Sea end of the Northern Sea Transfer. In February 1957, the USS *Tirante* was scheduled to carry out the first "northern patrol" in what the ONI hoped would be "a series of patrols to provide thorough coverage of the Northern Fleet by submarine reconnaissance."[125] According to the British officer briefed about the US operations, the reason for initiating these patrols was twofold. First, Britain, having cancelled a programme of operations along the Murmansk coast, was:

> no longer providing sufficient cover in an area where we have hitherto been a productive and reliable source; secondly, having recently been given access to the reports of our own submarine operations off the Murmansk coast, the USN have been able to persuade the State Department of the feasibility and value of such operations, and that the risks of detection are negligible.[126]

In 1956–57 both SOSUS and submarine patrols were supplemented by electronic intercepts of submarine communications from Norway covering the Northern Fleet area.[127] In 1956, the Norwegian Defence Intelligence Staff stepped up its seabased electronic surveillance when a US-equipped vessel, *Eger*, was launched and began monitoring Soviet naval activity in northern waters.[128]

Aerial reconnaissance was a further source of information on submarine developments in the high north, though the U-2 flight in October 1957 referred to earlier was, as far as it is known, a relatively rare operation.[129]

Norway's contribution to the monitoring of submarine activity can be gauged by a survey of the monthly scores of submarine contacts, which the ONI began to publish in September 1958.[130] On 11 September 1958, for example, ONI records show that a submarine was "contacted" by a Norwegian trawler off the Norwegian coast.[131] On 24 March, 1959, a Norwegian radar station spotted a submarine on the north east coast of Norway.[132] Both these cases show that the reporting system between Norwegian and US authorities had improved markedly since the early attempts at co-ordinating intelligence efforts in the area.[133]

Norway also held a particularly close watch on the Soviet Union's north Atlantic fishing fleet. From 1957 onwards, as increasing attention was paid to limited war scenarios in the NATO area, the US Army, Marine Corps and Navy displayed an ever-growing concern about the "real intentions" of the Soviet merchant and fishing fleets in the Norwegian and Barents Sea. They were seen as an "ever-present threat to the military security of certain sensitive areas, such as North Norway and Iceland."[134] In early 1957, over 2000 ships were assigned to Soviet shipping companies in Northern Europe, with as many as 300 trawlers observed together in the Norwegian sea at one time. In June 1957 the ONI noted how the Soviet fishing fleet had begun to appear in large numbers year-round in the Norwegian sea in 1950–51. While the report was careful to conclude that the Soviet vessels were not "necessarily" engaged in "sinister, political or intelligence activity," the fleet did have every opportunity to "obtain up-to-date and detailed information on coastline beaches, and water depth for possible future amphibious landings on Iceland, the Faroes, the Norwegian coast, and other northern European areas."[135] Norwegian authorities were also concerned about the activities and potential wartime role of the Soviet fishing fleet, and in 1959 a committee was set up by the Defence Intelligence Staff to study questions relating to the "use of fishing vessels in an attack against Scandinavia".[136]

Conclusion

American concerns about the growth of Soviet naval power in the Northern Fleet area had two basic consequences for Norway. First, it gave Norway a vital part to play in American efforts to keep abreast of Soviet military, commercial and scientific activities in the north-east Atlantic and Arctic regions. In particular, US attempts to monitor the expansion of the Soviet long-range submarine fleet and naval aviation in the Arctic, came to depend crucially on close collaboration with the Norwegian Defence

(a)   **Soviet submarine order of battle, 1953–60:**

Date:	Number:
February 1950:	255
October 1953:	358
January 1955:	368
February 1956:	421
January 1959:	443

(b)   **Distribution of long-range submarines, 1953–60:**

Date:	Northern Fleet Long-Range Submarines (Total Number of Long-Range Submarines)	Percentage of Long-Range Submarines Assigned to the Northern Fleet
October 1953:	26 (77)	33.8 %
February 1956:	79 (208)	38 %
January 1960:	132 (280)[138]	47.1 %

Table 3.1: Soviet submarine order of battle, 1953–60[137]

Intelligence Staff. Second, the increasing significance of the Northern Fleet in the mid-fifties meant that the US Navy began to concentrate a greater share of its *strategic* and *logistic planning* efforts towards sustaining operations in the Arctic. This and the consequent increase in US operational activities in the area from 1955 onwards reflected Norway's changing role in US maritime strategy.

In addition to the "W" and "Z" class of submarines which constituted the bulk of the long-range submarine force, a much smaller number of long-range second-line submarines were kept operational and in some cases modernised in the 1950s. In the spring of 1956, the ONI estimated that the classes likely to or thought to have been modernised (e.g. fitted with snorkel) included: "K-1", "L II", "L III" and "S-1", all of which had been produced before or during the Second World War.[139] The majority of these, 29 in 1956, were deployed with the Northern Fleet.[140]

Part III: Norway and American Maritime Strategy, 1954–60

The Northeast Atlantic – Norwegian Sea – Barents Sea area may well be the area of decision with respect to the success of any United States operations to maintain the flow of supplies to our European allies and to our US forces in Western Europe. This area is of twofold importance – first as an avenue for the movement of US shipping; secondly, as the area from which the Soviet submarine threat may be stopped at its source...[1]

> Strategic Plans Division,
> US Navy, October 1953.

INTRODUCTION

The preceding chapter traced developments within the Soviet Northern Fleet area between 1954 and 1960, and the concomitant growth of US and Norwegian intelligence and reconnaissance activities in the north-east Atlantic. Part III explores how US naval commitments and activities in the area changed from an initial awareness of the strategic importance of the "northern seas" to specific requirements for wartime bases and facilities in Norway and an increased level of operational activity in the North Atlantic. In short, it details the US Navy's adjustment after 1954 to what Michael Palmer has described as "a Northern strategy".[2] It focuses on the manner in which the process of adjustment, especially the increasing emphasis on forward nuclear strike operations, came to influence Norway's place in American strategic calculations. This involves a closer look both at the precise role of Norway in US naval war plans under the "New Look", and the augmentation of operational activity in and around Norwegian territory between 1954 and 1960. It also requires a closer look at British naval policy between 1953 and 1960 and its implications for Norway and, above all, American commitments in the North Atlantic. Finally, Part III assesses the impact of new and rapidly changing technologies on the perceptions and dispositions of the American administration and military planners. Of particular importance in this respect was the growing evidence of Soviet advances in the areas of missile and submarine technology following the successful launch of Sputnik in late 1957. The challenges which the forward maritime strategy after 1954 posed for Norway's commitment to a policy of maintaining "low tension" in northern Europe are considered more fully in Part IV.

4 The US Navy, Norway and the New Look: Adjusting to a "Northen Strategy", 1954–57

I US MARITIME STRATEGY, THE NEW LOOK AND THE NORTHERN SEAS

Post-war American Maritime Strategy and the New Look

To President Eisenhower, the Korean War had demonstrated that conventional wars against communist-inspired forces were likely to be both costly and inconclusive.[3] By 1954, the new Republican administration had completed its first review of "basic national security policy," designed to solve Eisenhower's great equation of maintaining a strong defence at a bearable cost. To do this, emphasis was to be placed on strategic air power, the integration of nuclear weapons into tactical units and the establishment of a strategic reserve in the continental United States.[4] At the same time, overall manpower ceilings were to be substantially reduced and greater reliance placed on allies for initial ground defence. A JCS Memorandum for the Secretary of Defense in December 1953 succinctly summarised the rationale behind the change of policy.

> ...there is a need for a reorientation of our military strategy toward placing greater reliance upon the capabilities of new weapons as a means for exploiting our technological advantages over the USSR, of reducing the effect of the manpower differential between us and the Soviet bloc, and of enabling us to reduce our over-all military expenditures. To this end, our superiority in atomic weapons must be exploited to the maximum.[5]

The force levels agreed by the JCS in December 1953 reflected these priorities, with the Air Force as the main beneficiary.[6] In terms of actual reductions, the Navy was less severely affected than the Army, with force levels for 1957 set at 1030 active ships and a personnel strength of

650,000.[7] However, in order to secure its share of future defence appropriations, it was forced to adapt to the new priorities of the administration. This it did by upgrading its *overall* nuclear strike capability and by publicly presenting its carriers as thermonuclear weapons systems essential to the strategic deterrence mission.

Although the Navy had developed a rudimentary atomic capability in 1949 (using a modified version of the Neptune patrol bomber (P2V-3C)), in September 1951 it still only had 48 aircraft (AJ-1 Savage) designed to deliver the atomic bomb.[8] Only 27 of these had been assigned to operating squadrons.[9] In 1952 no allocation of weapons to various commanders had been agreed upon, nor had a "procedure for the use of atomic weapons in direct support of land operations" been established.[10] The following year, however, a JCS report on the status of US military programmes as of June 1953 noted that:

> ...the Navy has acquired a powerful and flexible atomic weapon delivery capability within its carrier task forces and this capability is increasing. Atomic weapons are available on very short notice in the forward areas, where attack carriers are deployed.[11]

By 1955 all attack carriers – fifteen were in commission – carried nuclear weapons.[12] In March of the following year the A3D-1(A-3) Skywarrior all-weather heavy attack bomber entered operational service. In September 1956, the entry into service of the A4D Skyhawk, further strengthened the nuclear projection capabilities of the Navy.[13] In the mid-1950s the Navy also revised the composition of its carrier air groups by increasing the ratio of nuclear attack squadrons to fighter aircraft.[14]

Although the Navy made "every effort ... to conform to the national security policy adopted in October 1953,"[15] the *basic reorientation* of post-war maritime strategy did not fundamentally change. This reorientation, which had crystallised in 1946–47 during Admiral Forrest Sherman's tenure as Deputy Chief of Naval Operations,[16] was succinctly described in an article by Samuel Huntington published in the May 1954 issue of *US Naval Institute Proceedings*.[17]

The article examined the emergence of a "new naval doctrine" evident in the "writings of postwar naval writers and leaders."[18] At the root of the new doctrine was "the theory of the transoceanic navy, that is, a navy oriented away from the oceans and towards the land masses on their far side."[19] America's ideological and military adversary in the Cold War was above all a *continental power* and not a *maritime power*. Indeed, in 1955, the US Secretary of the Navy acknowledged that shortcomings in surface and air striking power meant that the "Soviet navy could not hope to guarantee the safety of shipping far beyond its coasts or to make landings and support land forces at points far removed from its Eurasian bases."[20] Thus, the purpose of the post-war transoceanic Navy was:

> not to acquire command of the sea but rather to utilize its command of the sea to achieve supremacy on land. More specifically, [it was] to apply naval power to that decisive strip of littoral encircling the Eurasian continent.[21]

While Staff Colleges were reluctant to reject the supposed "underlying fundamentals of universal application" identified by Mahan, internal documents show that the Navy leadership had come to view power projection along the Eurasian littoral as the principal mission of the navy in war.[22] A report by the Joint Strategic Plans Committee in July 1954 stated that in the event of war, the US Navy would have to control the "sea areas and salients around and into the enemy homeland." This, the committee noted, required the:

> ... maintenance of striking forces in being and in readiness, capable of immediate offensive operations to effectively deny to the enemy use of those sea areas that he wishes to use and to permit their use by our naval forces as avenues to project military power into enemy territory.[23]

In a study completed in 1956, Admiral Jerauld Wright, SACLANT and Commander of the US Atlantic Fleet, stated that to gain and maintain "sea control of vital areas in the Atlantic" he would "destroy Soviet naval and air bases and other sources of Soviet sea power threatening ACLANT."[24] Furthermore, he would "participate in the general nuclear offensive by use of sea-based delivery systems ... support NATO land and air campaigns, and ... conduct amphibious operations and counter enemy amphibious operations."[25]

This predilection for forward offensive operations represented the logical outcome of a redefinition of the relationship between two of the traditional functions of sea power in war: *sea control* and *power projection*. These tasks were increasingly seen, by the US Navy in particular, as mutually reinforcing, that is, *power projection* against submarine and bomber bases on land had become an integral part of securing *sea control*.[26] As Sokolsky makes clear, throughout the 1950s the battle for the control of the Atlantic was not conceived of in terms of major fleet action on the high seas. It would instead be "a question of projecting American power on to the periphery of Europe in the face of formidable Soviet undersea forces."[27]

The tendency for sea control and power projection functions to merge was not, however, merely a reflection of changed geopolitical circumstances. It was also a result of the impact which rapid technological change was exerting on fleet action, especially in the areas of firepower, ship propulsion, jet-aircraft and guided missile technology, sensors and communications.[28] In his semiannual report for 1956, the Secretary of Defense, Charles Wilson, took note of the progress which had been made in the "Navy's gradual transition from steam to nuclear power, from guns to guided missiles, from TNT to atomic weapons, and from propeller to jet aircraft."[29] And Admiral Wright, in his aforementioned study, claimed that, given the "trends in technological developments," attacks at source were the "only effective counter to the ballistic missile in sight."[30]

The basic structure of the post-war Navy reflected the shift in thinking, with fast attack carrier task forces forming the centrepiece of the surface fleet.[31] So did changes in *tactical doctrine* away from the traditional concern with the concentration of force at sea in preparation for a decisive engagement, to an increasing emphasis on the principle of dispersion for defensive purposes at sea (to minimise the dangers of atomic destruction), and "concentration at or over the target on land."[32]

In early 1947 Admiral Sherman's specific ideas for war with the Soviet Union had focused on forward employment of *conventional* carrier task forces in the Mediterranean theatre. By 1954, *power projection along the littoral* was still a central feature of US maritime strategy, though carrier task forces were now heavily oriented towards nuclear operations. There was one further important difference between the situation in 1947 and 1954: the Mediterranean was no longer viewed as the single most important theatre of operations.

SACLANT and the Northern Seas as a "Critical Area"

In late 1953, as the governing directives for the New Look were being finalised by the JCS, the Navy's Strategic Plans Division had designated the "Northern Seas" (the north-east Atlantic, Norwegian and Barents Seas), as a "critical area" to the security of the United States.[33] Its "critical" nature derived from the fact that:

> the Barents Sea is the attack route to the only significant submarine base for Atlantic submarines now available to the Soviets. With the Bosphorus and Baltic exits sealed, Soviet submarines must be operated from their northern bases.[34]

Since long-range submarine bases in the Kola Inlet and the White Sea areas were "sufficiently remote to preclude almost all air attacks with fighter cover save those from mobile bases," preparations had to be made for the US to conduct forward offensive carrier operations to neutralise the submarine threat at source.[35] Outlining the rationale for such operations, the Strategic Plans Division concluded:

> The destruction of Soviet submarine bases by air attack is now possible using penetration type atomic bombs. Positive and accurate results can be assured by the use of dive-bombing delivery tactics with adequate fighter escort. Similar tactics against Soviet naval airfields are the answer to the Soviet naval air threat to shipping. In this manner, the Soviet submarine and air threat can be reduced to such an extent that the Allied shipping on the high seas can be adequately protected by the relatively meagre escorting forces which will be available. Europe is a large peninsula attached to the Eurasian continent. Carrier-based aircraft with their fighter escort, can successfully attack this European peninsula operating from the Mediterranean, and the Barents and Norwegian Seas.[36]

These views reflected a growing appreciation within the naval establishment, and especially within ACLANT, of the strategic significance of the north-east Atlantic.[37] In September 1955, Admiral Robert Carney, having just retired as the Chief of Naval Operations, published a long essay in *Proceedings* on the "Principles of Sea Power." Summarising his ideas on sea power in the nuclear age, Carney emphasised how the future of Denmark and Norway, as well as that of Germany and Britain, "would be gravely threatened without Allied ability to control both the North and Norwegian Sea areas."[38] Not surprisingly, therefore, when the Joint Strategic Plans Committee the following month recommended that the Navy Department re-appoint to Norway a Chief of the MAAG with the rank of Rear Admiral, it emphasised that departmental interest in the appointment derived from the relationship of the country in question "to the strategic plans and military objectives of the United States."[39]

It was, above all, the "strategic plans and military objectives" of SACLANT (who was also Commander of the US Atlantic Fleet) which impinged upon Norway's place in US strategy. And it is important, therefore, to consider briefly the relationship between SACLANT's *national* and *alliance* command responsibilities. Although the title of SACLANT implied international command responsibilities, both Admiral Lynde McCormick and his immediate successor, Admiral Jerauld Wright, acted first and foremost as *national* commanders. In part, this was because they only exercised peacetime command authority over the employment of the US Atlantic Fleet. Equally important, however, was the assumption that a general war would necessarily involve an intense initial nuclear exchange and a *fast-moving* land-battle in Europe. This expectation led Admiral Wright in 1955 to state that all his plans were predicated on the assumption that "initial deployments and operations are the same in almost all cases whether forces remain under US command or are transferred to NATO commanders."[40] A final factor which also had the effect of reinforcing American dominance within the ACLANT planning process arose from the fact that the principal naval force at the disposal of the Alliance in the event of war, the Strike Fleet Atlantic, was organised as a *separate operational command* directly subordinate to SACLANT.[41] Thus, whereas political and national sensitivities invariably intruded into SACEUR's planing process, SACLANT's concept of operations came to reflect more closely the strategic priorities and interests of the US Navy.[42]

II   NORWAY IN US NAVY WAR PLANS

SACLANT's Strategic Concept and the Changing Role of Carrier Task Forces Under "New Look"

When Allied Command Atlantic was activated in April 1952, US Navy planners envisaged two broad roles for attack carrier task forces in the North Atlantic. First, they would serve as mobile platforms for the conduct of offensive air operations against enemy threats at their source, attacking bases and facilities from which Soviet submarines and naval aviation derived operational support.[43] The second major role envisaged for heavy carriers was "in support of and augmentation of allied land-forces participating in the land-air battle in Europe."[44] Indeed, when General Eisenhower in 1951 presented his estimated force requirements for the defence of Western Europe, he informed the Standing Group that these were predicated on the assumption that the "primary role of aircraft carriers" would be to assist in the defence of his northern and southern flanks.[45]

By 1954, however, both strategic planning and operational exercises placed primary emphasis on strike operations and the projection of "nuclear offensive power ... into the heart of the enemy naval bases and airfields."[46] This shift was caused both by *strategic* considerations and by a perceived need from 1954 onwards to prioritise naval tasks in the face of a growing Soviet naval threat.[47]

In 1951 General Eisenhower's requirements for 16 attack carriers – eight of which would be deployed on the Northern Flank thirty days after the outbreak of war – had been tailored to the conventional strategy favoured by the Alliance between 1950–1952.[48] The post-Korean build-up notwithstanding, by late 1953 actual US attack carrier commitments to NATO were two ships on peacetime station in the Mediterranean, and wartime commitments in the Atlantic significantly below what SACEUR, now the President, had been asking for in 1951.[49] Reporting on the status of US military programmes as of December 1954, the Navy stated it was able to keep only one or two attack carriers in the Atlantic fully ready for use in the initial phase of a general war.[50] Instead of two striking fleets in the Atlantic, only one would be available after one month of war "at the earliest."[51] In March 1955 Admiral Jerauld Wright informed the Chief of Naval Operations that he did not possess sufficient carrier forces to ensure early destruction of targets in the Baltic, Barents and White Sea area "within an acceptable period after D-Day."[52] A diversion of resources away from the nuclear strike role was rejected. The following month, in April 1955, Rear Admiral McCorckle, Director of Fleet Operations, in discussing capabilities for amphibious operations, reported that attack carriers were now "heavily committed" and could therefore not be used to support amphibious operations "in the early days of an emergency without unacceptable curtailment of the primary offensive tasks of these ships."[53]

An additional factor which was increasingly seen to militate against carrier operations primarily in support of the land-battle, especially in Denmark and South Norway, was the perceived vulnerability of carriers operating in the confined waters close to the Baltic approaches. In March 1953 an air target study produced by US naval intelligence for use by SACLANT had assumed that carriers would operate from the "entrance to the Baltic Sea or from 5 miles off the coast of Norway."[54] This assumption was rejected by Arleigh Burke, the head of the Strategic Plans Division and later CNO, on the grounds that it was "considered improbable" that "carriers would conduct flight operations at the entrance to the Baltic Sea, i.e. within the Skagerak and Kattegat."[55]

The emphasis on nuclear power projection and the corresponding downgrading of the support role for carriers, meant that operational planning and exercise patterns came to focus predominantly on preparations for the tactical employment of nuclear weapons against Soviet targets in the Northern region. According to Sokolsky, US carriers earmarked for SACEUR in the Mediterranean had by 1954 "begun to shift their primary focus from battlefield support to nuclear strikes."[56] At about the same time, a corresponding shift occurred in the north. In early 1955 SACLANT, in co-ordination with SAC, was scheduled to attack submarines, surface and air forces in being and "the bases from which they derive their operational support and protection" in the Baltic, Norwegian Barents and White Sea area.[57] In March 1955 there were an estimated 18 target complexes of interest in the Baltic, the Barents and the White Sea capable of supporting enemy submarine or other offensive forces. All these targets would, according to Admiral Jerauld Wright, have to be "destroyed by atomic attack in order to ensure that Soviet shore-based potential for support of naval forces may suffer maximum possible reduction."[58] The key role of nuclear weapons for tactical as well as strategic missions during this period can be seen in CINCNORTH's Atomic Strike Plan for 1956 which outlined the details of the so-called "Plan Jutland Charlie". This involved the use of nuclear weapons to eliminate Soviet Sverdlov-class cruisers attempting to move from the Baltic into the Northern Sea in the event of war.[59]

The strategic rationale for the shift towards strike operations was the conviction within the US Navy that, as one internal report in 1955 put it, "attack at source" by carrier striking forces represented the "Navy's first line of defence against enemy submarines."[60] Norway's role became one of sustaining and supporting these operations. It is worth noting in this context that in December 1954, planning started for the *first* joint atomic command post exercise held by CINCNORTH. The exercise, known as Sky Blazer, was held in late February 1955, and involved the practice of all "atomic support procedures."[61]

As the submarine threat from Soviet northern bases was seen to increase further after 1955, even greater emphasis was placed on "forward operations" in the northern seas. In December 1956, this emphasis was enshrined in NATO's new "Overall Strategic Concept for the Defence of the NATO Area (MC 14/2)." To further NATO's strategic objectives in the Atlantic ocean area, it was:

> essential to have a timely projection of Allied sea-borne nuclear offensive power against enemy naval and other agreed targets; and also to engage the enemy as soon and as far forward as possible so as to reduce to the minimum the number of his units which can penetrate to the broader reaches of the Atlantic and threaten the vital Allied sea lines of communications.[62]

Outlining the concept of operations in SACLANT's EDP for 1957, Wright emphasised that initial priority would be given to "nuclear strikes against Soviet naval and air power in a position to contest his use of the Norwegian Sea."[63] Once the air threat had been sufficiently reduced, SACLANT's main nuclear targets would be "submarine bases, units at sea, naval bases, and supporting communication complexes."[64] The British Joint Planning Staff, commenting on SACLANT's plans, noted that his

EDP now placed even "greater emphasis on offensive operations by the Striking Fleet."[65]

All of these developments were to have important consequences for Norway. In the first place, although Eisenhower's original flank concept was not formally abandoned, fewer resources were available for direct support of the land-air battle in Norway.[66] While it is true that the US Navy after 1957 displayed growing concern with the dangers of a direct threat to North Norway, this was not sufficient to detract from the primary emphasis on strike operations.[67] Yet, as will be seen, the failure to meet what turned out to be unrealistic requirements after the post-Korean build-up and the subsequent emphasis on nuclear strike operations, did not lead to any corresponding diminution of interest within the US Navy for Norway and the contiguous seas. On the contrary, the construction of airfields and other shore-based facilities supporting the Strike Fleet, especially in North Norway, gave Norway a vital role in US maritime strategy.

Planned Wartime Operations from Norwegian Air Bases

As the US Navy increasingly turned to the North Atlantic, bases in north Norway appeared particularly suitable as staging areas for operations against targets on the Kola Peninsula and long-range submarines transiting the northern approaches. As early as in 1951 it had been recognised that existing plans for "submarine mining ... of selected Barents – White Sea targets" were inadequate. In a memorandum in December 1951, Rear Admiral Frank Akers, responsible for the US Navy's undersea warfare effort in the early 1950s, pointed out that no clear requirement had been "established" for "patrol bomber" bases within "effective range" of targets in the Barents – White Sea area. Admiral Akers noted further that

> It is considered that the Barents – White Sea area may well be the most important from which Soviet submarines will operate against the Allies in the Atlantic. It is emphasized that mining of selected targets in the area is a requisite of maximum anti-submarine effort.[68]

Akers concluded by recommending that "further study be made of the requirements for conducting mining operations in the Barents – White Sea area, particularly with a view to accomplishment within naval capabilities."[69]

Although the US Navy in 1951 did recommend that wartime base rights be obtained in North Norway to assist Norwegian forces in "ASW, search barrier patrols, mining and electronic search," no request was made for formal negotiations with Norwegian authorities.[70] The need to modify and expand air bases for use by the US Navy was reiterated in 1952 and 1953, though no *effective* action was taken until 1954.[71] By late 1954, however, CNO had officially incorporated three "maritime air facilities" in Norway – Andøya, Bodø and Ørlandet – as key wartime operating bases for the US Navy. In September 1955, Admiral Jerauld Wright, Commander of the Atlantic Fleet, sent the newly appointed Chief of Naval Operations, Admiral Arleigh Burke, a detailed list of his requirements for all three airfields. By the end of the year, the general function of each airfield had been clarified and was spelled out in CNO's amended list of naval base requirements overseas.[72]

The decision to concentrate preparations for immediate wartime deployment to bases in North Norway was directly related to the growth of the Soviet northern submarine fleet discussed in the previous chapter. Apart from serving as staging bases for peacetime reconnaissance and ASW training missions, Bodø and Andøya, in particular, were assigned an important wartime role in the offensive directed against the Soviet submarine threat from northern bases.[73] The chief purpose of these bases was to act as a final staging area for offensive aerial mining operations in northern waters; operations which, according to Rear Admiral Akers, were likely to "yield more profitable immediate results than any other attacks undertaken to counter submarine capabilities."[74] By 1955, detailed plans had been worked out and SACLANT's mining plan for 1955 gave a precise indication of the role of Norwegian air bases in the event of war. According to the plan, aircraft deployed to Norway would:

> conduct an early mining campaign in order to inflict maximum casualties on enemy ships, particularly U-boats, and to limit the freedom of movement of enemy shipping.[75]

Assuming that northern parts of Norway, the Baltic exits and the channel ports would be held by NATO forces during the first 60 days of war, and that Sweden would remain neutral, SACLANT forces would at the outset of hostilities initiate an extensive aerial mining campaign. The object of this campaign, which would be closely co-ordinated with Strike Fleet and SAC operations, was to:

(1) establish "sustained attrition minefields" off Arkhangelsk and Belomorsk in the White Sea Area by Neptune (P2V) sorties from Andøya.

(2) establish "limited attrition minefields" off Polyarnyy, Vayenga, Tyuva Guba in the Kola Inlet and off Pechenga and Yokanga by Neptune (P2V) aircraft from Andøya and "other Norwegian bases."

(3) establish "transitory attrition fields" in the White Sea entrances off the Murmansk Coast and the Kola Inlet and Pechenga approaches by US and UK submarines based on the Clyde.[76]

However, effective utilisation of Norwegian bases by the US Navy for the accomplishment of these tasks was seen to require significant modifications of existing airfields. In terms of immediate post-D-Day deployment, Andøya was the most important airfield. According to CNO plans, the maritime air facility at Andøya, which had been included in SACLANT's 1953 infrastructure programme, was to receive one squadron for offensive mining operations "immediately available post D-Day" (D+1), to be *augmented rapidly* thereafter.[77] The aircraft in question, Neptune (P2V) maritime patrol bombers, would be deployed from Iceland, and their missions as listed by CNO included ASW-mining, air early warning, and photo-reconnaissance operations.[78] The size of the prospective wartime deployment to Andøya can be seen in the Navy's requirements for construction of installations and infrastructure facilities to support wartime operations in the area. According to CINCLANT, Andøya required prior construction of "austere national support facilities" including base administration and housing facilities for 1100 men (825 for support and 275 for the flight crews). When, in October, the Strategic Plans Division was asked to comment on CINCLANT's requirements for wartime detachment to Norway, special emphasis was placed on the need for a pre-D-Day mine storage and assembly facility "to support naval plans."[79] In his mining plan for 1955, SACLANT noted that difficulties of shipping mines after D-Day, required pre-D-Day deployment of a one month's supply of mines to Andøya and Clyde. Those at Andøya were to be ready mines, and facilities had to include storage, test assembly and handling facilities.[80]

The deployment of patrol bombers and supporting units to Bodø, which only became fully operational in 1955, was planned for D+6 months, hence there was no requirement for pre-D-day construction beyond existing infrastructure programmes.[81] Post-D-day construction required for support of wartime deployments, however, included base facilities for 1200 men (825 support personnel and 375 for flight crews). In CNO's final list of overseas base requirements for 1955, Ørlandet in the Trøndelag area, which had originally been included as a NATO airfield in

SACEUR's infrastructure programme for 1952 (third slice), was to serve as an advanced maintenance base for aircraft deployed further north at Andøya and Bodø.[82] The airfield at Ørland was to receive aviation repair personnel "on D-Day for overhaul and major repair of US aircraft based at Andøya."[83] Full support facilities were needed for 400 men since these were to be deployed immediately after D-Day.

In order to prepare air crews for operations in and around Norway, the expansion of facilities between 1955 and 1960 was accompanied by a significant increase in operational activity. In early August 1955 a US memorandum presented to the Norwegian Ministry of Foreign Affairs requested "authorization of indoctrination flights of two US Navy P2V aircraft based at Keflavik to Bodø, Andøya and Bardufoss about every three weeks."[84] The memorandum noted further that in view of the planned wartime missions of these aircraft, it was desirable that US Navy personnel should have some "familiarity with NATO airfields in Norway and the flight conditions adjacent thereto."[85] After discussion between Foreign Minister Halvard Lange and the US ambassador to Norway, Lester Corrin Strong, the request was formally granted in an exchange of notes on 17 August.[86] The agreement formed the basis for a steady expansion of US maritime air operations in and around Norway in the latter half of the decade. Less than two months after this initial agreement, Admiral Wright informed CNO that "additional agreements" had to be negotiated.[87] In his detailed list of requirements for Norway in September 1955, Wright stated that agreements would have to be obtained for "up to thirty training and familiarisation flights per month ... for all types of naval aircraft" in connection with negotiations for all three airfields (Bodø, Andøya and Ørlandet).[88] An indication of the scale of US activity in and out of Norway by September 1956, is found in a Norwegian Foreign Ministry memorandum which refers to US requests for clearance of American aircraft being made "several times per week if not daily."[89] As will be seen in subsequent chapters, US activity was further stepped up in late 1957 and early 1958.

There is a further consideration here. In the mid-1950s Neptunes were specially equipped to carry atomic depth charges (Mk 90 "Betty") for use in anti-submarine transit operations.[90] At Hvalfjordur in Iceland, where the British had built a naval base during the war, the US Navy constructed an atomic ammunition facility (known as "AUW shops") for servicing atomic depth bombs "to support the special weapons operations of the Second Fleet."[91] As noted above, patrol bombers stationed in Iceland were earmarked for operations in Norway in the event of war, and exercised there with increasing frequency in the latter half of the decade. Although there is no evidence to indicate that "special weapons assembly facilities" were constructed in Norway, the central role envisaged for nuclear weapons in naval operations in the 1950s, does raise important questions about the *tension* between declaratory and operational policy. At the first NATO Heads of Government meeting in December 1957, Prime Minister Gerhardsen declared that nuclear weapons of any kind would not be stationed on Norwegian territory. The Neptunes almost certainly carried their nuclear payload on missions in the North Atlantic and into Norwegian airfields. Interestingly, in 1995 it was also publicly revealed for the first time that the US stored nuclear weapons at Thule Air Force base in Greenland in the period between 1958 and 1965, and that this had been done with the knowledge and acceptance of the Danish government in spite of its public commitment to a non-nuclear policy.[92] The evident difficulties of pursuing a non-nuclear policy within a nuclear alliance at the *operational* as opposed to the *declaratory* level of policy, are also brought out by a closer look at Norway's relationship to Strike Fleet operations in the North Atlantic.

Norway and Strike Fleet Operations

From 1954 onwards Norwegian territory also became increasingly important for the support of Strike Fleet operations. One reason for this was that special arrangements were made for northern Norwegian air bases to be used as staging points for carrier-based attack aircraft operating with the Fleet. Although this function was incidental to the primary role which the aforementioned airfields played in aerial mining operations, the US Navy in 1953–54 did formulate plans for carrier-based aircraft to use Norwegian air bases for "atomic strikes on the USSR."[93] The requirement for "periodic support of carrier-based aircraft" from Norwegian airfields was first stated in 1953 and provoked strong reactions from the US Air Force which felt that the Navy was seeking to usurp traditional Air Force missions.[94] In December 1954, Admiral Carney nonetheless approved SACLANT's recommendation that airfield facilities on Andøya be used by aircraft of the Carrier Striking Forces provided this did not interfere with maritime/patrol aircraft operations.[95] The use of airfields for carrier-based aircraft was, however, only one of the ways in which strike fleet operations benefited from access to "facilities" on Norwegian territory. Far more important was the assistance provided in areas of communications and navigation.

Communications

In the 1950s communications problems in the Arctic represented a major impediment to large-scale fleet operations. As a result, the US Navy devoted much attention and resources to remedy existing deficiencies.[96] The adverse impact of abnormal ionospheric conditions (auroral disturbances) and the effect of the ship's roll and pitch in heavy Arctic weather on the directivity pattern of antennas, were not new problems.[97] They had, however, acquired new importance "because of the necessity to maintain large scale continuous operations in ... Arctic areas with the greatest emphasis on continuity and reliability."[98] In August 1956 exercise Gulf Stream was held in the far north in order to test communications with the Strike Fleet. The exercise only served to demonstrate the "very unsatisfactory" communications in the area, and confirmed that the northern waters were "in many respects the very worst area for reliable, long range communications."[99] As a direct result of this exercise, rhombic aerials for communications with the Strike Fleet were installed at two places along the North Norwegian coast; Bodø and Helgelandsmoen.[100] These stations were tested again the following year in a series of major exercises in the North Atlantic – Strikeback, Counterpunch and Northback. But again, disturbances "almost completely severed communications between shore and fleet for long periods."[101] The importance attached to establishing reliable communications between shore stations in Norway and the Strike Fleet in the North Atlantic was related to two specific developments after 1955.

In the first place, as the shore-based facilities became tied to the integrated air defence system set up between 1955–57 throughout Northern Europe, the Strike Fleet could be provided with vital air defence early warning information. The requirement for such information was seen to increase significantly in 1956–57 when "Badger" aircraft entered the Soviet Northern Fleet Air Arm. At the sixth annual SHAPE-SACLANT planning co-ordination conference in late 1956 – shortly after "Badgers" were first reported to be operational in the Northern Fleet area – representatives for SACLANT's Strike Fleet established requirements for exchange of information with shore installations in Norway.[102] To this *defensive* requirement, however, was soon added an *offensive* requirement. In November 1958 representatives for the Commander of Allied Forces in the Eastern Atlantic informed NEC staff that they were planning to utilise control and reporting systems within the NEC area for routing tactical bombing aircraft.[103] The value of shore installations in Norway, for both *defensive* and *offensive* purposes, increased steadily throughout the decade.

Navigational Support

The navigation system which the US Navy relied upon in the late 1940s and 1950s, known as Loran (Long-Range Aid to Navigation), had first been developed during the Second World War at the MIT Radiation Laboratory. By recording time differences between the arrival of radio signals from various land-based transmitters, positional fixes were made. A report by the Joint Communications-Electronics Committee to the JCS in October 1955 emphasised that Loran was the only precise all-weather navigational aid which had extensive coverage and which could be used by aircraft and vessels, and was therefore "an important defensive and offensive weapon."[104] In the report, the JCS also stated that Loran coverage "would be immediately required in the North Atlantic, North Sea, Norwegian Sea and the Mediterranean areas upon the outbreak of war in Europe."[105]

The system was developed and expanded throughout the 1950s, and in July 1955, SACLANT in a signal requested that "Loran site surveys be made as soon as possible" in Norway.[106] From 29 August to 12 September preliminary site surveys were made at Austkapp on Jan Mayen, Bø in Vesterålen and Bjugn in South-Trøndelag by Norwegian authorities assisted by technical experts from the US Coast Guard. In December the Chief of Naval Operations, in his recommended changes to the Navy's overseas base requirements, requested 30 acres of land on each location for construction of the Loran system. The "planned occupancy date" was 1958.[107] All three stations were approved under the fifth slice of NATO's infrastructure programme. It should be noted that the date of CNO's request for the stations in Norway preceded the accelerated phase of the Polaris programme and certainly preceded the decision to deploy the first boats in the Norwegian Sea.[108] The 1955 requests were for Loran-A stations designed to support Strike Fleet surface and air operations in the Norwegian Sea and the north-east Atlantic. As will be seen, in connection with the establishment of a navigational support system for the Polaris submarines, US authorities in March 1958 formally approached the Norwegian Foreign Ministry with a request for the construction at Bø in Vesterålen of a more advanced long-range navigation system, the Loran C.

Conclusion

This chapter has looked, first, at the broader background to the growth of US naval interests in the high north, and, second, at the specific ways in which Norway entered into the strategic calculations of the US Navy. By

1956, CINCLANT and OPNAV had specified their requirements for airfield construction in North Norway. Maritime air squadrons based in Iceland had been assigned wartime missions in Norway whence they would carry out offensive mining operations in the Kola Inlet and the entrances to the White Sea. Site surveys had been completed for Loran A stations in Norway designed to support Strike Fleet and tactical air operations. Similarly, communication facilities were also under continuous construction, testing and improvement. The basis for a new and expanded role for the US Navy in the north-east Atlantic had been laid.

Nevertheless, the growth of US activity between 1954 and 1957 was more pronounced in the areas of intelligence and reconnaissance than in forward operational deployment. A basic reason for this was that until late 1957 the US still relied strongly on the presence and capabilities of the Royal Navy in the north-east Atlantic. In late 1957 and early 1958, however, changes in British naval policy, the impact of technological developments and growing concern about Soviet guided-missile submarines led the US Navy to step up its activities in the far north markedly.

This chapter has also emphasised the extent to which US naval planning between 1954 and 1960 was biased in favour of nuclear operations. This vital aspect of the period and its consequences for Norway's role in US nuclear strategy is further explored in the following chapters.

5 British Naval Policy, 1953–60: Implications for Norway and American Commitments in the North Atlantic

In Chapter One it was observed that, even after the reorganisation of NATO's command structure in 1951, the British COS as a *collective body* showed little interest in reassessing the place of Norway in its defence priorities. By late 1951 and early 1952, however, such lack of interest no longer applied to all three services. In the early 1950s, Admiralty thinking – specifically as it applied to the employment of the Fleet Air Arm – evolved in a manner which again led to an emphasis on the importance of Norway and its contiguous seas in British naval policy. This chapter addresses three issues. First, it looks at the principal reasons – strategic, political, and bureaucratic – for the resurgence of the Royal Navy's interest in Norway before the 1957 Defence Review. Second, it examines the impact of Sandys's Defence Review on British naval policy, looking in particular at the American reactions to the changes in the Royal Navy's NATO commitment. Finally, it explores some of the additional factors which, in 1957–58, further increased Norway's importance in US maritime strategy.

I THE ROYAL NAVY AND NORWAY, 1953–57

British Sea Power and Norway

When General Eisenhower, in a letter to his former mentor General Marshall in March 1951, described the command arrangements he envisaged for Europe, he wrote how in "the North ... the only disposable strength will, of necessity, be furnished by the British Navy."[1] Eisenhower wrote that he also hoped to "get the agreement of the British Admiralty to provide, in operational emergency, naval strength to support Norway and Denmark."[2] This was not surprising since the maritime area was one in which Britain, especially before the full impact of the *Radical Review* process that began in January 1953, was still a source of very considerable strength. During the Atlantic-wide NATO exercise Mariner in September and October 1953 – the largest international manoeuvre since the end of the Second World War – Britain participated with 117 ships of all types and 20 air squadrons. By comparison, the US committed 78 ships and 11 air squadrons.[3] In a major tactical exercise held in the Norwegian Sea two years later, the British naval contingent included no less than *five* carriers, six submarines and 25 ships of other types.[4]

Already in connection with NATO's Medium-Term Defence Plan, approved by the Council in December 1950, Britain had stressed the importance of offensive operations in the Baltic Sea, and had committed one cruiser and 59 destroyers to a Scandinavian convoy system. The *continued* interest in Norway on the part of the British Naval staff throughout the 1950s suggests that the restricted nature of COS interests in Scandinavia, outlined in Chapter One, did not apply to all the Services.[5] Indeed, as Clive Archer has noted, the Royal Navy was the one service which remained committed to the defence of Norway in the 1950s.[6] Yet, effectively this commitment only lasted until the British Defence Review of 1957, at which point retrenchment in naval establishments began in earnest, and, more importantly, the "centre of gravity of future naval deployments would move significantly eastward."[7]

As Eisenhower's letter to Marshall indicates, the establishment of NATO's integrated command structure was a key factor in ensuring that the Royal Navy again took more than a declaratory interest in Norway after its immediate postwar concentration on the Middle East and the Mediterranean. In spite of Churchill's public misgivings about Anglo-American naval command arrangements in the Atlantic, both the Commander-in-Chief Eastern Atlantic (CINCEASTLANT) and the Commander, Allied Naval Forces Northern Europe (COMNAVNORTH), were British Admirals, thus confirming the Royal Navy's pre-eminent interest in the region. Renewed concern about the Soviet submarine threat and the emergence for the first time of a credible Soviet surface capability following the appearance of the Sverdlov-class cruiser in 1951, also led the naval staff to take a more direct interest in Northern Europe. So did clearly the experience of the Korean War as well as the earlier than antici-pated Soviet nuclear test breakthrough in late August 1949.[8] Both these developments heightened the sense of vulnerability to Soviet military power in Europe and served to concentrate Navy opinion to a greater degree than before on the requirements of defending Western Europe and the "home base" Against the background of these general considerations, however, naval interest in Norway should be understood in relation to three more specific factors.

The first of these was the adoption of what Eric Grove has referred to as a "British Atlantic strike fleet strategy" in the early 1950s, centred around the contribution of British fleet carriers to NATO's Strike Fleet.[9] The argument that Norway had to be defended, or at least denied as a "secure" staging area for air and naval operations against Britain, was thought to be particularly persuasive by the Admiralty in its struggle to preserve the Fleet Air Arm.[10] This, however, changed after 1957 when the rationale for maintaining larger carriers shifted to an emphasis on their limited and Cold War functions in the Middle East, the Indian Ocean and South East Asia, that is east of Suez.

Second, the Navy's attachment to the concept of broken-backed war, a lengthy section on which had been included in the 1952 Global Strategy Paper, also ensured continued interest in Northern Europe. More specifically, Admiralty planners argued that the decisive importance of the submarine campaign in the period of broken-backed war heightened the need to prevent the Soviet Navy from establishing forward submarine bases in North Norway.

Third, in arguing the case that the Royal Navy maintained an operational as well as a declaratory interest in Norway, it is important to stress that until the Defence Review of 1957 all three Services retained a considerable degree of operational and planning autonomy. This had a direct impact on the strategic priorities and dispositions of each service.[11] As Martin Navias has pointed out, long before Sandys's White Paper of April 1957 there had been "an irrevocable movement towards a declaratory stress on massive retaliation and changes in force posture" within the British defence establishment.[12] At the operational level, however, services continued to fight for policies that would protect their particular programmes, one result of which was that no significant change in Britain's force posture accompanied the strategic consensus that appeared to have been reached with the Global Strategy Paper of 1952. While the Defence White Papers of both 1955 and 1956 stressed a "war preparation priority list" reflecting increased emphasis on strengthening the deterrent, the Navy "continued to attempt to prevent the implications of such an ordering from undermining its favoured roles and capabilities."[13] It was partly for this "bureaucratic" reason that the Navy was able to maintain a commitment to Norway. Advances in weapons technology, opposition by the other Chiefs of Staff to the concept of broken-backed hostilities, balance of payments difficulties and unrelenting financial pressure notwithstanding, the defence of Norway remained a central argument in favour of maintaining the Fleet Air Arm.

British Strike Fleet Strategy in Northern Waters, 1952–57

Under the "three-pillar strategy" adopted by the COS in June 1947 – protection of sea communications, defence of the home base and the Middle East – the Navy concentrated its efforts on the protection of shipping by emphasising counter-mine and convoy escort forces.[14] Accordingly, the principal role of British fleet carriers between 1947 and 1952 was the protection of Mediterranean convoys from air attack. By 1952, however, the Admiralty was arguing increasingly in favour of a more offensive concept of operations based around fleet carriers in the Atlantic, capable of launching direct attacks against Soviet naval targets on the Kola Peninsula and in the Baltic area, as well as dealing with the threat posed by Soviet long-range cruisers. The strike fleet strategy, with an increasing emphasis on the carrier's usefulness as a nuclear platform alongside the American component of the Striking Fleet, thus signified a shift in British naval doctrine away from a concept of carrier operations primarily geared towards the direct defence of shipping. As Admiral Sir Michael Denny put it in 1956, the Strike Fleet would "undertake offensive and support operations, rather than the direct defence of the Atlantic trade routes."[15]

The activation of ACLANT, the first NATO command post on American soil and the first peacetime international ocean command, was a factor of major importance in terms of moving towards a Strike Fleet strategy on the part of the Admiralty. The NATO commitment, William Crowe observed, "signified a marked change in the Board of Admiralty's attitude. It was envisaging naval forces carrying the war to enemy territory, attacking land targets, and supporting troops."[16] The Navy's reorientation towards offensive operations in northern waters appears also to have been influenced by the appointment in 1951 of Admiral Rhoderick McGrigor to the post of First Sea Lord. Admiral McGrigor who replaced Admiral Bruce Fraser, had been involved in carrier operations in northern and Arctic waters during the war and was a strong advocate of the offensive use of carriers. Admiral Fraser, on the other hand, had operated with battleships in the far north, and this appears to have made him far more "convoy-minded" than McGrigor.[17]

In early 1953 the Mediterranean was no longer envisaged to be the principal theatre of operations for British fleet carriers, which had become *Carrier Group Two* of the Strike Fleet.[18] The Strike Fleet mission in war was, according to Crowe, to "deploy to the North Atlantic and attack targets in Northern Russia with atomic bombs and hopefully to support landings in the Scandinavian area."[19] On the eve of the Radical Review process British war-plans had assigned two operational fleet carriers to the group, whose mission included covering SACLANT's Scandinavian convoys. In these plans the carriers were given a very wide range of tasks, including "fighter and ASW support, as well as "attacking at source', supporting NATO land forces and attacking surface raiders."[20] In addition to the fleet carries, the British element of the planned wartime composition of the Strike Fleet thirty days after the outbreak of war included one battleship, four cruisers and fifteen destroyers.[21]

Although SACEUR's "flank concept" was never properly implemented, the Admiralty, like the US Navy, *continued* to stress the Navy's responsibilities in northern waters. With the Radical Review process now under way, the Admiralty's Plans Division in the summer of 1953 listed the need to ensure "the supply and possible reinforcement of the NATO allies in Scandinavia to prevent its use as an enemy base against the United Kingdom"[22] as one of five naval tasks to be carried out in the first six weeks of a war. Another important naval task in the early stages of a war was the "deployment of minelaying and light surface forces to shut the Baltic for as long as possible."[23] In an important Radical Review meeting held on 10 November 1953, Duncan Sandys, Minister of Supply, and a strong opponent of the carrier programme, stated that "as he understood the position, fleet carriers were required for three main purposes."[24] These were: firstly, the defence of Norway; secondly, offensive operations against enemy bases in the Baltic and the North Sea, and thirdly, protection of Atlantic convoys against long-range Soviet raiders. According to Sandys, none of these constituted valid reasons for maintaining fleet carriers with their full complement of advanced and costly aircraft. Offensive operations against enemy bases and convoy protection against raiders could be performed by land-based aircraft. Moreover, with respect to the protection of convoys, Sandys added that "the US Fleet could also be relied upon."[25] Most interesting, however, were Sandys's grounds for dismissing the first argument which in his opinion sustained the requirement for heavy carriers: the defence of Norway. His expressed view in this respect is of particular significance in view of his subsequent appointment, under the premiership of Harold Macmillan, to the post of Minister of Defence. The defence of Norway, in the words of Sandys, "might or might not be a feasible operation but it was…one which as matter of strategic priority bore no relation to the defence of Western Europe or of the United Kingdom."[26]

In spite of Sandys's open attack on the carrier programme in late 1953, the Naval Staff continued to argue that Britain's strike fleet contribution should constitute the Navy's principal wartime commitment. The chief strategic rationale for maintaining fleet carriers as part of the Strike Fleet was that only the Royal Navy would be able to operate in northern waters during the first fifteen days of war, the critical opening phase of a conflict. This was stressed repeatedly by Admiralty representatives in COS and Cabinet discussions about the future of Britain's heavy carriers. In a memorandum prepared in time for the aforementioned Radical Review meeting, the First Lord of the Admiralty, James P.L. Thomas, argued that until the American attack carriers could reach the Eastern side of the Atlantic, "the British element will need to hold the ring."[27] This was reiterated by Thomas a month later when he stressed that without fleet carriers, the East Atlantic would be without a covering force for the first crucial fourteen days of war.[28] Moreover, by giving up fleet carriers, Thomas argued, "we should cease to be able to influence American naval planning in NATO."[29]

The wartime role envisaged for British fleet carriers was to attack at source all "threats to sea communications", the principal categories of which included: submarines and their base facilities, surface vessels in harbour, airfields and aircraft on the ground, and communications and waterways such as the Baltic – White Sea Canal.[30] In late December 1953, the Admiralty, somewhat surprisingly, received support from the Air Ministry for the claim – which Sandys had tried so hard to undermine – that carrier-based aircraft were in fact better suited to undertake missions in northern waters and Scandinavia than were shore-based aircraft.[31] In a meeting, on 22 December, between the First Sea Lord, Admiral Sir Rhoderick McGrigor, and the Chief of Air Staff, Sir William Dickson, the latter agreed that for "attacks on Russian northern bases and communications," fighter escorted strikes from carriers might be more effective than attacks at extreme range by Bomber Command. Furthermore, the CAS agreed that carrier aircraft were better suited for "accurate minelaying" in the Norwegian leads.[32]

Still, between 1952 and 1957, Britain's *actual* contribution to Strike Fleet was confined largely to the provision of fighter cover and anti-submarine protection.[33] Admiralty planners, however, argued that technological advances in the field of aircraft and carrier construction, guided weapons and submarines would place an even greater premium on *offensive strategies* for the control of sea communications in the future. A staff paper forwarded to Admiral McGrigor in February 1954, dealing with the likely effects of scientific developments "on the pattern of naval warfare", observed:

> In war it will again be imperative to develop at the earliest propitious moment offensive operations against the enemy's maritime forces at sea and in their bases and to destroy the enemy bases.
>
> As part of such an offensive strategy for the control of sea communications, attacks by a Carrier Striking Force will be necessary to supplement attacks by land based aircraft.[34]

It was on the basis of these arguments that the Naval Staff stressed the importance of developing nuclear-capable fighter aircraft, such as the N113 (Scimitar) and DH110 (Sea Vixen), and strike aircraft such as the NA39 (Buccaneer). The N113 and DH110 would be designed specifically to counter the growing strength of Soviet naval aviation operating with the 4th Fleet Air Force (South Baltic Sea), 8th Fleet Air Force (North Baltic Sea) and the Northern Fleet Air Force (White Sea).[35] As noted earlier, British, American and Norwegian concerns about the growing potential of Soviet naval aviation increased markedly after the emergence of the "Badger" medium bomber, and the gradual introduction of the Mig-19 ("Farmer") and Yak-25 ("Flashlight") fighters into naval units. In late 1953 J.P. Thomas warned that even at present, Russian Type 35 ("Bosun") bombers from "bases in Norway or northern Denmark" could reach most of the south western approaches to the UK without flying within the combat range of any shore-based fighters.[36] Only the development of the DH110 and the N113 could meet the requirement generated by the Soviet threat from Soviet Baltic and northern bases. More advanced British *strike* aircraft, such as the NA39, would represent an effective "anti-*Sverdlov*" platform, while also being capable of dropping "small atomic bombs ...within a few hundred miles of the enemy coast."[37] With these weapon systems fully developed, the Admiralty argued, Britain would be in a much stronger position to influence the conduct of strike fleet operations and NATO naval strategy more generally.

Between 1954 and 1957 the Admiralty continued to argue in favour of a Strike Fleet strategy.[38] An important victory seemed to have been won in early 1955 when the Defence Committee accepted the arguments of the Navy when it ruled out cuts in the fleet air arm as a means of saving money.[39] Having been asked to consider the long-term strategic role of the Fleet Air Arm, the Minister of Defence, Harold Macmillan, produced a memorandum on the subject for the Defence Committee on 7 January 1955. In the memorandum the Defence Minister specifically mentioned the need to consider the effect of any change of plans concerning carriers to NATO on the Scandinavian members of the Alliance. Macmillan concluded by arguing that savings incurred by converting heavy carriers into light carriers without a full complement of aircraft, would not outweigh the benefits of continuing to produce two heavy carriers for the Strike Fleet (a third, Macmillan pointed out, had already been asked for by SACLANT). The Committee accepted that Britain's commitment of fleet carriers to NATO put her in a position to influence overall NATO naval strategy and thus to affect decisions concerning the employment of the Strike Fleet itself.[40] As with the carrier debate in late 1953, it was successfully argued that without British carriers on the European side of the Atlantic there would be no means of "operating in waters subject to heavy enemy air attack and outside the range of shore-based air cover" until the US section of the fleet arrived. In the debate on the Naval Estimates in the House of Commons some months later, the First Lord, J.P. Thomas, again stressed the virtues of the carrier battle group as "a self-protecting, largely self-contained mobile airfield" in a nuclear war.[41]

What, then, can be said about the specific tasks assigned to British maritime forces in the north, tasks involving Norwegian territory, bases and supply facilities in the event of war?

British documents from late 1953 do refer to the existence of "a SACLANT plan" in which the Royal Navy was to take part in carrying out "attacks on Russian Northern bases."[42] The actual plan and the targets involved are not specified, though a good indication of the mission envisaged for the British in the Far North and Norway's role in it, can be found in the 1955 US Navy brief on allied mining plans discussed in the previous chapter.[43] As indicated above, one of SACLANT's highest priorities in the "emergency phase" (D-Day through D+6 months) of general war was to reduce substantially the Soviet "submarine menace" through offensive aircraft, surface and submarine mining operations.[44] In this endeavour, Norway played a critical role, providing staging bases for US Navy and RAF "patrol bombers" assigned targets on the Kola Peninsula, in the Kola Inlet and in the White Sea Entrance. In SACLANT's offensive mining plan for 1955, 20 British Lincoln bombers under national control would be assigned to SACLANT for "specific Pechenga-Murmansk mining."[45] More specifically, two wartime missions, to be initiated immediately upon the commencement of hostilities, were given to the Lincoln bombers of Bomber Command. The first was to establish "sustained attrition minefields" in the Murmansk approach channel by aircraft staged through north Norway. The second task was to establish "limited attrition minefields" on both sides of the Kola Inlet and off Yokanga on the Barents

Sea coast. The second task would be done by aircraft staged from Andøya and other "Norwegian bases."[46] With the Strike Fleet itself, the UK had assigned 28 Wyvern strike aircraft and 16 turbo-prop Gannets, carrier-based aircraft also designed to participate in the early and critical mine-laying campaign. In addition, British submarines based on the Clyde would establish transitory attrition minefields in the White Sea entrance, off the Murmansk coast, in the Kola Inlet and the Pechenga approaches. Furthermore, allied submarines would lay deep anti-submarine barriers in portions of the Greenland – Iceland – Scotland area; one in the Denmark Strait and one east of Iceland.[47] Finally, SACLANT forces would assist SACEUR in establishing a mine barrier in the Baltic exits.

Direct Assistance to Norway and the Concept of "Broken-Backed" Hostilities

The Strike Fleet strategy advocated by the Admiralty was essentially con-cerned with the first phase of global war. Though the Navy placed much emphasis on attack at source at the outset of a war, the war-time roles envisaged for fleet carriers in "Northern waters" spelled out in late 1953 also included the disruption of "any attempt by the enemy to support land and amphibious operations with major surface units."[48] The principal reason put forward by the Admiralty in favour of maintaining direct com-mitments to Norway was this: successful land operations in Norway, espe-cially in the far north, would give the Soviet Navy extremely valuable submarine bases, from which they could prosecute the war during the period of "broken backed" hostilities.[49] This concept of broken-backed warfare had successfully been championed by the First Sea Lord, Admiral McGrigor, during the global strategy discussions held by the COS in 1952. In their final paper it was concluded that:

> future war would begin with a short period of great intensity which would be followed, if a decision had not been reached in the first period, by an indefinite period of broken-backed hostilities during which both sides would seek to recuperate from the wounds they had sustained and to recover strength from a further intensive effort.[50]

It was acceptance of this long-war scenario by Sir John Slessor (CAS) – allowing for the possibility that conventional operations would still follow a post-nuclear exchange – which had enabled the First Sea Lord to accept the overall conclusion of the Global Strategy Paper: increased emphasis on nuclear weapons in British strategic policy. The term "broken-backed" appeared in the 1954 Defence White Paper, and though it was removed from the Defence White Paper for 1955 in favour of a more exclusive stress on "the deterrent", the Navy continued to stress the importance of sea power in "a period of broken-backed warfare ... during which the opposing sides would seek to recover their strength" in preparation for the decisive battle.[51] Even during the White Paper discussions of April 1957, the Navy showed no intention of abandoning its commitment to broken-backed warfare; after the nuclear exchange phase, it was argued, the Navy would still have to confront the Soviet submarine threat.[52]

From the Admiralty's point of view, endorsement of this concept heightened the importance of providing assistance to NATO allies in Scandinavia, since during the phase of "broken-backed" war the main theatre of operations would be at sea. The very large number of Soviet submarines, having survived the initial phase, would then be in a position to conduct an intensive campaign against sea communications. Moreover, the Admiralty, having confronted the German fleet-in-being strategy in the North Atlantic during the Second World War, was, unlike the US Navy, far more concerned about the threat posed by Soviet surface raiders of the 16,000-ton Sverdlov class. If these cruisers succeeded in dispersing before the outbreak of a conflict, they could be tucked away in Norwegian fjords, as had German major surface combatants, including *Tirpitz, Admiral Hipper, Lützow, Admiral Scheer* and *Prinz Eugen*, during much of the war. Against this background of a dual surface and subsurface threat, closing the Baltic and preventing the Soviet Northern Fleet from acquiring bases along the north Norwegian coast became stated Admiralty objective in war.[53]

During NATO's annual Command Post Exercise in April 1957 (CPX 7), Lord Mountbatten spent some time explaining his case to SACLANT and other senior NATO commanders. The Soviet submarine fleet, Mountbatten argued, was the "master card" which the Russians held up their sleeve. The reason for this was simple: after the first exchange of thermo-nuclear bombing "the Russian submarines, all of whom will have been at sea before the war started, if the Russians started it ... will still be there." The second stage of war, Mountbatten argued, not wanting to be "alarmist," could "go on for a year at least, perhaps two." The Russians had already built 27 submarine depot ships and they were building more. Moreover, submarines could be "tucked away in all the inlets of the North Coast of Russia, and indeed, if they have Norway in their hands, in Norway."[54]

However, it should be added that while these considerations led the Naval Staff to stress the need for *direct* support to Norway, as seen in the preceding chapter, the unavailability of fast carriers in "sufficient" numbers (as defined by SACLANT) and the growth of Soviet naval-power, meant that priorities had to be spelled out more explicitly. Although plans still emphasised the importance of carrier-based support for the land-battle in Norway,[55] the need to secure sea control by "materially reducing" land-based threats to sea communications received higher priority than the direct defence of Norway. When the First Sea Lord countered criticism of the Fleet Air Arm raised by the Swinton Committee in 1954, he argued that as an "extra role" British carriers would help defend Norway against amphibious attack. But this, he stressed, was "only incidental to the primary strategic role of defeating the Soviet surface fleet."[56] Still, joint planning and combined exercises involving maritime support to the land areas of Norway and Denmark continued after 1953, though not on the same scale as Mainbrace. In May 1954, a "major conference" was held at Northwood with CINCNORTH representatives discussing the employment of the UK element of the Strike Fleet in the NEC area.[57] The tasks which the Admiralty Plans Division had outlined in the summer of 1953 were rehearsed by British forces in a NATO exercise, Morning Mist, in September 1954. One phase of this exercise (Northern Mist) was conducted by COMNORLANT and practised the sailing of a convoy from Methil (Scotland) to Kristiansand (South Norway) in conjunction with minelaying and mine sweeping activities.[58]

The Appeal to History and Opposition to Naval Commitments in the North

The Strike Fleet concept, with its emphasis on offensive operations alongside US carriers, clearly had greater appeal to the Naval Staff than the earlier post-war emphasis on convoy escort tasks to protect shipping. The Strike Fleet was more of a "battle fleet', whose mission would be to seek out and destroy the enemy, thus acting more in the Mahanian tradition of gaining command of the sea through decisive fleet action. It is important to note here that the Royal Navy had a historical tradition of involvement and responsibility in "Northern Waters" to which the Admiralty consciously appealed when arguing their case for a Strike Fleet strategy, preparations for broken-backed war, and, more generally, for a "commitment" to allies in Scandinavia.[59] Of particular importance were the recent experiences of wartime operations in the Norwegian and Arctic seas. During the Second World War, one of the major Anglo-German naval engagements in European waters had taken place in the approaches to Narvik in April 1940.[60] Furthermore, Germany's fleet-in-being strategy had forced the Royal Navy to maintain a strong presence in the North

Atlantic throughout the war, both to support the convoy runs to Murmansk and to seek out enemy surface raiders.[61] Combined Operations had been carried out along the Norwegian coast, and Lord Mountbatten himself, as Commodore Combined Operations, planned the raid against the Norwegian island of Vågsø in late 1941. This was significant as "the first operation in which all three Services were truly interwoven in planning and execution".[62] In the first week of May, 1945, the last major wartime operation carried out by the Home Fleet was led by Rear-Admiral Rhoderick McGrigor and took place in the Vestfjord. In a series of accurate and successful attacks, Avengers and Wildcats of the Fleet Air Arm inflicted heavy damage on base installations supporting the German Arctic U-boat flotilla, including the destruction of the submarine depot ship *Black Watch* in the Kilbotn Fjord.[63]

Given this legacy of involvement in the North, it is not surprising that the appeal to history was used by Navy representatives when they stressed the strategic value of Scandinavia and the consequent need to maintain commitments in the area.[64] It was typically expressed in an aforementioned memorandum by the First Lord of the Admiralty, J.P. Thomas, concerning the role of carriers. Having described the "main function of our Fleet Carriers ... as a contribution to the "Striking Fleet," Thomas went on to portray the role of the Strike Fleet as:

> analogous to that of the Grand Fleet of World War I and the British Home Fleet of World War II, namely the offensive force for Atlantic and Northern Waters.

There was more to this, however, than simply the question of previous involvement in the area. During the Second World War, lessons had been learned which Admiralty planners felt were highly relevant to an understanding of the implications of growing Soviet Naval power in Northern Europe in the 1950s.[65] First, the experience of operating in Norwegian and Arctic seas after the end of the Norwegian campaign had left the Admiralty staff keenly appreciative of the enormous tactical advantage held by the Germans in combining shore-based air reconnaissance and strike forces, powerful surface raiders and submarines, all operating out of bases in Norway.[66] If enemy forces were to acquire bases in northern Norway, they would not only advance their bomb line further west but their submarines and surface raiders would pose a most serious threat to Allied sea lanes of communications.[67]

Secondly, the Norwegian campaign in the spring of 1940 had also brought home more general lessons, two of which were pointed out by

Captain S.W. Roskill in his influential study of the war at sea, the first volume of which appeared in 1954:

> The first concerned the effect of air power on the control of the sea. It could no longer be doubted that if effective air cover was lacking, warships could not operate protractedly and the Army could not be maintained overseas. Secondly, there was the old lesson that if a secure base cannot be established in an overseas theatre of war, the land campaign cannot prosper.[68]

According to the Admiralty, technological advances since the war had only accentuated the relevance of these lessons.

Given the financial pressures and competing strategic priorities that existed between 1952 and 1957, it is not surprising that Navy opinion favourable to greater strategic priority for Norway met with resistance from other quarters within the British political and defence establishment.[69] Even before the Defence Review of 1957, it was becoming clear that British defence priorities were likely to change in a way that would affect the Royal Navy's traditional commitment in the North. The British Prime Minister, Anthony Eden, meeting with the Norwegian Prime Minister, Einar Gerhardsen, raised the issue in October 1956. Under the discussion item entitled "NATO, The Strategic Reappraisal," the PM's brief read:

> The means of defence have changed with the vast increase in nuclear weapons; and so has the nature of the threat, which is now more strongly directed through economic means towards Asia and the Middle East. This problem is of particular interest to the United Kingdom. We should be doing a disservice to our NATO partners if we overestimated our own economy and had not the economic resources and military strength to support our friends and guard our interests in those areas.[70]

II SCALING DOWN BRITISH NAVAL COMMITMENTS IN THE NORTH ATLANTIC, 1957–60

Naval Implications of the 1957 Defence White Paper

In early January 1957 the financial crisis precipitated by the Suez debacle prompted Harold Macmillan to accelerate the Long-Term Defence Review process initiated by Churchill's Conservative administration in 1952. To co-ordinate the process, Macmillan appointed Churchill's son-in-law, Duncan Sandys, as his new Minister of Defence. The outcome of the review was the April 1957 Defence White Paper, designed to "revise not merely the size, but the character of the defence plan."[71] Sandys's White Paper, as it came to be known, argued centrally that advances in weapons technology meant that "the only existing safeguard against major aggression is the power to threaten retaliation with nuclear weapons." Greater emphasis on the "deterrent" and nuclear weapons in British strategic policy would ensure substantial savings in defence expenditure. In fact, the *principal* rationale behind the White Paper was Sandys's and Macmillan's desire to secure financial savings by reducing manpower. As such, the document was motivated more by economic factors than by any coherent set of strategic considerations.[72]

There was, in essence, nothing radically new about these arguments. The Defence White Paper codified ideas that had first been adumbrated in the Global Strategy Paper of 1952, namely, that "while conventional forces were to be retained to guard against threats to Britain's world-wide interests and as a partial deterrent to aggression in Europe, the main emphasis of Britain's global strategy was to be placed on the deterrent and operational capabilities of nuclear weapons with conventional forces of reduced size."[73] Yet, while Sandys's ideas may not have been very novel, the original Global Strategy Paper had not been followed up by any significant change in the balance of conventional and nuclear forces.[74] Concessions made to the Army and the Navy, such as the concept of "broken-backed" hostilities, meant that little actual change had taken place in Britain's overall force posture between 1952 and 1957. The real significance of Sandys's reforms, therefore, lay in the fact that only in 1957 did "a major change in the extant equilibrium of nuclear-conventional forces ... take place and a "New Look" force posture reflecting added emphasis on nuclear weapons and decreased conventional forces ... come into being."[75] Unlike Lord Alexander and Anthony Head before him, Duncan Sandys, with enhanced institutional power and strong personal backing from Macmillan, was able to impose his priorities on the services. This meant that forces designed for use in global war would have to be cut or, where possible, redirected towards limited and cold war functions in support of residual colonial commitments and treaty obligations outside Europe.[76] In a report circulated to the COS on 8 May 1957, the Joint Planning Staff noted that:

> the Defence White Paper, which is based primarily on economic necessity, assumes that since global war is unlikely so long as the deterrent

remains effective, priority in the deployment of our resources after our contribution to the deterrent, must be geared to cold and limited war tasks.[77]

On the basis of these priorities and Sandys's known hostility to the carrier, the Naval Staff had to provide a case for the retention of carriers which *did not* emphasise their role in a general war with the Soviet Union. Consequently, the Admiralty chose not to stress the value of carriers as nuclear platforms in global war, even though advanced fighter and strike aircraft – the Scimitar, the Sea Vixen and NA39 – were all in advanced stages of development. Sandys's hostility to the strike fleet concept made it imperative for the Naval Staff to find an alternative basis on which to rest the case for the Fleet Air Arm.[78]

Stressing the value of carriers as "means of applying air power in areas where other means cannot be efficiently or economically based,"[79] the Admiralty chose to focus on their role in limited war and cold war operations east of Suez. In a report by the Joint Planning Staff circulated for consideration by the Chiefs of Staff on 18 February 1957, the east-of-Suez scenario was prominent. Whilst stressing the "serious blow" to political cohesion within NATO, resulting from removal of carriers from the Strike Fleet, the report placed primary emphasis on the contribution that carriers would make to the "maintenance of the territorial integrity and internal security of colonial territories and dependencies overseas."[80] It was an effective argument seen in the light of Sandys's insistence on maintaining *all* British defence commitments in the Middle and Far East while simultaneously reducing the size of army garrisons overseas.[81] The report's conclusion, that the Fleet Air Arm should be retained, was unanimously approved by the COS Committee the following day; a "major victory" for the Admiralty.[82] While the White Paper envisaged reductions in the reserve fleet and the Navy's shore establishments and ruled out renewal of the cruiser fleet, British naval strength east of Suez was to be maintained at *existing levels*. Cutbacks would have to be made in the Mediterranean and Home Fleets.[83]

The White Paper and Britain's Contribution to NATO

The centrality of the "deterrent" in the White Paper notwithstanding, the basis for Britain's naval contribution to NATO was justified by a reference to what was, in effect, a watered-down version of the broken-backed war argument championed by the Navy since 1952. Although the term itself was not used, and had not appeared in any White Paper since 1954,

Sandys did allow for the "possibility that the nuclear battle might not prove immediately decisive; and in that event it would be of great importance to defend Atlantic communications against submarine attack." The logic of the argument was for Britain to concentrate more exclusively on anti-submarine warfare operations using light carriers. The consequent process of reordering naval priorities continued throughout 1957, and, in November of that year, Lord Mountbatten formally accepted that forces west of Suez should be geared towards anti-submarine operations.[84] This was confirmed in January 1958 in the first draft of the 1958 Defence White Paper on the role of the Navy. The draft explained how the "Western Fleet" of the Navy should concentrate on strengthening NATO's ASW capabilities and that this effort would be "at the expense of the air defence and strike role in the Atlantic."[85] The principle of balanced collective forces was not, however, to be applied east of Suez, where "all-purpose naval forces at about their present level" would be maintained.[86] Even though Sandys emphasised the ASW commitment to NATO, this role was clearly secondary to the focus on limited-war scenarios east of Suez. As a result, the Royal Navy, according to Crowe, "turned away from NATO," and continued to do so under Sandy's successor, Harold Watkinson, who assumed office in 1959.[87] While this reordering of priorities was neither as dramatic nor as sudden as Crowe seems to suggest, the general change of priorities heralded by the Defence White Paper could not be denied. Moreover, although British defence officials did stress their continued commitment to NATO, there is little doubt that the *perception* that Britain was reducing her alliance commitments too rapidly was taking root within NATO (however unjustified in terms of Britain's economic predicament). In January 1959 Admiral Jerauld Wright told the *Draper Committee* that he expected "no help in the offensive campaign except for the *possible* contribution of one UK carrier and the Dutch cruisers."[88]

In late January 1957, John Foster Dulles, in a meeting with Duncan Sandys in Washington, "expressed the hope" that the "proposed UK armament cuts ... could be worked out in a way which would minimize the shock to NATO."[89] Sandys replied that while he certainly hoped this could be done, the "cut had to come, irrespective of NATO."[90] Reactions within NATO, as Dulles had predicted, were felt almost immediately. In a Chiefs of Staff meeting on 12 April, Lord Mountbatten referred to a telegram he had received from CINCAFMED saying "there had been a profound shock throughout his NATO command at what was regarded as a unilateral action by one member nation which could not but weaken the structure of NATO."[91] Referring to further British naval cuts in early 1958, one American commentator wrote how a "growing body of NATO opinion feels the economy-backed British Navy has left a gaping hole in the North

Atlantic."[92] As British representatives presented the "United Kingdom case" during NATO's *Annual Review* meetings between 1957 and 1960, growing allied concern about what was seen to be a diminishing NATO commitment on the part of Britain was registered by the Chiefs of Staff. The COS nonetheless reaffirmed the strategic priorities laid down in the 1957 White Paper.[93]

British naval cuts and re-deployments in the period between 1957 and 1960 had direct and indirect consequences for Norway. *First*, the emphasis on naval responsibilities east of Suez, a policy to which the Government's commitment only increased in the years following the defence review, inevitably meant a reduction of Britain's naval contribution in the North Atlantic. When preparing the UK reply to the 1958 Annual Review, the COS noted how "as a result of recent decisions ... the Far Eastern Fleet has increased at the expense of the Home and Mediterranean fleets."[94] In view of the maritime nature of the Northern European Command area, this was in itself a disconcerting trend. *Secondly*, changes in British naval policy also had more direct consequences. When in 1960 the fast minelayer HMS *Apollo* was decommissioned, CINCNORTH's mining plan for the Kattegat, known as the "Apollo Plan", became obsolete.[95] The successful accomplishment of this plan in war was deemed to be vitally important in terms of "bottling up" the Soviet Baltic Fleet. As the plan became obsolete, General Norstad was requested, in May 1961, to review all mining plans for the Kattegat with a view to possibly reducing the total mining requirement and to approach the Norwegian Ministry of Defence asking that it assume user nation functions.[96] The third and most important consequence for Norway of changes in British naval policy was *indirect,* namely, the growth of American military activity and commitments in the North Atlantic. It is worth noting here that during the defence review process Mr Sandys, according to Sir Richard Powell's recollection, "felt that if the need arose the Americans could and would fill any gaps in Atlantic naval defences that the reductions in British naval strength had opened."[97]

III   US NAVY REACTIONS TO BRITISH NAVAL CUTS: IMPLICATIONS FOR NORWAY AND THE MARITIME BALANCE IN NORTHERN WATERS

The reactions of the US Navy to the naval implications of Sandys's defence review and the pressure for further cuts after April 1957 may usefully be seen as going through two stages.

The first of these lasted through the summer of 1957 and started even before the White Paper was publicly presented. This was a period of *clarification* – that is, a period during which American officials, representing not only the Navy but also other branches of the administration (notably the White House itself and the State Department), sought to establish exactly what would be the size, nature and implications of the proposed cuts. The second phase ran through the autumn of 1957 and into the first half of 1958 and was characterised by a sense of deepening American concern about changes in the balance of maritime forces in the eastern Atlantic area. In the autumn of 1957, it was the conclusions drawn from an analysis of two specific events which most strongly influenced the development of American attitudes. The first of these was a series of NATO maritime exercises – Strike Back, Sea Watch and Stand Firm – all of which were held in the eastern Atlantic in September.[98] The second event, in October, was the successful launching of Sputnik I from a rocket test facility near Tyuratam in Soviet Central Asia.

January 1957 – September 1957

When Harold Macmillan met with President Eisenhower at Bermuda in March 1957 to repair relations after Suez, he used the opportunity to inform the President about the estimated reductions associated with the forthcoming White Paper. With regard to naval forces, Macmillan told Eisenhower that the British D-Day contribution to SACLANT would be cut by *one third*, though more detailed disclosures were not made.[99] The President for his part raised the issue of the "reductions in the Royal Navy and the gap that they would leave in the North Atlantic."[100] In particular, Eisenhower stressed the importance of the United Kingdom controlling the sea area between Scotland and Iceland, and Sir Richard Powell, then Permanent Secretary at the Ministry of Defence, told the COS on 12 April that the Prime Minister had personally accepted this as an "undertaking."[101] In spite of Macmillan's promise, Admiral Sir Michael Denny, UK Standing Group representative and Head of the British Joint Services Mission in Washington, told the COS that while the Bermuda conference had been useful in terms of outlining the logic behind the White Paper to the Americans, there was likely to be "strong criticisms from the Departments of Defence when they realised the ultimate reductions in the size of our forces."[102] In particular, Denny noted, there would be "strong repercussions when the United States Navy appreciated the magnitude of our reductions."[103] At the conclusion of the meeting, the Chiefs endorsed Sir Richard Powell's suggestion that Lord Mountbatten and the Chief of Air Staff, Sir Dermot Boyle, should inform SACLANT "candidly ... at the first convenient opportunity" what the British reductions in naval forces and maritime air were going to be.

The opportunity to do so arose on 7 May when Admiral Jerauld Wright, hoping for more details about the schedule and scale of UK naval reductions, met with the COS in London.[104] Admiral Wright was particularly anxious to know whether British carriers allotted to his command would be *strike* or *ASW* carriers. Lord Mountbatten explained that their precise role could not be stated since they also had to be prepared to undertake "various roles in cold and limited war."[105] Still, two carrier groups would "probably" be made available for SACLANT in the event of global war. Sir Dermot Boyle was more specific and reported that maritime aircraft for SACLANT, most of which were assigned missions in and around Norway, were to be reduced to 72 in 1957, to 54 by December 1958 and to 42 by December 1959.[106]

The source of SACLANT's worries at this particular time was clearly revealed to the COS the following day in a report circulated by the Joint Planning Staff concerning SACLANT's recent deployment plans. The Planning Staff pointed out how the "introduction of the missile-carrying submarine has caused SACLANT to place increased emphasis on the importance of the Forward Defence Zone," and that he "now indicates that he will require considerable United Kingdom naval forces to be stationed in peacetime to detect submarines and prevent their deployment to wartime stations."[107] In fact, Admiral Wright had told members of the COS the previous day, that, given the potential threat from Soviet guided missile submarines, UK naval reductions had come at a time when D-Day force readiness "was even more important and force requirements were in fact increasing."[108] As the Planning Staff pointed out, however, British long-term defence policy foresaw a marked reduction in the number of United Kingdom naval forces earmarked for the eastern Atlantic.[109] The Planning Staff could see no likelihood of British anti-submarine vessels being made available in "peacetime for the specific task of detecting the deployment of Russian missile submarines."[110] Lord Mountbatten's comments at the COS meeting convened to discuss the report clearly point to the tensions that had arisen between American and British priorities. According to the First Sea Lord, SACLANT wanted:

> ships and maritime aircraft permanently available in peacetime to give early warning of the move of Soviet submarines. These we should not be able to provide. SACLANT also wanted all D-Day naval forces on station in peacetime. Such a requirement would conflict with our policy

of earmarking the majority of our naval forces to NATO, and using them world wide.[111]

September 1957 – May 1958

The second leg of the US Navy's response to British cuts occurred in the autumn and were related to the "semi-successful" conclusion of a series of maritime exercises held in the North Atlantic.

The main aim of Strike Back, which began on 19 September, was to practise offensive carrier operations against shore targets while "avoiding attacking submarines, hostile surface ships and beating off attacks by land-based aircraft."[112] The Strike Fleet – commanded by Vice Admiral Robert Pirie on board the flagship USS *Northampton* and with air power provided by the new American "super-carriers," USS *Forrestal* (CVA-59) and USS *Saratoga* (CVA-60), as well as by the British fleet carrier *HMS Eagle* – simulated nuclear attacks against land-targets in Norway. Exercise Strike Back, during which the Strike Fleet operated in the North Norwegian Sea with some units crossing the parallel of 70 degrees north, revealed serious deficiencies in communications and logistics under Arctic conditions.[113] Abnormal ionospheric conditions at times completely severed communications between shore and fleet. This led to increased efforts to upgrade communication facilities and installations in Norway in order to provide support for both defensive and offensive Strike Fleet operations.[114]

It was, however, in exercise Sea Watch that the "most glaring weakness in NATO's naval capability was uncovered."[115] The exercise was designed to test the ability to keep sea lines of communications across the Atlantic open through the conduct of aggressive anti-submarine warfare. In this exercise, however, "opposing" submarine forces – including the first nuclear-powered submarine, USS *Nautilus* – "racked up a high score of kills" and inflicted unacceptable losses on the defending force.[116] It is important to stress here that the performance of the USS *Nautilus* during all phases of the exercise left a deep impression on both American and British officials. In the years that followed, the experience was to have a very powerful influence, especially on American views about the possibilities for submarine operations in the Arctic. A report by Sir John Eccles, Commander of the Home Fleet, on the performance of *Nautilus* in exercise Strike Back, concluded that the "US Navy, originally sceptical of its capabilities, now regard the nuclear submarine as an entirely new weapon of war."[117] The US submarine had successfully simulated attacks against 16 different ships, including two carriers. According to the report, the *Nautilus* alone had "constituted a greater threat to opposing forces than did all other 21 snort fitted submarines put together."[118]

So depressing were the results from Sea Watch, that Sir John Eccles and Air Marshal Sir Bryan Reynolds, who jointly led the exercise, were prompted to issue a statement which had the effect of seriously embarrassing the Government by linking the outcome of the exercise to British naval cuts.[119] At the press conference, Eccles was even more outspoken in his criticism, saying that "we have got nothing like enough forces with which to carry out our primary task, either in the air, under the sea or on the sea. We are desperately short of all the hardware needed to fight this battle."[120] Clearly aiming his criticism at the Government, Eccles added: "I am not in a position to criticise political decisions, but I say this as a professional man with 40 years" experience. I cannot carry out my task as given to me at the moment without more forces."[121]

To the Americans, Admiral Eccles's remarks strongly reinforced existing worries about the debilitating impact of defence cuts on the ability of Britain to carry the initial burden of defence "in its own backyard."[122] In a separate statement, Admiral Jerauld Wright further embarrassed the British Government by openly supporting Eccles's comments concerning the inadequacy of forces in the "front line trenches" of the Eastern Atlantic.[123] In Admiral Wright's opinion, the problem of containing the Soviet submarine "menace" from bases at Murmansk and to a lesser extent the Baltic, which is what this debate was essentially about, was further complicated by the weakness of the Norwegian and Danish navies. In November, this view was publicly supported by CINCNORTH, General Sir Cecil Sugden.[124]

James Grant, a reporter for *The Register* in London, seeking to place Eccles's comments within the broader context of British naval policy in 1957, captured the mood and the general conclusions reached by US defence and administration officials after the exercises:

> Despite the defense economy measures here, it had been commonly accepted myth that Great Britain's naval power could act as the backbone of the bulwark against Soviet sea strike in the critical opening period.
>
> No matter what some authorities contend, it is now glaringly obvious that this is impossible.
>
> The crippling cutback in both British naval strength and the slow down in the development of more advanced naval weapons has taken its toll. This policy is, of course, in line with the notion that Western Europe is indefensible anyhow in the face of an all-out assault.
>
> For months now, high-ranking British naval men have been bridling in private at this scuttling of UK sea might.

..The lid finally blew off this pressure cooker of frustration with the jolting declaration of Admiral Eccles.[125]

These American worries were strongly reinforced by the demonstration of Soviet advances in missile technology in early October. The launching of Sputnik I and II, while not directly relevant to navy assessments, contributed to a *psychological environment* which seemed to magnify the significance of every measure that appeared to weaken Western capabilities. The threat of Soviet missile-guided submarines – for which there was, as we have seen, very little hard intelligence – at once seemed more credible. Most importantly, Sputnik showed that the continental United States was no longer impervious to a direct strategic attack. The fact that the Soviet Union was at least three years away from an initial operating capability for ICBMs did not really matter; the crucial premise of "massive retaliation" which had provided it with a *degree* of credibility – that is, the relative invulnerability of the American home land to direct strategic attack – had been removed.

While the shock of Sputnik appears to have influenced Eisenhower in the direction of increasing defence co-operation with Britain,[126] it did not have any appreciable impact on the trends in British naval policy. In February 1958, following the publication of the new White Paper and the announcement of further cuts,[127] the Chief of Naval Operations, Admiral Arleigh Burke, in a letter to Lord Mountbatten expressed his disappointment:

> From many previous indications I was aware that you would be forced into accepting significant reductions in your forces, but I was not quite prepared for the shocker contained in the recently published "White Paper".
>
> It would be inappropriate for me to offer my condolences on this turn of events, and yet I must in all sincerity say I am disturbed to see these drastic reductions in your naval forces at the very time when navies are so important to the accomplishment of our common objectives.[128]

In May, the *Manchester Guardian* reported on the "disappointment" with which Admiral Jerauld Wright had received the news that Britain would turn carriers west of Suez into helicopter carriers for anti-submarine warfare, thus effectively relinquishing the strike role option.[129] According to the article, this decision had come as a surprise since plans had been far advanced "for the incorporation of some of the finest ships of the Royal Navy into the Atlantic striking fleet, which is now entirely American."[130] The US Navy had been particularly keen to draw upon the "excellent capabilities" of the Royal Navy in air defence, including recent developments in radar.[131] In February 1959 Admiral Robert Carney, the former Chief of Naval Operations, noted in a letter to the *Draper Committee* that

> The UK is still reducing its Naval strength and appears to be placing dependence on ASW protection of its home waters by US forces. Furthermore, no UK Naval Forces are committed to NATO general use in the Med or elsewhere. This is a touchy point, but our own security is involved ... and our policy toward the UK should be re-examined to make sure that US interests are not jeopardized by US Navy make-up of British deficiencies created by shift of British effort to other defense activities.[132]

The extent to which the Royal Navy's strategic concepts and priorities were changing in the period after Sandys defence review, and the impact of this change on traditional commitments in the far north, are clearly seen in the minutes of a Cabinet Defence Committee meeting held at Chequers in February 1963. Discussing future defence policy, the First Sea Lord (Sir Caspar John), stated that the Navy's:

> ... role in support of NATO required us to subscribe paying lip service to two strategic concepts which were no longer sound the concept that naval forces might be required to carry on a "broken-backed" war after a strategic exchange between Russia and the West and the concept that on the outbreak of a war a powerful naval strike force should mount an attack on Russia from northern waters.[133]

Conclusion

Shortly before the disclosure of the 1958 White Paper, which so "shocked" Admiral Burke, the Chief of Naval Operations had written to Lord Mountbatten explaining that the frankness with which he felt obliged to express his views was needed "because any great modification to your forces will directly and immediately affect the tasks and responsibilities of our Navy."[134] The weakening of the British position in the Atlantic was not, however, the only reason for the change in American policy in 1957–58. The performance of USS *Nautilus* in the autumn exercises and the launching of Sputnik had the very important effect of demonstrating just how formidable was the potential threat presented by nuclear-powered submarines. The events in the autumn of 1957 were also highly significant in another respect. During Strike Back, the USS *Forrestal* and USS *Saratoga* received their first operational work-outs in the North Atlantic.

These ships were not only larger than the British fleet carriers, but their improved nuclear projection capabilities along with the prospective deployment of Fleet Ballistic Missile submarines in the Norwegian Sea greatly alarmed the Soviet Union. This, along with other developments (such as the intensification of US air operations in the Arctic after 1957), brought Norway more directly into the nexus of superpower military confrontation in the late 1950s.

6 American Forward Maritime Strategy in the North Atlantic, 1957–60

According to some observers, Admiral Sir John Eccles's "frank admissions" about British naval weakness in late 1957, marked the first step in a campaign to have the US Navy assume additional duties in the Atlantic, much as the Sixth Fleet had done in the Mediterranean after the Second World War.[1] And, indeed, in June 1960, the *Daily Telegraph* reported that for the first time the US was about to have a "continuously operational carrier striking fleet in the North Atlantic."[2] This chapter examines the growth of US naval activities and interests in the North Atlantic between 1957 and 1960, and assess their direct and indirect implications for Norway. In this context, three key areas merit particular attention: (1) the measures introduced to strengthen American anti-submarine warfare capabilities, (2) the deployment of Fleet Ballistic Missile submarines (Polaris) in the Norwegian Sea, and (3) the growing concern within the US Navy about possible limited war scenarios on the Northern Flank. The chapter also examines signs of growing Soviet concern about US maritime strategy in the far north after 1957.

I ANTI-SUBMARINE WARFARE AND LIMITED WAR CONTINGENCIES

Meeting the Soviet Submarine Challenge: Offensive Operations and Organisational Change

Although Admiral Burke had reinstated anti-submarine warfare as the Navy's first priority in 1955, the events of 1957 infused the naval establishment with a new sense of urgency.[3] In the Atlantic the weaknesses revealed in Sea Watch and the belief that Soviet nuclear-powered and missile-carrying submarines would soon become operational, dramatically increased the US Navy's perceived need for a sustained effort to improve ASW capabilities.[4] Testifying before a Congressional subcommittee in

February 1959, Admiral Jerauld Wright reported that "almost all components of the Atlantic Fleet" were now engaged towards the destruction of Soviet submarine power.[5]

In a paper sent by Admiral Burke to Eisenhower's administrative assistant, Bryce Harlow, in mid-November 1957, the Chief of Naval Operations outlined the "submarine problem" and the basic tenets of the Navy's anti-submarine philosophy.[6] From this and similar documents, the US ASW programme can be seen as centring on three major tasks, each corresponding to layers of defence against the submarine threat.[7] First, Admiral Burke expected that most submarines would be hidden in dispersed coves and fjords. The "first line of defence", therefore, would be direct nuclear attack against submarine bases. Carrier striking forces, in co-ordination with SAC, would be required to "search out and destroy these small hidden bases, as early as possible in war, to reduce the menace at its source."[8] Second, if submarines survived the initial attack, they would have to sortie through minefields laid at the exits from home waters. In these offensive mining operations, conducted by aircraft and submarines, Norway's role was considered extremely important.[9] Third, if submarines did succeed in dispersing into larger ocean areas, they would be sought out by hunter-killer task forces consisting of lighter ASW-configured carriers (CVS), attack submarines and surface ships. These would be aided by sea-based aircraft and shore-based patrol bombers in Scotland, Iceland and Norway.[10] Although it is true that these principles of ASW had been emphasised earlier, the organisational effort put into strengthening capabilities in each of these areas increased substantially in 1957, with important consequences for both Britain and Norway.

In the first place, nuclear strike operations against targets on the Kola peninsula and at the White Sea entrances were assigned higher priority. The extreme difficulties which the US Navy encountered in its own exercises when trying to detect, classify, track and locate nuclear-powered submarines for kill led the Navy to place an even greater emphasis on attack at source.[11] Commenting on Admiral Wright's concept of operations in his EDP for 1958, the British Joint Planning Staff noted that:

SACLANT considers that the Striking Fleet should launch its nuclear attacks from the Norwegian Sea. Priority will be given, in the early stages, to strikes against Soviet naval and air power which might contest the use of the Norwegian sea ... As the Soviet air threat is reduced to manageable proportions, their main nuclear targets will be:

(a)   Submarine bases and supporting installations.
(b)   Submarine and surface forces at sea.

    (c)   Naval bases, shipyards and supply installations.
    (d)   Lines of communications supporting the above.[12]

The perceived importance of destroying targets in the initial period of conflict is illustrated by SACLANT's insistence that "if the deployment of the Striking Fleet is significantly delayed, external assistance will be sought to deal with the above primary targets by nuclear attacks."[13]

Joint exercises reflected the heavy emphasis on nuclear operations. In the autumn of 1960, during a series of large-scale exercises collectively known as Fallex 60, the Strike Fleet moved into the Norwegian Sea through the Iceland – Faroes Gap and simulated nuclear strikes against the continent in face of undersea and air opposition.[14] Similarly, exercise Riptide II, in the summer of 1961, was specifically "designed to perfect nuclear strike operations and to test strike co-ordination in a hostile, air, surface and submarine environment."[15]

Yet, the clearest indication of the evolving emphasis on strike operations in the north can be seen in the growth of targets identified for nuclear attack by American forces in the first phase of war. In January 1951 there were five targets in the "Barents Sea area" recommended by the ONI for "immediate" attack, whose destruction would seriously weaken the Soviet submarine offensive.[16] Some four and half years later, in July 1955, a list of targets drawn up for the Regulus nuclear surface-to-surface missile, contained 19 targets, all part of the "Murmansk complex."[17] Targets included airfields and storage facilities as well as naval bases. Finally, in April 1959 the ONI presented a detailed study, based on JCS guidance for "reducing the Northern Fleet threat," on the vulnerability of the Soviet Northern Fleet to air attack.[18] This study provides a unique insight into the operational plans of US naval forces and indicates clearly just how important the northern area had become by the end of the decade. The ONI quoted 54 "fixed installations that control or support Northern Fleet naval forces ...[as] the most likely targets."[19] This figure included four naval headquarters, 21 naval operating bases, 11 major ports and ship-yards, six naval supply depots and 12 "major" fuel stores. This dramatic increase corresponded to changes made in SACEUR's and CINC-NORTH's Atomic Strike Plans (ASP), which in 1959 were also revised to take account of the "large number of additional targets" in the NEC area.[20]

Another aspect of the programme to strengthen US capabilities was a series of organisational changes designed to improve centralised direction and co-ordination of the overall ASW effort. Most significant in this respect was the establishment in July 1957 of an entirely new *functional* command under Admiral Wright, known as the Anti-Submarine Defence

Force, Atlantic.[21] The first commander of the force, Admiral Frank Watkins, was given centralised authority for all anti-submarine efforts in the Atlantic, with special responsibility for co-ordinating the operations of three anti-submarine defence groups established in the course of 1957 and 1958.[22] The first of these, designated Task Force Alpha under Admiral John S. Thach, was established in 1957 with the specific objective of developing hunter-killer group tactics, doctrines and procedures. In the autumn of 1958, Admiral Wright established two new ASW defence groups. One of these, Group Bravo, specialised in ASW protection of fast carrier forces (i.e. the Strike Fleet) operating in the North-east Atlantic. The second task force, designated Group Charlie, was set up in order to develop convoy tactics and protect amphibious force convoys.[23] These major changes were accompanied by an increased level of operational activity in the eastern Atlantic, which was immediately felt by the British, the Norwegians and the Soviet Union.

Britain and US Forward Strategy

In late 1957 and early 1958 the US Navy began to press for greater command responsibilities in the eastern Atlantic, commensurate with the increase in operational activity of US naval forces in the area. In a note to the COS in April 1958, Lord Mountbatten said there was "increasing evidence that the Americans desire a Command on this side of the Atlantic and are determined to control their own forces employed on Forward Defence operations in northern waters."[24] At the same time, the US Navy was hoping to obtain base rights in Scotland in support of northern operations. As early as December 1956, the "matter of the Clyde base" had briefly been discussed between the Minister of Defence, Anthony Head, and Admiral Wright. When Sir Michael Denny in Washington wrote to Mountbatten about the meeting, he described how

> Wright made a very good dissertation and established that the need arose from the forward strategy concepts leading to the application of the Atomic Strike from the Strike Fleet Atlantic at the earliest moment from D-Day.[25]

Following the "semi-successful" ASW phase of 1957 autumn manoeuvres, Admiral Wright's major objective became one of *preventing* Soviet Northern Fleet submarines from entering into the Atlantic, where the task of locating them would be much more complex. The routes of entry into the North Atlantic he considered to be, first, through the Greenland– Faroes–Scotland–Norway area and, second, the Spitsbergen-

North Cape area. In both of these approaches Wright in late 1957 proposed to set up peacetime "Detection Zones."[26] According to the British Joint Planning Staff:

> Upon "general alert" being declared, SACLANT plans to create a barrier by reinforcing the Greenland-Iceland area and to establish patrols in the Spitsbergen-North Cape area. By creating a barrier at the outbreak of war, he plans to contain the enemy's naval forces within the Barents and Norwegian Sea. He considers this forward defence plan gives the best hope of neutralising the Soviet submarine threat with the forces likely to be at his disposal.[27]

The COS, however, showed little enthusiasm for the "barrier" concept. As for establishing peacetime detection zones, Lord Mountbatten thought that instituting "the first supervisory detection patrol at sea to be operated clearly to detect Russian movements ... might be considered provocative."[28] The Joint Planning Staff believed such zones might provide useful intelligence, but foresaw many "political difficulties such as Norwegian objections."[29] Moreover, the COS felt that there was a risk that if the US Navy chose to concentrate on the entrances to the North Atlantic, the forces available in the initial phase for the direct protection of shipping, seen as vital to Britain, would be diminished. The US Navy, however, was determined to implement the forward strategy concept in spite of British reservations, and succeeded in enshrining an emphasis on "forward operations" in MC 70 (NATO's Minimum Essential Force Requirements, 1958–63). This key NATO document stated that submarine gap patrols should be established in the Greenland–Iceland–Faroes–Norwegian Gap, to serve as early warning barrier in peacetime and "firm barrier in war."[30]

In January 1958 Lord Mountbatten, in a letter to the Chief of the Air Staff, Sir Dermot Boyle, informed him about a recent visit by Admiral Eccles to the United States. Eccles noted that Admiral Wright was now "sold on the forward strategy concept and intends to adopt it gradually from now on."[31] Moreover, he felt "reasonably convinced" that Wright was intending to set up a separate command under a US Flag Officer to conduct the anti-submarine forward barrier in the NORLANT area.[32] Eccles concluded:

> To sum up – with the increasing preponderance of US air and surface forces in the EASTLANT area, they are determined to increase their operational control in the front line areas, this in spite of their holding command of the Strike Fleet ... The impending decrease in British forces and influence in the area is a strong factor in hardening their attitude.[33]

A personal letter from Burke to Mountbatten the following month confirmed Eccles's conclusion. Burke stressed that "any diminution in the Royal Navy or in the strike role or the anti-submarine warfare role means that the tasks which must be done will fall more heavily on our shoulders."[34] On 11 April 1958 Admiral Woods, a submariner and the British Deputy to Admiral Wright, wrote to the First Sea Lord, explaining how SACLANT was becoming ever more concerned about the Soviet SSBN threat, pointing out that:

> the Submarine transit offensive in the northern narrows will become increasingly important as the Russian SSN and SSG potentiality grows in the next five years.[35]

It was against this background that the COS met to discuss a specific US request for "agreement in general principle" to base naval forces in Britain in support of "forward defence operations in Northern waters."[36] The initial request was for stationing six radar picket frigates, 24 naval patrol and 12 early warning aircraft, one submarine depot ship and a squadron of about 12 hunter-killer submarines.[37] Additionally, it was understood that the US Navy and the Third Air Force had also approached the Air Ministry with regard to similar facilities for US aircraft.[38] The American submarines were intended to form the nucleus of the submarine detection zone in the Greenland–Iceland–Faroes Gap.[39] The following month, when the Admiralty Board met to discuss changes in NATO naval commands, it took note of the "desire of the United States Navy to provide considerable forces for the Northern sub-area and to base some of the forces of ships concerned in this country in peacetime."[40] Lord Mountbatten believed that the Americans wanted to have at least one or two commands on the Eastern Atlantic seaboard with front line operational responsibilities.[41]

When the issue of naval command structures came up again for consideration by the Board in October, the US proposal for a "North Atlantic barrier force" was discussed. The Board expressed concern about the growing US dominance of all naval arrangements in the North Atlantic. The minutes record that:

> unless the United Kingdom could soon make a concrete proposal for the integration of the command of the barrier force in the NATO structure, the United States Navy would proceed to set up the command as a purely functional one, responsible directly to the Commander-in-Chief, Atlantic.[42]

Partly because of the advantages which the Royal Navy thought it would gain by closer *operational* co-operation with the United States, it was decided to accept the US request for shore facilities.[43] The govern-ment granted the US request for shore installations "to date from about 1960."[44] The *actual* US forward submarine patrols, however, began much earlier. In fact, the submarine/air barrier patrols between Greenland and the Faroes were instituted in the summer of 1958, using submarines and aircraft based on Keflavik in Iceland. Twelve submarines and two squadrons of maritime patrol aircraft were involved in these patrols. When Admiral Burke asked the Admiralty whether the Royal Navy could take over the patrols for three weeks starting in early August 1958, the Admiralty found that the required deployment of UK forces would have absorbed "all the operational submarines in Home waters."[45]

There is some evidence that US concern about the Soviet sea-launched missile threat to its eastern seaboard led the US Navy to consider withdrawing a large number of surface ships from the eastern Atlantic. The fact that this did not happen was partly attributable to British pressure. More important, however, as the Joint Planning Staff rightly pointed out:

> irrespective of the threat to the eastern seaboard of America, they [US Navy] regard the eastern side of the Atlantic as the main battle area.[46]

Norway and US Forward Strategy

On 13 May 1958 President Eisenhower met with Norwegian Prime Minister Einar Gerhardsen and Sam Rayburn, the Speaker of the House of Representatives, in the White House. After the meeting, Eisenhower in a letter to Rayburn wrote that it had been "a fortuitous circumstance" that both of them had been able to talk to Gerhardsen, whose country was "a particularly important factor in all our calculations concerning the defense of the North East Atlantic."[47] That Eisenhower chose to emphasise this particular aspect of Norway's contribution to US strategy was clearly neither fortuitous nor a matter of political tactics.

Between 1957 and 1960 there were four specific areas in which Norway made an increasingly important contribution to US maritime strategy. First, intelligence activities and co-operation in northern waters intensified. Second, maritime and tactical airfields in the northern part of the country continued to be modified to meet US Navy standards and also saw a marked increase in operational activity. Third, shore-based commu-nication facilities, capable of providing operational support to the Strike Fleet, were improved, while storage depots for naval forces were con-structed in south Norway. Fourth, infrastructure facilities to meet the navigational requirements of the Fleet ballistic missile submarines deployed in the North Atlantic were constructed on Norwegian territory.

The estimated difficulties of detecting nuclear-powered submarines in ocean areas increased the importance of *current intelligence* gathered near the submarine base area. For this reason, Admiral Wright noted in 1959, he would now "have to keep even closer anti-submarine watch on the coastal areas around NATO borders."[48] Similarly, the ONI study on the vulnerability of the Northern Fleet to air attack in April 1959 concluded that the value of current intelligence on the disposition of forces could not be overemphasised.[49] As a result, technical intelligence operations, especially ELINT flights from the UK and Norwegian bases into the Barents Sea, increased towards the end of the decade. In late 1959 and early 1960 both British and US authorities asked for permission to increase the number of ELINT flights staged from Norway. It was now proposed that the British would conduct six "reconnaissance flights" per year while the Americans would launch flights every two weeks from Norwegian airfields.[50] This proposal was, however, quickly rejected by the Norwegian authorities on political grounds, that is, the scale of the programme might increase tension in the area.[51] By the late 1950s HF/VHF SIGINT stations at Vadsø and Vardø in Finnmark were providing the US with vital information about Soviet missile test activity in the Barents and White Sea area, while intercepting Soviet ship-to-ship, ship-to-shore and air-to-ground communications in the same area.[52]

Of particular concern to US naval intelligence appears to have been Norway's Arctic possessions, especially the Svalbard archipelago, whose strategic location and political status made it a particularly sensitive area.[53] An ONI report back in August 1954 had appraised the military significance of the archipelago. The report emphasised that it provided an ideal site for "air facilities, guided missile emplacements, weather and Loran stations and radar posts."[54] The ONI singled out two specific reasons for a naval interest in the archipelago. First, the islands could provide extremely valuable bases for anti-submarine operations, potentially offering harbours and airfields year round "only 700 miles from Murmansk and only 480 miles from the northernmost part of Norway." Secondly, as long as Svalbard remained "in neutral or friendly hands", carrier task forces could attack the Soviet Union from the Barents Sea with much less risk, since "nowhere else could the carriers approach so close to vital targets in the Soviet Union."[55] As well as identifying three possible locations offering "excellent possibilities" for construction of air strips, the ONI observed that since many of the intercontinental bombing routes passed "over or within fighter range of Svalbard," air bases for refuelling and for fighter escorts "would be very advantageous."[56] This evident interest in Svalbard continued throughout the decade, and developments on the archipelago were closely monitored by service intelligence branches.[57] It is clear also that the more senior levels of the US administration were seriously concerned about threats to the islands emanating from the Soviet Union itself or orchestrated by the Russian community already present on the archipelago. Specific policy guidance with respect to Scandinavia, drawn up by the NSC in the spring of 1960 and amended in October, contained a separate paragraph emphasising the importance of urging "Norway to maintain effective surveillance of Soviet activities in Spitsbergen."[58] Additionally, the NSC agreed that the US would have to "be prepared to concert with Norway and other interested nations in protesting any Soviet violations of the demilitarisation provisions of the 1920 treaty and in refusing to consider any revision of the Treaty that would permit the establishment of Soviet political authority or military bases in the Archipelago."[59] This paragraph in the NSC report was, according to Robert Cutler, one of only four extensions of present policy contained in the NSC review of US policy towards Scandinavia.[60]

Construction of maritime and tactical airfields in North Norway intensified after 1957, and by 1960 "final acceptance inspection on major items" and off-base facilities at Bodø, Ørlandet, and Andøya could take place.[61] Apart from actual construction, US maritime patrol and mining aircraft also increased the rate of operational sorties and training missions out of Norway. In January 1958 Admiral Eccles told the First Sea Lord that the post of Commander of US Navy maritime air squadrons in Iceland would be upgraded to Rear Admiral, and that this was a further sign of US commitment to the forward strategy concept.[62] During a planning conference held in Norway in 1958 "plans, not yet finally ratified by SACLANT, for an increased war deployment by CINCAIREASTLANT aircraft on Norwegian bases, were analysed in detail and the operational implications assessed."[63] The time phasing of these plans was such that "undue interference" with tactical air operations was foreseen. Hence, "several conferences" were held to study the necessary infrastructure facilities and logistics requirements, and "some major construction projects for SACLANT" were agreed.[64] This suggests that the wartime importance of the bases was being upgraded.[65] Finally, northern Norwegian airfields continued to be available for carrier-based aviation when the Strike Fleet was operating in the north-eastern Atlantic. Against this background of increased activity, the 5th and 6th planning co-ordination meetings between SACLANT and SACEUR in 1958 specifically discussed the co-ordination of SACLANT's air activity in the Northern Command area. According to the NEC annual report, one of the major items:

> concerned the SACLANT pre-planned targets in the area adjoining the Northern Command, on which more detailed information was sought. This information, previously withheld, may now be forthcoming.[66]

Whereas long-range submarines were still considered by SACLANT to be the greatest threat confronting the ACLANT naval forces after 1957, two additional threats are given greater prominence in his 1958 Emergency Defence Plan. First, the air threat was assumed to have "considerably increased" with the introduction of "Badger" medium bombers into the naval air arm.[67] The main threat was thought to emanate from naval and air units with the Northern Fleet, "probably augmented prior to D-Day by some units of their Baltic Fleet and their Long-Range Air Force."[68] For this reason, specific air defence requirements for the Strike Fleet to receive early warning information from shore-installations (Sector Operating Centres) in Norway were agreed in 1958 between SACLANT and national authorities. In addition to the air defence information, in November 1958, representatives from SACLANT reported that they were planning to utilise air control and reporting (C&R) systems in Norway for routing tactical bombing aircraft to forward directors.[69] In 1958, infrastructure funds were also specifically allocated to "improve communications with SACLANT" from Norway.[70] The second additional threat that was emphasised in SACLANT's 1958 EDP also had a direct bearing on Norway. For the first time SACLANT listed the existence of a "limited amphibious threat ... in the north-eastern part of the ACLANT region."[71]

Limited War on the Northern Flank?

As long as "massive retaliation" retained at least an element of credibility, very little attention was paid in Washington or in Paris to Norway's relationship to the central European front. Nor, as indicated in preceding chapters, was there much concern about *direct* threats to Norwegian territory. Indeed, John Foster Dulles, in his so-called "massive retaliation" speech before the Council on Foreign Relations in January 1954, stressed that a continuation of traditional American policies would have forced the United States:

> to be ready to fight in the Arctic and in the Tropics; in Asia, the Near East and in Europe; by sea, by land and by air; with new and old weapons.[72]

The budgetary, economic and social consequences of such an effort would, according to Dulles, inevitably result in self-exhaustion.

By late 1957 and early 1958, however, the premises of massive retaliation were increasingly being questioned not only by Democratic Senators and influential academics, but also by critics within the administration.[73] Already in June 1956 the Joint Intelligence Committee, reviewing the Joint Strategic Capabilities Plan for 1 July 1956 to 30 June 1957, pointed out how "military conflict short of general war may become more likely as both sides achieve the capability to destroy each other even after surprise attack."[74] It was, however, the Soviet ICBM announcement in August 1957, and, more significantly, the launching of Sputnik in October, which most crucially undermined a central assumption of US nuclear strategy since late 1953: the relative invulnerability of the North American continent to *direct* strategic attack. Once Sputnik demonstrated that the continent was no longer impervious to a direct strategic threat, the implications of a "nuclear stalemate" with the Soviet Union gradually came to affect perceptions about Norway's vulnerability to Soviet military and political pressure. In the wake of Sputnik, the dangers of Soviet "operations with limited objectives, such as infiltrations, incursions or hostile local actions in the NATO area" became a subject of greater concern within the US and especially among Norwegian military and government officials.[75] When the Norwegian Chiefs of Staff argued for the need to strengthen defences in the border areas with the Soviet Union, they emphasised that

> The development of modern weapon systems has, among other things, led to a situation where the border area between Norway and the Soviet Union has acquired a considerably greater significance (en vesentlige større betydning) for Norway – and therefore for NATO – than it has had in the past. With its dominant position, the Soviet Union – if it wishes – can easily create "episodes" and even "provocations" which would require swift, independent and considered responses on the Norwegian side. What happens in the border area can therefore quickly acquire a significance outside the purely local context (trans.)[76]

Similarly, when British defence officials visited Oslo in May 1960 to discuss UK defence policy at the invitation of the Norwegian Defence Minister, "they found that the principal Norwegian preoccupation was the effect of a possible limited incursion into northern Norway."[77] The British, however, especially under Duncan Sandys's tenure as Defence Minister, were strongly opposed to any concept of limited war in the NATO area, and it was the US Navy which appeared most receptive to Norwegian concerns.[78] In fact, the US Navy had long been concerned about potential

Soviet interests in North Norway.[79] In late 1953 Arleigh Burke had emphasised that the "critical" importance of the northern waters derived in part from the fact that:

> the northwestern and northern coasts of Norway are extremely attractive sites for submarine bases. The fjords are ideal places to construct sub pens tunnelled into cliffs rising from the sea. Were the Soviets to capture these coastal areas by amphibious operations, they could construct submarine bases in the fjords that would be all but invulnerable to air attack.[80]

As the Soviet submarine fleet increased and the ability of naval infantry forces on the Murmansk coast to conduct amphibious operations improved, the Chief of Naval Operations became more concerned about direct threats to North Norway.[81] Capturing Norway's northern coastline, it was argued, would enhance possibilities for dispersing the Northern Fleet, thus reducing its vulnerability to Strike Fleet attack. More generally, Navy representatives argued that a condition of "true nuclear stalemate" would "result in added stimulus to actions short of all-out war – stepped-up cold war activity and increased likelihood of local or limited wars."[82] And this prospect was assumed to give the Navy, especially its carrier striking force, added importance, given its capacity for "precise and discriminate delivery of weapons, conventional as well as atomic."[83] According to an internal Navy report which Burke sent to Mountbatten in early 1958, it was argued that

> Recent Soviet developments and acceleration of ballistic missile programs will result in a more complete condition of thermonuclear stalemate sooner than originally anticipated. All-out war will be more unthinkable, but at the same time added stimulus will be given to cold war activity and increased likelihood of limited war...
>
> The carrier striking force will become more indispensable than ever for countering limited war situations, but at the same time will retain a versatility to meet the demands of all-out nuclear war if such should occur.[84]

The following year Admiral Wright, testifying before Congress, specifically referred to the desolate, trackless and thinly-inhabited provinces of North Norway as a "sensitive area of NATO" which, along with Berlin and the Turkish frontier, might in the future be subject to Soviet "probing actions."[85] This so-called "Finnmark grab" scenario under conditions of nuclear stalemate also received some attention from professional commentators. In a paper in September 1959, Captain Liddell Hart wrote that "no area so easily lends itself to, and invites, this kind of "twenty-four-hour pounce" as does the Scandinavian stretch on the Northern Flank of NATO, especially in its present state of acute weakness."[86]

In spite of the US Navy's interest in the problem, however, until the Kennedy administration assumed office, only very limited measures were undertaken in order to prepare for limited war contingencies on the Northern Flank. Furthermore, none of these measures appear to have gone far beyond the planning stage in the 1950s. On 13 June 1953 SACEUR directed CINCNORTH to outline operational plans and logistic requirements for the employment of US Marine forces in Norway and Denmark.[87] Over the next two years a series of co-ordination and planning conferences were held by the principal commanders concerned but no substantive progress appears to have been made. In late 1957 the Norwegian MOD approved a visit by 21 US Marine Corps officers from Fleet Marine Force Atlantic to observe exercises in North Norway. The purpose of this visit, which took place in early 1958, was to "observe tactics, equipment, weather and terrain" in connection with SACEUR's Strategic Reserve Plan No. 1 for North Norway."[88] Preliminary studies for the concept of employing ACE Mobile Forces in North Norway were only completed in 1960, and these studies were deemed to require further detailed area studies of North Norway, again covering terrain, weather, logistic and support facilities.[89] By 1960, no firm decision had been made about the pre-stocking of heavy equipment in North Norway.[90]

An important reason for the lack of progress in this area was that Eisenhower himself remained very sceptical about diverting resources toward limited war planning in Europe. But more importantly, even after 1957 the US Navy was not prepared to divert resources away from its *primary* commitment to nuclear strike operations against Soviet targets in the northern region. In this they were in full agreement with the British. In November 1958 the First Sea Lord circulated a letter from the Commander-in-Chief, Home Fleet, which accurately summed up both American and British attitudes. The letter noted that "Jerry Wright very wisely refuses to commit himself to support of North Norway regardless of other factors."[91]

II NORWAY AND THE US FLEET BALLISTIC MISSILE PROGRAMME

Norway and US Nuclear Strategy

It has already been argued that Norway between 1954 and 1960, by virtue of the operational support given to the Strike Fleet from its territory, was inextricably tied, albeit indirectly, to US nuclear strategy. Norway's relationship to the Polaris programme further demonstrates the difficulty, when operational policy is taken into account, of pursuing a non-nuclear policy within a nuclear alliance.

Although the actual basing of Polaris submarines in Norway was considered as an option by the US Navy, no formal approach about this was ever made to Norwegian authorities.[92] The Norwegian base policy, as well as the agreements about bases at Holy Loch in the Clyde Estuary and at Rota in Spain, militated against a formal approach to the Norwegians.[93] The advantage of basing SSBNs in Norway was that it would have permitted submarines more time on station and less in transit to station. With the first generation of submarines, the need to reduce the period spent transiting from base to patrol areas was a particularly important consideration. This was because each submarine carried single-warhead Polaris A-1 missiles with a range of only 1200 miles. As the target system for the Polaris was the Soviet "industrial base and government control structure," it meant that the submarines had to operate far forward in the Arctic ocean.[94]

Although the question of basing was not pursued, Norway did become tied to the Polaris programme through its provision of infrastructure facilities designed to support accurate submarine navigation. The need to ensure the highest degree of accuracy in launching the missile into the right trajectory was an urgent concern in the early phase of the Polaris project. A major research and development programme was initiated to that end.[95] One important way of ensuring accuracy was to base navigation on the principle of infrastructure redundancy. This meant that parallel communication and navigational aid systems were built and operated.[96] Redundancy allowed the *principal* navigational system for the Polaris-type submarine, the inertial navigator known as the Ships Inertial Navigation System (SINS), to be supplemented by independent sources of position and velocity data.[97] Along with its nuclear propulsion plant the SINS was designed to give the Polaris submarine a maximum degree of independence from its environment. However, because of inevitable accumulation of errors caused by the effects of gravity anomalies ("gyro drifts"), the SINS could not operate autonomously for an indefinite period of time.[98] In the case of Polaris, information from external sources of navigation or "periodic resets" were required every eight hours.[99]

Two specific sources of "external fixes" involved Norway directly in the FBM programme. The first of these was the Loran-C, a far more accurate version of the Loran system, which was originally developed during the Second World War. In a Defence Department memorandum for the Secretary of State in June 1959, Loran-C was described as a "highly accurate, ground-based, long-range radio navigation system ... being installed overseas by the US Coast Guard at the request of the Department of Defence to fulfil a military requirement generated by the Polaris program."[100] By the late 1950s Loran-C receivers were able to provide navigational accuracy of about a quarter of a mile at 1000-mile range and they were sensitive to differences of thirty to forty feet.[101] This satisfied the "fix-accuracy" requirement for the Polaris which was set at plus – minus a quarter of mile within the operational area of ground wave coverage.[102] By constructing a series of Loran-C networks, it was therefore possible continuously to monitor SINS performance.[103]

The Loran-C stations built in Norway, however, were originally set up to assist in the establishment of a second source of "external fix" for submarine navigation, namely, detailed knowledge about the ocean bed in which the submarine would operate. An Admiralty document in June 1958 explained that for Polaris submarines to "position themselves with absolute accuracy in Northern waters," the US Navy was now planning to chart the ocean floor so that submarines could "establish their position by echo sounder without surfacing."[104] In order to provide accurate reference for the necessary survey, the US Navy planned to build two Loran-C stations in the areas concerned to support the oceanographic survey ships.[105]

Mapping the distinctive topographical features and gravity anomalies on the ocean floor also had another potential function in relation to the Polaris project. As an Admiralty paper pointed out, such information made it possible to calculate "ballistic trajectories from fixed positions to preselected targets."[106] A report approved by the COS on the "strategic implications of Polaris-type missiles" requested by the Minister of Defence, noted that the use of "pre-selected firing stations which have been clandestinely marked before hostilities would substantially simplify the navigational aiming problem."[107]

When the State Department instructed the US Embassy in Oslo in March 1958 to request permission to build Loran-C systems in Norway, the stations were justified in terms of assisting "special survey ships to locate themselves with a high degree of accuracy in preparing charts of the ocean bottom."[108] The Embassy was further instructed to point to the importance of Loran-C stations to the Polaris programme only in the most general terms. If, however, elicitation of Norwegian co-operation necessitated more specific details, Ambassador Frances Willis was empowered to "disclose to a very few highly placed and reliable Norwegian officials the concept of using this charted data as a navigation method for Polaris submarines."[109] On 19 May 1958 Halvard Lange was handed an aidemémoire by the US ambassador with the official request for a site survey to be made with a view to establishing a "Loran-C installation" on Norwegian territory.[110] The *aide-mémoire* stated: "The Top Secret military requirement will necessitate the operation of the station for a minimum period of about two years."[111] In July 1958 the Security Committee of the Norwegian Government approved the request. Following a survey by US technical personnel in August 1958, it was decided that Kleppelven near Bø on the island of Langøy in North Norway would be the site of the "transmitter station" and a temporary "monitor" station would be set up on the same island while a permanent "monitor" station would be constructed on the island of Jan Mayen. In January 1959 a formal Memorandum of Understanding was exchanged between the two Governments, whereby it was agreed that the station would be manned by Norwegians and that the US would cover the costs of constructing and operating it. In the summer of 1959 complete Loran-C coverage was scheduled in the North Sea–Barents Sea–Greenland area by 1 January 1960, using a four-station chain.[112] The station at Bø became operational in late 1959, but was followed in June 1960 by another "urgent" request, this time for a station on Jan Mayen. The request was discussed in the Security Committee in late July and during this meeting Lange informed the committee that, according to Willis, the station was needed for a period of 18 to 24 months in order to support ocean surveys in the North Atlantic "with a view to the possible deployment of SLBMs of the Polaris type in the area."[113] The construction of the Jan Mayen station and an associated control station at Bjugn was approved by the Government in August and became operational as early as December 1960.

In February 1960 the US formally approached Norwegian authorities about the planned operations of US oceanographic survey ships in the Norwegian Sea. Norwegian officials were told that the surveys were related to the Loran-C project and that it would be desirable to use Norwegian ports for replenishment while the ships were operating in the Norwegian sea. The Norwegian Government accepted the request for a nine-month period.[114] The ships involved, *Dutton*, *Michelson* and *Bowditch*, were all converted from Victory hulls in late 1958 in order to "support the Fleet Ballistic Missile Programme."[115]

There can be little doubt that the US regarded the establishment of Loran-C stations in Norway as a matter of major importance for the success of the first generation of the Fleet Ballistic Missile system.[116] A report by the Joint Staff in June 1959 described Loran-C as the "only available system that will satisfy the ground-based electronical navigational aid requirements of the Polaris programme and the seaward extensions of the DEW [Distant Early Warning] Line."[117] Since the Norwegian Sea had been chosen as the initial area of operational employment, Norway's contribution was of great importance. This was acknowledged in the comprehensive and "top secret" review of US overseas military bases prepared under the auspices of William Lang, Assistant Secretary of Defence in April 1960. The report stated that "by way of new facilities, Loran-C stations, essential to the Polaris mission, are being established in Italy, Turkey and Libya and in Iceland, Norway and the Faeroes."[118]

The construction of the Loran-C stations in Norway was not, however, a matter of public debate at the time, nor did it provoke much discussion within the Government. The reason for this was simple: the relationship of the Loran-C stations to the Polaris programme was an extremely closely guarded secret, with the State Department hoping that details could be confined "to a very few highly placed and reliable Norwegian officials." Wilkes and Gleditsch have in their detailed study emphasised (if only implicitly) that secrecy stemmed from US concern shared by Halvard Lange about domestic and internal Labour party opposition to closer integration into US nuclear strategy. Domestic political considerations in Norway do not in fact appear to have been a major motivation behind the American or Norwegian emphasis on maintaining secrecy. The need for secrecy had as much to do with the perceived importance of avoiding any leaks about the true purpose of these vulnerable and important stations. This can be seen in the fact that insistence on secrecy in negotiations over Loran-C was observed equally strictly with respect to Britain, which was, after all, going to provide bases for the actual submarines.[119] There are two further considerations here. First, the Defence Department was most anxious to ensure that the cover story for Loran-C – "an experimental navigational system" – was kept, in part because the government had to secure international frequency allocation for the operation of Loran-C in the 90–110 Kc band. As a top secret Defense Department memorandum for the Secretary of State in June 1959 pointed out:

> Should governments unfriendly to United States ascertain the real purpose of Loran-C, an effort may be exerted ... to eliminate navigation systems from the 90 to 110 Kc band. Forced withdrawal of Loran-C from this band would create unacceptable complications in the Polaris program.[120]

Second, the obvious vulnerability of the system to Soviet counter measures was clearly an overriding consideration in maintaining secrecy.

III   THE SOVIET UNION AND "US ARCTIC STRATEGY"

The strategic survey by the JWPC in 1947 (discussed in Chapter One) had observed that "the Murmansk – Kola Peninsula area offers one possible route of approach to the heart of the USSR where entry might be made directly on Soviet soil."[121] In fact, ever since the Civil War and the British-led intervention through the ports of Murmansk and Arkhangelsk in the spring and summer of 1918, the Soviet government had remained acutely aware of its vulnerability in this part of Russia.[122] It was hardly surprising, therefore, that the dramatic technological advances of the 1950s and the concomitant growth of US military interests in the Arctic should generate such concern among Soviet military commentators.[123] In terms of US maritime strategy, Soviet military writings – appearing in specialist journals such as *Soviet Fleet* (*Sovietsky flot*) and the armed forces newspaper *Red Star* (*Krasnaja svesda*) – tended to concentrate on two developments.[124] First, there was deep concern about the emphasis, in US deployments and NATO maritime exercises, on forward nuclear carrier operations in the Atlantic. Second, Soviet writers devoted much attention to the strategic implications of the employment of the Polaris submarines in the Norwegian Sea.

In August 1958, shortly after the polar voyages of USS *Nautilus* and USS *Skate*, an article in *Soviet Fleet* about the Polaris programme observed that the US was now placing great hopes in the nuclear submarine as "a new weapon that can effectively be used in the vast and difficult-to-reach Arctic areas on the northern seacoast of the USSR."[125] The *Red Star* also viewed the *Nautilus* voyage under the ice-cap as exclusively a military adventure. The specific objective had been to find:

> ways of using atomic submarines in polar areas for combat actions, and particularly ways of employing rocket weapons by such submarines against the most important centres of the Soviet Union.[126]

Another article in *Soviet Fleet* in November 1958 on the significance of these trans-polar journeys, argued that the specific purpose of the trips had been to "determine the state of the ice cover of the Arctic basin" in order to prepare for strikes against the northern regions of the Soviet Union.[127] The previous month an article entitled "The Arctic Strategy of the United States" described the prospective deployment of nuclear powered submarines with missile capabilities as part of a comprehensive "Arctic strategy."[128] Most of these articles referred explicitly to open US literature. And there was no shortage of material indicating that the US Navy was exploring the military potential of the Arctic.[129]

The concerns of the Soviet military about American maritime strategy in the North, however, were most authoritatively expressed in Marshal V.D. Sokolovsky's influential book, *Military Strategy*, which appeared in 1959.[130] According to Sokolovsky, the most important task for the Soviet Navy from the outset of any war would be to "destroy enemy carrier-based units ... before they come within launching range; ... destroy their protective forces and supply sections; and ... destroy the regions where they are based."[131] Sokolovsky specifically referred to NATO's FALLEX 60 exercise, in which a carrier-based strike unit from the Norwegian Sea had made 200 simulated nuclear attacks against coastal objectives and other "targets deep within our territory." In war, Sokolovsky argued, the enemy would attempt to "deploy these units in the most important theatres near the socialist countries and to deliver surprise nuclear attacks against coastal objectives (naval bases, airfields, missile installations)."[132]

In most of the Soviet writings there was naturally a strong propaganda element emphasising the ability of the Soviet armed forces to meet the Arctic challenge. Nikonov, for example, wrote that US plans to utilise the Arctic as a theatre of war were "frankly adventuristic" since the Soviet Union had

> all the necessary and perfectly up-to-date forces and means to nip in the bud any aggressive operations of the imperialists and doom their reckless Arctic strategy to failure.[133]

Nonetheless, the Soviet Union was clearly deeply concerned about the growing might of US sea power close to their vulnerable northern perimeter, and began to adjust their own naval plans accordingly. According to Michael McGwire, the perceived need to meet the threat from US carriers led to a change in policy in 1957-58, at which point primary emphasis was placed on the nuclear submarines and anti-carrier operations.[134] This shift can be seen in NATO's Annual Standing Group intelligence assessment for 1959, which estimated that about fifty per cent of the Northern Fleet submarine force would be employed for attack on Carrier Strike Forces.[135]

Conclusion

By late 1960 the US Navy had considerably expanded its role in northern waters. On 15 November 1960 the first nuclear-fuelled ballistic missile submarine, USS *George Washington*, commenced its first operational patrol in the Norwegian Sea. Since 1957 the US Navy had also significantly enhanced the striking power of its heavy attack carriers, whose ability to operate for extended periods north of the Arctic circle had improved dramatically over the course of the decade.

These developments were clearly of great concern to the Soviet Union. On 9 November 1960, Sir Frank Roberts, the newly-appointed British Ambassador to Moscow, called on his Norwegian counterpart, Oscar Gundersen, to discuss the wider significance of the latest "awkward exchanges" between the Norwegians and the Russians about Spitsbergen and northern Norway. The Norwegian ambassador told Roberts that the "advent of the Polaris submarine and the recent Anglo-American agreement on a Clyde base had made the Russians particularly sensitive as regards their northern sea approaches."[136] Their sensitivity, Gundersen argued, "was all the greater because they realised they could not hope to keep under control by threat of nuclear retaliation submarines cruising in the Arctic in the same way that they hoped they could keep under control missiles in fixed positions in Turkey."[137]

Growing Soviet sensitivity about its northern frontier, however, was also related to other developments. Most important in this respect was the noticeable expansion of American air operations (both reconnaissance and SAC airborne alerts) in the Arctic in the wake of the Sputnik launches. The combined impact of these developments on bilateral relations between the Soviet Union and Norway on the one hand, and between Norway and the United States on the other, will be examined further in the last chapter.

Part IV: The Political Context

Among the Nordic countries Norway has continued to lead in so far as NATO is concerned. If Norway's support of NATO should be seriously weakened or disappear, it is likely that similar trends would appear in Denmark and probably Iceland.[1]

> Frances Willis, US
> Ambassador, Oslo,
> 1958

Time after time, as in Pakistan or Okinawa, the maintenance and development of military or air bases would be stubbornly pursued with no evidence of any effort to balance this against the obvious political costs. Political interests would continue similarly to be sacrificed or placed in jeopardy by the avid and greedy pursuit of military intelligence ..."[2]

> George F. Kennan,
> *Memoirs: 1950–1963*

INTRODUCTION

Previous chapters have focused on the evolution of Norway's place in American strategic policy essentially from a military-strategic perspective. Although Norway's chief importance to the United States undoubtedly lay in this area, its role as a political ally should not be neglected. A study of NSC, State Department and MAAG reports all suggest that Norway was regarded as a potentially useful and influential supporter of American political objectives in the Cold War. The administration fully appreciated, however, that the weight which the opinions and actions of the Norwegian government carried internationally, and consequently the degree of influence which Norway could hope to exert on behalf of the US, depended crucially on the *institutional* and *geographic* context in which Norway operated at any given time. Most important in American eyes was Norway's position within the Nordic region, especially its relationship to

Denmark and Iceland on the one hand and to Sweden (outside the formal alliance structure) on the other.

The ever closer involvement of Norway in American plans and activities described in preceding chapters also, however, placed growing demands and, at times, strains on the bilateral management of relations between the Eisenhower administration and the Norwegian authorities. Chapter Eight examines the nature of those relations in greater detail.

7 Norway as a Political Ally: The US and the Nordic Region

I AMERICA, NORWAY AND THE NORDIC REGION

Norway, the UN and the European Social Democratic Movement

Ever since the establishment of the United Nations in 1945, Norway had been strongly committed to, and participated extensively in, the activities of the organisation and its associated agencies. The Eisenhower administration's policy paper on Scandinavia in April 1960 acknowledged this fact. It also emphasised that the "considerable prestige" which all three countries enjoyed in the international community meant that their support of US policies was "valuable in international organisations and for general propaganda purposes."[3] The NSC noted further that the Scandinavian countries were of political interest to the United States, since they were regarded "throughout the world as prime examples of Western democracy."[4] Outside the NATO context the administration did not usually distinguish between the different Scandinavian countries. Indeed, it was usual for Sweden, Norway, Denmark and Iceland to confer on policy issues and, where possible, to develop a common position.[5] Isolated reports nonetheless attributed special importance to the positions taken by Norway on the grounds that its support "on major international issues in the UN [had] served as a valuable example to other Scandinavian countries."[6]

Although the administration rightly viewed Norway as among the "staunchest supporters" of the United States in international organisations, there were issue areas where American and Norwegian views did not converge.[7] According to the Special Assistant for National Security Affairs, Robert Cutler, one of the "few notable exceptions" where Norwegian views "diverged radically" from the US was the question of admitting the People's Republic of China to the UN.[8] The divergence was brought out clearly in 1959 when Lange openly argued that had China's membership been admitted it might have facilitated the solution of problems in Laos, Indo-China and Tibet.[9] On the question of Chinese admission, Norway followed the more pragmatic British line, as indeed it did on several other foreign policy issues in the 1950s.[10] The Eisenhower administration, however, was anxious to enlist continuing Scandinavian support in denying membership of the UN and associated agencies not only to the PRC, but also to East Germany, North Vietnam and North Korea. The State Department was particularly concerned lest increased commercial, technical and cultural contacts with East Germany should bring about a *de facto* recognition of the country. On this issue, however, the State Department did little more than state its views and concerns clearly to Norwegian authorities.

In the UN Norway also took an active interest in questions of disarmament, particularly the issue of international regulation of nuclear tests. An obvious source of Norwegian interest in this question was the fear of "possible dangers to herself from fall-out due to Soviet tests nearby."[11] In the autumn of 1956 the Norwegian UN delegation was instructed to present a draft General Assembly resolution on a system of advance registration and international observation of nuclear testing. However, before the technical details and inspection provisions of the Norwegian proposals were known, Henry Cabot Lodge Jr, America's UN ambassador, suggested to John Foster Dulles that he should present to the Norwegian delegation "on a strictly informal and personal basis, a draft resolution which would be acceptable to us."[12] Lodge felt that unless the US sought to direct the "Norwegians along lines most acceptable to us ... we may very possibly end up with a General Assembly adoption of a more radical proposal in which we may be forced to acquiesce."[13] In the end, the US endorsed a proposal for registration and limited international observation of tests, cosponsored by Norway, Canada and Japan.[14] The incident is indicative, however, of a greater Norwegian willingness to explore avenues in the field of disarmament than the US in the mid-1950s was prepared to consider.

In spite of these differences on isolated issues, the US administration appears to have taken for granted Norwegian support on "major issues" relating to the East–West confrontation. And, indeed, Halvard Lange was always most anxious to avoid open disagreement with Western allies in international fora.[15]

A second arena where the members of the administration evidently believed that the Norwegian Labour government could serve American interests was in relation to other Social Democratic parties in Europe. Norwegian views, according to one report, were thought to carry "an influence in European Social Democratic circles far out of proportion to the country's size."[16] It was on the basis of this assumption that John

Foster Dulles in March 1953 wished to enlist Halvard Lange's help in persuading Socialist leaders in Germany and France to take a more favourable position on EDC ratification.[17] The administration also hoped that the "strongly anti-communist" feeling prevalent in Scandinavian labour unions might be of "value to the United States in combating Communist labour influence in third countries, particularly Iceland and Finland."[18] Yet, although US labour and embassy representatives in the 1950s enjoyed close relations with the Norwegian trade union leadership, there is little evidence to suggest that the US pursued any clear-cut policy aimed at deriving political benefit from Norway's presumed standing within the European Social Democratic movement.[19] As with the case of the UN, one must be careful not to *exaggerate* American interest in or the importance they attached to Norway's potential value as a political ally in these areas.

Norway and the Nordic NATO Members

According to Jens Boyesen – personal adviser to Halvard Lange in 1949–51 and Permanent Representative to NATO between 1955 and 1963 – the United States viewed Norway as a "path-setter" within the Nordic region.[20] From the perspective of US policy interests, there were two dimensions to Norway's "special position."[21] On the one hand, Norway was seen to exercise a determining influence on the alliance policies of Denmark and Iceland. On the other, Norway served as a "point of contact"[22] with Sweden, notably in the highly sensitive areas of defence and intelligence.[23] These considerations raise two basic questions. First, why did Norway occupy this position in US perceptions? Secondly, was the administration justified in believing that Norway did in fact hold a "special position" in the region? The latter question will be examined in greater detail by looking at Norway's role with regard to US – Icelandic relations.[24]

Three closely related factors produced and conditioned contemporary American perceptions of Norway's status within the Nordic region. The first had to do with Norway's part in rejecting a purely Scandinavian security option in 1948–49, thus opening the way for full Norwegian, Danish and Icelandic membership of NATO. The second factor was the exceptionally high regard in which the Norwegian Foreign Minister from 1946 to 1965, Halvard Lange, was held by US and NATO officials. The third and less immediately apparent factor concerned American assessments of Norway's performance during World War II.

Norway and the Intra-Scandinavian Negotiations, 1949

The failure to find a common basis for a "Scandinavian defence alliance" in 1948–49 arose out of the basic difference which emerged in the course of negotiations between the Norwegian and Swedish governments with respect to the *fundamental character* of such an alliance.[25] As Lange himself put it some years later in a Chatham House address:

> Whilst Sweden wanted the alliance to have no ties whatsoever with other Powers, Norway was not prepared to enter into an alliance that would exclude practical co-operation with other defence groupings of the Western democracies.[26]

Although the Danish Prime Minister at the time, Hans Hedtoft, channelled his diplomatic skills towards reconciling Swedish and Norwegian views, Denmark, along with Iceland, decided in the end to follow Norway and opt for full membership.[27] The events of early 1949 had the effect of demonstrating to the State Department that Norwegian commitment to NATO was an essential precondition for membership by Denmark and Iceland.[28] Whether or not Norway's decision was in fact the *decisive* element in either Danish or Icelandic considerations, the US administration clearly assumed this to be the case, and *continued* to do so in the 1950s.

During talks between General Eisenhower and Norwegian Government officials in May 1952, the future president told his Norwegian hosts that he was "impressed" with how close the Danes felt to the Norwegians. On the issue of the possible stationing of tactical air units in Norway and Denmark, Eisenhower said that the Danes were "anxiously looking to Norway to lead the way."[29] In a cable to Washington in September 1955 the US ambassador to Britain, Aldrich, observed that Norway held

> a key position in relation to Iceland and Denmark, and [the] latter [countries] are influenced by Norwegian advice and example. Any actions tending to weaken Norwegian support for NATO ... would have adverse repercussions going beyond Norway.[30]

Finally, in a despatch in June 1958, Frances Willis in Oslo observed that "Norway's decision to join NATO was determinative in bringing in Denmark and probably also an important influence on Iceland's decision."[31] According to Willis, Denmark and Iceland continued to "follow the Norwegian lead" in matters of alliance policy.

Halvard Lange and Norway's "Atlantic policy"

In the American perception, the actual circumstances of Norway's accession to NATO were closely tied to the second factor referred to above: the
attitudes and influence of Halvard Lange. In fact, the Norwegian government's decision to reject a Scandinavian solution came to be associated
very largely with Lange's *personal* role in the negotiations.[32] Between
1954 and 1960 Halvard Lange's standing both within NATO and in the
US remained "out of all proportion to Norway's Alliance contribution," let
alone to its place in NATO's Continental Strategy.[33] Two other factors
account for Lange's personal and political standing. *First*, his reputation
rested in part on his impressive academic background, diplomatic style
and experience. He was a trained historian, fluent in English, German and
French, and had spent much of the war in German concentration camps.
He possessed an instinctive preference for "quiet diplomacy," and strongly
emphasised the virtues of alliance cohesion and the avoidance of purely
demonstrative stances on policy issues.[34] After the first NATO Heads of
State and Government meeting in December 1957, when the relationship
between Prime Minister Gerhardsen and Lange at the Foreign Ministry
became noticeably more strained, the State Department, aware of the
developing tension, viewed Lange's presence at the helm of Norwegian
foreign policy as even more important.[35] This was related to the second
source of Lange's standing within the US and NATO: his unwavering
commitment to an "Atlanticist" line in foreign policy. The fundamental
belief upon which Norwegian "Atlanticism" in the 1950s rested was the
idea that Norway was historically and culturally tied to an "Atlantic community" *(Atlanterhavssamfunn)* of democratic nations and that a natural
community of interests did exist among nations bordering the North
Atlantic.[36] The "association of Atlantic powers", as Lange himself put it,
was an "historic fact, unshaken by and independent of policy on individual concrete questions in regard to which we might disagree pro-
foundly."[37] Hence, a central feature of his Atlantic policy was a greater
readiness to "accept a growing degree of integration within the framework of the North Atlantic Community than within the confines of continental Europe."[38] It was these views which naturally led Lange to
become the alliance's most ardent advocate of expanding work in the
non-military, political and cultural fields.[39] In September 1951 he joined
the so-called Pearson Group set up in Ottawa in order to explore the possibilities of deepening Atlantic co-operation in non-military areas.[40]
More significantly, in 1956 he was appointed member of the Committee

of Three on Non-Military Co-operation established by the North Atlantic Council. His involvement with both groups was clear testimony to his high standing within NATO. It is interesting to note in this connection that "Lange's name had been mentioned in connection with the Secretary-Generalship since the creation of the position."[41]

There can be little doubt, then, that Lange's commitment to expanding transatlantic co-operation, his reputation for sagacity in foreign affairs and the high regard in which he personally came to hold the US were deeply reassuring to the administration.[42] This could be seen, for example, in Dulles's positive response to the creation of the Committee of Three in 1956. Reporting to the NSC on the May 1956 NATO meeting, Dulles said he thought "this was a good committee and one which would be sympathetic to the goals we have in mind."[43]

Norway and World War II

The third, less tangible, factor which appears to have influenced US perceptions of Norway's "path setting" role among the Nordic NATO allies was its performance during World War II and its experience of occupation rule. Norway's determination to resist German aggression in April 1940 and the two months of struggle which ensued seem to have left US decision-makers with the impression that once attacked, Norway would resist Soviet aggression. This issue was *distinct* from the question of Norway's peacetime defence contribution with which the administration was never entirely satisfied.[44] In various estimates, reports and commentaries, allusion was made to Norway's performance during the war, and this was contrasted, somewhat unjustifiably, with the Danish failure to offer any immediate resistance to the German attack. A CIA report in February 1949, analysing the effects of US military aid to European countries, is indicative of American attitudes. "Norway," the report noted, was "disposed to resist aggression in *any case*."[45] Denmark's "will to resist Soviet aggression," on the other hand, was "qualified by a sense of futility of armed resistance in the event of war."[46] For similar reasons, a detailed study by the State Department in 1955 of various currents of neutralism in Western Europe expressed greater concern about the political consequences of neutralist sentiment in Denmark than in Norway:

> That such sentiments have been less extensive than in Denmark was shown by Norway's effort to fight off the German invasion in 1940. That neutralistic attitudes are now less effective than in Denmark is largely attributable to the greater harshness of Norway's experience under German occupation.[47]

Similarly, in April 1959, a study by the State Department Bureau of Intelligence and Research of the pressures for disengagement in Western Europe, expressed the view that "many Norwegians, influenced by their own experience in World War II, no longer profess the same faith in formulas of neutralization."[48]

The US, Norway and Sweden

As indicated above, the actual degree to which Norway was able to promote US policy objectives will be examined in greater detail with respect to Iceland. It is necessary, however, briefly to consider the position of Sweden in relation to Norway and the US. A major problem here is the fact that relations in the defence and intelligence fields between Sweden, Norway and the US in the 1950s are still shrouded in much secrecy. Because of the sensitivity of the subject, many details remain obscure, and it is still not possible to reconstruct a fully satisfactory picture of the *extent* and *precise nature* of Swedish co-operation with Norway and the United States. One of the important questions that remains unresolved concerns the degree of knowledge which Swedish political authorities – most notably Foreign Minister Østen Undén, who came to personify Sweden's commitment to "armed neutrality" – had about bilateral service-to-service co-operation, especially between the US Air Force and its Swedish counterpart. In spite of these limitations, some tentative assessments can be made the on basis of existing sources.[49] Our knowledge of the subject has also recently been enriched by the publication of the Report of the Commission on Neutrality Policy established by the Swedish Government in 1992.[50]

Available documents suggest that it was official US policy to encourage the highest degree of *interdependence* in terms of equipment, force posture and planning between Norway and Sweden. The importance which the US attached to strengthening ties with Sweden through the "instrumentality" of Norway is well illustrated in an embassy telegram from the American ambassador in Stockholm, Butterworth, to the State Department in April 1953.[51] In the telegram, Butterworth observed that "varying degrees of covert or semi-covert collaboration are believed to exist between Norwegians and Swedes at certain levels of their military establishments ... [and] there are close relations between civilian leaders of the two countries ..." Butterworth went on to argue that "these and other reasons make it logical and desirable that joint planning efforts between Sweden and the West be undertaken through the instrumentality of the Norwegians."[52] To what extent did the State Department act upon Butterworth's recommendation?

The desire to draw upon the resources of Sweden seemed most natural to the US, which regarded the Swedish armed forces, particularly the Air Force, as a formidable obstacle to any Soviet operation in Scandinavia.[53] This view was also shared by Norwegian officials who, since 1949, had urged both the US and the British to take account of Sweden in NATO military planning.[54] Both General Gruenther and General Norstad were anxious to explore the possibilities of enlarging tacit military co-operation between Sweden and Norway as a means of strengthening the Northern Flank.[55] This is reflected in the fact that Norwegian defence planning, especially after 1955, when the focus shifted towards North Norway, was predicated on the assumption of Swedish "rear cover" in south and central Norway.[56]

The activities and papers of Colonel Bernt Balchen show clearly that the Swedish Air Force, in particular, was keen to expand contacts and practical co-operation with Norway and the US. Reporting on talks held with senior Swedish officers in late 1951, Balchen wrote: "It was obvious from my conversation with General Nordenskjold [Chief of the Swedish Air Force] that Sweden is anxious, in his opinion, to effectuate a secret mutual defense agreement with Norway which in turn should be coordinated with the NATO overall plans."[57] As seen in Chapter Two, General Nordenskjold also informed Balchen that, in the event of an "immediate emergency," seven Swedish airfields could be made available to NATO beyond those needed for the Swedish Air Force. In August 1952 the American ambassador to NATO, William Draper, according to Balchen, "outlined the possibilities for an increased military capability in Scandinavia by effecting a mutual defence agreement between Norway and Sweden."[58] Colonel Balchen's role in the policy-making process in Washington is still unclear, and there is no evidence suggesting that such a "treaty" was ever concluded.[59] In an interview, Jens Boyesen referred to Balchen's idea of a "secret mutual defense agreement between Norway and Sweden coordinated with NATO plans," as an expression of "gigantic naivety" on Balchen's part. It would indeed appear that Balchen was too optimistic about the possibilities of formalising defence co-operation with Sweden in the early 1950s. Nonetheless, there can be little doubt that Balchen's activities did reflect growing co-operation between the US and Sweden, especially in the field of intelligence.[60] An internal Defense Department reference, recording Balchen's activities in 1952, noted that he had been provided with "highly classified information from Swedish military leaders," and that he had held "special conversations with Norwegian and Swedish officials, all of which have been made available to Air Intelligence and, through channels, to the CIA."[61] The Report of the Commission on Neutrality also notes that Sweden, in the late 1940s, "entered into intelligence collaboration with Norway" and that this relationship was strengthened in the 1950s.[62]

US Air Force documents in 1960 also speak of "technical assistance and security agreements" between Sweden and the US, with the USAF acting as an executive agent for the implementation of the agreements.[63] The ties which existed between the Swedish and the US air forces appear to have been particularly close under General Nordenskjold's and, especially, General Ljungdahl's periods as Commanders of the Swedish Air Force. A revealing reference is found in a letter from the Commander of the USAF Air Development Division to Thomas White, the Air Force Chief of Staff, in which he describes the outcome of a recent visit to Sweden by him and members of his staff:

> Especially significant was General Ljungdahl's address to us and his staff at a dinner where he deliberately "laid it on the line," unequivocally pointing out the reliance he placed upon our goodwill and strategic strength. To his entire staff he indicated that Sweden's best national interests would be served by their understanding and endorsement of US Air Fore efforts.[64]

The Report of the Commission on Neutrality Policy also found Swedish defence staff collaboration with the US Air Force in Germany to be particularly close. Indeed, in the early 1960s cooperation was close enough to warrant the establishment of a "crypto-telex link ... from the Defence Staff headquarters building to the USAF in Wiesbaden".[65]

There is one further factor to be considered in this picture. Apart from practical service-to-service and intelligence co-operation, US strategic planning and weapons export policy made allowance for Sweden as a "functional ally" and provisions were made which reflected this status. NSC 6006 of April 1960 listed as an aim of US policy the need to assist in the "establishment by Sweden of early warning, air control and advanced weapons systems which are *compatible with and complementary to* those planned for installation in the territory of neighbouring countries."[66] Sweden was, moreover, "the only non-allied country" to which the US was willing to sell "modern weapons" and release highly classified research and development information.[67] It is also worth noting that the only issues which, during the course of preparing NSC 6006, generated substantive discussion between agencies leading to amendments of earlier drafts, concerned Sweden. There were two issues that generated discussion at the NSC meeting convened to discuss policy towards Scandinavia. The first was a proposed "new policy directive" which maintained that the

US should "be prepared to come to the assistance of Sweden against Soviet Bloc aggression, if possible in co-operation with appropriate NATO countries."[68] Eisenhower felt that the problem of the defence of Sweden had to be raised in NATO, and the original paragraph was amended to reflect this. The new paragraph, finally agreed in the autumn, held that "in the event of Communist domination of Finland," the US should "consider promoting Sweden's membership to NATO."[69] The second issue concerned US military assistance, where the JCS expressed concern lest "too much research and development data" be shared with Sweden.[70] This concern should be understood in light of the extremely favourable treatment which Sweden as a "non-allied country" received in the 1950s.[71]

To sum up, then, it is clear that running parallel to Sweden's official policy of "armed neutrality" in the 1950s was a degree of functional co-operation with the United States, the full extent of which is not known. In an interesting comment, Helge Pharo, a leading Norwegian historian, has recently argued that Sweden in 1948–49 "in reality" chose the policy which Norway had pursued until 9 April 1940, that is, the "implicit guarantee line" and belief in automatic protection described by Olav Riste.[72] In this, as Butterworth put it, Norway was seen as a vital "instrument" through which co-operation with Sweden could be effectuated.

II NORWAY AND THE ICELAND BASE CRISIS, 1956

The Strategic Importance of Iceland to the United States, 1954–60

In a list of post-war overseas base requirements approved by the JCS in late October 1945, the Joint Planning Staff included Iceland as a "primary base area" vital to the security of the United States.[73] And in June 1946, Iceland, Greenland and the Azores were all on a list of six "essential" places where permanent peacetime base rights had to be secured.[74] At this early stage, however, American interests in Iceland derived primarily from the perceived need to protect the approaches to the American continent and to secure communications to US forces in Europe.[75]

The growing influence of the polar concept on US strategic policy after the outbreak of the Korean War further heightened Iceland's and Greenland's strategic significance in American eyes. In May 1951 the US – Icelandic Defence Agreement was signed, providing for the peacetime stationing of American forces and the construction of military facilities on the island.[76] The following year the US Minister in Iceland approached the Icelandic Foreign Ministry with a list of further military requirements "over and above those negotiated the previous year."[77] These involved a doubling of the number of troops on the island and included a request for the right to build another SAC base in the south-western part of the country. In May 1954, following several delays and "complicated" negotiations, a set of "supplementary understandings" was reached between the US and Icelandic governments. Under this agreement the overall US personnel ceiling was raised from 3900 to 6200; rotational training of air units was accepted and provision was made for the construction of a port and logistic facilities for the Strike Fleet. Shortly after reaching this accord, the first of three NSC policy papers on Iceland completed during the Eisenhower administration was presented to the President by the NSC Planning Board. The paper, NSC 5426, described the island as a vital "base area for offensive operations in conjunction with NATO, for air and naval defence of the approaches to North America and for maintaining sea communications between the United States and Europe."[78]

Between 1954 and 1960, however, the strategic importance of Iceland to the US increased further as a direct consequence of two developments. First, between June 1955 and February 1959, SAC gradually replaced its heavy type B-36 bomber with the new long-range B-52. During this transitional period, the mainstay of the bomber force consisted of the B-47, SAC's first all-jet medium bomber, introduced in late 1951. Its more limited range meant there would be greater reliance on overseas bases for refuelling of aircraft *en route* to the Soviet Union from bases in the US.[79] In an article circulated to the members of the Operations Coordinating Board (OCB) Working Group on Iceland in December 1955, Joseph Alsop wrote that

> The loss of Keflavik alone would be enough to highlight the appalling problem which increasingly confronts the Strategic Air Command. The fact that the SAC is entering a period when it will be almost wholly dependent on the medium range B-47 bomber.

Against this background Alsop emphasised the profound impact which the loss of the Icelandic air base would have on the US ability to "retain our dwindling margin of superiority in the atomic-air race."[80]

The second development which had the effect of significantly upgrading the strategic value of Iceland to the US has already been examined: the growth of the Soviet Northern Fleet submarine force and the concomitant adjustment of the US Navy to a northern strategy after 1955. This was clearly evident in the Planning Board's revised policy paper on Iceland, NSC 5712/1, submitted to the President in May 1957. Iceland now provided: (1) a vital link in the early warning system for the US and NATO; (2) an important base for anti-submarine operations; (3) important forward logistic support facilities for Strike Fleet operations; (4) a significant air base, and (5) a "key communications link between the United States, the United Kingdom and other NATO countries."[81] As in the case of Norway after 1954, the US Navy gradually replaced the Air Force as the service with the greatest strategic interest in Iceland.[82] This process culminated in 1960, when an agreement between Iceland and the US was reached whereby the US Navy took over the operation of the defence bases in Iceland which had previously been under the command of the USAF.[83] The *New York Times* reported that the transfer of principal responsibility for the operation of existing defence installations in Iceland from the Air Force to the Navy was described as "desirable in view of the Navy's increasingly active role in defence of the northern flank of NATO."[84]

The discussion within the NSC on the contents of NSC 5712/1 provides perhaps the most revealing insight into the importance which the US military, in particular, now attached to the retention of military facilities in the island. An early draft of the NSC paper had stated that the denial of the aforementioned advantages to the US "would result in an unacceptable weakening of the North Atlantic Defence system."[85] At the NSC meeting John Foster Dulles questioned whether the term "unacceptable" was appropriate. The Secretary of State wondered whether the term implied that the US, if asked to leave, would in fact resort to the "use of force to compel Iceland to permit our troops to remain?"[86] Robert Cutler, Special Assistant for National Security Affairs, said he did not believe the Planning Board had envisaged the use of force under this circumstance but "thought that perhaps the Joint Chiefs of Staff feel that force was justified in the circumstance envisaged."[87] General Twining's specific response to Cutler's query is partly sanitised, though it is clear from the context and related documents that the armed services did indeed hold the view expressed in the draft position.

Norway and Iceland

In the 1950s Norwegian authorities were acutely aware of the fact that any weakening of the American position in Iceland would seriously threaten the security of air and sea lanes linking Britain and Scandinavia to the US. Norway's peripheral status in NATO's continental strategy during this period reinforced a vested Norwegian interest in Iceland's continued commitment to NATO.[88] The interdependence of Iceland and Norway in US air and maritime strategy was also recognised by the Icelandic government. Partly for this reason, the Icelandic government in 1952 insisted that a senior Norwegian military representative should review the US request for additional military rights on the island over and above the Defence Agreement of 1951.[89] The decision to have the US request for military rights evaluated by a Norwegian "military adviser" reflected the Icelandic Government's fear that further installations would accentuate the country's role merely as a *defensive* outpost for the US and as a staging base for *offensive* operations.[90] The Norwegian representative, General Bjarne Øen, arrived in January 1953 and stayed in Iceland for three weeks, conferring with American and Icelandic officials before submitting his report.[91] General Øen's mission, however, should also be seen as a clear indication of Norway's special status in relation to Iceland, a fact which the US readily recognised.

This can be seen in the first comprehensive policy paper on Iceland produced by the NSC Planning Board in July 1954, NSC 5426. The Planning Board noted in its report that the Icelandic Government "observes closely the activities and policies of the Norwegian Government ... in connection with NATO affairs and is inclined to follow the direction set by that country."[92] The NSC also noted that "much of this attitude" came from "the very high respect" which the Icelandic Foreign Minister had for Halvard Lange. Lange had also strongly influenced the Icelandic government's decision to join NATO in the first place.[93] Although Iceland viewed Danish policies "with some interest", it did not attach "nearly as great an importance to decisions by that country," and there was "little influence on Icelandic policies or attitudes attributable to Denmark."[94] It is clear, therefore, that the US government in its troubled dealings with Iceland in the 1950s attached particular importance to consultations with Norway. This link became particularly important in 1956 when the Icelandic parliament voted in favour of actually removing US troops from the island. It is necessary, however, first to consider briefly the sources of the US – Icelandic discord in this period.

The principal reason for the American concern about its long-term presence on Iceland stemmed from the fluid internal political situation in the country. A widespread pro-neutralist sentiment was sustained by a deeply-held fear of being culturally "overwhelmed" by the large American troop presence on the island.[95] Moreover, the Icelandic communist party, *Kommunistaflokkur Islands*, was seen by the American administration (and Norwegian intelligence) as an instrument of Soviet subversion, skilfully exploiting the appearance of an American "protective hegemony" on the island by presenting itself as the "true protector of Icelandic sovereignty."[96] In February 1955 the OCB progress report on American policy toward Iceland noted that "the communist infiltration of organised labor in Iceland progressed to such an extent that the federation of trade unions is essentially now controlled by a Communist coalition."[97]

What complicated matters further was the vulnerability of Iceland's single-product economy to Soviet bloc economic penetration, especially after British fishing interests in 1953 imposed an unofficial but highly effective embargo on Icelandic fish. This British action was a retaliatory boycott against Iceland's unilateral extension in 1952 of its territorial limits calculated on extended new base lines. The consequent loss of the British market – traditionally some thirty-five per cent of the total catch was marketed in the UK – led to a Soviet offer to Iceland in August 1953 of favourable bilateral trading arrangements. The percentage of Iceland's exports to the "Soviet bloc" rose from 5–7 per cent in 1949–52 to 30 per cent in 1956. Measures to counteract Soviet economic and political overtures towards Iceland – specifically, what could be done to provide more markets in non-Communist countries for Icelandic fish – occupied a remarkable amount of time for the NSC in the Eisenhower period.[98]

The Icelandic Base Crisis of 1956

In March 1956 the Althing passed a resolution "calling for discussions with the United States for revision of the defence agreement, aiming at withdrawal of US forces and having Iceland assume responsibility on behalf of NATO for maintenance of the defence installations."[99] On 11 June Foreign Minister Kristinn Gudmundsson, in a note to the US ambassador in Iceland, John Muccio, formally proposed that the US and Iceland should open negotiations by 1 August with a view to revising the 1951 Defence Agreement.[100]

The Althing resolution led to an immediate suspension of negotiations for new defence construction, and to the creation by the OCB of an "Iceland Operational Control Group" headed by a senior State Department official. The Group, working within the NSC machinery, was charged with co-ordinating specific programs "on a crash basis" and would "function on a day-to-day basis."[101] The basic reason for the Icelandic action in 1956 appears to have been the conviction that international tensions had relaxed sufficiently since the Geneva summit of 1955 for a reassessment of US requirements to be made. As the final policy paper on Iceland under Eisenhower noted, Icelandic politicians were "particularly sensitive to any feeling in Europe or elsewhere" of any relaxation of world tensions.[102] The NSC also felt that "lack of understanding of the increased long-range air and sea capabilities of the Soviets" had contributed to the demand for a withdrawal.

A key instrument in the American "crisis" diplomacy was the attempt to encourage Norwegian authorities, especially Foreign Minister Lange, to influence the Icelandic government's position. Given Norway's "special relationship" with Iceland, the US hoped that the Norwegian authorities could act as a positive influence on the Icelandic government by urging it to reconsider its decision. This hope was bolstered by the fact that the Norwegian government itself expressed "great concern" about the Icelandic decision in view of the extreme difficulties which any withdrawal would create for the defence of the Northern Flank and the contiguous sea areas.[103] In an article circulated by the OCB in April, it was stated that "officials in Washington" were hoping that Norway might be able to persuade Iceland to reconsider its position.[104] Similar stories appeared in the Norwegian press and were not without foundation in fact.[105] The available evidence shows that throughout the spring and summer of 1956 the US State Department, especially through its representative in Iceland, Ambassador John Muccio, continued to consult closely with Norwegian authorities over developments in US – Icelandic relations.

On 29 May Muccio called on his Norwegian colleague, Torgeir Anderssen-Rysst, to discuss developments in Iceland. Ambassador Muccio, who had recently returned from consultations in Washington, told Anderssen-Rysst that John Foster Dulles had expressed his personal appreciation for the advice given by Halvard Lange at the NATO ministerial meeting earlier in the month.[106] Dulles had told Muccio that the Norwegian Foreign Minister had had a "very positive influence" on Dulles's assessment of the situation in Iceland.[107] More specifically, Lange appears to have urged Dulles to consider the official US response carefully and not to "overreact" as this would only have strengthened anti-American sentiment in Iceland.[108] The initial US response to the Althing decision was in fact clearly measured and no "agonizing reappraisal" was held out as a means of exerting pressure on the Icelandic government. This initially restrained US response, however, changed after the Icelandic elections in July and the formation of a new cabinet which included two members of the communist-front Labour Alliance (*Althydubandalag*).[109]

US – Norwegian consultations, if anything, intensified after the elections. When on 23 July Iceland's new foreign minister, Gudmundur Gudmundsson, made a private visit to Oslo to discuss the base question with Halvard Lange, the Americans were kept closely informed by the Norwegians about the content of the talks.[110] On 4 August the US ambassador to Oslo, Lester Corrin Strong, was briefed by Lange about the meeting which he had held with the Icelandic minister.[111] The State Department subsequently expressed its "great appreciation" for the information provided by Lange to Strong about the meeting with Gudmundsson.[112]

A clear example of the manner in which Norway was seen to be of use by the US can be found in a memorandum of conversation between Corrin Strong and a senior Foreign Ministry official, Skylstad, in late august. Strong told Skylstad that the Icelandic suggestion that Keflavik could perhaps be maintained by civilian personnel only was not acceptable to the US government. Strong added that he hoped the Norwegians could inform the Icelandic government about this, since the US itself did not wish to appear to be exerting pressure on Iceland.[113]

Norway did not, however, merely act as an intermediary. It also sought to influence US policies. On 1 August Corrin Strong informed Norwegian officials that "the US government could not initiate negotiations with Iceland about the defence agreement as long as there were communists in the government."[114] Both bilaterally and through NATO, Norway strongly urged the US to show restraint in its approach to Iceland, arguing that ill-considered initiatives would have the opposite effect of what was intended. American authorities were particularly concerned about the problem of maintaining security within NATO and proposed sweeping measures which would effectively have excluded Icelandic representatives from all important fora and discussions in the alliance. The Norwegian government reacted strongly against the US proposal for an "American security system" and Ambassador Corrin Strong was told to inform the State Department that such measures by the US would drive Iceland out of NATO altogether.[115] The State Department appears to have accepted Norwegian arguments and the question of excluding Iceland from NATO fora was postponed until Iceland's position in the Alliance was further clarified.[116]

In the end, however, the resolution of the Icelandic base crisis did not depend crucially on Norwegian mediation. Following the disturbances in Poland and the Hungarian uprising in October 1956, the Icelandic government suspended the implementation of the *Althing* resolution, and did not pursue the issue further.[117] The US – Icelandic negotiations, which had started in early October, were completed in December 1956 and enabled US forces "to remain in Iceland under substantially the same conditions provided for in the original agreement of 1951," only establishing a "procedure for subsequent high-level consultation."[118] In a "progress report" in May 1957, the situation was reported to have "improved significantly" with the communists "effectively isolated from the conduct of foreign affairs."[119] Still, troop–community relations continued to be a major problem throughout the 1950s, reaching a low point in the latter half of 1959.[120] Only in the 1960s, once the US had substantially reduced its presence on the island by withdrawing all Army units, did tensions ease significantly.

Conclusion

In the 1950s the State Department recognised that Norway's "special position" among the Nordic countries – a function of geostrategic location, history and Halvard Lange's international standing – offered significant opportunities for promoting other policy objectives in the region. In view of the extreme importance which the US Air Force and Navy attached to maintaining and developing early warning installations on Greenland and facilities to support forward maritime operations in Iceland,[121] the influence which Norwegian actions were assumed to have on Danish and Icelandic policies, gave Norway a particularly important role in US calculations. This was most clearly the case with respect to Iceland, which maintained a "special relationship" with Norway and whose place in American maritime and air strategy was closely related to that of Norway. Less is known about Norway's precise role in relation to Sweden, though there can be little doubt that close functional ties developed between Sweden and the US in the 1950s, and that the US regarded Norway as a key link in this relationship.

8 Norway, the United States and the Management of Bilateral Relations, 1954–60

Norwegian security policy in the Cold War has traditionally been described as a function of two sets of considerations. On the one hand, membership of NATO implied a policy of *deterrence* vis-à-vis the Soviet Union. The necessary corollary of this was a high degree of *integration* into the Western defence system. On the other hand, measures of deterrence and integration have been pursued alongside policies of *reassurance* vis-à-vis the Soviet Union and *screening* with respect to the Western alliance, above all to the United States.[1] The overall aim of Norwegian policy has been to integrate these elements into a "composite security posture" geared towards sustaining a "pattern of restraint and mutual consideration in Northern Europe."[2] This chapter focuses on the reassurance element of Norwegian policy, with special reference to those developments in the maritime and intelligence sphere discussed in the preceding chapters. More specifically, it examines the degree of understanding shown by the US administration for Norway's desire to keep its confrontation with the Soviet Union at a low level. This will be done by addressing three related questions. First, what were the American attitudes to Norwegian base policy and associated operational restrictions on US and allied military activity? Second, using the U-2 and RB-47 incidents of 1960 as a case study, how did the US *manage* its relations with Norway in the highly sensitive area of intelligence co-operation? Finally, which other broader policy considerations influenced the conduct of US policy with respect to Norway?

I THE UNITED STATES AND NORWEGIAN BASE POLICY

Norwegian Base Policy, 1954–1960

In the spring of 1952, as the alliance sought to implement a conventional strategy for the defence of Europe, Norwegian policy regarding the stationing of foreign military units on its territory came under direct pressure. At issue was the question of how to make up for what was seen as a major deficiency in the alliance's force posture: the lack of tactical air forces in Northern Europe.[3] The proposal to deploy one US tactical fighter wing (75 aircraft) in Norway would indeed have represented a departure from the declared policy that Norway would not allow foreign bases on its territory in peacetime. In May 1952 Eisenhower told Norwegian government officials "that the US could not be expected to provide funds for air base development in Norway until there could be some announcement of Norway's intention to revise their policy."[4] In the following month, Dean Acheson told Anthony Eden in London that the "Norwegians were asking for two contradictory things ... They wanted the aircraft to be near at hand, and at the same time they were unable to agree to their being stationed on Norwegian territory."[5] Throughout the autumn of 1952 the State Department continued to entertain the hope that Norwegian policy would be changed, possibly after the parliamentary elections the following autumn.[6] By early 1953, however, SACEUR's "flank concept" had been quietly buried, both US and NATO strategy was under review and Allied interest in the Northern Flank was fast diminishing.[7] Partly for this reason, there was no longer the same interest in establishing permanent bases in Northern Europe, particularly in the face of political opposition.

Between 1954 and 1960 no US initiative comparable to that of 1952 was made to alter Norwegian base policy. The reason for this was threefold. First, as indicated above, with the changes in alliance strategy and the down-grading of the Northern Flank in land operations, the question of revising the policy lost much of its relevance. Second, as will be discussed later in this chapter, the State Department gradually came to appreciate the potentially adverse effect that a change of policy might have on stability in Northern Europe. The third factor, which will be examined here, had to do with the specific operational requirements of the US and the extent to which these could be accommodated *within* the existing policy framework laid down by Defence Minister Jens Chr. Hauge in his 1951 statement on Norwegian base policy.

Throughout the 1950s official statements of the Norwegian basing policy, whether uttered in public or in response to a particular Soviet note, consistently emphasised its *political* motivation and *conditional* nature. As with Hauge's original declarations in 1949 and 1951, the government carefully avoided any precise and exclusive definition of the policy. In particular, no attempt was made to specify the degrees and types of foreign access associated with the terms "bases," "installations" and "facilities." Such definitional ambiguity served two purposes. In the first place, the Norwegian government did not wish to be tied to a specific and restrictive interpretation on which would then be conferred a contractual or semi-legal status by Soviet authorities. Indeed, the single most persistent theme of Soviet diplomacy towards Norway between 1954 and 1960 was the attempt to transform Norway's unilateral policy on bases into a bilateral understanding.[8] For example, in discussions with Prime Minister Gerhardsen in May 1957, the Soviet ambassador to Oslo, Gribanov, suggested that it would perhaps now be an idea to "formalise Norwegian declarations on base policy in treaty form."[9]

As indicated above, however, definitional ambiguity also served another purpose. It enabled Norwegian authorities to provide the US with strategic access, facilities and services so long as these were not seen to challenge the underlying political consideration which informed the base policy. A memorandum in January 1960 from the Norwegian Minister of Defence, Nils Handal, to SACEUR and SACLANT illustrates this clearly. The document laid out the principles governing the maintenance, control and operation of NATO infrastructure in Norway "with particular reference to projects which have been, or will be provided *over and above the requirements of the Norwegian NATO forces*."[10] It thus provides an instructive insight both to the areas in which Norway contributed "over and above" her own requirements, and to the different "categories of facilities" which were not precluded by the base policy. According to the document, the facilities included: the forward scatter system; the early warning chain; signal communications; Tacan stations (tactical aircraft beacons); Loran stations; radio stations; war headquarters; storage facilities; tactical and maritime airfields, and, finally, naval bases.[11] A closer look at the construction of maritime and tactical airfields in North Norway and their use by the US Navy, confirm the view that a formal change in base policy was not deemed necessary by US authorities.

US Naval Plans and the Base Policy

When the Director of the Strategic Plans Division, Admiral Dennison, in October 1955 was asked to review CINCLANT's detailed list for requirements in Norway, he noted that it was

> ... unfortunate that Norway, our NATO partner, refuses the US the right to operate from and to station personnel at the NATO fields pre D-day. Since the strategic requirement exists for these installations, some pre-D-day construction of national infrastructure is required to support D+1 day operations.[12]

Dennison's comments should not, however, be seen as reflecting more than a professional and almost instinctive military response to politically motivated restrictions.[13] Such attitudes, which could be found among British, US and Norwegian officers, also stemmed from certain inevitable *practical* problems which the policy created. One of these was that eligibility for NATO common infrastructure funds laid great stress on multinational use. Whereas other NATO commands could quote several other user nations, CINCNORTH could refer only to "possible outside support in time of war from unspecified nations."[14] While this criterion did not apply to airfields, CINCNORTH's annual report noted that there had been difficulties "in the case of naval bases, war headquarters, and POL projects other than jet fuel type."[15] In spite of this, however, the naval requirements prepared by Admiral Wright in late 1954 were not seen to demand any fundamental change in the Norwegian policy. In connection with US Navy requirements at Andøya, which necessitated bilateral negotiations with Norway, the Chief of Naval Operations emphasised that the policy on bases "does not prevent the building of support facilities pre-D-Day for forces to be employed in Norway in the event of war."[16] And "support facilities" is precisely what SACLANT was anxious to obtain. In the case of Andøya, the single most important maritime airfield for SACLANT in Norway, this included storage facilities and assembly equipment for mines to be used in the aerial mining campaign. It also included the provision of major fuel stores, maintenance facilities, mountain hangars and ground navigation aids allowing aircraft to operate by night and in all weathers. The expansion and standardisation of material and procedures, which the construction of facilities and the provision of services amounted to, meant that maximum interoperability for SACLANT forces in the north-east Atlantic could be achieved.

Yet, although bilateral arrangements accompanying the growth of naval US activity in North Norway did not require any basic revision of policy, the *political* factors which had dictated caution in 1952 still very much applied. The Norwegian government was most anxious to ensure that increased activity on the part of the US Navy in the north did not appear unduly "provocative" to the Soviet Union. Bilateral arrangements, therefore, had to take cognisance of political factors which the Norwegian government considered to be essential to the preservation of the state of "low tension" in the region. These considerations were incorporated into specific operational directives that aimed both at minimising the chances of "incidents" and, more importantly, sought to avoid the impression that Norway was allowing US aircraft unrestricted access to bases in Norway. In addition to specific and standard directives, the Norwegian Foreign

Ministry considered each individual US or British application for "reconnaissance flights" in the light of political considerations. A key concern was to avoid the appearance of *regularity* in the pattern of allied flight operations since this could be interpreted as a fixed arrangement which was at variance with the "spirit" of the base policy.[17]

On 19 January 1951 "Norwegian Regulations for the Admittance of Foreign Warships and Military Aircraft into Norwegian Territory in Times of Peace" was established by Royal Decree.[18] According to the rules laid down, all flights by allied aircraft into Norway had to be cleared *directly* through the Protocol Office of the Norwegian Foreign Ministry at least 72 hours in advance. In January 1952 the Norwegian Ministry of Defence, in a letter to the Foreign Ministry, raised the question of whether these rules were not too cumbersome and should therefore be simplified with regard to allied aircraft.[19] The Foreign Ministry, however, advised strongly against any modification "out of consideration for our base policy."[20] The only change that was made in response to the MOD query was that *allied aircraft taking part in NATO manoeuvres* could be cleared through the Ministry of Defence rather than the Protocol Office of the Foreign Ministry.

In September 1956 the US air attaché in Norway, Colonel Flanagan, approached the Foreign Ministry asking whether these existing regulations could not be simplified in view of the increased frequency of US flights into Norway. Flanagan felt the procedure was perhaps too cumbersome, since each request had to go via diplomatic channels rather than through the MOD or, preferably from a US point of view, the Norwegian Air Force High Command. Existing procedures meant that US requests for clearance had to be considered "several times per week if not daily."[21] However, the Foreign Ministry again rejected any modification of the policy laid down in the Royal Decree of 1951 and clearances continued to be passed through the Foreign Ministry. Earlier in the year, a British request for a relaxation of the existing rules with regard to "informal naval visits" was turned down by the Foreign Minister on the same political grounds.[22]

Some modification to the 72-hour rule appears to have been made with respect to maritime aircraft in the latter half of the decade. In 1959, under an agreement between US and Norwegian authorities, the specific directive for US Navy maritime patrol flights to Norway from Iceland (code-named "Neptune Journey") required that all flights be cleared with Norwegian regional air commanders at least 24 hours in advance. Other restrictions, however, remained intact. Before each flight the US Navy had to make prior notification of aircraft type, number of aircraft, POL requirements and route plan. Limits were also placed on the payload of each aircraft.[23] Most significantly, "Neptune Journey" flights would not be cleared to the East of 24 E longitude or "...within 20 nautical miles from the Finnish–Swedish border."[24] As indicated above, this longitudinal restriction was part of a wider set of conditions and operational parameters placed on allied military activity in the far north in the early 1950s. These included the prohibition against using Norwegian territory for overflights of Soviet territory and that there should be no allied military manoeuvres in the county of Finnmark.[25]

In summary, therefore, the absence of any clear-cut distinction between various categories of "facilities" allowed for flexibility in operational policy, and no approach was made by the CNO to the State Department suggesting that a change of base policy was needed to accommodate a greater forward presence for the US Navy. Although the US Navy would have preferred a greater number of familiarisation flights and a simplification of the rules governing the clearance of individual sorties, the growth of American maritime activity described in Chapter Six did not create serious bilateral complications or US "pressure" on Norway. The restrictions imposed on *regular* operations and training activities – be they ASW air patrols, NATO exercises or familiarisation flights – were observed by the US Navy. American intelligence activities in and around Norway, however, presented a very different problem.

II INTELLIGENCE COOPERATION: THE U-2 AND RB-47 INCIDENTS

Background to the Incidents: Arctic Air Operations After 1957

In early May 1960 a U-2 high-altitude reconnaissance aircraft, piloted by CIA officer Gary Powers, was shot down by Soviet air defence forces near Sverdlovsk. The incident precipitated a sharp deterioration in US–Soviet relations, culminating in the collapse of the Paris summit later in the month. The U-2, which had taken off from Peshawar, was scheduled to land at the Norwegian airport of Bodø, a fact which, according to the official Soviet note of protest, made Norway "an accessory to provocative actions by the United States against Norway's neighbour, the Soviet Union."[26] Less than two months later another US intelligence-gathering aircraft, an ELINT-configured RB-47H of the 55th Strategic Reconnaissance Wing operating out of Brize Norton, was shot down outside Soviet air space in the Barents Sea. Following this incident, the Soviet government issued another protest charging Norway with continued complicity in American reconnaissance and espionage operations.[27] The details and wider international implications surrounding the U-2 incident in particular are well documented and need not be recounted.[28] The concern here is to examine and assess the US *handling* of the two incidents vis-à-vis Norway. This, however, must be done against the background of three specific developments that emerged in the far north after 1957: (1) the increase in SAC operations in the Arctic regions, (2) the "Bodø affair", (3) the issue of possible airfield construction on Svalbard between 1958 and 1960. Along with US naval activities described in preceding chapters, all three issues not only bore witness to the growing American involvement in the area but also placed a perceptible strain on Soviet–Norwegian relations.[29]

SAC arctic operations

In a letter to the Chairman of the United Nations Security Council on 18 April 1958, the Soviet ambassador at the UN requested a meeting to consider "urgent measures to put an end to flights by United States military aircraft armed with atomic and hydrogen bombs in the direction of the frontiers of the Soviet Union."[30] The continuation of such flights, the Soviet representative argued, "might lead to a breach of world peace and the unleashing of an atomic war of annihilation."[31] The Soviet Union was particularly worried about SAC flights in the polar regions which had been instituted regularly in the wake of the Sputnik launches and the Gaither Committee's demand for "prompt and aggressive implementation of the SAC 'alert' concept."[32] These flights, which were designed to "permit a more rapid response to enemy surprise attack and to decrease vulnerability,"[33] continued and even increased in regularity when, in 1958, so-called "positive control exercises" were instituted by SAC.[34] Erik Himle, appointed State Secretary at the Norwegian MOD in July 1958, could not recall that Soviet authorities expressed concern about SAC's Arctic alert procedures *directly* to the Norwegians.[35] On a visit to Norway after the U-2 incident, however, Anastas Mikoyan did convey the concerns of the Soviet military to the Norwegian authorities.

In addition to SAC operations, Soviet authorities were also deeply troubled and embarrassed by U-2 overflight operations which the CIA had been able to carry out with impunity since July 1956. In a note delivered to the State Department only three days after the call for a Security Council meeting, the Soviet Union secretly protested against a recent overflight by "an American military reconnaissance aircraft of the

Lockheed U-2 type."[36] The reason for the intensity of Soviet concern regarding U-2 flights was expressed to the Norwegians after the U-2 incident in May 1960. In June 1960 a senior Norwegian official, Asbjørn Engen, informed his American colleague in Paris that the head of the Scandinavian department of the Soviet Foreign Ministry had told him that:

> the reason Khrushchev made so much of the U-2 over-flight was because Soviet military leaders had told Khrushchev that they "could not and would not" live with situation in which over-flights by single plane might be made for purpose of "leading in" a flight of bombers.[37]

The "Bodø affair"
On 23 December 1958 *Sovietsky Flot* carried an article, allegedly based on Finnish and Norwegian press reports, about reconnaissance flights by British and American aircraft over northern waters staged from Norwegian airfields. The following month, on 19 January 1959, Deputy Foreign Minister Valerian Zorin formally summoned the Norwegian ambassador, Oscar Gundersen, to discuss the matter.[38] According to *Izvestiya*, which wrote about the meeting on 21 January, Zorin was said to have "expressed the hope that the Norwegian Government would take necessary steps to prevent future use of Norwegian aerodromes by American and British military aircraft for purposes hostile to the Soviet Union."[39] As seen earlier, U-2 aircraft had been deployed to Bodø for close to two months in the autumn of 1958. Gundersen, in his oral reply to Rodionov, the head of the Scandinavian section of the Soviet Foreign Ministry, stated that neither US nor British aircraft had been transferred to Bodø or any other airfield in Norway.[40] He did add, however, that Allied aircraft were occasionally allowed to utilise Norwegian airfields for brief periods in connection with regular NATO exercises. When such permission was granted, no flying over Norwegian territory east of 24 degrees was permitted. A few weeks later Khrushchev, in a conversation with ambassador Gundersen in Moscow, again expressed concern about American intelligence flights along Russia's borders.[41] In a discussion that went on for more than two hours Khrushchev also raised the issue of an American aircraft which had recently "come from Norway" over Finland and had then for a brief period flown over Soviet territory.[42] The Norwegian ambassador replied that his government had denied that such a flight had been launched from Norway. Both Khrushchev and Rodionov, however, thought it immaterial whether the aircraft were permanently or temporarily deployed to Norwegian

airfields as long as they transgressed Soviet territory or had "anti-Soviet intentions."

The airfield question on Svalbard, 1958–59
In November 1958 the activities of two Norwegian entrepreneurs and Arctic enthusiasts who, since 1956, had been exploring ideas for a civilian airfield on Svalbard, prompted the Soviet government to issue a note to Norway.[43] The note reiterated the Soviet position that Norway had unlawfully included the archipelago in SACLANT's area of responsibility in 1951. It stated further that the "planned construction of an aerodrome on the Spitsbergen archipelago could be regarded in no other way than as a link in the construction of a network of military airfields conducted in the NATO programme."[44] The Norwegian response, conveyed in a note on 10 January 1959 and later elaborated in an address by Lange before the Storting, maintained "that Norwegian authorities at present have no plans in general for building aerodromes on Spitsbergen or assisting in this."[45]

It was Oscar Gundersen's impression that, until May 1960, Soviet authorities had broadly accepted Norwegian reassurances with respect to both the "Bodø affair" and the airfield question. Following the U-2 and the RB-47 incidents, however, Gundersen felt that "our so-called good neighbourly relationship to the Soviet Union ... had seriously deteriorated."[46]

The Soviet Reaction and the Norwegian Response to the U-2 and RB-47 Incidents

Soviet reactions to Norway's involvement in the U-2 operation in May assumed two forms. On the one hand, a series of direct and menacing threats were issued. On the other hand, Soviet authorities sought to exploit Norwegian embarrassment by extracting a more narrow and precise definition of Norwegian base policy.

On 9 May 1960, four days after Khrushchev had first referred to the "downing of a US military aircraft," he declared:

> From the lofty rostrum of the Supreme Soviet we once again warn those countries that make their territory available for the take-off of planes with anti-Soviet intentions – do not play with fire, Gentlemen![47]

That same evening, at a Czech embassy reception, Khrushchev, in the words of Sir Patrick Reilly, "gave a solemn warning to the countries which hire out their bases to other powers, and made explicit threat of direct retaliation against bases used for such flights."[48] On 13 May an official Soviet protest was delivered to the Norwegian ambassador. The note drew attention to the fact that in January 1959, having received "exact and verified information about deliberate reconnaissance flights" from the Bodø airfield, the Soviet Government had told the Norwegian ambassador that "such a state of affairs was intolerable."[49] In a strongly worded note the Soviet government now warned that if provocations continued from Norwegian territory, it would be "obliged to take appropriate measures in reply."[50]

Soviet attempts to extract a more narrow definition of the base policy were most evident during Anastas Mikoyan's three-day visit to Norway not long after the U-2 incident and the collapse of the Paris summit.[51] Reporting on Mikoyan's visit to Norway before the North Atlantic Council in Paris, Mr Arne Gunneng, Acting Permanent Representative, stated that "to Norwegian authorities the purpose of the visit, apart from opening the Industrial Exhibition, seems primarily to have been to press Norway for a narrower interpretation of our base policy as well as for a continuation of our policy as regards atomic weapons."[52] Mikoyan was also disturbed by Norwegian "advances" towards the Federal Republic in connection with plans for the establishment of a NATO Baltic Command.

Although the shooting-down of the RB-47 over the Barents Sea was clearly outside Soviet territory, a fact that was confirmed by Norwegian SIGINT sources, the Soviet Union immediately linked the two incidents and protested officially to the Norwegian Government on 11 July.[53] The Soviet protest note to the US, delivered on the same day, concluded:

> The Soviet Government with deep regret has to state that Governments of some states who are allies of the USA in military blocs have not yet drawn necessary conclusions from known facts connected with aggressive actions of the US Air Force ... and through this bring great danger upon peoples of their countries.[54]

The following day, Khrushchev reaffirmed Defence Minister Malinovski's threat to "launch retaliatory missile blows at the take-off bases of American planes which violate Soviet air space."[55]

On 9 May Halvard Lange told the Storting that civilian and military authorities in Norway had "absolutely no knowledge" of the fact that Gary Powers was on his way to Bodø.[56] He emphasised further that permission had "never been granted for Norwegian flying fields to be used as the starting point for missions which violate other states' territory."[57] Recent work by Rolf Tamnes shows that although "principal political leaders" knew that a "reconnaissance operation in the North" was scheduled for April, they had no knowledge of the aircraft involved and had no reason to believe that the operation would involve overflying of Soviet territory, something which the US in any event had been expressly barred from if it involved Norwegian territory.[58] As for "military authorities," however, Vilhelm Evang, the powerful Head of the Defence Intelligence Staff, *appears* to have known rather more about US plans than he was prepared to admit during internal investigations at the time. Evang had first been approached in early April by the CIA representative in Oslo, Louis C. Beck, with a request for flight operations, preferably out of Andøya, involving two U-2s and three C-130s. Although neither Evang nor the Air Force Commander in North Norway, General Einar Tufte Johnsen, knew the exact details of US plans, according to Tamnes, Evang must have surmised that the operation would involve some penetration of Soviet territory, possibly along the lines of the U-2 operation in the north in 1957.[59] Norwegian political leaders, however, clearly felt that they had not been adequately informed and Sir Peter Scarlett, the British ambassador to Oslo, was right in deducing "that confidence must have been impaired as between the Norwegians and the Americans, especially in the conduct of intelligence activities."[60] Norwegian authorities did indeed set out to re-examine existing mechanisms for ensuring political control over intelligence operations and reconnaissance flights in the Arctic seas, in particular, were subject to closer scrutiny.[61] Moreover, the number of US technical experts attached to airfields in North Norway and to the Loran-C installations in Vesterålen was reduced during the course of the summer and autumn with a view to replacing them completely with Norwegian personnel.[62]

In spite of the genuine consternation felt by the Norwegian Government for not having been fully informed, Lange did not, however, wish to exacerbate the strain in relations with the US as this could only benefit the Soviet Union.[63] Although Lange was described in the press as having issued a "protest" to the US, the British ambassador understood it was "rather an aide-mémoire setting out the Norwegian attitude."[64] Paradoxically, the menacing language which Khrushchev and especially Malinovsky directed towards Norway made it easier for US and Norwegian authorities to manage the crisis both vis-à-vis each other and internally.[65]

US Crisis Management

Unlike the JCS and the intelligence community, Eisenhower, who had closely controlled the U-2 programme from the White House, had in fact long been worried about the political consequences should one of the U-2s be shot down in denied territory.[66] In late 1958 he told a small group of officials that since the U-2 was being tracked, he was no longer sure "whether the intelligence which we receive from this source is worth the exacerbation of international tension which results."[67] Three months later he again expressed reservation about a request from Secretary of Defense Neil McElroy to continue reconnaissance flights on the grounds that it was "undue provocation."[68] The President's concern explains, in part, why he was so anxious to repair the damage done in relations with Norway.

The Norwegian involvement in the episode was a major embarrassment for the United States and the President quickly imposed restrictions on "all intelligence operations of a 'provocative' nature," including Air Force "ferret" operations.[69] On 10 May the Norwegian ambassador to Washington, Paul Koht, called on Secretary of State Christian Herter to present the statement which Lange had delivered to Parliament the previous day. Herter told Koht that Khrushchev's accusations against Norway had been discussed with Congressional leaders, and that he had assured members that the Norwegian Government "knew nothing about this flight and was in no way involved."[70] Herter added that CIA Director Allen Dulles (who certainly must have known about Norway's exact involvement in this and previous operations), said it could perhaps be admitted that "Bodø Airport may have been one of several alternative fields given to the pilot where he might ask permission to land in case of emergency."[71] Herter further told Ambassador Koht that he could tell the press that he had assured him that "the Norwegian Government knew nothing about the flight."[72] In response to the Norwegian "protest", delivered on 13 May, the State Department replied with an aide-mémoire, in which it confirmed that the Norwegian authorities had not been requested to grant permission for American aircraft of the U-2 type, and had such a landing been made, it "would have been contrary to principles followed by Norwegian authorities."[73]

The determination of Eisenhower not to involve or further embarrass Norway can also be seen in the internal US debate in the wake of the incident. Republican Senators complained about the lack of commitment shown by US allies on the periphery of the Soviet Union.[74] Influential representatives of the Republican Right had on previous occasions demonstrated a lack of understanding of the situation in Northern Europe and the sensitivities of US allies in the area. In 1957, for example, the Senate Minority Leader, William Knowland of California, eager "to take up Khrushchev on his offer to withdraw troops from Hungary,"[75] had publicly proposed that if the Russians would quit Hungary, Norway should leave NATO.[76] John Foster Dulles called on the Senator and told him "the Senator's reference to Norway might not be well received in Norway," and that he ought to have expressed himself more "tactfully."[77] During a meeting with congressional leaders after the U-2 incident, Eisenhower said that U-2 flights had involved the use of friendly bases and that in order to avoid embarrassment he had decided to suspend further flights.[78] On this occasion another prominent member of the Republican "Old Guard," Styles Bridges of New Hampshire, was anxious to know "why some of our allies protested about the use of bases on their soil."[79] Eisenhower defused the question and responded that some of these nations were militarily weak and close to the borders of the Soviet Union.[80]

The US handling of the U-2 incident must also, however, be seen in the broader context of the, at times, problematic history of US–Norwegian intelligence co-operation in the 1950s. The failure of the US properly to inform Norwegian political authorities about the U-2 operation was not an isolated incident, and the US concern about Norwegian reactions must be understood against the background of a similar lack of consultation in the past.

On 4 December 1952 Norwegian authorities reported US aircraft over Norwegian territory without prior clearance. The aircraft involved, a KB-29 and an RB-45 based at Lakenheath, were configured for SIGINT operations. The RB-45 was sighted at intervals near Stavanger, Trondheim, Bodø and Harstad, and caused a Norwegian west-coast alert. The Commanding General of the 7th US Air Division in Britain, to which the aircraft belonged, informed Curtis LeMay that the Norwegian Foreign Ministry was "considering a formal protest in view [of] *previous violations*."[81] In a later despatch, the Commanding General reported that the US air attaché in Oslo believed he could "prevent a formal complaint provided he admits that the aircraft involved were USAF aircraft and commits us not to repeat the infringement."[82] In the spring of 1954 US reconnaissance aircraft again violated Norwegian air space without prior clearance in connection with radarscope and visual photography missions over the Kola Peninsula.[83] The State Department subsequently acknowledged that "a few unauthorised" missions had transgressed Norwegian air space.[84] In early October 1957 a U-2 mission launched from Giebelstadt into the Barents Sea again violated Norwegian air space, resulting in an official Norwegian protest. Later, in the same month, the Chief of the Norwegian Air Force informed the Minister of Defence that an unidentified aircraft had been reported on a radar screen in South Norway.[85] The aircraft, approaching from the south at an altitude of 60 000 feet, could not be intercepted and must either have been a U-2 or possibly a British Canberra, which was also capable of reaching this operating altitude.

Several factors, some of which were alluded to in Chapter Two, made it inevitable that the kind of incidents and friction referred to above would occur. These included: the lack of congressional or any other form of oversight; the very powerful position of service intelligence branches before the establishment of the DIA, and, finally, the state of technology for technical intelligence gathering in the 1950s. Related to this was, of course, the "cult of intelligence permissiveness" so characteristic of the "Allen Dulles era."[86] And, although Eisenhower was acutely aware of the political dangers involved, he nonetheless felt the operations he had sanctioned and encouraged were necessary. Intelligence-gathering activities, such as the U-2 operations between 1956 and 1960, were, as he put it in a press conference on 11 May 1960, "a distasteful but vital necessity."[87]

Signs of US Concern about Soviet Pressure on Norway in the Wake of the Incident

Although the State Department and the President fully appreciated the difficulties which the incidents had caused for Soviet–Norwegian relations and the need, therefore, to rebuild confidence in Norway's "low-tension" policy, senior State Department officials did voice their concern about the consequences of continued Soviet pressure for a narrowing of Norwegian policy on bases. Expressions of concern by the State Department followed the re-emergence of the issue of airfield construction on Svalbard. On 26 October 1960 the Soviet Government issued another note of protest to the Norwegian Government about the existence of "definite plans ... for the construction of a number of aerodromes on Spitsbergen."[88] The protest cited British and Norwegian press reports in September 1960 on the activities and "real motives" of a Norwegian-led scientific expedition to the island in the summer of 1959. According to the Soviet note, the expedition, "largely financed by Americans," had "carried out a broad survey of the possibilities of building aerodromes on the Spitsbergen archipelago with landing strips of up to 3000 metres and capable of receiving modern heavy jet bombers."[89] The note appeared to be based specifically on an article in the *Daily Express* of 22 September 1960, which described "secret plans for the construction of six aerodromes ... worked out for the Arctic Institute of North America." Through the intermediary of Colonel Joseph O. Fletcher, who became head of the Air Force section of MAAG Norway in the late 1950s, the Arctic Institute of America had indeed provided funds for a research trip on the island.[90] Reporting on the incident before the North Atlantic Council on 9 November, the acting Norwegian representative, Ulstein, confirmed that a Norwegian expedition financed by the Arctic Institute of the United States had visited the island, but that the Norwegian Government had not been informed that among the expedition's objectives was the exploration of possible airfield sites.[91] Ulstein added that the Norwegian Chief of Staff was in any event strongly opposed to the construction of airfields since in war "they would be a present to the Soviet Air Force."[92]

In late November ambassador Koht in Washington reported that the US was following Norwegian declarations about "our base policy with the greatest interest." Particular attention had been given to the reply following the latest Soviet protest regarding Svalbard. He had gained the impression that senior State Department officials were now concerned lest the:

> declarations given by our side in response to repeated Soviet enquiries about our base policy, can lead us into a situation where the government is tied in its relations to the Soviet Union to a far greater degree than was originally envisaged...
>
> The Americans admit that the Norwegian declarations have not gone beyond the very first statements on base policy, but they are nonetheless concerned that the Soviet Union, by repeatedly forcing new reassurances from the Norwegians, are achieving what they intend to achieve: frequent repetitions can easily give a declaration a more contractual character than its form would suggest.[93]

These concerns were in fact shared by the Norwegian Foreign Ministry, and they did not signify any American critique of the base policy *per se*.

The lack of evidence suggesting American pressure for a change of Norwegian policy and the efforts put into repairing relations after the incidents in 1960, must also be seen in the context of a broader set of considerations which the State Department brought to its analysis of US–Norwegian relations.

III   SOURCES OF US POLICY TOWARDS NORWAY

In April 1960 the NSC Planning Board emphasised the need for the US to "make every effort to ensure the continued availability ... of military facilities on the territory of Denmark and Norway."[94] With this objective in mind the administration was naturally anxious not to encourage, by its own action, *domestic political* or *regional* developments that might endanger existing ties to these countries. The State Department appears to have appreciated this demand for sensitivity in relations with Norway in two respects. First, it was recognised that "isolationist and neutralist sentiment" was a still potent force in Norwegian political culture and that it might be fuelled by fear of nuclear war, nationalism, and negative reactions to US leadership. "The tradition of neutrality," a State Department study in 1955 observed, exerts a "continuing impact on public thinking in Norway."[95] American concerns centred specifically on the attempts of the Soviet Union to exploit this tradition, which was assumed to be especially prominent within sections of the ruling Labour Party. Second, and not unrelated, the State Department gradually came to appreciate that there was an interdependence of security policy orientations within the Nordic region which it was in the US interest to preserve. More specifically, it was recognised that the "delicate balance of Soviet–Finnish relations"[96] was related *both* to Sweden's status as a neutral nation and to the degree of military integration which Norway and Denmark were prepared to accept within the Western Alliance.

The Fear of "Neutralism" After the Geneva Summit

The attitudes of the Eisenhower administration towards *neutralism* have been reassessed by scholars working on the Eisenhower presidency.[97] In a detailed study of both the Truman and Eisenhower administrations, W.H. Brands argues that "American policy, as distinct from the rhetoric in which that policy was sometimes shrouded, demonstrated a pragmatic ability to deal with neutralism on its merits."[98] Brands thus rejects earlier simplified assessments, particularly those dealing with John Foster Dulles's views on the subject.[99] Brands' work, however, concentrates largely on the Third World and no comparable study has been made of US attitudes towards neutralism in Europe.

The significant easing of international tension in the spring of 1955, culminating in the Geneva Summit in late July, provided a strong impetus for the US to assess the potential influence of the various "currents of neutralism" in Western Europe. Growing high-level concern about the strength of "neutralist attitudes" and Soviet attempts to foster dissension among allies can be seen in the annual revisions of the Basic National Security Papers from the period. In early January 1955, NSC 5501 stated that

> The Soviet leaders have almost certainly regarded their "peace offensive" as their most important effective present tactic for dividing the free world and isolating the US from its allies.[100]

The revised paper, approved by the President in March 1956, was far more specific, arguing that

> In 1955 Communist tactics against the free nations shifted in emphasis from reliance on violence and the threat of violence to reliance on

division, enticement and duplicity ... They are seeking to use to their advantage the greater prestige and acceptance among the family of nations which resulted from the Summit Conference and thus overcome the stigma of Godless barbarism which they have borne in varying degree ever since the Russian revolution.[101]

Indicative of US concern in 1955 was also a lengthy report about neutralism in Europe produced by the State Department on the assumption that it was now a subject deserving "careful and continuing attention by US policy makers."[102] The first problem was how to *define* "neutralism" for purposes of policy-making. Distinguishing it from "neutrality" and "neutralization," the report defined it as any attitude which involved "a disinclination to cooperate with US objectives in the cold war and in a possible hot war combined with either a similar disinclination or, at worst, a hesitation to go so far as to cooperate with USSR objectives."[103] It was stressed that this was a broad definition, which in practical terms embraced such diverse manifestations as "third-force thinking, passive resistance to international commitments, support of non-alliance policies, egocentric nationalism and similar influences that impede or inhibit co-operation with the US."[104] It was also emphasised that policy had to take account of the many forms and shadings which neutralism assumed in different countries. Ultimately, however, the growth of neutralism and its "ability to attain major political influence" would depend on the degree to which "communist strategy gives priority to stimulating and exploiting neutralism."[105]

What, then, about US perceptions of "neutralist" sentiments in Norway? In a despatch from Oslo to the State Department in July 1955, ambassador Corrin Strong referred to the "co-existence blandishments of the Soviet Union."[106] Following a visit to Norway shortly after the Geneva summit, Dr Gabriel Hauge wrote to the President and told him that the Russians were now "actively wooing the Norwegians."[107] Hauge, who was personally close to Eisenhower and his foremost economic adviser at the time, told the President that the US

> must not make the mistake of thinking friendly Norway is always and forever in the bag. If the Russians are successful in their efforts, Norway's contribution to NATO could be affected.[108]

The following year the MAAG Mission Chief's programme review for Norway recommended that present objectives be changed with a greater emphasis on combating the Soviet "charm" offensive.[109] Ambassador Willis also stressed the importance of taking measures that would "counter the Russian offensive in Norway."[110]

Both Hauge's and Willis's remarks must be seen against the background of a significant shift of style in Soviet foreign policy towards Norway, which was symbolised by the official Soviet coverage of Gerhardsen's first visit to Moscow in November 1955.[111] Emphasis was now placed on the promotion of "good neighbourly" relations to be further developed on a bilateral basis.[112] This shift in policy formed part of a more general reappraisal of the Soviet Union's external relations following Khrushchev's consolidation of power and Malenkov's removal as Chairman of the Council of Ministers in February 1955.[113] An important aspect of this "new line" was the reassessment of "neutrality" which came to be described, not as a retrograde phenomenon, but as a "positive force, creating a zone of peace between the two blocs."[114] The signing of the Austrian State Treaty in May 1955 and the Soviet "neutrality campaign" in Scandinavia in 1955–56 were both expressions of the change in Soviet thinking.[115]

The decision by the Icelandic parliament in March 1956 to re-examine the Defence Agreement with the US was widely seen as the first victory of Soviet "new look" tactics, and "evidence of the effectiveness of Soviet propaganda about the relaxation of international tension."[116] According to the *Washington Post*, the "seeming defection" of Iceland was the "direct result of the 'summit' conference at Geneva."[117] According to the *New York Herald Tribune* the significance of the Althing resolution went far beyond the value of the base itself. It involved the "psychological question of the precedent such a withdrawal could set for other NATO powers, especially Norway and Denmark" which had been under "particularly intensive Soviet pressure to reduce, and indeed eliminate, NATO commitments."[118]

Similarly, Soviet policies in the Baltic area were seen by the US as a deliberate and calculated attempt to encourage "neutralist sentiment" in Norway and Denmark. In 1958 a report by ONI argued that the most important Soviet aims, in sponsoring the "Baltic Sea of Peace Campaign" in 1957–58, were twofold. First, it hoped to weaken Danish and Norwegian ties to NATO. Secondly, a parallel aim was the extension of neutrality in northern Europe. The ONI study concluded:

> By using Finland as an example, the USSR has tried to persuade Denmark and Norway of the advantages of neutralism ... The achievement of an enhanced degree of [Soviet] co-operation with Scandinavia would also give the USSR an effective talking point for efforts elsewhere to encourage neutralism and weaken collective defence efforts.[119]

The State Department was principally concerned, however, about "forms of neutralist expression ... relating to political activities and affecting governmental policies."[120] In the case of Norway, the subject of concern was the possible challenges to Lange's Atlanticism emanating from within the ruling Labour Party. Opposition to Lange's line was initially most prominent within the Parliamentary Labour party and among a relatively small circle of intellectuals, many of whom were associated with a fortnightly journal, "Orientering" (Orientation), which began to appear in 1952–53.[121] But from 1955 onwards, friction emerged within the party leadership itself, that is, between Halvard Lange at the Foreign Ministry and Prime Minister Gerhardsen and his key advisers, most notably Andreas Andersen, in the Prime Minister's Office.[122] The publication of Konrad Nordahl's diaries throws an interesting light on emerging tensions within the Labour Party leadership on the subject of foreign and defence policy after 1955. Nordahl was leader of the Confederation of Trade Unions (Landsorganisasjonen) from 1945 to 1965. Along with Party Secretary Haakon Lie, he belonged to the "right" of the Party on foreign policy issues. He was a strong and loyal supporter of Halvard Lange and, as his diaries demonstrate, he displayed a similar concern about the evolution of Gerhardsen's views about the Soviet Union.[123] The tension between Lange and Gerhardsen – the first signs of which were reflected in disagreements over the timing and purpose of Gerhardsen's visit to Moscow in 1955 – stemmed from basic differences in both background and outlook.[124] And these came out most clearly in connection with preparations for Gerhardsen's address at NATO's first Heads of State and Government meeting in Paris in December 1957. The NATO summit was widely seen as a response to the Sputnik launches and the associated Soviet propaganda campaign in the autumn of 1957. Both Eisenhower and Foster Dulles viewed the meeting as a response to "the continuing and increasingly menacing attitude of the Soviet Union."[125] They felt it was necessary therefore to "reaffirm Atlantic solidarity."[126] The meeting was also crucial in another respect. The US was to announce plans for the deployment of MRBMs in Europe and the creation of a NATO atomic stockpile.[127]

Having put aside a more cautious Foreign Ministry draft, Einar Gerhardsen in his address reaffirmed Norwegian base policy, ruled out the stationing of MRBMs in Norway and said his government had no plans about establishing atomic storage sites on its territory. Furthermore, Gerhardsen suggested that disengagement proposals aimed at thinning out forces in central Europe (such as the Rapacki plan) should be given more sustained consideration. He also expressed the opinion that the decision to deploy MRBMs ought to be delayed until the prospect for negotiations had been explored more fully.[128] Although the speech had been slightly modified, Lange "did not care very much for it" since the impression given was that "a new and personal bridge-building policy" was now being pursued by the Norwegian Prime Minister.[129] It was, above all, the tone and timing of Gerhardsen's address which upset Foreign Ministry officials.

What about the US reactions to Gerhardsen's speech? At the NSC meeting convened to discuss the issues to be decided at the December meeting, John Foster Dulles had foreseen political opposition among opposition parties in Europe as a "real danger."[130] The *significance*, however, which Dulles and Eisenhower attached to Gerhardsen's Paris speech is more difficult to assess, even though the address was widely interpreted as having made a strong impact. Nordahl recorded in his diary that it "had caused a great stir and was viewed by many as a sign that Norway was on its way out of NATO, adopting instead a neutralistic attitude like that of Sweden."[131] According to Drew Middleton of the *New York Times*, writing on 18 December:

> The exposure of political weaknesses on the Northern Flank of the Atlantic alliance was regarded today by military and diplomatic sources as perhaps the gravest development of the North Atlantic Council meeting.[132]

Middleton reported further that political sources in the US delegation feared the "encouragement of strong neutralist forces in both countries [Denmark and Norway] as a consequence of the attitude taken by their delegations."[133] According to William H. Stoneman, a former secretary to Trygve Lie at the UN writing in the *Philadelphia Inquirer*, Gerhardsen had "scared the daylights out of American officials" with his speech in Paris.[134] Although there is little evidence to support Stoneman's bombastic assertion, it is reasonable to assume that Gerhardsen's speech reinforced existing concerns about the potential strength of opposition in Norway to closer Allied integration.[135] This view is also supported by isolated reports after 1957.

In a State Department background paper for NATO's Ministerial meeting the following year, "political problem areas" included

> Certain other countries (particularly Norway, Denmark and Canada) [which] may call for revisions of certain NATO policies which they feel have hindered relaxation of tensions and for greater efforts in the disarmament field.[136]

In early 1959 Dulles, in a letter to Selwyn Lloyd, expressed his deep concern about Soviet attempts to weaken the alliance by encouraging divisions among its members. In particular, he saw:

> very great danger for our alliance in the Soviet device of writing simultaneous letters to our several members and getting separate replies, with the inevitable divergencies which the Soviets can exploit.[137]

Some months later, a study by the State Department Bureau of Intelligence and Research of pressures for disengagement in Western Europe pointed out that while many Norwegians might no longer profess the same faith in "formulas of neutralization," there was still a "favorable disposition toward the principle of disengagement because of widespread anti-militaristic and neutralistic sentiments" in all three of the Nordic NATO countries.[138] A year later the NSC Planning Board recommended that US policy towards Scandinavia should "stress the danger to Scandinavian and Free World security of unilaterally neutralizing or demilitarizing Scandinavia."[139]

It would clearly be an exaggeration to argue that US concern about the resurgence of isolationist and neutralist sentiment was the sole, or even principal, determinant of US sensitivity regarding Norway. Nonetheless, the State Department in 1955 did assume that "neutralism" was exerting a "considerable influence upon present governmental policies," and this factor had to be taken into account by US policy makers. Moreover, as indicated earlier, the perception of Norway as having a "determining influence" on Danish and Icelandic alliance policies gave added significance to developments within Norway. The available evidence also makes it clear that the State Department was keenly aware of the domestic and party-political constraints in which Norwegian foreign and defence policies were formulated.[140] Back in August 1952 Trygve Lie had told US and UK ambassadors that although Oscar Torp, Gerhardsen and Lange "understood clearly the need for foreign troops," they also felt that to grant base rights for tactical aircraft might split the Labour Party. Hence, they felt that "the possible loss of party control was too high a price to pay for the base."[141] The State Department country study of neutralism in Norway in 1955 emphasised that effective opposition to adequate Norwegian defence measures, which was described as the foremost expression of neutralist sentiment, was concentrated within the Labour Party itself.[142] At the Northern European Chiefs of Mission Conference in London, held before the Paris meeting, Frances Willis indicated that "pacifism and neutralism remains a latent force in Norway, particularly in the Labour Party."[143]

US Understanding of the "Nordic balance"

The pressures which US officials exerted for base rights in Denmark and Norway in 1952 suggests little consideration for possible regional implications of the deployment of Allied units in Scandinavia. Precisely this point was made by Trygve Lie in the aforementioned meeting with US and UK ambassadors. Lie stated that "Sweden would prefer that Norway not permit foreign troops on its territory in peace, since Sweden would not care to see Russian defences pushed any closer to its territory."[144] Between 1954 and 1960 Norwegian officials impressed upon their US counterparts – both in private discussion and openly – that the self-imposed limitations on Norway's policy did serve the wider purpose of preserving regional stability and a low level of tension. In an address at Chatham House in March 1954, Halvard Lange said that the principal consideration behind the Norwegian base policy was that the "stationing of allied units in Norway might cause a heavy strain, not only on Norwegian–Soviet relations but also on the relationship between the Soviet Union and the Atlantic Alliance as a whole."[145] He went on, however, to point out that

> The Norwegian Government maintains in particular that the permanent stationing of allied units on the Scandinavian peninsula might provoke increasing Soviet pressure on Finland, and possibly occupation of Finnish bases near the Norwegian and Swedish borders, a development which would not only seriously impair the strategic position of both Norway and Sweden, but also cause a serious deterioration of the international situation in general.[146]

Whilst Norway fully recognised the objections which could be raised against the policy from a "purely military point of view," Lange insisted that political considerations were of "overriding importance."[147]

A study of NSC papers on US policy towards Finland between 1954 and 1960 suggests that the US did come to appreciate the security linkages in the region. The first NSC policy paper dealing exclusively with Finland, NSC 5403, in January 1954, emphasised the need for the US to "avoid any steps which could threaten the delicate balance of Finnish–Soviet relations and call forth drastic measures inimical to Finnish independence."[148] The paper did not, however, specify which "steps" might upset the balance. In a revised policy paper, presented to the President in October 1959, Finland was described as "an unwilling pawn in Soviet efforts to demonstrate the virtues of 'peaceful co-existence' and to weaken Scandinavian ties with the west."[149] It was also recognised that any drastic

Soviet move, either militarily or politically, against Finland would probably force Sweden into closer co-operation with the West and even with
NATO.[150] Again, one should be careful not to exaggerate the importance
of these considerations on US policy. Nonetheless, although it is difficult
to determine the precise impact of these considerations, by 1960 the NSC
certainly recognised the interdependence of security postures in Northern
Europe:

> Scandinavian policy toward Finland seems to be based on acceptance of
> the status quo in which Swedish neutrality is balanced off against
> Finnish neutrality. Desire not to provoke Soviet reaction on Finland,
> undoubtedly is a factor in Swedish neutrality and Scandinavian caution
> in building up offensive military strength. Conversely, Soviet restraint
> with respect to Finland may reflect a desire not to push Sweden into
> NATO or to accelerate Scandinavian military preparations.[151]

Conclusion

It has been argued in this chapter that US attitudes towards and basic
acceptance of Norway's "low tension policy" (*lavspenningspolitikk*)
stemmed from different sources.

There was, after 1952–53, no US interest in acquiring permanent bases
in Norway. In part, this was because US operational requirements could be
accommodated within the framework of the self-imposed restrictions laid
down by the Norwegian government in 1951. Although greater Norwegian
flexibility in terms of facilitating the peacetime use of Norwegian airfields
was seen as desirable, there was no US "pressure" for the Norwegian
authorities to change their declared policy concerning the stationing of
foreign armed forces on their territory. The evidence indicates that the US
Navy accepted and adhered to the restrictions imposed on its operations
involving Norwegian territory. Nevertheless, a distinction should be drawn
between an evolving pattern of *regular* peacetime military activities, on
the one hand, and intelligence operations on the other. Between 1954 and
1960, intelligence co-operation – as the U-2 and RB-47 incidents illustrate – remained the single most problematic aspect of US–Norwegian
bilateral security relations.

With respect to Norway's "nuclear ban" policy enunciated by
Gerhardsen in Paris in 1957, the first thing to note is that the US *never*
regarded Norway as a potential site for the deployment of MRBMs.[152] As
for the construction of atomic storage sites in Norway, US and British military officials – including Generals Norstad, Twining and CINCNORTH,

Sir Cecil Sugden – certainly did emphasise the importance, especially to the defence of North Norway, of incorporating nuclear weapons in Norwegian units.[153] But this, as Tamnes has shown, did not amount to US pressure.[154]

Finally, it has been argued that US policy towards Scandinavia as a whole was influenced by a broader set of considerations, though it has been stressed that the precise impact of these considerations is difficult to appraise. Tom Hetland has argued that Soviet policies towards Scandinavia in 1955 were influenced by "Nordic balance" considerations. More specifically, he notes that the Soviet Union, by easing its pressure on Finland in 1955 (allowing Finnish membership of the Nordic Council and returning Porkkala), hoped to strengthen Sweden's position and at the same time boost anti-NATO forces in Norway and Denmark.[155] The fact that the US also appears to have recognised Nordic interdependence in the field of security suggests that a symmetry in the perceptions of the main external powers about security linkages in the region emerged in the 1950s and facilitated the maintenance of low tension in the area.[156]

Conclusion: The US–Norwegian Alliance, 1954–1960

> The full substance and significance of an alliance is seldom revealed in the formal contract or treaty for military co-operation, any more than the essence of marriage is revealed in the marriage certificate.[1]
>
> Robert E. Osgood

NORWAY'S VALUE AS AN ALLY OF THE UNITED STATES

Alignment with the Western powers in 1949 enabled Norway – a country with meagre resources, recently occupied by a foreign power and bordering a major *potential* adversary – to become a "consumer" of the collective good of security.[2] The fact that the "Scandinavian option" represented, in the words of Holst, a "perfectly valid alternative" in terms of association with a political community only demonstrates that Norway's decision to join NATO was more the "result of security calculations than of a commitment to community building."[3] By the early 1950s, the United States had largely replaced Britain as the principal underwriter of Norwegian security. Although the Royal Navy remained actively committed to Norway until Sandys's defence review, the 1950s as a whole saw the "continuation of the trend established in the late 1940s – a shying away by Britain from any serious commitment to the defence of Norway with the United States taking on an increasing burden."[4]

The nature of an alliance relationship involving "small" and "great" powers cannot, however, be understood merely in terms of a dichotomy between consumers and suppliers of security. To view small-power alignment simply as a means of acquiring "drawing rights" on the military capabilities of greater powers overlooks the contribution which a small power can make towards the strategic objectives of the larger power. One difficulty here is that the alliance literature rarely separates "small" states analytically from "weak" states, the result of which has been to focus mainly on the *net* security benefits accruing to small alliance partners.[5] This has obscured the degree to which "strength" and "weakness" are not only related to "size" as an independent variable, but are also influenced by the structure of the international system; the state of weapons technology; the geographic position of the small state; the policies of and the specific role conceptions held by decision-makers in the small state. The interaction of these factors produces an "exchange relationship" even between manifestly unequal powers and may, under certain circumstances, give smaller allies a role disproportionate to the actual distribution of material and political resources in the alliance.[6] As relations between Norway and the US demonstrate, the smaller power may be in a position to lend *political support* and provide *capabilities* and *access* enabling the larger ally to project military power more effectively. Thus, Norway was not only contributing towards the local containment of Soviet power but was also enhancing the overall deterrent posture of the alliance. In addition to this, Holst has pointed to yet another, though less apparent, role which smaller allies may play. In an area of potential great power conflict, small allies may "contribute to the provision of security in a broader context through the engagement in the shaping of a pattern of security."[7] As suggested by this study, the distinctive policies adopted by a smaller power within an alliance may indeed facilitate the maintenance of regional order by encouraging "low tension" and a stable pattern of behaviour on the part of outside powers.

Norway's Role in US Strategic Policies, 1954–60

In light of these considerations, Norway's role in the strategic policies of the US between 1954 and 1960 is apparent in three areas.

(1) By rendering operational support and permitting limited access to its territory, Norway enabled the US Navy, Air Force, and the CIA, to carry out their prescribed roles and missions in a more efficient manner.

(2) By providing political support and playing a "special role" within the Nordic region, Norway allowed the US to consolidate and develop strategically important ties to other powers in the area, above all to Iceland and Denmark.

(3) By adopting a set of unilateral restraints in the realm of military policy, Norway contributed towards a pattern of security in Northern Europe which the US administration *gradually* came to recognise as a source of regional stability.

It is useful to look at each of these three areas in turn and relate them to the questions set out in the introduction to this book.

Operational support

In an attempt to account for "the big influence of small allies," Robert Keohane has identified three distinct "levels of action" through which small powers have sought to influence US foreign policy. Although Keohane classifies Norway as a "loyal ally" thereby excluding it from his analysis, the distinction he draws between the various levels at which relations are maintained between the US and its allies, highlights an important and neglected aspect of bilateral security relationships involving the US during the Cold War.[8] One of the levels examined by Keohane – informal bargaining with separate elements of the US government – points to a central feature of US–Norwegian relations in the 1950s.[9] According to Keohane, a small states' representative:

> may try to develop close working relationships with interested sub-units of the US Government, appealing to the Army, Navy, or Air Force, the CIA or AID. Co-operation may be implicit as well as explicit; but in either case, common interests – in bases, military strength, aid programs or intelligence information – are the ties that bind. The success of the strategy is determined largely by the extent to which the American Government agencies are dependent on the small ally for the performance of their missions.[10]

According to Keohane, it follows from this that the "over-all dependence of the small ally on the United States is reversed" in so far as CIA and the Defence Department is concerned.[11] This, he adds, is "particularly true for the Navy and Air Force, which require bases, overflight rights and port of call privileges abroad."[12] The book has emphasised three interrelated areas where these "sub-units of the US Government" saw themselves as "dependent" on Norwegian co-operation "for the performance of their missions."

The first of these was Norway's role in providing basic and current intelligence on military and scientific developments in the Soviet Union. Second, Norway served as an early-warning outpost for *direct strategic* threats against the North American continent during a period which Admiral Arleigh Burke described as "an era of national preoccupation with the threat of Soviet surprise attack."[13] Finally, there was, from late 1954 onwards, the ever growing importance of Norway in US maritime strategy, including the provision of infrastructure facilities to support the operational deployment of the first generation of US nuclear-fuelled ballistic missile submarines. By the end of the decade, Norway had also acquired a key role in the nuclear-oriented ASW strategy of the US Navy.[14]

Norway's significance in each of these areas resulted from the interplay between geography and rapidly changing military technologies occurring within a bipolar context of intense ideological rivalry. Erling Bjøl has noted that *geography* has been neglected as an analytical category in attempts to explain the "power of the weak" in international relations.[15] Geographic location alone, however, is not necessarily a source of small power strength. Instead, the broader notion of a country's "general security geography" should be seen as a dynamic factor shaped by the political constellations between great powers, technological developments and geographic position in the system.[16] That Norway's value to the US was crucially determined precisely by these factors is clearly evident throughout the 1950s. The fear of surprise attack which gave Norway such a key role in the realm of early warning and intelligence gathering, stemmed in part from the state of nuclear and ballistic missile technology which in the 1950s appeared to place a premium of first strike options. Rapid technological advances in other areas – most notably the advent of nuclear propulsion for submarines – also decisively influenced Norway's place in American strategic calculations. The impact of the interaction between technology and geography on Norway's position in US strategy, is also apparent when one considers two developments at the end of the period covered by this study. First, the emergence of dependable photo-satellite reconnaissance systems in 1960–61 reduced the significance of Norway's geographic location as far as the US strategic reconnaissance programme was concerned. As a result, operations involving Norway in the 1960s became less "provocative" than they had been under Eisenhower.[17] Second, with the acquisition of a secure second strike capability, achieved partly through deployment in northern waters of the Polaris submarines, the US relaxed its overriding concern about the threat of a surprise attack.

Political support

As indicated above, Norway's role in US strategic policy was not only a function of its geography. The State Department and the NSC also attached importance to securing political support from Norway in international organisations and fora where it "could stand up and be counted" as a supporter of American policies.[18] Even more important to the administration was the "special role" which Norway played within the Nordic region. In view of the critical priority which the Eisenhower administration attached to maintaining bases and facilities on Greenland and Iceland, the *perception* of Norway as having a determining influence on Danish and Icelandic alliance policies added significantly to Norway's importance as an ally. The administration also encouraged the development of close "functional ties" between Norway and Sweden; ties which it hoped would strengthen the overall defence posture of the Western Alliance and facilitate closer US – Swedish collaboration in the areas of defence and intelligence.[19] In all this, Norway's strong commitment to an "Atlanticist" foreign policy in the 1950s, personified in the attitudes of Halvard Lange, served as an "ideological factor" reinforcing US perceptions about Norway's value as an ally. However, in terms of explaining the strength of US – Norwegian alliance ties in the period, "ideological similarity" or the "commitment to shared values" was not a major determinant.[20] This is also borne out by the fact that the documentary record and interviews indicate that Norwegian decision-makers and military officials still felt "politically and ideologically" much closer to Great Britain. Reporting on Lord Alexander's visit to Norway in 1954, the British Commander of Allied Naval Forces in Northern Europe captured Norwegian sentiments when he wrote that his "impression" was that "if the gale is going to blow, the Norwegians would like a sheet anchor down in England".[21] Norwegian attitudes in the 1950s were still powerfully influenced by the legacy of wartime co-operation, a fact which was recognised by US officials. In 1955, a US Navy brief on a forthcoming visit by the Chief of the Norwegian Navy, Admiral Johannes Jacobsen, observed:

> It is suspected that any leaning he may have might be more toward England than toward America largely due to his association and contacts with the British Navy during and since the last war.[22]

These Norwegian attitudes persisted throughout the 1950s, even though the British COS displayed a very limited interest in the defence of Norway and the US had become the principal external guarantor of Norwegian security.[23]

Regional security
The third area identified above in which Norway's role as a small ally should be assessed was the part it played in shaping a pattern of regional security in Northern Europe by balancing policies of deterrence and reassurance vis-a-vis the Soviet Union. It is difficult on the basis of available evidence to say how much *direct* influence Norway's role in this respect had on US policy making towards Norway. It is clear, however, that certainly by 1960, the NSC recognised that the reservations which Norway had placed on its alliance membership were part of a wider pattern of mutual restraint observed in the Nordic region. Attitudes to Norway's unilateral policies of restraint were thus partly based on the understanding that major changes in the balance of external influences bearing on the

region might generate instability and provoke compensatory Soviet pressures.

The ever closer relationship which developed between the US and Norway during this period raises two further questions. In the first place, what role did the Alliance framework play in the development of bilateral ties between Norway and the US? Secondly, what was the place of Norway in US nuclear strategy, and to what extent was declaratory policy at odds with operational activities given the centrality of nuclear weapons in American and allied planning in this period?

NATO as a Legitimising Framework for Bilateral Co-operation

For the US administration, NATO provided a multilateral framework for bilateral collaboration with Norway in areas deemed to be of particular significance to the US. This was recognised by the NSC, whose "major" policy recommendations in April 1960 included an emphasis on the need "to ensure the continued availability to the United States of military facilities located on the territory of ... Norway, utilizing to this end our NATO relationship with them."[24] Several projects in the 1950s illustrate this. The Forward Scatter communications system established in Norway was funded by the US to support "allied" air operations in the North European theatre. The system, however, was also considered by US authorities to be vitally important for relaying current intelligence and early warning information of possible air attack directed towards the North American continent. The Loran-A stations at Jan Mayen, Bø and Bjugn, built under Slice Five of NATO's infrastructure programme, were designed primarily to support US fleet operations in the North Atlantic. Similarly, the negotiations on pre-D-day construction of facilities and access for US naval aircraft to airfields in North Norway were conducted under the formal auspices of SACLANT, even though the operational requirements were drawn up by the Strategic Plans Division and the Chief of Naval Operations in Washington.

NATO's role as a collective framework for co-operation with US services and agencies was of even greater importance to Norwegian authorities. Here, the Alliance offered a broader context in which bilateral arrangements of a politically sensitive nature could be worked out. Reporting on discussions with Norwegian government officials about "the question of SAC and TAC air requirements in Norway" in 1952, the head of the Navy's Foreign Military Rights Branch observed that the "implications were carefully considered by the Norwegians who felt some form of relationship to SHAPE and NATO planning should be shown."[25] The statement is indicative of Norwegian concerns but also illustrates how these could be assuaged by placing bilateral arrangements within a multilateral framework. These considerations indicate an additional *function* of alliances other than the aggregation of power and the promotion of international order.[26]

Norway and US Nuclear Strategy: Declaratory versus Operational Levels of Policy

The outstanding feature of US military policy in the period between 1954 and 1960 was preparation for the employment of nuclear weapons in the widest possible range of wartime contingencies.[27] Although by late 1957 the premises of the New Look were widely seen to have been undermined, the "massive retaliation idea", as Bernard Brodie wrote in 1959, had become the "basic orientation of American defence policy."[28] Even the US Navy, which after 1957 showed most concern about limited war scenarios in areas such as North Norway, continued to emphasise nuclear responses in the event of war.

It has traditionally been argued, if only implicitly, that by adopting a "non-nuclear policy" in the 1950s, Norway was able effectively to dissociate itself and remain separate from the nuclear dimension of US strategy.[29] Even with respect to the 1950s Tamnes argues that Norway "never attained an important role in US and British nuclear war plans."[30] It certainly is true that Norway rejected the permanent stationing in peacetime of both MRBMs and tactical nuclear weapons on its territory.[31] However, merely to focus on these two categories obscures the fact that, at the *operational* level, Norway's role in American strategy inevitably involved a nuclear dimension. In December 1954 Norway, along with all other NATO countries, formally accepted the "necessity and desirability of basing NATO military plans and preparations on the concept that an effective atomic capability is indispensable to a maximum deterrent and essential to defence in Western Europe."[32] With allied acceptance of the New Look as the basis for Western defence planning, a nuclear orientation was built into the NATO force structure which became ever more pronounced as the decade wore on.[33] Under these circumstances, the distinction between facilities designed to support *only* conventional as opposed to nuclear operations is an artificial one, especially with regard to non-strategic operations.[34] For the US Navy and Air Force to carry out their operational tasks in Northern Europe, a high degree of integration was required to ensure effective communications, command and control of forces. There can be little doubt that the operations which this integration was designed to support were overwhelmingly nuclear in nature. The Loran-A stations and shore-based communications facilities were built to support Strike Fleet operations in northern waters, and the Loran-C stations were considered "essential" to the Polaris mission. The scatter communication system constructed in Norway was designed to support "atomic strike co-ordination and control." Towards the end of the decade, the US Atlantic Fleet was utilising air control and reporting systems in Norway for routing tactical bombing aircraft to forward directors. In addition to this, the 1950s saw the "integration of warning and intelligence with nuclear forces," a development which arose "out of the need to establish control over the operating environment in which these weapons found themselves."[35]

It does not follow from this, however, that extensive co-operation at the operational level invalidates the importance of *declaratory* policy which has as its aim political and psychological effects.[36] There are two considerations here. In the first place, co-operation at the operational level was usually conducted in secrecy, and details about the *precise* role of Norwegian facilities in US plans necessarily remained highly classified. Second, as indicated above, it is important to distinguish between the *functions* of declaratory and operational policy. Whereas operational policy was geared towards maximising military effectiveness in the event of conflict, Norway's declaratory policy was aimed both at the *external* and *domestic* environment. Domestically, declaratory policy was designed to reassure those elements within Norway, especially inside the ruling Labour Party, which remained sceptical of too close an association with the US in the realm of military policy. In the 1950s the Norwegian government did indeed succeed in preserving a broad domestic consensus on matters of defence and security.[37] In its external dimension, declaratory policy was intended to *reassure* the Soviet Union about the defensive character of the US–Norwegian alliance. The unilateral measures of restraint and confidence-building and the official commitment to a "low tension policy" contributed towards this objective. As for the attitudes of the Soviet Union towards Norway's security policy, especially its role in American strategy, a more definitive judgement must await a study of the Soviet archives.[38]

When, in 1949, Norway was invited to join the Atlantic Alliance, there were those in the US, including most prominently John Foster Dulles and George F. Kennan, who questioned the wisdom of incorporating whole or parts of Scandinavia into the Western collective defence system. In 1949, the strategic rationale for bringing Norway into the alliance was seen to lie almost exclusively in the *denial value* of its membership. By 1960, however, the political and strategic value of Norwegian membership was no longer questioned by the US administration. Indeed, there can be little doubt that Norway had come to assume an important, albeit in many areas a discreet and indirect, role in US strategic policy as a result of the developments explored in this book.

Notes

INTRODUCTION

1. John L. Gaddis, *Strategies of Containment: A Critical Appraisal of Post-War American National Security Policy* (Oxford: Oxford University Press, 1982), p. 4.
2. E.M. Earle, ed., *Makers of Modern Strategy* (Princeton: Princeton University press, 1971), p. viii.
3. For a collection of the Basic National Security Policy papers under Eisenhower, see Marc Trachtenberg, ed., *The Development of American Strategic Thought: Basic Documents from the Eisenhower and Kennedy Periods* (New York: Garland Publishing, Inc. 1988). For NSC 162/2, see pp. 35–67.
4. JCS 2101/113, Enclosure "A" Military Strategy to Support National Security Policy Set Forth in NSC 162/2, 10 December 1953, ccs 381 US(1-31-50) sec. 32 JCS (Geographic File) 1954–56, Box 2, Rg. 218, NARA, and Gaddis, *Strategies of Containment*, pp. 148–150. For an excellient account and analysis of the administration's approach to national security policy see Gaddis, *Strategies of Containment*, chapters 5 and 6.
5. Gaddis, *Strategies of Containment*, p. 146.
6. Ole Holsti, T. Hopmann and J. Sullivan, *Unity and Disintegration in International Alliances: Comparative Studies* (New York: John Wiley & Sons, 1973), especially chapter one. See also Erling Bjøl, "The Power of the Weak," *Cooperation and Conflict* 3, (1968).
7. Geir Lundestad, *America, Scandinavia and the Cold War 1945–1949* (New York: Columbia University Press, 1980), p. 338.
8. Helge Pharo and Knut E. Eriksen, *Norsk sikkerhetspolitikk som etterkrigshistorisk forskningsfelt* (Bergen: LOS-senter Notat 92/13), p. 41. Certain aspects of Norway's relationship to the US have been subject to scrutiny. A good example is provided by Gleditsch's work on the military importance of radio navigation aids in Norway. See Owen Wilkes and Nils P. Gleditsch, *Loran-C and Omega: A Study of the Military Importance of Radio Navigation Aids* (Oslo: Norwegian University Press, 1987).
9. Rolf Tamnes, *The United States and the Cold War in the High North* (Oslo: Ad Notam, 1991). See also "Doktordisputas, 12 oktober 1991, på avhandlingen *The United States and the Cold War in the High North*," *Historisk Tidsskrift* 2 (1992).
10. Lundestad, *America, Scandinavia and the Cold War,* p. 346. See also Dean Acheson, *Present at the Creation: My years in the State Department* (New York: Norton & Company Inc., 1969), pp. 277–279.
11. Memorandum of Conversation, 26 May 1960, Staff Notes May 1960(1), Box 50, DDE Diary Series, Papers of Dwight D. Eisenhower as President, DDEL, and letter to author from Harold E. Stassen, 15 April 1991.

12. Memorandum for the President, 3 March 1953, Norway (3), Box 37, International Series, Papers of Dwight D. Eisenhower as President, and, Briefing Note for NSC Meeting of 1 April 1960, Attachment to Summary of Discussion 439th Mtg of the NSC, Box 12, NSC Series, Papers of Dwight D. Eisenhower as President, DDEL.

13. Gordon Gray, "Organising for Total Defence," *The General Electric Defence Quarterly* 3 (July–September 1960). For a more recent account of the workings of the NSC under Eisenhower, see Anna Kasten Nelson, "The 'Top of Policy Hill': President Eisenhower and the National Security Council," *Diplomatic History* 7 (Fall 1983).

14. NSC, Vol. I Geographical Area Policies (Part VI, Europe, Scandinavia), NSC 121, 1 November 1952, 001028 DDC, 1989. NSC 6006/1, 6 April 1960, NSC 6006/1 Scandinavia, Box 29, NSC Series, Policy Papers Subseries, WHO: Office of Special Assistant for National Security Affairs, DDEL.

15. These include: *Study of Continental Defence for the Interim Subcommittee on Preparedness of the Senate Armed Services Committee by Robert Sprague, February 1954*; *The President's Citizen Advisors on the Mutual Security Programme, 1956 (Fairless Committee)*; *Report to President on United States Overseas Bases, December 1957 (Nash Report)*; *The President's Committee to Study the US Military Assistance Programme, 1958–1959 (The Draper Committee),* and *Review of United States Overseas Military Bases (Lang Report), April 1960,* DDEL.

16. Memorandum for the President, 24 November 1954, Dulles, John Foster Nov.' 54(1), Box 3, Dulles-Herter Series, Papers of Dwight D. Eisenhower as President, DDEL.

17. Paul Nitze, "Atoms, Strategy and Policy", *Foreign Affairs* 34, No. 2, (1956).

18. Ibid., p. 187.

19. In a key article which differentiates explicitly between different "levels" of "strategy" and "decision-making", Rosenberg argues that "nuclear strategy does not, in reality, consist of concepts or even policy statements. It consists of concrete decisions regarding war plans, budgets, forces, and deployments." See David Rosenberg, "Reality and Responsibility: Power and Process in the Making of United States Nuclear Strategy 1945–68," *Journal of Strategic Studies* 9 (March 1986), p. 35.

20. David Rosenberg, "The Origins of Overkill: Nuclear Weapons and American Strategy, 1945–1960," *International Security* 7 (Spring 1983). See also David Rosenberg, "US Nuclear Stockpile 1945 to 1950," *The Bulletin of Atomic Scientists* (May 1982).

21. Martin S. Navias, *Nuclear Weapons and British Strategic Planning, 1955–1958* (Oxford: Clarendon Press, 1991), chapter three.

22. Olav Riste, "Relations Between the Norwegian Government in Exile and the British Government," Paper presented to colloquium on Anglo-Norwegian Relations during the Second World War, Oxford, 25–27 September 1991. Riste's observation was made with reference to the nature of the wartime alliance between Britain and Norway, another alliance relationship between highly "unequal" powers.

23. George Liska, *Nations in Alliance: The Limits of Interdependence* (Baltimore: The Johns Hopkins Press, 1962), pp. 116–117.

24. Ibid.

25. Ibid.
26. Ibid.
27. See discussion in Chapter One.
28. Nitze, "Atoms, Strategy and Policy", p. 188.
29. Johan J. Holst, "The Security Pattern in Northern Europe: A Norwegian Perspective," in *Britain and NATO's Northern Flank,* ed. Geoffrey Till (London: Macmillan Press, 1988).
30. For a comprehensive treatment of these issues, see Rolf Tamnes, "Handlefrihet og lojalitet: Norge og atompolitikken i 1950 årene," in *Historiker og Veileder: Festskrift til Jakob Sverdrup,* eds. H. Pharo and Trond Bergh (Oslo: Tiden Norsk Forlag, 1989).

1   ANGLO–AMERICAN STRATEGIC POLICY AND NORWAY, 1945–54

1. State Department, Policy Statement: Norway, 15 September 1950, File 611.57/9-1550, Rg. 59, NARA.
2. See for example Roald Berg, "'Det land vi venter hjælp af.' England som Norges beskytter 1905–1908," in *Defence Studies IV,* ed. Rolf Tamnes (Oslo: Tano, 1985), and Jens Petter Nielsen, "Ønsket tsaren seg en isfri havn i nord?" *Historisk Tidsskrift,* no. 4; (1991).
3. Olav Riste, "Fra integritetstraktat til atompolitikk: det stormaktsgaranterte Norge, 1905–1983," in *Defence Studies 1983–4,* ed. Rolf Tamnes (Oslo: Tanum-Norli, 1984), p. 42. See also Olav Riste, "Isolationism and Great Power Protection: The Historical Determinants of Norwegian Foreign Policy," *FHFS Notat* 2, 1984 (Oslo: Research Centre for Defence History, 1984), p. 3.
4. Olav Riste, *Isolasjonisme og stormaktsgarantiar* (Oslo: Institutt for Forsvarsstudier, 1991), p. 47.
5. For an account of the development of the government's "Atlantic Policy" see Olav Riste, "The Genesis of North Atlantic Defence Co-operation: Norway's 'Atlantic Policy', 1940–45," in *Defence Studies 1981,* ed. Rolf Tamnes (Oslo: Tanum-Norli, 1982).
6. For the strategic rethinking which lay at the root of the Atlantic policy see Foreign Minister Trygve Lie's article in *The Times* (London), 14 November 1941, entitled "A Community of Nations: Plans for lasting peace after victory."
7. See *Instilling fra Forsvarskommisjonen av 1946, Del 1: Grunnleggende synspunkter og forslag* (Oslo: Arbeidernes Aktietrykkeri, Oktober 1949), p. 67.
8. Ibid., pp. 37–40.
9. Nils Morten Udgaard, *Great Power Politics and Norwegian Foreign Policy: A Study of Norway's Foreign Relations November 1940–February 1948* (Oslo: Universitetsforlaget, 1973), p. 92.
10. Riste, "Isolationism and Great Power Protection," p. 10.
11. St.meld. nr.32, (1945–46) *Plan for en første reisning av Norges Forsvar (Treårsplanen), Stortingsforhandlinger 1945–46, 2.Bind* (my emphasis).

See also Memorandum of Conversation with Norwegian Government and Defence Officials, 13 January 1951, Trips: SHAPE no. 1, Round Robin, Box 201, Dwight D. Eisenhower Pre-Presidential Papers, DDEL.

12. On the issue of functional ties, see Magne Skodvin, *Norden eller NATO? Utenriksdepartementet og alliansespørsmålet, 1947–1949* (Oslo: Universitetsforlaget, 1971), pp. 33–34, and Olav Riste, "Functional ties: a semi-alliance? Military co-operation in north-west Europe 1944–1947," in *Defence Studies*, ed. R. Tamnes (Oslo: Tanum-Norli, 1981), pp. 37–50.

13. Olav Riste, "Was 1949 a turning point? Norway and the Western Powers 1947–50," in *Western Security: The Formative Years*, ed. Olav Riste (Oslo: Universitetsforlaget, 1985), p. 137.

14. Anthony Eden, *The Eden Memoirs: The Reckoning*, Vol. 3 (London: Cassell & Company Ltd., 1965), p. 291. See also *The Diaries of Sir Alexander Cadogen, 1938–45*, ed. David Dilks (London: Cassell, 1971), p. 420.

15. Udgaard, *Great Power Politics and Norwegian Foreign Policy*, p. 41. For an account of Soviet-Norwegian relations during the war, see Sven G. Holtsmark, *The Norwegian Government and the Soviet Union, 1940–1945* (Oslo: Institute for Defence Studies, 1988).

16. Thus in March 1944, Trygve Lie told the Soviet ambassador, Victor Lebedev, that the Norwegian Government was prepared to discuss the issue of letting Norwegian police forces stationed in Sweden participate in the fight against Germany on the Northern Front under Soviet command. On 25 April 1944 the Norwegian Government offered the Soviet Union a treaty similar to that presented to Britain and the United States about the arrangements for civil administration and jurisdiction in the parts of Norway liberated by an Allied expeditionary force.

17. Udgaard, *Great Power Politics and Norwegian Foreign Policy*, pp. 45–46.

18. Daniel Yergin, *Shattered Peace: The Origins of the Cold War and the National Security State* (London: Andre Deutsch Ltd., 1979), p. 9, and John L. Gaddis, "Spheres of Influences: The United States and Europe, 1945–1949," in *The Long Peace: Inquiries into the History of the Cold War* (Oxford: Oxford University Press, 1987), pp. 48–71.

19. Lundestad, *America, Scandinavia, and the Cold War*, p. 43.

20. Ibid., pp. 52–53.

21. *FRUS 1948, Vol. III*, pp. 46–48. The ensuing domestic and intra-Scandinavian debate about Norway's future position in a Western security system and the road to alliance membership have been dealt with elsewhere and need not be recounted here. See particularly Skodvin, *Norden eller NATO? Utenriksdepartementet og alliansespørsmålet, 1947–1949* (Oslo: Universitetsforlaget, 1971); Knut Einar Eriksen, *DNA og NATO: Striden om norsk NATO-medlemskap innen regjeringspartiet, 1948–1949* (Oslo: Gyldendal, 1972); Knut Eriksen and Magne Skodvin, "Storbritannia, NATO og et skandinavisk forbund," *Internasjonal Politikk* no. 3 (1981); Nikolaj Petersen, "Britain, Scandinavia and the North Atlantic Treaty, 1948–49," *Review of International Studies* 8 (1982); Kersti Blidberg, *Just Good Friends: Nordic Social Democracy and Security Policy* (Oslo: Institutt for Forsvarsstudier, 1987); Magne Skodvin, *Nordic or North Atlantic Defence? The Postwar Scandinavian Security Debate* (Oslo: Institutt for Forsvarsstudier, 1990).

22. NSC 28/1, 3 September 1948, President's Secretary's Files, Harry S. Truman Library. Parts of this document is reproduced in *FRUS 1948, Vol. III*, pp. 232–233.
23. Ibid.
24. Lawrence Freedman, "The first two Generations of Nuclear Strategists," in *Makers of Modern Strategy*, ed. Peter Paret (Oxford: Oxford University Press, 1986), p. 743.
25. Notat, Norske og sovjetiske uttalelser om Norges sikkerhets - og basepolitikk, 31 oktober 1950, 33.6/14, UD (my emphasis).
26. Ibid.
27. Howard Turner, "Britain, the United States and Scandinavian Security Problems, 1945–49," (Ph.D. diss., Aberdeen University, 1982), p. 354. See also Riste, "Was 1949 a Turning Point?", p. 145.
28. Nils Ørvik and Niels J. Haagerup, *The Scandinavian Members of NATO*, Adelphi Paper no. 23 (London: IISS, 1965).
29. Quoted in Johan J. Holst, "Norwegian Security Policy," *Co-operation and Conflict II* (1966), pp. 70–71.
30. John K. Skogan, "Norsk sikkerhetspolitikk i brytning mellom allianse og nøytralitet," in *Norsk Utenrikspolitikk*, eds. J.J. Holst and D. Heradstveit (Oslo: Tano, 1985), pp. 35–36.
31. Halvard Lange, "Scandinavian Co-operation in International Affairs," *International Affairs* (July 1954), p. 292.
32. Riste, "Isolationism and Great Power Protection," p. 12.
33. Clive Archer, "The Lessons of War: Norway in Postwar Allied Strategy," paper presented to Colloquium on Anglo-Norwegian Relations during the Second World War, Oxford, 25–27 September 1991.
34. See Chiefs of Staff discussion on "Future Strategy" in March 1948, COS(48), 39th meeting, 17 March 1948, DEFE 4/11, PRO. See also Alan Bullock, *Ernest Bevin – Foreign Secretary* (Oxford: Oxford University Press), pp. 348 and 470–73.
35. "Some Notes on the Defence Problem of Britain, by Field Marshal The Viscount Montgomery of Alamein," 30 December 1947, BLM 183/12 (MF), The Montgomery Papers, Imperial War Museum.
36. "The Problem of Future War and the Strategy of War With Russia, Memorandum by GIGS," 30 January 1948, BLM 183/17 (MF), The Montgomery Papers, The Imperial War Museum.
37. COS(48), 39th meeting, 17 March 1948, DEFE 4/11, PRO.
38. "Scandinavian Defence: Strategic Considerations," 4 June 1947, FO 371/65961, PRO. The study had been requested by Robin Hankey, Head of the Northern Department in the Foreign Office.
39. Ibid.
40. Ibid.
41. "Scandinavian Defence: Questionnaire by Norwegian Minister of Defence," 12 March 1948, DEFE 4/11, PRO.
42. Ibid.
43. Ibid.
44. Eric Grove and Geoffrey Till, "Anglo-American Maritime Strategy in the Era of Massive Retaliation, 1945–60," in *Maritime Strategy and the Balance of Power*, eds. J. Hattendorf and R. Jordan (London: Macmillan/St. Antony's

College), p. 276. The plan was later renamed 'Speedway' by the British and 'Trojan' by the Americans. For US war planning in this period, see K.W. Condit, *The History of the Joint Chiefs of Staff: The Joint Chiefs of Staff and National Policy, Vol. II 1947–1949,* and W.S. Poole, *The History of the Joint Chiefs of Staff: The Joint Chiefs of Staff and National Policy, Vol. IV 1950–1952* (Washington, DC: Historical Division, JCS, 1978 and 1979).

45. This plan was referred to as 'Galloper' by the British and 'Offtackle' by the Americans.

46. JP(49)134(Final), Plan Galloper, 1 March 1950, DEFE 6/11, PRO.

47. Ibid.

48. Rolf Tamnes, "Integration and Screening: the two faces of Norwegian alliance policy," *FHFS Notat* 5. 1986 (Oslo: Research Centre for Defence History, 1984), p. 10.

49. The first MTDP proposal, to be implemented in phases by 1954, was approved in May 1950 and illustrated the enormous gap between aspirations and the likelihood of the plan ever being implemented; the plan assumed ninety ready and reserve divisions and a tactical air force of 8000 planes. See Lawrence S. Kaplan, *NATO and the United States: The Enduring Alliance* (Boston: Twayne Publishers, 1988), pp. 39–40.

50. Rolf Tamnes, "The Struggle for the Northern Flank," in *Western Security: The Formative Years,* ed. Olav Riste (Oslo: Norwegian University Press, 1985), pp. 219–222.

51. Earlier emergency plans assumed that Scandinavia would fall within 2–3 months, though a bridgehead might possibly have been held in the Stavanger area, later in the Trondheim area further north.

52. As will be argued, although the COS as a collective body continued to show little interest in reassessing the place of Norway in its defence priorities, in late 1951 Admiralty thinking evolved in a manner which again led to an emphasis on the importance of Norway to Western security.

53. Tamnes, "Norway's Struggle for the Northern Flank," p. 219.

54. Memorandum for General Gruenther, 12 March 1952, Gruenther, A. (1), Box 48, Dwight D. Eisenhower Pre-Presidential Papers, DDEL. On the restricted nature of COS interests in Norway see also Notat, Muligheter for forsvar av Norge i tilfelle av krig, 12/2–1952, 33.2/18, Bind I, UD.

55. Interview with Sivert Nielsen, 16 April 1991. Throughout the 1950s CINC-NORTH, his Chief of Staff and Commander Allied Naval Forces Northern Europe (COMNAVNORTH), were all British officers.

56. Notat, Forsvarsplanen og Nordkommandoen, 10 mars 1954, 33.2/18, Bind I, UD.

57. "Staff Visits," AFNORTH Historical Reports, 1 January 1954–30 June 1954, SECCOS, HQ AFNORTH.

58. Ibid.

59. Notat, Forsvarsplanen og Nordkommandoen, 10 mars 1954, 33.2/18, Bind I, UD, and interview with Sivert Nielsen, 16 April 1991.

60. See, for example, Selwyn Lloyd to Prime Minister, 14 April and 18 May 1953, FO 800/819, PRO.

61. It must also be added that British references to "Northern Europe" for much of the 1950s tended to reflect a more narrow concern with the security of the Baltic Approaches; for this, Denmark was the key and defence was best

conducted in Germany. See Notat, Forsvarsplanen og Nordkommandoen, 10 mars 1954, 33.2/18, Bind I, UD, and, JP(49)149(Final), "Strategic Guidance from the SG to Regional Planning Groups of NATO," November 1949, DEFE 6/11, PRO.

62. Letter from COMNAVNORTH to Sir Rhoderick McGrigor, 26 March 1954, ADM 205/102, PRO.
63. Interview with Jens Boyesen, 15 April 1991.
64. Quoted in Lawrence Freedman, *The Evolution of Nuclear Strategy* (London: The Macmillan Press Ltd., 1983), p. 80.
65. JWPC 474/1, "Strategic Study of Western and Northern Europe," 13 May 1947, ccs 092 USSR (3-27-45), sec. 20, Geographic File, 1946–47, Rg. 218, NARA.
66. For the background to Pincher and early US war plans, see Steven T. Ross, *American War Plans, 1945–1950* (New York and London: Garland Publishing Inc., 1988).
67. JWPC 474/1, 13 May 1947, ccs 092 USSR (3-27-45), sec. 20, Geographic File, 1946–47, Rg. 218, NARA.
68. Ibid.
69. "Norway: Airfields and Seaplane Stations," 1 November 1948, AFOIN/ONI, (MF) Roll no. A1297, 142.609-26 (R), Office of Air Force History, Bolling AFB.
70. "Requirements for US Air Forces in Europe During the Occupational Period," 23 May 1945, SWNCC 134, ccs 686.9 European Theater (4-30-45), sec. 1, Geographic File, 1942–45, Rg. 218, NARA.
71. State Department concern was partly based on the fact that Soviet troops had not yet withdrawn from Finnmark, a consideration which was impressed upon Washington by its Oslo embassy.
72. Riste, "Was 1949 a Turning Point?", p. 143.
73. The restrictions were basically twofold: the archipelago could not be used for "warlike purposes", and signatories to the treaty were granted equal access to economic exploitation of the island's resources.
74. Rolf Tamnes, *Svalbard og stormaktene: Fra ingenmannsland til Kald Krig, 1870–1953* (Oslo: Institutt for Forsvarsstudier, 1991), pp. 50–51.
75. On 15 February 1947 the Norwegian Parliament rejected a Soviet request for negotiations on the status of Spitsbergen. See Knut E. Eriksen, "Svalbard 1944–1947: Et brennpunkt i øst-vest rivaliseringen," *Internasjonal Politikk*, no. 1, 1977. The British Joint Intelligence Committee, in August 1947, believed that the long-term aim of Soviet Union in Spitsbergen was the "acquisition of base facilities for Russia herself by an arrangement for "joint defence" with the Norwegian Government." See "Soviet Interests, Intentions and Capabilities," JIC (47) 7/1 Final, 6 August 1947, (MF) BLM 188/72, The Montgomery Papers, Imperial War Museum.
76. NSC 28/1, 3 September 1948, President's Secretary's Files, Harry S. Truman Library.
77. Riste, "Was 1949 a turning point?", p. 144.
78. For SAC evaluation of the possible advantages of establishing air bases on Spitsbergen, see "The Significance of Spitsbergen (Svalbard) As a Strategic Air Base," 26 January 1948, Headquarters SAC, Intelligence Brief No. 32, (MF) Roll no. A4020-416.606-32, Office of Air Force History, Bolling AFB.

79. Ambassador to Norway (Bay) to Secretary of State, 19 February 1948, *FRUS 1948 Vol. III*, pp. 24–26, and interview with Jens Chr. Hauge, 10 April 1991, Oslo.
80. Ibid.
81. It may be useful, even at this stage, to say a few words about Colonel Bernt Balchen. Bernt Balchen was born in Norway and acquired US citizenship in 1930. Before the war he had been involved with Norwegian aviation and during the war he had been Chief, Allied Air Transport Command for Scandinavia, Eighth Air Force. Recalled to active duty in 1948, he went on to serve as project officer for the construction of the Thule Air Base and as Special Assistant, Arctic Affairs at the HQ Northeast Air Command in 1955–56. He worked closely with the USAF Directorate of Intelligence. An interesting article, which appeared in *Literaturnaja Gaseta* in connection with Balchen's return to active duty, suggests that Soviet authorities had a clear idea about the nature of his work for the USAF. See To: Director of Installations, Subject: Commendation for Col. B. Balchen, 9 June 1952, Military Matters, 1927–78, and "The Strange Transformation of a Colonel," *Literaturnaja Gaseta*, 18 August 1948, The Papers of B. Balchen, Manuscript Division, Library of Congress.
82. "Evaluation of Military Capabilities from Norway," 9 October 1950, (MF) Roll no. 30926, Col. Bernt Balchen Collection, Office of Air Force History, Bolling AFB.
83. "Military arrangements for the utilization of certain Norwegian airfields for the attainment of NATO objectives in case of hostilities," 18 October 1952, Luftforsvaret (overkommandoen), FD; Royal Military Decree 17 October 1952, FD.
84. Ibid.
85. Ibid. The USAF Mobilization Plan 1952 included in its requirements for Gardermoen a "medium bomber and 1 Fighter Escort Group. " To: OP-30B From: OP-301, Subj: Tactical Air Force Base Rights in Norway, 29 August 1952, A-14, Box 271, Strategic Plans Division, NHC.
86. It should be added that, in 1953, 49 American military personnel were stationed at Sola and Gardermoen. These were primarily attached to "communication facilities" established close to the airports and designed to support SAC operations.
87. A.J. Wohlstetter, F.S. Hoffman, R.J. Lutz, H. S. Rowen, "Selection and Use of Strategic Air Bases," R-266, RAND report, April 1954. p. v. See also Memorandum for the Record, ND, Ts. No. 3-2700 to 3-3499 (1953), Folder no. 34, Entry 214, Rg. 341, NARA.
88. "Meeting the Threat of Surprise Attack, (Killian Report) 14 February 1955," reprinted in *The Development of American Strategic Thought: Basic Documents from the Eisenhower and Kennedy Periods*, ed. Marc Trachtenberg (New York: Garland Publishing Inc., 1988), p. 406.
89. This will be discussed in more detail in the following chapter.
90. "Summary of Discussion between General Eisenhower and Norwegian Governmental Officials, 9 May 1952," 10 May 1952, Conversations, Memos of (SHAPE) 1951–52, Box 136, Dwight D. Eisenhower, Pre-Presidential Papers, DDEL.

91. Halvard Lange quoted in Tamnes, "Norway's Struggle for the Northern Flank," p. 239.

92. James Forrestal, who had been appointed Secretary of the Navy in April 1944, went on to serve as the first Secretary of Defence from September 1947 to March 1949. See Yergin, *Shattered Peace*, pp. 204–208, and Michael Palmer, *Origins of the Maritime Strategy: American Naval Strategy in the First Postwar Decade* (Washington, DC: Naval Historical Center, 1988), pp. 4–6.

93. *The Forrestal Diaries,* 7 February 1945, quoted in Lundestad, *America, Scandinavia and the Cold War*, p. 40.

94. Yergin, *Shattered Peace*, pp. 208–11.

95. See Vincent Davis, *Postwar Defence Policy and the U.S. Navy* (Durham, NC: University of North Carolina Press, 1966), pp. 147–150, 163–66; Michael S. Sherry, *Preparing for the Next War: American Plans for Postwar Defence, 1941–1945* (New Haven: Yale University Press, 1977), p. 218; Gregg Herken, *The Winning weapon: The Atomic Bomb in the Cold War, 1945–1950* (New York: Vintage Books, 1982), pp. 202–204.

96. David Alan Rosenberg, "American Postwar Air Doctrine and Organization: The Navy Experience," in *Air Power and Warfare, Proceedings of the Eighth Military History Symposium* (Washington, DC: Office of Air Force History, 1978), pp. 251–254.

97. Davis, *Postwar Defence Policy and the Navy*, pp. 222–223.

98. Palmer, *Origins of the Maritime Strategy*, pp. 21–23, and *The Forrestal Diaries*, ed. Walter Millis (London: Cassel & Co. Ltd., 1952), pp. 209–210. See also R.G. Albion and R.H. Connery, *Forrestal and the Navy* (New York: Columbia University Press, 1962), pp. 185–190.

99. Presentation to the President, 14 January 1947, Vice Admiral Forrest Sherman, Appendix to Palmer, *Origins of the Maritime Strategy,* pp. 85–91.

100. Ibid.

101. Admiral Sir Michael Denny, "The Atlantic in a World War: What Does it Mean?", *The RUSI Journal*, no. 603 (August 1956). For the background to the establishment of SACLANT, see also Robert Jordan, *Alliance Strategy and Navies: The Evolution and Scope of NATO's Maritime Dimension* (London: Pinter Publishers, 1990), pp. 11–16 and 34–35.

102. Annex J to HIST/NORTH/1952–53, History of Northern European Command, SECCOS, HQ AFNORTH, and "Carriers to the Rescue?", *Air Force* (December 1952).

103. Notes on a Meeting at the White House, 31 January 1951, *FRUS 1951, Vol. III, part 1*, p. 454. See also Memorandum, From: CNO, to JCS, 29 April 1952, Subj: JCS 2073/349–Naval support of SACEUR's Northern Flank, A–1, Box 271, Strategic Plans Division Records, NHC.

104. D/OP-30 (Arleigh Burke) to Distribution List, enclosing "Study of Attack Carrier Force Levels (Cold War)," 13 October 1953, A4, Box 280, Strategic Plans Division Records, NHC.

105. General Eisenhower to Admiral W.M. Fechteler, December 1951, The *Papers of D.D. Eisenhower: NATO and the Campaign of 1952: XIII* (Baltimore: The Johns Hopkins University Press, 1989), p. 769.

106. "The Defence of the Free World," Address by Lt. General Alfred M. Gruenther to the American Club of Paris, 28 June 1951, Gruenther, Alfred M. (1) [Aug. 1950–April 1952], Box 48, Dwight D. Eisenhower, Pre-Presidential Papers, DDEL.

107. War Plans Division, D/Plans, Info., 5 October 1951, Subj: Employment of Aircraft Carriers in the North Sea and North East Atlantic, 7c Carrier Papers, Box 84, Papers of General H.S. Vandenberg, Manuscript Division, Library of Congress.

108. Quoted in "Study of Attack Carrier Force Levels (Cold War)," 13 October 1953, A4, Box 280, Strategic Plans Division Records, NHC.

109. "There is No Easy Way Out: A Second Look at Mainbrace," *Air Force* (January 1953). For Navy commitment to SACEUR's Flank Concept, see Memorandum, From: D/Operational Readiness To: D/Strategic Plans, 12 December 1952, Subj: Intelligence Estimate for JSOP, A16-12, Box 274, Strategic Plans Division Records, NHC.

110. For details about the organisational structure of the U.S. Navy since 1946, see Thomas C. Hone, *Power and Change: The Administrative History of the Office of the Chief of Naval Operations, 1946–86* (Washington, DC: Naval Historical Center, 1989).

111. "The Kola Inlet and its Facilities," *The ONI Review,* vol. 4, no. 9, 1949, NHC.

112. Ibid.

113. Annex, "Targets recommended for immediate effect," 24 January 1951, ONI Ts Records, NHC.

114. Hearings before the Subcommittee on Appropriations House of Representatives, Eighty-Third Congress (First Session), Department of Navy Appropriations for 1954, 3 March 1953, (Washington: USGPO, 1953), pp. 76–78.

115. Ibid., p. 76.

116. Ibid., p. 78.

117. "Study of Attack Carrier Force Levels", 13 October 1953, A4, Box 200, Strategic Plans Division Records, NHC. Admiral Burke served as Chief of Naval Operations from 17 August 1955 to 1 August 1961.

118. Ibid.

119. A few figures suffice to illustrate the magnitude of the US build-up in the early 1950s. The number of Air Force wings increased from 48 in 1950 to nearly 100 in 1953. The number of ships in the navy increased from 671 to more than 1100 by the summer of 1952. The number of US forces stationed in Europe grew from 145,000 men in 1950 to 427,000 by the end of 1953. See Seyom Brown, *The Faces of Power* (New York: Columbia University Press, 1983), p. 52, and Jeffrey Record, *Revising US Military Strategy* (New York: Pergamon Brassey's, 1984), p. 19.

120. James A. Huston, *One For All: NATO Strategy and Logistics through the Formative Period, 1949–1969* (Newark: University of Delaware Press, 1984), p. 43. Mutual defence assistance agreement between the United States and Norway was signed in Washington, DC, 27 January 1950. In the period between 1951 and 1962, US aid through the MDAP accounted for 30% of Norway's total defence expenditure.

2   INTELLIGENCE AND AIR STRATEGIES IN THE ARCTIC,
    1954–60

1. Special Estimate No. 35: The World Situation over the Next Decade, IAC,
    quoted in "D/I, USAF Comments to Certain Questions Posed by the
    Honourable M.C. Smith," 26 May 1953, Ts. No. 3-1900 to 3-2699 (1953)
    Folder 21, Entry 214, Rg. 341, NARA.
2. Hanson W. Baldwin, "What Kind of Defense in the Atomic Age?" *New
    York Times Magazine*, 17 May 1953, reprinted in Robert Divine, ed.
    American Foreign Policy Since 1945 (Chicago: Quadrangle Books, 1969),
    pp. 79–86.
3. While *strategic* intelligence is required for the "formation of policy and mil-
    itary plans at national and international levels," *tactical* intelligence is
    intended to support "military plans and operations at the military unit level."
    In actual practice these two categories "differ only in scope, point of view
    and level of employment." Wolfram F. Hanrieder and Larry V. Buel, *Words
    and Arms: A Dictionary of Security and Defence Terms* (Colorado:
    Westview Press, 1979), p. 124 and p. 120.
4. Memorandum, 12 September 1953, Ts. No. 3-3300 to 3-3399, Entry 214,
    Rg. 341, NARA. North of 53 degrees latitude these three Military Districts,
    with headquarters at Riga, Leningrad and Petrozavodzk respectively, com-
    prised what the Norwegian Defence Intelligence Staff referred to as the
    Norwegian "area of interest." See Fst/E til FD/III, 25 januar 1960, enclosure
    "Sovjets krigspotensial innen vårt interesseområde," FD A/H 000849/60, FD.
5. "Statement by Allen W. Dulles," 31 May 1960, U-2 [Vol. II], Box 25,
    Subject Series Alpha Subseries, WHO: Office of the Staff Secretary, DDEL.
6. Memorandum, D/I action on NIE 11-3-55, 16 May 1955, TS No. 5-531 to
    5-1431 (1955), Box 81, Entry 341, Rg. 341, NARA.
7. Paul B. Stares, *The Militarization of Space: US Policy, 1945–84* (Ithaca,
    New York: Cornell University Press, 1985), pp. 44–45.
8. For balloon reconnaissance operations from Norway see Roger W. Sørdahl,
    "Den store hvite hvalen: Amerikansk etterretning fra Gardermoen 1956,"
    PRIO Report 5/1984 (Oslo: PRIO, 1984).
9. According to operative US definition in 1958, SIGINT comprised both com-
    munications intelligence (COMINT) and electronic intelligence (ELINT).
    COMINT derived from the interception and processing of communications
    passed by radio, wire and other electromagnetic means. ELINT was based
    on the collection and processing of "non-communications electromagnetic
    radiation emanating from other than atomic detonation or radioactive
    sources." NSCID No. 6, "Communications Intelligence and Electronic
    Intelligence," Effective 15 September 1958, Rg 273, NARA.
10. For the classic distinction between forms of strategic intelligence: "basic
    descriptive," "current repertorial" and the "speculative-evaluative," see
    Sherman Kent, *Strategic Intelligence for American World Policy* (Princeton,
    NJ: Princeton University Press, 1966.)
11. D/Intelligence to D/Operations, Subj: Gopher Project, 9 June 1953, Ts.
    No. 3-1900 to 3-2699 (1953), folder no. 23, Box 73, Entry 214, Rg. 341,
    NARA.

12. Ibid.
13. Memorandum for D/Plans, Subj: Reconnaissance, 3 October 1953, Ts. No. 3-3500 to 3-4399 (1953), Box 75, Entry 214, Rg 341, NARA.
14. Memorandum from Actg. D/Intelligence, USAF, 8 April 1954, Ts. 4-6A to 4-1050 (1954), Entry 214, Rg. 341, NARA. Herbert York, *The Advisors: Oppenheimer, Teller and the Superbomb* (San Francisco: W. H. Freeman and Co., 1976), pp. 89–93.
15. CIA, Subject: SNIE 11-8-54, 10 September 1954, (SNIE No. 11-8-54), WHO: Special Assistant for National Security Affairs, DDEL.
16. Paragraph C. 7, "Meeting the Threat of Surprise Attack," quoted in "Evaluation and implementation of the TCP Report," Memo to D/P, 28 March 1955, Ts. No. 5-31 to 5-1431 (1955), Entry 214, Rg. 341, NARA.
17. "Capabilities of Soviet Long Range Aviation to Attack the North American Continent," *The ONI Review: Secret Supplement*, Midsummer 1957, NHC.
18. See Harry H. Ransom, "Strategic Intelligence and Intermestic Politics," in C.W. Kegley, Jr. and E.R. Wittkopf, eds. *Perspectives on American Foreign Policy: Selected Readings* (New York: St. Martin's Press, 1983), p. 306.
19. Jeffrey T. Richelson, *The US Intelligence Community, Second Edition* (Cambridge, MA: Ballinger Publishing Company, 1989), p. 35. Attempts at "internal oversight" and co-ordination through such mechanisms as the 5412 Group proved unsuccessful. See here John Prados, *President's Secret Wars: CIA and Pentagon Covert Operations Since World War II* (New York: William Morrow and Company, Inc., 1986), pp. 146–148, and Stephen Ambrose, *Eisenhower, Volume II* (New York: Simon and Schuster, 1984), pp. 506–507.
20. Harry H. Ransom, "Secret Intelligence in the United States, 1947–1982: the CIA's Search for Legitimacy," in *The Missing Dimension: Governments and Intelligence Communities in the Twentieth Century,* eds. C. Andrew and D. Dilks (London: Macmillan, 1984), p. 205.
21. See for example Memorandum, From: D/Naval Intelligence, To: D/CNO (Administration), 13 November 1953, Subject: Requirement for Expansion of Air Section (OP-322v) Naval Intelligence Division, A-8, Box 283, Strategic Plans Division Records, NHC. This document details an internal Navy request for expanding the air section of the Naval Intelligence Division on the grounds that USAF intelligence is unwilling to co-operate and share intelligence with the Navy.
22. Bilag 1, til Stabsnotat av 8 juni 1957, Forsvarstaben til FD, Forslag om kontrollsone nord for polarsirkelen. A/H-06502, FD, and Chr. Christensen, *Vår Hemmelige Beredskap* (Oslo: Cappelen, 1988), pp. 148–49
23. Memorandum for Mr. Strauss, 15 April 1957, Subject: Soviet Weapons Tests Announcements, Box 6, Nuclear Weap. Tests, April–May 1957 (2), WHO: Office of Special Assistant for Disarmament (H. Stassen), DDEL.
24. David Holloway, "Research Note: Soviet Thermonuclear Development," *International Security* 4 (Winter 1979/80), p. 197.
25. "Brief for the Prime Minister's talks with the Norwegian Prime Minister," 27 October 1956, PREM 11/2437, PRO. See further discussion in Chapter Seven.
26. QIR (Quarterly Intelligence Report), January to March 1958, No. 15, 10 April 1958, ADM 223/241, PRO. Allen Dulles in his briefing for the

President after the launching of Sputnik in October 1957, referred to this particular test ("a large-scale hydrogen bomb at Novaya Zemlya") as one element in a "trilogy of propaganda moves." The other two "Soviet moves" were the Sputnik launch itself and the successful testing of an ICBM in August. See Summary of Discussion, 339th Mtg of the NSC, 11 October 1957, Box 9, NSC Series, Dwight D. Eisenhower Papers as President, DDEL.

27. Christensen, *Vår Hemmelige Beredskap,* pp. 148–153.
28. Ibid.
29. Department of State, Nov. 1963–Jan. 1969, ND, Vol. I Administrative History, Bilateral Relations with Western Europe, Scandinavia, DDC 002087, 1985.
30. The HASP programme started in 1954 and was sponsored by the Defence Atomic Support Agency. The programme was initially designed to "determine the role played by the stratosphere in the world-wide distribution of fission products from nuclear explosions." See Jay Miller, *Lockheed U-2* (Austin, Texas: Aerofax Inc., 1983), p. 37. See also Dick van der Art, *Aerial Espionage: Secret Intelligence Flights by East and West* (Shrewsbury: Airlife Publishing, Ltd., 1985), p. 31.
31. Miller, *Lockheed U-2,* p. 30, and Tamnes, Cold *War in the High North,* p. 133.
32. Robert Divine, *Eisenhower and the Cold War* (Oxford: Oxford University Press, 1981), p. 128.
33. Miller, *Lockheed U-2,* p. 30.
34. Interview with Erik Himle, 11 April 1991, ("Norge bidro i betydlig grad til a kartlegge utviklingen på rakkettområde.")
35. One of the first successful satellite discoveries, made by *Discoverer 29* in August 1961, was that *Plesetsk* was indeed the first Soviet ICBM site. See Lawrence Freedman, US *Intelligence and the Soviet Strategic Threat* (London: The Macmillan Press Ltd., Second Edition, 1986), p. 73.
36. This U-2 operation lasted for two months in the late summer and autumn of 1958, but according to Tamnes there is no evidence to corroborate Beerli's assertion which is denied by others who participated in the operation. Tamnes, *Cold War in the High North,* p. 133.
37. John Prados, *The Soviet Estimate: US Intelligence Analysis and Russian Military Strength* (New York: The Dial Press, 1982), p. 97. An estimate produced by the Norwegian Defence Intelligence Staff in May 1959 observed that: "although confirmatory information was lacking, is was reasonable to assume that permanent installations for launching intercontinental missiles had been constructed (or were in the process of being constructed) on the Kola Peninsula" (my trans.), Fst/E, Notat. Truselen mot Skandinavia, 28 may 1959, FO.
38. It is worth noting here that the decision to allow Powers's flight to go ahead less than two weeks before the Paris summit is seen by many as a mystery, especially in view of Eisenhower's known concern about the consequences of any one of the U-2s being shot down over the Soviet Union. Memorandum for the Record, 12 February 1959, Intelligence material(8), [Jan–Feb. 1959], Box 15 Subject Series Alpha, WHO: Office of the Staff Secretary, DDEL.

39. Michael R. Beschloss, *Mayday: Eisenhower, Khrushchev and the U-2 Affair* (London: Faber and Faber, 1986), pp. 241–242.

40. Tamnes, *Cold War in the High North*, p. 133. If the target was Saryshagan (46 12 degrees north, 73 38 degrees east) it is highly unlikely that the U-2B could also have covered Plesetsk given its range (estimated) of 4,125 miles without using an operating location in Western Europe. See "Performance Data" for U-2B/C/D, in Mike Spick, *American Spyplanes* (London: Ospery Publishing Ltd., 1986), p. 19.

41. This is one of several points that emerge from two Norwegian Foreign Ministry memoranda, Notat, Rekognoseringsflyvninger, 1 desember 1959 and Notat, Rekognoseringsflyvninger 9 desember 1959, 33. 6/14b, UD.

42. For growing concern about Soviet progress in the ICBM field in the second half of 1959, see Allen W. Dulles (CIA) to President, 18 August 1959, Allen W. Dulles (1), Box 13, Administration Series, Dwight D. Eisenhower Papers as President, DDEL.

43. Memorandum for Assistant Secretary of the Air Force (R&D), Subject: Soviet Guided Missile Developments, 15 September 1955, Ts. No. 5-1478 to 5-2957, Box 82, Entry 214, Rg. 314, NARA.

44. Another missile test site, Kapustin Yar on the Volga, was identified by Western analysts in 1953. Semipalatinsk, a nuclear test facility, was constructed in 1948 and was the site of the first detonation of a Soviet nuclear device. An ABM test site was located at Saryshagan and a weapons production line near Alma Ata. Steven J. Zaloga, "The Soviet Nuclear Bomb Programme: the First Decade," *Jane's Soviet Intelligence Review* 3 (April 1991), pp. 174–181, and Prados, *The Soviet Estimate,* p. 103.

45. Tamnes, *Cold War in the High North*, p. 128.

46. "Future of the Agency's U-2 Capability," 7 July 1960, Intelligence Matters (15) [June–July 1960], Box 15, Subject Series Alpha, WHO: Office of Staff Secretary, DDEL.

47. "How US Taps Soviet Missile Secrets," *Aviation Week*, 21 October 1957, and "Red Missiles Trailed By US Radar Based in Turkey for 2 Years," *Washington Post and Times Herald*, 21 October 1957. *Jane's Weapon Systems, 1969–70* (London: Sampson Low Marston & Co., Ltd, 1969), p. 581.

48. Robert J. Watson, *History of the Joint Chiefs of Staff, Volume 5, The Joint Chiefs of Staff and National Policy, 1953–1954* (Washington DC: Historical Division, JCS, 1986), pp. 34–35.

49. For the increased importance of the polar regions within the US Air Force and Navy after 1950, see Joseph O. Fletcher, "The Arctic: Challenge to the Air Force," *Air University Quarterly Review* 6 (Fall 1953); Charles T. Myers, "Defence Strategy Looks to the Northeast," *Army Information Digest* 9 (January 1954). For increased Soviet activity and interest in the region, see "Foreign Activities in the Arctic," *The ONI Review*, vol. 10, no. 6, 1955, NHC. For a more limited British perspective on the Arctic in the 1950s, see Peter W. Ellis (RAF), "A Realistic Arctic Strategy," *Military Review* (August 1956), pp. 94–98.

50. Memorandum for General Twining, Subj: General Kepner's Lecture on the "Strategic Importance of the Arctic," ND, March 1952, Box 51, The Papers of Hoyt S. Vandenberg, Manuscript Division, Library of Congress.

51. Ibid.

52. See Clive Archer, "The United States Defence Areas in Greenland," *Cooperation and Conflict* No. 3 (September 1988), pp. 125–127.

53. Sherry, *Preparing for the Next War*, p. 204.

54. Lundestad, *America, Scandinavia and the Cold War*, p. 75, and Archer, "US Bases in Greenland," p. 128. Air Force advocacy of the "polar strategy" must also be seen as a function of bureaucratic rivalry between the services in the US.

55. Also in October a report to the JCS outlined the present and future strategic importance of the Arctic, see JSPC 815/6, ccs 381 Arctic Areas (10-1-46), Rg. 214, NARA.

56. Lieutenant General Charles T. Myers, USAF, "Defense Strategy Looks to the Northeast," *Army Information Digest* 9 (January 1954), p. 24.

57. Nikolaj Petersen, *Denmark and NATO, 1949–1987* (Oslo: Institutt for Forsvarsstudier, 1987), p. 17. On the Arctic perspective and Thule, see "Arctic military ground and air operations," ND, and Memorandum for COS/USAF, Project "Robin," 16 March 1951, both documents in, Subject File: Reports and Tech. Data, 1937–71, Box 18, The Papers of Bernt Balchen, Manuscript Division, Library of Congress.

58. Joseph and Stewart Alsop, "Keflavik and Dahran," *New York Herald Tribune*, 4 December 1955. For the background to the construction of Thule Air Base which became operational in November 1952, see "Summary" 12 September 1952, Subject file: Reports and Tech. Data, 1938–1971, The Papers of Bernt Balchen, Manuscript Division, Library of Congress, and "US Creates Huge Air Base in Far North of Greenland," *New York Times*, 19 September 1952. The other main air base used by the US after 1951 in Greenland was Sondrestrom Air Base at Søndre Strømfjord, which was taken over by SAC in 1957. For a detailed account of these early developments, see Clive Archer, "Greenland and the Atlantic Alliance," *Centrepiece* 7 (Summer 1985), pp. 10–15.

59. JCS 1899/433, Enclosure, HQ SAC to C/JCS, Communications Deficiencies in the Northern Area, 4 February 1959, ccs 6420, JCS 1959, Box 88, Rg. 218, NARA.

60. John J. Teal, Jr., "The Rebirth of North Norway," *Foreign Affairs* 32 (October 1953), p. 123. For an indication of the growing importance attached to the Arctic areas in the mid-1950s, see "The Coldest Cold War," *Newsweek*, 15 November 1954.

61. Memorandum for COS/USAF, 15 January 1959, Subj: Changes in SAC War Plan, Command SAC, Box 27. Papers of General T.D. White, Manuscript Division, Library of Congress. See also Merton E. Davies and William R. Harris, *RAND's Role in the Evolution of Balloon and Satellite Observation Systems and Space Technology, R-3692-RC* (Santa Monica: The RAND Corporation, 1988), pp. 48–52.

62. Norman Polmar, ed. *Strategic Air Command: People, Aircraft and Missiles* (Annapolis, MD: The Nautical and Aviation Publishing Comp., 1979), pp. 40–41.

63. "Arctic Flying in the Next War – Interview with Colonel Bernt Balchen," US *News & World Report*, 28 January 1955.

64. Ibid. RAND estimated that two-thirds of the Russian target system was located above the fiftieth parallel of latitude. See Wohlstetter, et al. *Selection and Use of Strategic Bases*, p. 137.

65. Interview with Major General Bjørn Egge, 9 April 1991.
66. See also Bernt Balchen, "Lecture to NATO War College, Paris, April 1954," Col. Bernt Balchen Collection, (MF) Roll no. 30925, Office of Air Force History, Bolling AFB.
67. From US Embassy, Oslo, to Dept. of State, 18 June 1957, 757. 5 MSP/6-1857, DR, Rg 59, NARA.
68. For the most detailed insight into SAC war plans at this time, see David A. Rosenberg, "'A Smoking Radiating Ruin at the End of Two Hours': Documents on American Plans for Nuclear War with the Soviet Union, 1954–55," *International Security* 6 (Winter 1981/82), pp. 18–28.
69. Letter from C. Wilson to President, 24 June 1953, Air Bases – Outside USA, Box 1, Administration Series, Dwight D. Eisenhower Papers as President, DDEL.
70. JP(59)17(Final), 9 February 1959, PRO, DEFE 6/55.
71. It is interesting to note in this connection that in discussions between Colonel Bernt Balchen and senior Swedish military officials in December 1951, General Nordenskjold, Commanding General of the Swedish Air Force, stated "that in case of an immediate emergency, 7 air fields can be made available to NATO outside the ones needed for the Swedish Air Force." See Memorandum for Mr. Dickinson, Deputy for Installations, 10 December 1951, Col. Bernt Balchen Collection, Miscellaneous documents on defense of Norway, Sweden and Denmark, 40/04/24-65/08/23, (MF) Roll no. 30926. Office of Air Force History, Bolling AFB.
72. "DoD Report to NSC on Status of U.S.Military Programs as of 31 December 1954," 31 March 1955, NSC 5509 – Status of U.S.Nat. Sec. Pro. of Dec. 31, 1954, 1954 (1), Box 5, NSC Series – Status of Project Subseries, WHO: Office of Special Assistant for National Security Affairs, DDEL, and Tamnes, *Cold War in the High North,* pp. 102–103.
73. "USAF Strategic Communications System," *Signal,* May–June 1955.
74. Record of Government Meeting, 12 July 1960 (Regjeringskonferanse tirsdag 12 juli 1960 kl. 1300), Riksarkivet.
75. Tamnes, *Cold War in the High North,* p. 103.
76. Memorandum, 2 July 1953, Ts. No. 3-1900 to 3-2699 (1953), Entry 214, Rg. 341, NARA.
77. The Baltic Sea route, indicated by *Route Extra,* was also to be covered six times each 90 days. See Memorandum, 8 December 1953, USAF Electronic Reconnaissance Requirements, Ts. No. 3-3500 to 3499 (1953), Folder 43, Entry 214, Rg. 314, NARA.
78. "Requirement for Weekly RB-50G Electronic Reconnaissance Flight/Route Report," 25 May 1954, Ts. No. 1114 to 4-2146 (1954), Box 77, Entry 214, Rg. 341, NARA.
79. The RB-47K also featured high-resolution and side-looking radars. Marcelle S. Knaack, *Encyclopedia of US Air Force Aircraft and Missile Systems, Volume II* (Washington DC: Office of Air Force History, 1988), pp. 147–155.
80. Memorandum for D/Operations, USAF Electronic Reconnaissance Peacetime Program (RB-47H), 23 November 1955, Ts. No. 5-1478 to 5-2957, Box 82, Entry 214, Rg. 314, NARA. See also David Donald,

Spyplane: The Secret World of Aerial Intelligence-Gathering (London: Aerospace Publishing, Ltd, 1987), p. 23.
Program (RB-47H), 23 November 1955, Ts. No. 5-1478 to 5-2957, Box 82, Entry 214, Rg. 314, NARA. See also David Donald, *Spyplane: The Secret World of Aerial Intelligence-Gathering* (London: Aerospace Publishing, Ltd, 1987), p. 23.

81. Memorandum for Gen. A.J. Goodpaster, 17 August 1960, Subject: Navy Airborne Peripheral Operations, Intelligence material (17)[August 1960], Box 15, Subject Series, Alpha, WHO: Office of the Staff Secretary, DDEL.

82. Memorandum, Franz Josef Land Electronic Reconnaissance Flight of 20 May 1953, 26 May 1953, Ts. No. 3-1900 to 3-2699 (1953), Folder 21, Box 73, NARA.

83. TS Msg., From CG 7th Air Division, to CG SAC, 6 Dec. 1952, The Papers of Curtis LeMay, Manuscript Division, Library of Congress.

84. Memorandum, Recent Electronic Reconnaissance Flight, ND, Ts. No. 3-3500 to 3-4399(1953), Folder 32, Box 75, Entry 214, RG 314, NARA.

85. D/I, USAF Briefing for OASF Personnel, 23 January 1953, Ts. No. 3-1 to 3-399 (1953), Box 70, Folder No. 5, Entry 214, Rg. 341, NARA. This particular briefing stated that the "Soviet Union still is considered to lack the facilities, equipment and techniques required to exceed appreciably the relative effectiveness of German air defense of 1943."

86. "Closing the Arctic Gap," *The ONI Review,* vol. 13, no. 8, 1958, NHC.

87. Ibid. The Token radars located on the Peninsula gave ranges of around 100 nautical miles and a few extreme ranges of 200 nautical miles.

88. Ibid.

89. Bilag 1 til Stabsnotat av 8.juni 1957, "Sovjetiske styrker nord for Polarsirkelen fra norskegrensen til Ural," Fst/E, 8 juni 1957, A/H-06502–8. Jun 1957, FD.

90. Interview with Major General Bjørn Egge, 9 April 1991.

91. The argument was presented by Bjørn Egge, on behalf of the Defence Intelligence Staff, and was "listened to with interest" by the US, but less so by the French and the British.

92. Ibid.

93. *FRUS 1955-57*, Vol. IV, p. 621.

94. *Jane's Weapon Systems, 1969–70* (London: Sampson Low Marston & Co., Ltd., 1969), p. 581.

95. NEC Historical Reports, 1 July 1955–30 June 1956, Signals Division, SECCOS, HQ AFNORTH. At Bodø only the FPS-8 radar became operational in 1955.

96. NEC Historical Report, 1 July 1956–31 Dec. 1957, SECCOS, HQ AFNORTH.

97. Ibid.

98. Ibid.

99. NEC Historical Report (AIRNORTH), 1 July 1956–31 Dec. 1957, SECCOS, HQ AFNORTH and Amembassy (Oslo) to Department of State, no. 858, 18 June 1957, 757.5 MSP/6-1857, Rg. 59, NARA.

100. "Utskiftning av radarmateriell pa Vardø," 6 December 1956, Det Kgl. Norske Flyvåpen (Overkommandoen), Nasjonalt H-arkiv, FD.

101. As Paul Bracken notes, "the proliferation of listening posts and the U-2 constituted a forward deployment of warning sensors ... the U-2 and the listening posts around the Soviet border were intended to serve the warning needs of the military every bit as much as they did those of the CIA. Fierce jurisdictional battles between SAC and the CIA were fought as a consequence." Paul Bracken, *The Command And Control Of Nuclear Forces* (New Haven: Yale University Press, 1983), p. 13.

102. Prados, *The Soviet Estimate,* p. 103.

103. Memorandum for D/Plans from D/Intelligence, 4 March 1955, Ts No. 5-531 to 5-1431 1955), Box 81, Entry 341, Rg. 341, NARA.

104. Memorandum for Secretary Quarles re Detection Site in Sweden, 21 October 1955, Ts. No. 5-1478 to 5-2957, Box 82, Entry 214, Rg. 341, NARA.

105. *Had There Been a War... Preparations for the reception of military assistance 1949–1969* (Report of the Commission on Neutrality Policy, Stockholm 1994, SOU 1994:11), pp. 210–213.

106. Ibid., p. 211.

107. "Ionospheric Scatter Permits Long Distance Communications," *Signal* (November–December 1955), and "Forward Scatter of Radio Waves: A New Means of Communication," *Navigation* 5 (June 1956), pp. 107–113. Briefly, the forward scatter techniques used directional antennas with transmitter powers of 10-50kW (in either the VHF or UHF band) to produce radiation which would be received at the desired station after rebounding from the ionosphere or troposphere.

108. NEC Historical Report (Signals Division), 1 July 1955–30 June 1956, SECCOS, HQ AFNORTH. In February 1955 the Killian Report had expressed particular concern about the overseas communication system for early warning in view of the fact that the "network of Soviet jamming transmitters is very extensive and remarkably well co-ordinated." To overcome the problem of enemy jamming the Panel recommended that "the further development and application of ... 'Forward Scatter' transmission systems should be pushed with considerable vigor." See "Meeting the Threat of Surprise Attack (Killian Report)," reprinted in Trachtenberg, ed., *The Development of American Strategic Thought*, p. 354 and 482.

109. Annex I to AIRNORTH Historical Report, HQ AFNORTH Historical Report, 1 July 1956 to 31 December 1957, SECCOS, HQ AFNORTH. When completed in 1963, the communication system built upon the forward scatter principle was referred to as ACE High, and ran from North Norway to eastern parts of Turkey. See Huston, *NATO Strategy and Logistics,* pp. 170–171.

110. Report of OASD (R&D) Study Group on Certain Aspects of the Mutual Weapons Development Program in Western Europe, 19–30 March 1957, Missiles (March 1957), Box 1, Harlow Bryce Records, 1953–61, DDEL.

111. General Gruenther to SecDef Wilson, 7 Dec. 1955, ccs 092(8-22-46) (2) Sec. 21, Box 20, JCS 1954-56, Rg. 218, NARA. At the NATO ministerial meeting held in December 1955, Norway's importance in terms of providing early warning of air attack against the UK and the US. was again emphasised. See Nils Handal, "Aktuelle forsvarsproblemer i dag," (Speech 9 January 1956), *Norsk Militært Tidsskrift* 115 (1956), p. 80.

112. NEC Historical Report (Signals Division), 1 July 1955–30 June 1956, SECCOS, HQ AFNORTH. Between mid-1953 and 1958, the US MAAG also sponsored the construction of the "longest military microwave communications system in the world," running from the south of Norway past the Arctic circle. See "Microwave in Arctic," *Signal* (November 1958).

113. "NATO har bygd ut et nytt radiolinjesamband i Norge," *Arbeiderbladet*, 13 July 1958, and Huston, *NATO Strategy and Logistics*, p. 172.

114. F. Willis to State Department, Desp. 900, 18 June 1958, 757.5 MSP/6-1858, Rg. 59, NARA.

115. From MOD Norway to SACEUR, 17 November 1960, Norway (1) Box 49, General L. Norstad Papers, DDEL.

116. Estimate of Soviet Air Threat to the Continental United States, 1955–1961, 1 July 1955, Ts. No. 5-1478 to 5-2957 (1955), Entry 214, Rg. 341, NARA.

117. "Working Paper Prepared for Air Defence Development Planning Objectives Committee, Estimate of Soviet Intentions and Capabilities Against the US, 1958-1963," 17 August 1954, Ts. No. 1114 to 4-2146 (1954) Entry 214, Rg. 341, NARA, and, Memorandum, From: OP-03D3, To: AFOIN 3A1, 25 August 1952, Subject: A Study of Potential Soviet Action against the US from Northern Areas, EF-61, Box 289, Strategic Plans Division Records, NHC.

118. Ibid.

119. "Air Facilities on the Kola Peninsula," *The ONI Review,* vol. 7, no. 6, 1952, NHC. See Map 2.

120. Ibid.

121. "5 Soviet Airfields Near Norway Cited," *New York Times,* 19 January 1953.

122. Memorandum, 12 September 1953, Ts. No. 3-3300 to 3-3399, Entry 214, Rg. 341, NARA.

123. Admiral Espe had evidently not been briefed about these operations and the incident provides a good example of limited co-operation between the intelligence branches of these services. D/NI to D/AFOIN, 25 May 1954, Ts. No. 1114-to 4-2146 (1954), Box 77, Entry 214, Rg. 341, NARA.

124. In 1952 the Norwegian Defence Intelligence Staff initiated a HUMINT project, "Operation Uppsala", whereby Finnish "Mannerheim soldiers" were recruited by the Norwegians and sent into Soviet territory from Finland. The CIA provided technical assistance and equipment but the operations appear to have yielded only modest results. See C. Christensen, *Vår Hemmelige Beredskap,* pp. 70–81, and Svein Blindheim, *Offiser i Krig og Fred* (Oslo: Det Norske Samlaget, 1981).

125. "Report on Reconnaissance trip along Norwegian Soviet border," Miscellaneous Documents on Defence of Norway, Sweden and Denmark, 40/04/24–65/08/23, Col. Bernt Balchen Collection, (MF) Roll. no. 30926, Office of Air Force History, Bolling AFB.

126. CIA, Subject: SNIE 11-8-54, 10 September 1954, (SNIE No. 11-8-54), WHO: Special Assistant for National Security Affairs, DDEL.

127. CIA, Subject: SNIE 11-8-54, 10 September 1954, (SNIE No. 11-8-54), WHO: Special Assistant for National Security Affairs, DDEL, and "Development of Soviet Air Power in the Arctic," *The ONI Review,* vol. 10, no. 8, 1955, NHC.

128. NIE No. 11-3-55, 17 May 1955, NIE No. 11-3-55 (5), Box 11, NSC Series – Subject Series, White House Office: Office of Special Assistant for National Security Affairs, DDEL.
129. "Soviet May Day Air Show," *The ONI Review,* vol. 9, no. 5, 1954, NHC.
130. "A Review of Soviet Air Developments in 1955," *Secret Supplement of the ONI Review* (Spring 1956), NHC.
131. ONI observed in the summer of 1957 that "evidence of a rapid heavy bomber build-up is almost completely lacking." See "Capabilities of Soviet Long Range Aviation to Attack the North American Continent," *The ONI Review: Secret Supplement,* midsummer 1957, NHC. For an interesting account of Soviet air strategy see Raymond L. Garthoff, "Air Power and Soviet Strategy," *Air University Quarterly Review* 9 (Winter 1957–58), pp. 80–98.
132. For a good account of the bomber gap controversy, see Prados, *The Soviet Estimate,* pp. 39–50.
133. Interview with Major General Bjørn Egge, 9 April and 9 September 1991, Oslo.
134. Fst/E til FD/III, "1956 Intelligence Estimate," 18 February 1956, enclosing telegram to Admiral Storheil, Washington, DC, A/H 00158/343.1, FD.
135. Ibid.
136. Ibid. This figure was considerably higher than US estimates. See for example "Intelligence Aspects of US Continental Defence," 10 December 1954, A16-1, Box 300, Strategic Plans Division, NHC.
137. Interview Major General Bjørn Egge, 9 September, Oslo. See Map 2.
138. Egge described Norwegian authorities as being "very unhappy" with these reports, particularly as some of them even suggested that North Norway was "logistically impossible" to support, an assertion which German and Soviet Arctic operations in World War II demonstrated was clearly not the case. See James Gebhardt, *The Petsamo-Kirkenes Operation: Soviet Breakthrough and Pursuit in the Arctic, 1944* (Washington, DC: USGPO, 1989).
139. Fst/E til FD/III, "1956 Intelligence Estimate," 18 February 1956, enclosing telegram to Admiral Storheil, Washington, DC, A/H 00158/343.1, FD.
140. "Meeting the Threat of Surprise Attack (Killian Report)," reprinted in Trachtenberg, ed., *The Development of American Strategic Thought,* p. 346.

3   THE UNITED STATES, NORWAY AND THE SOVIET NAVAL THREAT IN NORTHERN EUROPE, 1954–60

1. Siegfried Breyer, *Die Seerüstung der Sowjetunion* (Munich: J.F. Lehmanns Verlag München, 1964), pp. 4–6. By 1960, however, the tonnage of the Northern Fleet about equalled that of the Baltic Fleet. See Wolfgang Höpker, "The Polar Sea Fleet of the Soviet Union," *The Fifteen Nations* (June 1960), p. 28.
2. Annex J. to Hist/North/1952–53, "Exercise BLUE MOON" History of Northern European Command, 1952–53, SECCOS, HQ AFNORTH. Rolf Tamnes, "Defence of the Northern Flank, 1949–56," paper presented to

conference on "The North Atlantic Alliance, 1949–1956," Freiburg, 11–13 September, 1990, p. 9.

3. See Tamnes, *Cold War in the High North*, p. 144.

4. See "Baltic Area – Military Importance and Defence," 13 December 1950, File TS No. 7988, ONI TS Records, NHC. A clear indication of high-level concern about the area can be seen in NSC 88, "US Courses of action in the event the Soviets attempt to close the Baltic," 17 October 1950, President's Secretary's Files, National Security Council Meetings, Harry S. Truman Library.

5. "The Armed Forces of The USSR," *Secret Supplement to the ONI Review*, midsummer 1954, NHC.

6. Ibid.

7. Ibid.

8. "Intelligence Briefs," *The ONI Review*, vol. 9, no. 10, 1954, NHC.

9. Interview with Vice Admiral Ronald Brockman, 18 March 1991. See also Commander T. Gerhard Bidlingmaier, "The Strategic Importance of the Baltic Sea," *USNIP* 84 (September 1958), pp. 23–31.

10. Keith Allen, "The Northern Fleet and North Atlantic Naval Operations," in *The Soviet Navy: Strengths and Liabilities,* eds. Bruce W. Watson and S.M. Watson (Boulder, Colorado: Westview Press, 1986), p. 183.

11. "Soviet Naval Developments Since World War II, Part II," *The ONI Review*, vol. 10, no. 5, 1955, NHC.

12. "Kola Inlet and its Facilities," *The ONI Review*, vol. 4, no. 9, 1949, NHC.

13. "Ports and Naval Bases of the Kola Inlet," *The ONI Review*, vol. 13, no. 3, 1958, NHC.

14. From its entrance to its head, south of Murmansk, the Kola Inlet is 30 miles long, 1 to 2 miles wide and has a limiting depth of 75 feet in fairway. The "base" in the Kola Inlet was therefore dispersed over a length of some 30 miles.

15. "Ports and Naval Bases of the Kola Inlet," *The ONI Review*, vol. 13, no. 3, 1958, NHC.

16. A.D.Nicholl, "Geography and Strategy," in *The Soviet Navy,* ed. M.G. Saunders (London: Weidenfeld and Nicolson, 1958), pp. 246–247.

17. Mokhnatkina Pakhta, one and a half miles west of Chelnopushka, was listed as a naval fuel annex and ammunition transfer point. Roslyakova close to Chelnopushka was another naval port "of some significance." See Map 4.

18. "Soviet Submarine Bases," *The ONI Review*, vol. 12, no. 8, 1957, NHC.

19. *Guba Dolgaya Zapadnaya* east of the entrance to the Kola Inlet was listed as a naval operating base for patrol boats controlling the approaches to the Inlet. "Ports and Naval Bases of the Kola Inlet," *The ONI Review*, vol. 13, no. 3, 1958, NHC.

20. QIR, April to June 1955, No. 4, 10 July, 1955, ADM 223/240, PRO.

21. Ibid. and "Naval Attaches Report on Russian Naval and Related Matters for the Third Quarter of 1955," ADM 1/26168, PRO. The British also reported that Severomorsk had been "considerably extended."

22. "Vulnerability of USSR Northern Fleet to Air Attack," *The ONI Review*, vol. 14, no. 4, 1959, NHC.

23. Until the anti-party purge in 1957, the yard was known as the Molotovsk yard. Its importance to the US stemmed from the fact that the first Soviet

SSN and SSBN projects were all concentrated at Severodvinsk. Between 1958 and 1963, all thirteen of the November-class submarines – the first nuclear-propelled attack submarine of the Soviet Navy – were built there. In 1959, the world's first SSBN, the Hotel-class submarine, was completed at Shipyard 402 at Severodvinsk. See N. Polmar and J. Noot, *Submarines of the Russian and Soviet Navies, 1718–1990* (Annapolis, MA: Naval Institute Press, 1991), pp. 294–296.

24. In the summer of 1951, two cruisers – *Chapayev* and *Zhelezniakov* – were transferred from the Baltic to the Northern Fleet. These were followed by a Sverdlov class cruiser a year later. Both transfers were described by ONI as being of "great naval significance". See "Soviet Naval Developments Since World War II, Part II," *The ONI Review*, vol. 10, no. 5, 1955, NHC.

25. JIC 558/392, "Intelligence Estimate of Soviet Bloc Capabilities and Probable Courses of Action between Now and the End of 1960," 6 February 1956, 334 JIC (12-7-55), JCS 1954–56, Rg. 218, NARA, p. 226.

26. "Developments and trends in the Soviet Fleet during 1955," *Secret Supplement of the ONI Review,* Spring 1956, NHC.

27. QIR, April to June 1955, No. 4, 10 July 1955, ADM 223/240, PRO.

28. QIR, January to March 1956, No. 7, 10 April 1956, ADM 223/240, PRO.

29. JIC 558/392, 6 February 1956, 334 JIC (12-7-55), Rg. 218, JCS 1954–56, NARA, p. 227.

30. See "Soviet Navy Sorties and Interfleet Transfers," in "Developments and Trends in the Soviet Fleet 1958," *The ONI Review*, vol. 14, no. 5, 1959, NHC.

31. Little is known in the West of the 'Bosun' (Type-35), although the figure of 700 is almost certainly too high. Between 400 to 500 would appear to be a more accurate estimate. Jean Alexander, *Russian Aircraft since 1949* (London: Putnam, 1975), pp. 363–65.

32. "Study of Attack Carrier Force Levels (Cold War)," A4, Box 280, Strategic Plans Division Records, NHC.

33. "Capabilities of the Soviet Type 39 against Allied Naval Operations," *The ONI Review: Secret Supplement*, midsummer 1954, NHC.

34. Ibid.

35. Det Kgl.Norske Flyvåpen (Overkommandoen) til FD, 6 December 1956, "Utskiftning av radarmateriell pa Vardø," A/H 011926, FD; and Fst/E to FD/III, "1956 Intelligence Estimate," 18 February 1956, A/H 001580, FD.

36. "Soviet Naval Developments Since World War II: Part II," *The ONI Review*, vol. 10, no. 5, 1955, and "Developments and Trends in the Soviet Fleet and Soviet Naval Air Force during 1954," *The ONI Review: Secret Supplement*, Spring 1955, NHC.

37. "Developments of Soviet Air Power in the Arctic," *The ONI Review*, vol. 10, no. 8, 1955, NHC. See also report on "significant airfield developments" in the Soviet Arctic in 1955 in "A Review of Soviet Air Developments in 1955," *The ONI Review: Secret Supplement*, Spring 1956, NHC.

38. "Soviet Naval Aviation," *The ONI Review*, vol. 10, no. 10, 1955.

39. Units training with Yak-25 ("Flashlight"), a twin-jet night and all-weather fighter-bomber, were active in the area round Severomorsk in 1955 and were considered operational with the Northern Fleet Air Arm the following year. Another fighter, the Mig-19 ("Farmer") also appeared in naval aviation

units for the first time in 1955. See "Soviet Air Developments, 1956," *The ONI Review: Secret Supplement*, Spring–Summer 1957, NHC.

40. Soviet radio and weather stations in the polar regions were assumed by the USAF to facilitate bomber navigation and operations in the Arctic. Similarly, studies of terrestrial magnetism in the Arctic were seen as important for assessing missile guidance requirements and extensive hydrological and bathometric measurements were designed to ensure safe submarine operations throughout the Arctic ocean. Drifting stations were organised regularly by the Soviet Union from 1954 onwards. See "Soviet Arctic Equipment," *The ONI Review* vol. 11, no. 7, 1956, and Pier Horensma, *The Soviet Arctic* (London and New York: Routledge, 1991), p. 111.

41. See Cmdr. Bernard M.Kassell, "Soviet Logistics in the Arctic," *USNIP* 85 (February 1959), pp. 88–95, and Capt. R.S.D. Armour (RN), "The Soviet Naval Air Arm," in *The Soviet Navy*, ed. M.G. Saunders (London: Weidenfeld and Nicolson, 1958), p. 196.

42. "Developments in Soviet Naval Aviation," in "Developments and Trends in the Soviet Fleets during 1956," *The ONI Review: Secret Supplement*, Spring–Summer 1957, NHC.

43. "Soviet Air Developments, 1956," *The ONI Review: Secret Supplement*, Spring–Summer 1957, NHC. The air-to-surface missile was the AS-1 (NATO name 'Kennel'), and was carried by "Bulls" and "Bagders" in the late 1950s. See Norman Polmar, *The Naval Institute Guide to the Soviet Navy*, Fifth Edition (Annapolis, MD: Naval Institute Press, 1991), p. 381.

44. "Developments and Trends in the Soviet Fleet in 1957," *The ONI Review,* vol. 13, no. 5, 1958, NHC.

45. "An Improved Capability of Soviet Naval Aviation," *The ONI Review*, vol. 13, no. 1, 1958, NHC.

46. "Soviet Navy "Badger" Threat Against Aircraft Carriers," *The ONI Review,* vol. 13, no. 12, 1958, NHC.

47. Ibid.

48. "Developments and Trends in the Soviet Fleet, 1958," *The ONI Review,* vol. 14, no. 5, 1959, NHC.

49. Consequently, the effectiveness of the Northern Fleet Air Force was "at least as high if not greater" than that of the numerically superior Baltic Fleet Air Force (ca. 800 versus 1100 aircraft). Fst/E to F. Ramm(FD), 25 January 1960, enclosing "Sovjets krigspotensial i vårt interesseområde. Luftmilitært." A/H 000849–26 Jan. 1960, FD.

50. JP(57)146(Final) 22 November 1958, SACLANT's Emergency Defence Plan for 1958, DEFE 6/44, PRO.

51. Fst/E, Notat: Truselen Mot Skandinavia, 28 mai 1959, FO.

52. Ibid.

53. "The Soviet Air Forces in 1959," *The ONI Review,* vol 15, no. 4, 1960, NHC.

54. Jay Wagner, "The West German response to Soviet naval activity in the north," in *Soviet Seapower in Northern Waters: Facts, Motivation, Impact and Responses,* eds. John K. Skogan and Arne O. Brundtland (London: Pinter Publishers, 1990).

55. Historical Report, HQ Allied Naval Forces Northern Europe, 1 July 1956–31 December 1957, SECCOS, HQ AFNORTH.

56. "Soviet Submarine Bases," *The ONI Review*, vol. 12, no. 8, September 1957, NHC.
57. "Russia's Growing Submarine Force Poses 'Definite Threat' To US; Now Totals 450,": *The Army-Navy-Air Force Journal*, 14 September 1957.
58. See for example presentation by the Chairman of the JCS, General N.F. Twining, before Senate Armed Services Committee on 20 January 1959; JCS (6), Jan-Feb 1959, Box 4, Subject Series, DoD Subseries, WHO: Office of the Staff Secretary, DDEL. The British, as will be seen later, did take the surface threat much more seriously.
59. "Major" warships included carriers, battleships and cruisers. Destroyers and escort vessels were counted as "minor". The Soviet Union had neither carriers nor battleships. "Comparative Tabulation of Armed Forces Strengths – 1955," JCS, 16 February 1956, (MF) (81) 57a, Declassified Documents Catalog, 1981.
60. R.W. Herrick, *Soviet Naval Strategy: Fifty Years of Theory and Practise* (Annapolis, MD: US Naval Institute, 1968), pp. 67–73. In 1956 the cruiser building programme ended and over the next four years the size of the Soviet surface fleet declined significantly. For a penetrating contemporary analysis of Soviet Naval strategy, see Raymond L. Garthoff, "Sea Power in Soviet Strategy," *USNIP* 84 (February 1958), pp. 85–93.
61. "Secret Testimony Cites 1960 Red Sub Peril," *The Register*, 6 September 1958.
62. JIC 436/2, "Implications of Soviet Armaments Programs and Increasing Military Capabilities," 16 January 1956, JCS 1954–56, JIC Committee Papers, (12–28–55 through 1–17–56), Rg. 218, NARA.
63. Memorandum, From: OP-60, To: OP-92, 17 December 1954, Subject: Recent Acceleration in the USSR Long-Range Submarine Building Program, EF-61 (Russia), Box 307, Strategic Plans Division Records, NHC.
64. "Developments and Trends in the Soviet Fleet and Soviet Naval Air Force during 1954," *The ONI Review: Secret Supplement*, Spring 1955, NHC.
65. COS(MA)(56)2(Final) "The Role of the Russian Submarine Fleet," Report by the Maritime Air Committee, DEFE 5/72, PRO.
66. *Jane's Fighting Ships, 1959–60* (London: Sampson Low, Marston & Co, 1959) p. 298.
67. "Developments and Trends in the Soviet Fleet and Soviet Air Force during 1954," *The ONI Review: Secret Supplement,* Spring 1955, NHC.
68. At the end of 1954, the Soviet Union was estimated to have over 24 000 torpedoes and 500 000 mines. "Soviet Naval Armaments Production," *The ONI Review: Secret Supplement*, Spring 1955, NHC. See also Polmar and Noot, *Submarines of the Russian and Soviet Navies,* pp. 145–50.
69. "Indicated Employment of Soviet Submarines," *The ONI Review: Secret Supplement*, Spring 1955, NHC.
70. "Developments and Trends in the Soviet Fleet during 1956," The *ONI Review: Secret Supplement, Spring* 1956, NHC.
71. JIC 436/2, 16 January 1956, JIC Committee Papers, (12–28–55 through 1–17–56), JCS 1954–56, Rg. 218, NARA.
72. "Vast Increase in Soviet Submarine Threat," *Secret Supplement of The ONI Review*, Spring 1956, NHC.

73. The peak of the German effort was reached in late April and early May 1943, when 240 U-boats were operational. The number of German U-boats on patrol never exceeded 120, this being the peak figure reported for 9 May 1943. J. Noakes and G. Pridham, eds, *Nazism 1919–1945 Vol. 3, Foreign Policy, War and Racial Extermination: A Documentary Reader* (Exeter: Exeter University Press, 1988), p. 853.

74. "Vast Increase in Soviet Submarine Threat," *The ONI Review: Secret Supplement* Spring 1956, NHC.

75. "Soviet Capabilities and Probable Courses of Action Through 1960," NIE. 11–3–55, 17 May 1955, NIE No. 11–3–55(5), Box 11, NSC Series – Subject Subseries, WHO: Office of the Special Assistant for National Security Affairs, DDEL.

76. Ibid., Table 7, Estimated Bloc Naval Forces, Mid-1955, Mid 1960.

77. "A Summary of Submarine Contacts during 1955," *The ONI Review: Secret Supplement*, Summer 1956, NHC.

78. Ibid.

79. Memorandum for Ass. Secretary of Defence (Supply and Logistics) from Director Communications-Electronics, USAF, 8 March 1956, 334 ccs (10–5–65), Box 52, JCS 1954–56, Rg. 218, NARA. Palmer, *Origins of the Maritime Strategy*, p. 82. The SOSUS line between North Norway and Bear Island, however, was not operational in the 1950s.

80. Staff Notes No. 23, 28 September 1956, SN 16–30, Box 24. WHO: Staff Research Group Records, DDEL.

81. "Naval Attache's Report on Russian Naval and Related Matters for the Third Quarter of 1955," ADM 1/26168, PRO.

82. QIR, January to March 1957, No. 11, 10 April 1957, ADM 223/240, PRO.

83. "Developments and trends in the Soviet Fleets during 1956," *The ONI Review: Secret Supplement*, Spring-Summer 1957, NHC.

84. "Developments and trends in the Soviet Fleet in 1957," *The ONI Review*, vol. 13, no. 5, 1958, NHC. It is worth noting that contemporary Western estimates of Soviet submarine strength were, on the whole, remarkably accurate. It is now believed that 26 Zulus and 236 Whiskys were completed. See Polmar and Noot, *Submarines of the Russian and Soviet Navies*, pp. 281–284.

85. "CIA Briefing for Preparedness Investigating Subcommittee of the Armed Service Committee of the Senate," 26 and 27 November 1957, A. Dulles/H. Scoville Comments before Senate Comt. (Nov. 57), Box 1, Bryce Harlow Records, 1953–61, DDEL.

86. "Transition Period in Soviet Naval Construction," *The ONI Review*, vol. 13, no. 9, 1958, NHC. See also QIR, January to September 1958, No. 17, 10 October 1958, ADM 223/243, PRO. As for surface ships, the reduction of earlier years continued with only the Kotlin class destroyer and Riga class escorts reportedly being built in 1957.

87. In 1959, the most authoritative open source, *Jane's Fighting Ships*, stated that there were 'about 500 submarinesó in the Soviet navy. *Jane's Fighting Ships, 1959–60* (London: Sampson, Marston & Co., Ltd., 1959), p. 298. Whilst reasonably accurate, Jane's did tend to err on the side of overestimation.

88. "Transition Period in Soviet Naval Construction," *The ONI Review*, September 1958, NHC. In testimony to the Senate Preparedness Sub-Committee in January 1958, Admiral H.G. Rickover, stated that a "number of Soviet submarines" were already fitted with missiles. D.W. Morley, "Technology and Weapons," in *The Soviet Navy,* ed. M.G. Saunders (London: Weidenfeld and Nicolson), p. 206.

89. "CIA Briefing for Preparedness Investigating Subcommittee of the Armed Service Committee of the Senate," 26 and 27 November 1957, A. Dulles/H. Scoville Comments before Senate Comt. (Nov. 57), Box 1, Bryce Harlow Records, 1953–61, DDEL.

90. See "Soviet Sub Capability Likened to Air Power of Reds by Admiral Wright," 8 February 1958, *Army-Navy-Air Force Journal,* and "NATO Chief's Warning on Submarine Threat," *Daily Telegraph,* 19 November 1959.

91. JP(57)59(Final), 8 May 1957, DEFE 6/41, PRO.

92. Vice-Admiral C. C. Hughes Hallett to First Sea Lord, 7 January 1954, ADM 205/102, PRO.

93. Ibid. Admiral Hallett went on to say: "These ideas, though they may not be widely held, affirm that the thought uppermost in some US Naval minds is that the defence of the continental United States is the primary role of its naval forces. "

94. JP(57)59(Final), 8 May 1957, DEFE 6/41, PRO, and QIR, January to March 1958, No. 15, 10 April 1958, ADM 223/241, PRO. This report stated that the era when Soviet nuclear submarines would enter the Fleet in "operational quantities" would only begin in 1961.

95. QIR, January to March 1958, No. 15, 10 April 1958, ADM 223/241, PRO.

96. Jan S. Breemer, "Estimating the Soviet Strategic Submarine Missile Threat: A Critical Examination of the Soviet Navy's SSBN Bastion Strategy" (Ph. D. diss., University of Southern California, 1987), p. 48.

97. Ibid. p. 44. In fact, in 1961 and 1962, technical difficulties encountered by the USSR with their SLBM programme is reflected in the fact that both the Zulus and Golfs ceased deployments outside "near-home operating waters."

98. Even here there were anomalies which did not appear to fit overall assessments. For example, in 1957 there was no confirmed information on the existence of submarine pens in the USSR. See "Soviet Submarine Bases," *The ONI Review*, vol. 12, no. 9, 1957, NHC.

99. For the problem of mirror-imaging in the area of intelligence, see Abram N. Shulsky, *Silent Warfare: Understanding the World of Intelligence* (Washington, DC: Brassey's, 1991), pp. 64–67.

100. Sir Richard Powell, letter to author, 14 November, 1991.

101. Memorandum, From: CNO, To: The Hydrographer, 13 July 1955, Subject: Submarine Control of Regulus (enclosing priority target list for Regulus), A–5, Box 315, Strategic Plans Division Records, NHC. See also Norman Friedman, U.S. *Naval Weapons* (London: Conway Maritime Press, 1983), pp. 218–220.

102. "Chronology of Significant Events in the US Intermediate and Intercontinental Ballistic Missile Programs," 8 November 1957, Missile Program (3), Box 4, OCB Series – Subject Subseries, WHO: Office of Special Assistant for National Security Affairs, DDEL.

103. Ibid.
104. Ibid.
105. See interview with Rear Admiral Charles E. Weakley, Anti-Submarine Warfare Readiness Executive, "Could Missile Subs Operate From the North Pole Region? – Red Submarine Threat Termed 'Unparalleled in History'," *The Register*, 29 March 1958.
106. This trip was immediately followed by another sub-polar voyage by the *USS Skate*. "Skate' Trip's Military Value Is Praised," ("Professional Notes"), *USNIP* 84 (October 1958), pp. 129–30.
107. Hanson Baldwin, "Strategic Value of the Arctic Proved – Suitable as a Site to Launch Guided Missiles," *The Daily Telegraph,* 9 August 1958.
108. Ibid. Similarly, on the perceived implications for the Arctic as an area of strategic pivot, see A. F. Talbert, "Polar Routes Envisioned As Increasingly Vital," *USNIP* 84 (October 1958), pp. 130–132.
109. "Secret Testimony Cites 1960 Red Sub Peril," *The Register*, 6 September 1958.
110. David A. Anderton, "Details of Sputnik Surprise Scientists," *Aviation Week*, 21 October 1957.
111. A good illustration of the public anxiety which the emerging "submarine peril" engendered after Sputnik can be seen in a *Newsweek* article devoted to the subject in August 1958. "Missile-Firing Sub: New Space-Age Weapon," *Newsweek*, 25 August 1958.
112. Ambrose, *Eisenhower: The President*, p. 423.
113. Polmar and Noot, *Submarines of the Russian and Soviet Navies*, p. 152.
114. "Aboard a Soviet Cruiser," (Excerpts from report by Capt. A.P.W. Northey, DSC, RN), *The ONI Review: Secret Supplement*, Autumn 1956, NHC.
115. Ibid. The British attaché also wrote that Khrushchev "appeared completely fascinated by the possibilities of guided missiles in any role."
116. "Soviet Propaganda on Missile Launching Submarines," *The ONI Review*, vol. 14, no. 2, 1959, NHC, and "Selected Quotations from Soviet Leaders' Statements," 23 January 1959, Committee mailings no. 33 thru no. 39, U.S. President's Committee to Study the U.S. Military Assistance Program (Draper Committee), Records, 1958–59, DDEL.
117. See for example article by Marshal Vasilevsky, "Dangerous Boasting," *Red Star*, 14 August 1957, and "Answers of General Commander of the Air Force Marshal K.A. Vershinin," *Pravda*, 8 September 1957 (both articles kindly translated by Maxim Shashenkov, Nuffield College, Oxford).
118. Memorandum, 16 July 1952, Subject: Possible Exit of USSR Cruisers from the Baltic Sea, A16–12, Box 274, Strategic Plans Division Records, NHC.
119. "The Changing Soviet Concept of Sea Power: An Editorial," *The ONI Review*, vol. 9, no. 11, November 1954, NHC.
120. Memorandum, CNO to CINCLANT, 9 November 1954, Subject: Reconnaissance of the East Norwegian Sea, North Cape Area, Folder TS 1955, Box 330, Strategic Plans Division Records, NHC.
121. From: CNO To: JCS, Subj: Reconnaissance of Uninhabited Areas, 14 April 1952, A1, Box 271, Strategic Plans Division Records, NHC.
122. Memorandum, CNO to CINCLANT, 9 November 1954, Subject: Reconnaissance of the East Norwegian Sea, North Cape Area, Folder TS 1955, Box 330, Strategic Plans Division Records, NHC.

123. Memorandum, CINCLANT to CNO, 28 January 1955, Subject: Reconnaissance of the East Norwegian Sea – North Cape Area, Folder TS 1955, Box 330, Strategic Plans Division Records, NHC.
124. From Vice-Admiral R.F. Elkins to First Sea Lord, 16 October 1956, ADM 205/110, PRO.
125. From Vice-Admiral R.F. Elkins to First Sea Lord, 31 September 1956, ADM 205/110, PRO.
126. Ibid. Britain had been gathering intelligence along the Murmansk coast in an operation called Pontiac. The cancellation of the operation and the American decision to conduct operations in the Murmansk area itself is yet another indication of growing American involvement in the region.
127. Norman Friedman, *The Naval Institute Guide to World Naval Weapons Systems, 1991/92* (Annapolis, MD: Naval Institute Press, 1991), p. 802.
128. Christensen, *Vår Hemmelige Beredeskap*, pp. 143–46.
129. Tamnes, *Cold War in the High North*, 1990, pp. 129–132. Plans were certainly considered for more U-2 flights in the "extremely important" northern sector in 1959 and 1960. Memorandum, 12 February 1959, Intelligence Material (8)[Jan–Feb. 1959], Box 15, Subject Series, Alpha, WHO: Office of the Staff Secretary, DDEL.
130. "Monthly Box Score of Submarine Contacts," *The ONI Review*, vol. 13, no. 9, 1958, NHC.
131. "Monthly Box Score of Submarine Contacts," *The ONI Review*, vol. 14, no. 3, 1959, NHC.
132. "Monthly Box Score of Submarine Contacts," *The ONI Review*, vol. 14, no. 7, 1959, NHC. Both these contacts were classified as positive by OPNAV.
133. A plotting of these ONI reports indicate clearly that the highest incidence of contacts occurred in the north Atlantic.
134. Jürg Meister, "The Soviet Merchant Ships and Fishing Fleets," in *The Soviet Navy*, ed. M.G. Saunders (London: Weidenfeld and Nicolson, 1958), p. 232. See also Hanson W. Baldwin, "Versatile Fishermen: But the Soviet Fleets Will Have a Task To Track New US Polaris Submarine," *New York Times*, 22 November 1960.
135. "The Soviet North Atlantic Fishing Fleet," *The ONI Review*, vol. 12, no. 5, 1957, NHC.
136. Fst/E, Notat: Truselen mot Skandinavia, 29 mai 1959, FO.
137. These figures are based on a cross-reference of US, UK and Norwegian declassified intelligence estimates. The most important of these include: "The Threat and Vulnerability of Soviet Submarines", Typed Brief, March 1950, File 4, Drawer 1, No. 7869/5, ONI TS Records, NHC; Annex A to Enclosure, OP-301D/jwl, 13 October 1953, A4, Box 200, Strategic Plans Division Records, NHC; "Vast Increase in Soviet Submarine Strength", *Secret Supplement of the ONI Review*, Spring 1956, NHC; Memorandum, D/NI to D/OP-30, 18 January 1955, "Acceleration in Soviet Submarine Building Program", EF-61, Box 327, Strategic Plans Division Records, NHC; QIR (Quarterly Intelligence Report), for January to March 1957, no. 11, 10 April 1957, PRO, ADM 223/240; Presentation by C/JCS, 20 January 1959, JCS (6), Jan.-Feb. 1959, Box 4, Subject Series-DoD Subseries, WHO: Office of the Staff Secretary, DDEL; Appendix to Annex

to JP(59)140(Final), "Likely Deployment for war of Soviet Submarines in the Atlantic Area", JP(59)140(Final), 20 November 1959, PRO, DEFE 6/58; "Order of Battle Northern Fleet, 22.1.60", enclosure to Letter Fst/E to FD, 25 January 1960, FD A/H 849/60, Fst/E 25/1-60, FD.

138. This figure includes "modern" submarines only, and leaves out 19 K,L,S,M submarines with the Northern Fleet in 1960. "Order of Battle Northern Fleet, 22.1.60," enclosure to Letter from Fst/E to F. Ramm (FD), 25 January 1960, FD A/H 849/60, Fst/E 25/1-60, FD.

139. "Vast Increase in Soviet Submarine Strength," *Secret Supplement of the ONI Review, Spring* 1956, NHC.

140. Increasingly, however, these obsolescent models were withdrawn from activate service. See "Vast Increase in Soviet Submarine Strength," *Secret Supplement of the ONI Review, Spring* 1956, NHC.

4 THE US NAVY, NORWAY AND THE NEW LOOK: ADJUSTING TO A "NORTHERN STRATEGY", 1954–57

1. "Study of Attack Carrier Force Levels (Cold War)," 13 October 1953, A4, Box 280, Strategic Plans Division Records, NHC.

2. Palmer, *Origins of the Maritime Strategy*, p. 77.

3. Dwight D. Eisenhower, *Mandate for Change 1953–1956* (London: Heinemann, 1963), p. 435.

4. Watson, *History of the Joint Chiefs of Staff, Volume 5,* pp. 35–37. For an interesting official account of the rationale behind the New Look, see "Strong US Defense for the 'Long Pull' – Interview with Admiral Arthur W. Radford, Chairman, Joint Chiefs of Staff," *US News & World Report*, 5 March 1954.

5. Memorandum for Secretary of Defense, 9 December 1953, Subject: Military Strategy and Posture, ccs 381, U.S.(1-13-50) sec 32., Box 2, JCS 1954–56 (Geographic file), Rg. 218, NARA.

6. JCS 2101/113, Enclosure "A" Military Strategy to Support the National Security Policy Set Forth in NSC 162/2, 10 December 1953, ccs 381 US(1-31-50) sec. 32, JCS (Geographic file) 1954–56, Box 2, Rg 218, NARA. See also Divine, *Eisenhower and the Cold War*, p. 37.

7. "Summary of Joint Papers Having to do with Naval Force Structures Since the 'New Look'," 9 December 1953, L(1), Box 322, Strategic Plans Division Records, NHC.

8. Memorandum, From: CNO, To: JCS, 7 September 1951, Subject: Navy Atomic Capability, A16-10, Box 264, Strategic Plans Division Records, NHC.

9. Ibid.

10. Memorandum, From: D/CNO(Air), To: D/CNO (Operations), ND Subject: Planning for the Use of Atomic Weapons, A16-10, Box 274 (1952), Strategic Plans Division Records, NHC.

11. JSPC 851/112, Status of US Programs for National Security as of 30 June 1954, ccs 381 US (1-13-50) sec. 41., Box 32, JCS 1954–56 (Geographic file), Rg. 218, NARA.

12. David Rosenberg, "Arleigh Albert Burke," in *The Chiefs of Naval Operations,* ed. Robert W. Love, Jr. (Annapolis, MD: Naval Institute Press, 1980), p. 276.

13. The first models of the Mark-5 bomb, a lightweight *strategic* nuclear weapon, and the Mark-7 bomb, the first truly *tactical* nuclear weapon in the US arsenal, were deployed with naval attack aircraft in 1952–53. The AJ-1, AJ-2 and, later, the A3D were designed to act as strategic bombers forming heavy attack squadrons (VHAs), while a range of other aircraft, including F2H, F3H-2N and FJ-4B, were assigned a tactical role. James N. Gibson, *The History of the US Nuclear Arsenal* (London: Bison Books Ltd., 1989), pp. 82–84, and George F. Eliot, "Sea-Borne Deterrent," *USNIP* 82 (November 1956).

14. Norman Polmar, *Aircraft Carriers: A Graphic History of Carrier Aviation and Its Influence on World Events* (London: MacDonald & Co. Ltd., 1969), pp. 596–601.

15. Rosenberg, "American Postwar Air Doctrine and Organization," p. 269.

16. Palmer, *Origins of the Maritime Strategy,* Chapter three.

17. Samuel P. Huntington, "National Policy and the Transoceanic Navy," *USNIP* 80 (May 1954).

18. Ibid., p. 488.

19. Ibid.

20. Semiannual Reports of the Secretary of the Navy, 1 Jan. 1954 to 30 June, 1954 (Washington, DC: USGPO, 1955).

21. Huntington, "The Transoceanic Navy," pp. 490–491. With the development of sea-based ballistic missile systems in the latter half of the decade, naval action would also have a potentially decisive bearing on operations in the *interior*.

22. Admiral Robert C. Carney, (CNO from 1953 to 1955), "Principles of Sea Power," *USNIP* 81 (September 1955). See also John Hattendorf, "American Thinking on Naval Strategy 1945–1980," in *Maritime Strategy and the Nuclear Age,* ed. Geoffrey Till (London: The Macmillan Press Ltd., 1984), p. 62.

23. JSPC 851/112, Status of US Programs for National Security as of 30 June 1954, ccs 381 U.S.(1-13-50) sec. 41., Box 32, JCS 1954-56 (Geographic file), Rg. 218, NARA.

24. Annex to JP(56)173(Final), "Pattern of Naval Forces For NATO Control of the Atlantic During the Next Decade," 16 November 1956, DEFE 6/37, PRO.

25. Ibid.

26. Norman Friedman, *The Postwar Naval Revolution* (London: Conway Maritime Press, 1986), pp. 22–23, and Wayne P. Hughes, Jr, *Fleet Tactics: Theory and Practise* (Annapolis, MD: Naval Institute Press, Maryland, 1986), p. 218.

27. Joel J. Sokolsky, *Seapower in the Nuclear Age: The United States Navy and NATO 1949–80* (London and New York: Routledge, 1991), p. 9.

28. L.W. Martin, *The Sea in Modern Strategy* (London: Chatto & Windus, 1967), p. 10, and, Malcolm W. Cagle, "A Philosophy for Naval Atomic Warfare," *USNIP* 83 (March 1957), pp. 250–51.

29. Semiannual Report of the Secretary of Defense, 1 Jan. 1955 to June 30, 1956 (Washington, DC: USGPO 1957), p. 4. The most notable signs of transition in the mid-1950s included the commissioning in September 1954 of the USS *Nautilus* (SSN-571), the first nuclear-powered submarine, followed shortly thereafter by USS *Seawolf*, launched in July 1955. The world's first guided missile cruiser, USS *Boston*, joined the fleet in 1956. And, finally, between 1955 and 1958, four new Forrestal class heavy attack carriers (*Forrestal, Saratoga, Ranger, Independence*) – authorised by Congress at the rate of one per year in the wake of the Korean War – joined the fleet.

30. Annex to JP(56)173(Final), 16 November 1956, DEFE 6/37, PRO.

31. Floyd D. Kennedy Jr., "The Creation of the Cold War Navy, 1953–1962," in *In Peace and War: Interpretations of American Naval History, 1775–1978*, ed. Kenneth J. Hagan (Westport, Connecticut: Greenwood Press, 1978), p. 310.

32. Huntington, "The Transoceanic Navy," p. 493; see also Semiannual Reports of the Secretary of the Navy, Jan.1 1954 to June 30, 1954 (Washington, DC: USGPO, 1955), p. 158.

33. "Study of Attack Carrier Force Levels (Cold War)," 13 October 1953, A4, Box 280, Strategic Plans Division Records, NHC.

34. Ibid.

35. Ibid.

36. Ibid.

37. Interview with Admiral Arleigh Burke, 18 July 1990, Fairfax, Virginia.

38. Admiral Robert B. Carney, "Principles of Sea Power," *USNIP* 81 (September 1955), p. 975.

39. JSPC 980/120, Selection of Chiefs JUSMAGS/MAAGS, 11 October 1955, ccs 092 (8-22-46)(2), sec. 18, JCS 1954–56, Rg. 218, NARA.

40. CINCLANTFLT's Annual Report for 1955, quoted in Sokolsky, *Seapower in the Nuclear Age*, p. 74.

41. Philip Wyman, "SACLANT: NATO's Atlantic Partner," *Military Review* 36 (October 1956), pp. 42–44. See also Jordan, *Alliance Strategies and Navies*, pp. 7–8.

42. This is evident in Admiralty papers for the period, especially after 1957, at which point British influence on the planning process appears to weaken. This will be discussed in greater detail in the following chapter.

43. D/Strategic Plans, to D/Naval Intelligence, Serials 000966P30 of 8 November 1950; and, 0001000P30, 24 November 1950, about "Target Data", both in A16-3, Strategic Plans Division Records, NHC.

44. War Plans Division, D/Plans, 5 October 1951, Subject: Employment of Aircraft Carriers in the North Sea and North East Atlantic, 7C Carrier Papers, Box 84, Papers of Hoyt S. Vandenberg (CS/USAF), Manuscript Division, Library of Congress.

45. Excerpts of letters from General Eisenhower to Admiral Fraser (First Sea Lord) and Admiral Fetchler (CNO), 24 September 1951, and SACEUR's reply to Standing Group request for estimate of force requirements based on D-Day 1 July 1954, quoted in "Study of Attack Carrier Force Levels (Cold War)," 13 October 1953, A4, Box 280, Strategic Plans Division Records, NHC.

46. Vice Admiral John McNay Taylor, "The Striking Fleet Atlantic," *NATO's Fifteen Nations* (April 1962), p. 37.

47. "Russia – Threat To US At Sea: Interview with Admiral Robert B.Carney, CNO," *US News & World Report*, 18 June 1954.

48. The ultimate expression of NATO's early conventional strategy was the February 1952 Lisbon force goals; nearly one hundred divisions backed up by naval and air power. In April 1953 the first downward revision of these force goals was approved. In December 1953 the NAC reduced previous force goals further, and in April 1954 the original Lisbon targets were formally abandoned. Watson, *History of the Joint Chiefs of Staff*, pp. 282, 287 and 299.

49. "Study of Attack Carrier Force Levels (Cold War)," 13 October 1953, A4, Box 280, Strategic Plans Division Records, NHC.

50. An additional factor which for much of the 1950s reduced the availability of carriers in the Atlantic was the continued deployment of Atlantic Fleet ships to the western Pacific. In his departing letter to President Eisenhower on 12 August 1955, Chief of Naval Operations, Admiral Robert Carney, felt "obliged" to state that "with the peacetime realities of deployments in the Pacific, we are not prepared to meet the Atlantic commitments which we have made to NATO; it is physically impossible to do so." See letter from Admiral Carney, CNO, to President, 12 August 1955, Admiral Carney, Box 10, Administration Series, Papers of Dwight D. Eisenhower as President of the US, DDEL.

51. NSC 5509, DoD Report to NSC on Status of United States Military Programs as of 31 December 1954, Part 1, 31 March 1955, NSC 5509 (1), Box 8, NSC Series–Status of Project Subseries, WHO: Office of Special Assistant for National Security Affairs, DDEL.

52. Letter from CINCLANT to CNO, 23 March 1955, Subject: US Atlantic Fleet Ability to Meet Post-D-Day Commitments to form Carrier Striking Forces, L(1), Box 322, Strategic Plans Division Records, NHC.

53. Memorandum, From: D/Fleet Operations Division, To: D/Strategic Plans, 4 April 1955, Subject: Mobility of Fleet Marine Forces, A16-12(2), Box 320, Strategic Plans Division Records, NHC.

54. Memorandum, From: D/Strategic Plans, To: D/Naval Intelligence, 17 March 1953, Subject: Air Targets Study, DDT No. 740; comments on, A-8, Box 283, Strategic Plans Division Records, NHC.

55. Ibid. and From: OP-55, To: OP-32, March 1953 Subject: Air Targets Study, DDT No.740, A-8, Box 283, Strategic Plans Division Records, NHC.

56. Sokolsky, *Seapower in the Nuclear Age*, p. 59.

57. Memorandum, From: D/Strategic Plans, To: D/General Planning Group, 18 February 1955, Subject: U.S.Navy Fixed Responsibilities in NATO Air Atomic Mission, A16-10, Box 319, Strategic Plans Division Records, NHC.

58. Letter from CINCLANT to CNO, 23 March 1955, Subject: US Atlantic Fleet Ability to Meet Post-D-Day Commitments to form Carrier Striking Forces, L(1), Box 322, Strategic Plans Division Records, NHC.

59. "Referat fra møte i den sentrale sjefsnemd, 8 mars 1957,–Sak. 213," FO.

60. "III. C. Evaluation of Capabilities of Antisubmarine Forces," in NSC 5509, Part 1, 31 March 1955, NSC 5509 (1), Box 8, NSC Series, Status of Project

Subseries, WHO: Office of Special Assistant for National Security Affairs, DDEL.

61. NEC Historical Reports, 1 July 1954–30 June 1955, "Training Activities," SECCOS, HQ AFNORTH.
62. Sections of MC 14/2 are cited in JP(57)124(Final), 6 November 1957, Allied Command Atlantic Minimum Forces Study, 1958–1962, DEFE 6/43, PRO.
63. JP(56)165(Final), SACLANT's Emergency Defence Plan for 1957, 1 November 1956, DEFE 6/37, PRO.
64. Ibid.
65. Ibid.
66. The 1953 report by the Strategic Plans Division stressed that "SACEUR has never deviated from his repeated statements that carrier task forces are vital to the security of his flanks." See "Study of Attack Carrier Force Levels (Cold War)," 13 October 1953, A4, Box 280, Strategic Plans Division Records, NHC.
67. This is discussed more fully in Chapter Six.
68. Memorandum, From: Assistant CNO, To: D/Strategic Plans 21 December 1951, Subject: Draft of Proposed Over-all Aerial Mining Plan; forwarding of, A4-3(1), Box 272, Strategic Plans Division Records, NHC.
69. Ibid. In 1952 the US Atlantic Fleet's "offensive mining plan" for the first month of war included only seven targets in the "Barents Sea – White Sea Area." See Brief of CINCLANT Mining Plan No.201-50, ND, A4-3 (1), Box 272, Strategic Plans Division Records, NHC.
70. Memorandum, From: OP-05, To: OP-04, 16 April 1951, Subject: Joint Military Rights Requirements in Norway, A14-1, Box 264, Strategic Plans Division Records, NHC. This memorandum was specifically referring to the airfield at Bodø which was then under construction. It was estimated that 175 officers and 1050 enlisted personnel would have to be accommodated at the base if agreement for basing was reached.
71. Memorandum, From: OP-301 To: OP-30B, 29 August 1952, Subject: Tactical Air Force Base Rights in Norway, A-14, Box 271; and Memorandum: From: OP-504E5 To: OP-301C, ND 1953, Subject: SACLANT Requirements Presentation, A14, Box 283, Strategic Plans Division Records, NHC. A maritime airfield was incorporated in the 1953 infrastructure programme (fourth slice), though detailed Navy requirements were only specified later (see below).
72. CNO's Recommended Changes to JSC 570/377 USBRO, December 1955, Box 323, Strategic Plans Division Records, NHC.
73. The special status of these two bases is also suggested by the existence of a document, "JCS 570/484, Status of Andøya and Bodø as Bases in Current War Plans," in the JCS "Hot Box" in 1958. The document is still classified, but the associated "flimsies" speak of the "extreme delicacy" of the paper (a Freedom of Information Act request for JCS 570/484 has been submitted).
74. Memorandum, From: Assistant CNO, To: D/Strategic Plans, 21 December 1951, Subject: Draft of Proposed Over-all Aerial Mining Plan, A4-3(1), Box 272, Strategic Plans Division Records, NHC.
75. "Brief of SACLANT Mining Plan 1-55," A16-12, Box 320, Strategic Plans Division Records, NHC.

76. Ibid.
77. CNO to CINCLANT, 6 December 1954, Subject: Base Requirements for Support of US Forces Earmarked for Assignment to SACLANT, JCS 1954–56, ccs 360 (12-9-42) Sec. 80, Rg.218 NARA, and Memorandum, From: Director, Strategic Plans, To: Director: Logistics Plans Division, 10 October 1955, Subject: Base Rights for Support of US Forces Earmarked for Deployment to Norway, EF, Box 325, Strategic Plans Division Record, NHC.
78. "Patrol bomber" was the US designation for what the British and the Norwegians simply referred to as "maritime patrol aircraft."
79. Memorandum, D/Strategic Plans to D/Logistic Plans Division, 10 October 1955, EF, Box 325, Strategic Plans Division Records, NHC. This requirement was added to CNO's list of overseas base requirements in December 1955.
80. "Brief of SACLANT Mining Plan 1-55," A16-12, Box 320, Strategic Plans Division Records, NHC.
81. From: CINCLANT, To: CNO, 16 September 1955, Subject: Base Rights for Support of US Forces Earmarked For deployment to Norway, (enclosure 3: Requirements for Bodø, Norway), EF, Box 325, Strategic Plans Division Records, NHC.
82. CNO's Recommended Changes to JSC 570/377 USBRO, December 1955, Box 322, Strategic Plans Division Records, NHC.
83. From: CINCLANT, To: CNO, 16 September 1955, Subject: Base Rights for Support of US Forces Earmarked For deployment to Norway, (enclosure 2: Requirements for Ørlandet, Norway), EF, Box 325, Strategic Plans Division Records, NHC.
84. Flyvåpenets overkommando, "Amerikanske flybesøk til Bodø, Andøya og Bardufoss," 13 Sept.1955, (ref. H 1111/55/005.I.3. JSB/EJ.), FD.
85. Ibid.
86. Ibid.
87. From: CINCLANT, To: CNO, 16 September 1955, Subject: Base Rights for Support of US Forces Earmarked For deployment to Norway, (enclosure 1: Requirements for Andøya, Norway), EF, Box 325, Strategic Plans Division Records, NHC.
88. Ibid.
89. Notat, 11 September 1956 (regler for fremmede skip og flys adgang til Norge i fredstid), 38.15/7, Bind. III, UD.
90. That is, atomic depth bombs would be employed against Soviet submarines in transit from northern bases to their patrolling areas in the North Atlantic. Memorandum, From: D/Undersea Warfare Division, To: Aviation Plans Division, Subj: AUW Shops for Servicing Atomic Depth Bomb, Mk-90 (Betty), A16-10, Box 319, Strategic Plans Division, NHC. See also "Soviet Sub Menace Cut by New Weapon," *The Register*, 2 November 1957.
91. Memorandum, From: D/Atomic Energy Division, To: D/Undersea Warfare Division, 25 November 1955, Subject: Permanent Facilities for Special Weapons Assembly Operations at Final Staging Bases, A16-10, Box 319, Strategic Plans Division, NHC. See also Sokolsky, *Seapower in the Nuclear Age*, p. 57.

92. The 48 nuclear warheads deployed at Thule between 1958 and 1965 were, in the event of war, to be used in the *Nike Hercules* missiles as part of the forward air defence of the US continent. See Ib Faurby, "Overraskelsen der ikke burde være kommet", *Politikken*, 15 July 1995, and "Regerings redegørelse til Folketinget om visse aspekter af Thule-sagen", 29 June 1995, Danish Foreign Ministry Memorandum.

93. Memorandum for General Vandenberg (CS/USAF), 18 February 1953, Subject: Navy Proposal for Shore Basing of Attack Aircraft in Northern Europe, 7c Carrier Papers, Box 84, The Papers of Hoyt S. Vandenberg, Manuscript Division, Library of Congress.

94. Ibid.

95. From CNO to CINCLANT, Subject: Base Requirements for Support of US Forces Earmarked for Assignment to SACLANT, 6 December 1954, JCS 1954–56, ccs 360 (12-9-42) Sec. 80, Rg. 218, NARA.

96. In December 1953, for example, the US Naval attaché in Oslo was requested to forward information to OPNAV about operating conditions in the Arctic. See Memorandum, For: OP-32 To: OP-30, 9 December 1953, Subject: Weather, Oceanography and Ship Operating Conditions in Arctic Regions, A16-1, Box 284, Strategic Plans Division Records, NHC.

97. Joseph A. Krcek (Office of Naval Research), "Communications in the Arctic," *Signal* 13 (September 1958), p. 41.

98. Ibid.

99. NEC Historical Reports, 1 July 1956–31 December 1957, SECCOS, HQ AFNORTH; Krcek, "Communications in the Arctic," p. 41.

100. NEC Historical Reports, 1 July 1956–31 December 1957, SECCOS, HQ AFNORTH.

101. History of NEC, 1 July 1956–31 December 1957 (signals division), Annex 8 to AFNORTH Historical Report, SECCOS, HQ AFNORTH. See also "Strike Back Paid Big Dividends, Reports Adm.Wright; Communications Is Problem," *Army-Navy-Air Force Journal,* 12 October 1957.

102. AIRNORTH, Historical Report, 1 July–31 December 1957, NEC Historical Reports, SECCOS, HQ AFNORTH.

103. NEC Historical Reports, 1 January 1958–31 December 1958, SECCOS, HQ AFNORTH. Use could here be made of the Tacan system, that is, the chain of tactical air beacons constructed in Norway in the mid- to late fifties under NATO's infrastructure programme. Moreover, the Loran stations constructed in Norway could also be used by aircraft for this purpose.

104. Report to JCS on Revised Loran Installation Plan, 19 October 1955, JCS 1954-56, ccs 676.3(8-25-42) sec. 12, Box 163, Rg. 218, NARA.

105. Ibid.

106. "Signals Chronological Order of Events," NEC Historical Reports, 1 July 1955–30 June 196, SECCOS, HQ AFNORTH.

107. The Navy requirements were for a "3-station chain." See "CNO's Recommended Changes to JCS 570/377 USBRO, December 1955," Box 323, Strategic Plans Division, NHC.

108. In early plans, Polaris submarines were scheduled for initial deployment *either* in the Norwegian Sea or Mediterranean. See Memo for SecDef, 5 May 1959, Subj: Statement of Navy Views on the Concept of

Employment and Command Structure for the Polaris Weapon System, ccs 4720, Box 62, JCS 1959, Rg. 218, NARA.

5   BRITISH NAVAL POLICY, 1953–60: IMPLICATIONS FOR NORWAY AND AMERICAN COMMITMENTS IN THE NORTH ATLANTIC

1. General Eisenhower to George Marshall, 12 March 1951, *The Papers of Dwight David Eisenhower: NATO and the Campaign of 1952: XIII,* (Baltimore: The Johns Hopkins University Press, 1989), p. 120.
2. Ibid. p. 120
3. *All Hands,* No. 442, December 1953, p. 36.
4. Exercise Sea Enterprise, 21–28 September, 1955, *The ONI Review,* vol. 10, no. 10, 1955, NHC.
5. Memorandum for General Gruenther, 12 March 1952, Gruenther, A. (1), Box 48, Dwight D. Eisenhower Pre-Presidential Papers, 1916–1952, DDEL.
6. Clive Archer, *Uncertain Trust: The British-Norwegian Defence Relationship* (Oslo: Institutt for Forsvarsstudier, 1989), p. 23. Interview with Vice-Admiral Ronald Brockman, 18 March 1991, London.
7. Eric J. Grove, *Vanguard to Trident: British Naval Policy Since World War II* (London: The Bodley Head, 1987), p. 204.
8. The success of carrier operations around the Korean peninsula, particularly close air support for the land-battle, was taken by both the Admiralty and the US Navy as a vindication of the utility of the carrier. See Bernard Brodie, *A Guide to Naval Strategy: Fourth Edition* (Princeton: Princeton University Press, 1958), p. 240. See also William J. Crowe, "The Policy Roots of the Modern Royal Navy, 1946–1962" (Ph. D. diss., Princeton University, 1965), pp. 128–131.
9. Grove, *Vanguard to Trident,* p. 98. On the various factors which contributed to pressure within the Admiralty for a more *offensively-oriented* Fleet Air Arm in the early 1950s, see also Crowe, "The Policy Roots of the Royal Navy," pp. 126–138.
10. Ibid., and interview with Vice-Admiral Sir Ronald Brockman, 18 March 1991.
11. Michael Dockrill, British Defence Since 1945 (London: Basil Blackwell, 1988), pp. 5–6, and Martin S. Navias, Nuclear Weapons and British Strategic Planning, 1955–1958 (Oxford: Clarendon Press, 1991), pp. 139–140.
12. Navias, *Nuclear Weapons and British Strategic Planning,* p. 67. Sir John Slessor also observed at the time that the White Paper of 1957 introduced "no basic revolution in policy," but merely rationalised tendencies "which have long been obvious." Sir John Slessor, "British Defence Policy," *Foreign Affairs* 35 (July 1957), p. 551.
13. Navias, Nuclear *Weapons and British Strategic Planning,* p. 77.
14. Future Defence Policy: Report by the Chiefs of Staff, 22 May 1947, reprinted in Dockrill, *British Defence Policy Since 1945,* pp. 132–138.
15. Denny, "The Atlantic in a World War," p. 353.

16. Crowe, "The Policy Roots of the Royal Navy," p. 136.
17. The author is grateful to Eric Grove for pointing out these possible connections.
18. The two fleet carriers available at the time were HMS *Eagle,* which had joined the fleet in October 1951, and the older HMS *Indomitable.* HMS *Ark Royal* followed some three-and-a-half years later. Fleet Carriers were functionally equivalent to US attack carriers (CVA), although they clearly did not match the USS *Forrestal* class of carriers. See B.B. Schofield, *British Sea Power: Naval Policy in the Twentieth Century* (London: B.T. Batsford Ltd. 1967), p. 221.
19. Crowe, "The Policy Roots of the Royal Navy," p. 133. This mission, according to Crowe, was "given number one priority among SACLANT's responsibilities."
20. Friedman, *The Postwar Naval Revolution*, p. 41.
21. Eric J. Grove, *Battle for the Fjords: NATO's Forward Maritime Strategy In Action* (London: Ian Allan Ltd., 1991), p. 10.
22. Quoted in Grove, *Vanguard to Trident,* pp. 91–2.
23. Ibid.
24. RDP/M(53)8, Radical Review, "Minutes of Meeting held 10 November 1953," 11 November 1953, ADM 1/24695, PRO.
25. Ibid.
26. Ibid.
27. Memorandum by the First Lord of the Admiralty, "The Role of Aircraft Carriers," 9 November 1953, ADM 1/24695, PRO.
28. Annex to RDP/P(53)32 "Admiralty replies to questions 1 to 11," 9 December 1953, ADM 205/93, PRO.
29. RDP/P(53)32, Memorandum by First Lord in Reply to RDP/P(53)30(R), 9 December 1953, ADM 205/93, PRO.
30. Attachment to Memorandum by the First Lord of the Admiralty, "The Role of Aircraft Carriers," 9 November 1953, ADM 1/24695, PRO.
31. "Enclosure to First Sea Lord's No. 2829 of 22nd of December, 1953," ADM 205/93, PRO.
32. Ibid.
33. Grove, *Battle for the Fjords,* p. 10.
34. Long Term Plans for the Navy, Enclosure, 28 January 1954, ADM 205/102, PRO.
35. In the spring of 1955 the ONI estimated that 660 aircraft were assigned to the 4th Fleet Air Force, 500 to the 8th Fleet Air Force and 498 to the Northern Fleet Air Force, see "Developments and trends in the Soviet Fleet and Soviet Naval Air Force during 1954," *The ONI Review Secret Supplement:* Spring 1955, NHC. The Scimitar was also to be given a nuclear ground support and interdiction capability. The Sea Vixen, to be developed with advanced airborne radar for all-weather performance, was regarded as having a potential nuclear delivery capability at the time.
36. First Lord to Minister of Defence, 23 December, enclosing "The Need for the DH 110 and the N 113," ADM 205/93, PRO.
37. The case for the NA39, see ADM 205/94, PRO.
38. The Navy case for the "aircraft-carrier striking force" in 1955 is clearly spelt out in an article representative of Admiralty opinion by Rear-Admiral

A.D. Torlesse, "The Role of the Aircraft Carrier," *Brassey's Annual 1955* (London: William Clowes & Sons, Ltd., 1956).

39. D(55) 1 Meeting, Memorandum by the Minister of Defence, Defence Policy: Heavy Aircraft Carriers, 7 January 1955, CAB 131/15, PRO.
40. D(55) 1st Meeting, Minutes of Meeting 13 January 1955, Minute no. 6.–Defence Policy: Heavy Aircraft Carriers, CAB 131/15, PRO.
41. Torlesse, "The Royal Navy in the Atomic Age," p. 155.
42. VCNS to First Lord, No. 631, 18 December 1953, ADM 205/93, PRO.
43. "Brief of SACLANT Mining Plan 1-55," ND, A16–12, Box 320, Strategic Plans Division Records, NHC.
44. Memorandum, From: C-in-C US Naval Forces Eastern Atlantic and Mediterranean, To: CNO, 14 December 1954 Subject: Priority List for Advanced Base Development, A4, Box 313, Strategic Plans Division, NHC.
45. "Brief of SACLANT mining Plan 1-55," ND, A16–12, Box 320, Strategic Plans Division Records, NHC.
46. Ibid.
47. Ibid.
48. Memorandum by the First Lord of the Admiralty, The Role of Aircraft Carriers, 9 November 1953, ADM 1/24695, PRO.
49. Interview with Vice-Admiral Sir Ronald Brockman, 18 March 1991, London.
50. Quoted in Navias, *Nuclear Weapons and British Strategic Planning,* p. 70.
51. Statement on Defence, Cmd. Paper No. 9075 (London: HMSO, 1954).
52. Navias, *Nuclear Weapons and British Strategic Planning,* p. 161.
53. On the dangers of Soviet submarine operations from the Norwegian coast, see "Remarks by First Sea Lord at CPX 7," 17 April 1957, MB1/I311, Mountbatten Papers, Archives and Manuscripts, Southampton University Library.
54. Ibid.
55. JP(54)107(Final), SACLANT's Emergency Defence Plan 1–55, 8 March 1955, DEFE 4/75, PRO.
56. Grove, *Vanguard to Trident,* p. 144; CC(54)73rd, Conclusions, CAB 128/27, PRO.
57. D/COS O&T, AFNORTH Historical Reports, 1 Jan. 1954–30. June 1954, SECCOS, HQ AFNORTH.
58. "Intelligence Briefs," *The ONI Review,* vol. 9, no. 9, 1954, NHC, and Historical Report, HQ Northern European Command, 1 July 1954–30 June 1955, SECCOS, HQ AFNORTH.
59. Interview Vice-Admiral Ronald Brockman, 18 March 1991, London.
60. S.W. Roskill, *The War at Sea 1939–1945, Volume I: The Defensive* (London: HMSO, 1954), pp. 169–178.
61. "Convoys to North Russia, 1942," p. 5141.
62. Philip Ziegler, *Mountbatten* (London: Fontana/Collins, 1986), p. 167, and, Roskill, *The War at Sea, Volume I,* pp. 513–514.
63. S.W. Roskill, *The War at Sea III, Part II: The Offensive,* (London: HMSO, 1961), pp. 262–263. This attack is particularly interesting in view of the Strike Fleet concept discussed earlier.
64. Many officers who had served with the Home Fleet in Norwegian and Arctic waters during World War II came into senior positions in the

Admiralty staff after the war. Best known, of course, were Admiral Sir Bruce Fraser who served as First Sea Lord from 1948 to 1951, and his successor in this position, Admiral Sir Rhoderick McGrigor, First Sea Lord from 1951 to 1955.

65. Interview with the Earl of Selkirk, 24 January 1991, London.
66. This had been learned the hard way through such disasters as the German attack on PQ 17 in July 1942.
67. See Captain H.H. McWilliam, "Sea Power and Aircraft," *Brassey's Annual 1953* (London: William Clowes & Son. Ltd.1954).
68. Roskill, *The War at Sea: Volume I*, p. 199.
69. For further discussion see Mats Berdal, *British Naval Policy and Norwegian Security: Maritime Power in Transition, 1951–60* (Oslo: Institutt for Forsvarsstudier, 1992), pp. 26–28.
70. Brief for Prime Minister's talks with Norwegian Prime Minister, 27 October 1956, PREM 11/2437, PRO.
71. Defence, Outline of Future Policy, Cmnd. 124, HMSO, April 1957, p. 1.
72. Wyn Rees, "The 1957 Sandys Defence White Paper: New Priorities in British Defence Policy?" *The Journal of Strategic Studies* 12 (June 1989), p. 226.
73. Navias, *Nuclear Weapons and British Strategic Planning*, p. 3.
74. David Greenwood, "Defence and National Priorities since 1945," in *British Defence Policy in a Changing World*, ed. J. Baylis (London: Croom Helm, 1977), pp. 186–188 and 195. For the "underlying tension between British doctrine and British practise" since 1952, see also R.N. Rosecrance, *Defence of the Realm: British Strategy in the Nuclear Epoch* (New York: Columbia University Press, 1968), pp. 178–180.
75. Navias, Nuclear *Strategy and British Strategic Planning*, p. 5.
76. Rees, "Sandys Defence White Paper," pp. 220–224.
77. JP(57)59(Final), SACLANT's Provisional Guidance for Earmarked UK Forces, 8 May 1957, DEFE 6/41, PRO.
78. Grove, *Vanguard to Trident*, p. 199, and, Crowe, "The Policy Roots of the Royal Navy," pp. 183–184.
79. JP(57)20(Final), The Fleet Air Arm, 18 February 1957, DEFE 6/40, PRO.
80. Ibid.
81. Rees, "Sandys' Defence White Paper," pp. 226–27 and Sir Richard Powell, letter to author, 14 November 1991.
82. Interview with the Earl of Selkirk, 24 January 1991, and Grove, *Vanguard to Trident*, p. 202.
83. Defence, Outline of Future Policy (5th Proof), March 1957, ADM 205/114, PRO, and, Defence, Outline of Future Policy, April 1957, Cmnd. 124 (London: HMSO, 1957). In response to further pressure for cuts, the Naval Staff produced a paper ("The Autumn Naval Rethink") in September 1957, which Sandys endorsed and which reiterated the importance of the limited war role and the carrier contribution to it.
84. Ziegler, *Mountbatten*, p. 553.
85. Defence White Paper 1958, 1st Draft, 1 January 1958, DEFE 7/986, PRO.
86. Ibid.See also Michael Carver, *Tightrope Walking: British Defence Policy Since 1945* (London: Hutchinson, 1992), p. 51.
87. Crowe, "The Policy Roots of the Royal Navy," pp. 195–97 and 212–215.

88. Admiral J. Wright to Mr. Draper, 28 January 1959, XV Letter to Adm.Wright Dec. 58 and Reply Jan. 59, Box 9, Draper Committee, Records, 1958–59, DDEL.(My emphasis).
89. Memorandum of Conversation, January 30, 1957, Memos of Conv. S(1), Box 1, General Correspondence and Memoranda Series, J.F. Dulles papers 1951–59, DDEL.
90. Ibid.
91. Confidential Annex to COS(57) 30th Meeting, "Meeting with Admiral Denny," 12 April 1957, DEFE 4/96, PRO.
92. James Grant, "New US Naval Task Force Seen as Essential for NATO," *The Register*, 5 April 1958.
93. "Suggested Outline of the United Kingdom Case," JP(58)149(Final), 28 October 1958, DEFE 6/52, PRO.
94. Annex to COS(58)158, UK Reply to 1958 NATO Annual Review, 17 June 1958, DEFE 5/84, PRO.
95. Allied Naval Forces Northern Europe, Historical Report for 1961, NEC Historical Reports, SECCOS, HQ AFNORTH.
96. Ibid.
97. Sir Richard Powell, letter to author, 14 November 1991.
98. In the press all three exercises were occasionally subsumed under the name STRIKE BACK. For the purposes of this argument, however, they should be seen as distinct since they were each concerned with a particular aspect of maritime operations in the North Atlantic.
99. Confidential Annex to COS(57) 30th Meeting, "Meeting with Admiral Denny," 12 April 1957, DEFE 4/96, PRO.
100. Sir Richard Powell, letter to author, 14 November 1991. Sir Richard Powell was present at the Bermuda meeting between Macmillan and Eisenhower.
101. Confidential Annex to COS(57) 30th Meeting, "Meeting with Admiral Denny," 12 April 1957, DEFE 4/96, PRO.
102. Ibid.
103. Ibid.
104. Without such details, Admiral Wright argued, he would have "no basis for accurate planning" in the years 1958 and 1959. COS(57) 34th Meeting, 7 May 1957, Minutes, DEFE 4/97, PRO.
105. Ibid.
106. Ibid.
107. JP(57)59 (Final), SACLANT's Provisional Guidance for Earmarked UK Forces, 8 May 1957, DEFE 6/41, PRO.
108. COS(57) 34th Meeting, 7 May 1957, Minutes, DEFE 4/97, PRO.
109. JP(57)59 (Final), SACLANT's Provisional Guidance for Earmarked UK Forces, 8 May 1957, DEFE 6/41, PRO.
110. Ibid.
111. COS (57) 35th Meeting, Minutes, 10 May 1957, DEFE 4/97, PRO.
112. Press Release, SACLANT Command Information Bureau Atlantic, "EXERCISE STRIKE BACK," 27 September 1957–No. 13.
113. Hanson W. Baldwin, "Weak Point in Fleet – An Analysis of Naval Communications and Other Facts Learned in Manoeuvres," *New York Times*, 2 October 1957.
114. This will be explored in greater detail in the following chapter.

115. James Grant, "NATO Naval Force Weakness Bared in Exercises," *The Register*, 19 October 1957.

116. Ibid.

117. "Performance of USS Nautilus," Extract from Report of 30th October by C-in-C Home Fleet, ADM 205/178, PRO.

118. Ibid. None of these results were publicised in the official press releases which only referred to the performance of conventional submarines. In January 1958 *Nautilus* was fitted with a new nuclear core, increasing her endurance by as much as 80%. See D.W. Morley, "Technology and Weapons," in *The Soviet Navy,* ed. M.G. Saunders (London: Weidenfeld and Nicolson, 1958), p. 204.

119. Press Release, SACLANT Command Information Bureau Atlantic, Joint Statement by Admiral Sir John Eccles and Air Marshal Sir Bryan Reynolds, 27 September 1957 – No. 15.

120. "'Grave Risk' in Naval Defence," *Times* (London), 28 September 1957.

121. Ibid. See also "Seadog off the Leash," *The Economist*, 5 October 1957.

122. James Grant, "New US Naval Task Force Seen as Essential for NATO," *The Register*, 5 April 1958.

123. "The Major NATO Naval Exercises in 1957," in *Brassey's Annual 1958* (London: William & Clowes, 1958), pp. 69–70.

124. Vice-Admiral B.B. Schofield, "Maritime Affairs," *Army Quarterly* (January 1958), and, "Navies 'Not In Good Shape' – NATO Commanders Complaint," *Manchester Guardian*, 22 November 1957.

125. James Grant, "NATO Naval Force Weakness Bared in Exercises," *The Register*, 19 October 1957. It should be noted that concern about the weakening of British defence efforts was not confined exclusively to the US Navy, but was in fact shared by the President himself. Referring to the period between May and September 1958, Steven Ambrose records that the President "was greatly concerned by the British military position, which the JCS told him was woefully weak." Ambrose, *Eisenhower: The President*, p. 478.

126. Wyn Rees, "Brothers in Arms: Anglo-American defence co-operation in 1957," in *Post-war Britain, 1945–64: Themes and Perspectives,* ed. A. Gorst, L. Johnman and W.S. Lucas (London: Pinter Publishers, 1989), p. 213.

127. Ziegler, *Mountbatten, p.* 554.

128. Admiral Burke to Lord Mountbatten, 23 February 1958, ADM 205/173, PRO.

129. "Use of British Carriers – US Surprised," *Manchester Guardian*, 12 May 1958.

130. Ibid.

131. Admiral Burke to Lord Mountbatten, 4 February 1958, ADM 205/173, PRO.

132. Admiral Robert Carney (Ret.) to W. Draper (Privileged Correspondence), Subj: Naval Aspects of Foreign Aid, 13 February 1959, Box 6, Draper Committee, Records 1958–59, DDEL.

133. Cabinet Defence Committee, Minutes of Meeting, 9th February 1963, CAB 131/28 PRO.

134. Admiral Robert Carney (Ret.) to W. Draper (Privileged Correspondence), Subj: Naval Aspects of Foreign Aid, 13 February 1959, Box 6, Draper Committee, Records 1958–59, DDEL.

6   AMERICAN FORWARD MARITIME STRATEGY IN THE
     NORTH ATLANTIC, 1957–60

1. "NATO Naval Force Weakness Bared in Exercises," *The Register*,
    19 October 1957.
2. "US Forming Carrier Striking Fleet for Atlantic," *The Daily Telegraph*,
    16 June 1960.
3. Rosenberg, "Arleigh Albert Burke," p. 277. See also *Semiannual Report of
    the Secretary of the Navy, 1 January 1957 to June 1957* (Washington, DC:
    UGPO, 1958), p. 176.
4. See US Naval Institute Oral History Programme, *Volume II of the
    Reminiscences of Admiral John S. Thach, USN* (US Naval Institute,
    Annapolis, 1977), p. 688, and *The Reminiscences of Rear Admiral Charles
    Elliot Loughlin, USN* (US Naval Institute, Annapolis, 1982), p. 255.
5. Presentation to Congress by Admiral Jerauld Wright, CINCLANTFLT,
    11 February 1959, CJCS 092. 2, JCS 1959, Box 12, Rg. 218, NARA.
6. Arleigh Burke to Bryce Harlow (enclosing "carrier paper"), 15 November
    1957, Missiles – Misc. Papers [1957–1958] (2), Box 2, Harlow, Bryce,
    Records 1953–61, DDEL.
7. See also, "US Navy ASW Programme" (OP-312), 17 January 1958, Navy
    Line Folder No. 3, Box 17, Papers of E.P. Aurand (Naval Aide to President,
    1957–61), DDEL.
8. Admiral Burke, "carrier paper," 15 November 1957, Missiles – Misc.
    Papers [1957–1958] (2), Box 2, Harlow, Bryce, Records 1953–61, DDEL.
9. The US referred to this phase of the ASW strategy alternately as "forward
    defensive operations" and the "barrier offensive." The Royal Navy preferred
    the older term "submarine transit offensive." Apart from the offensive
    mining, it involved, as the terms imply, *forward* operations against sub-
    marines in transit to patrol areas. See Vice-Admiral W. Woods to Lord
    Mountbatten, 11 April 1958, ADM 205/173.
10. For the distinctive US preference for Hunter-Killer as opposed to convoy
    operations favoured by the Admiralty, see the unofficial but highly repre-
    sentative article by A.L. Danis USN, "Offensive ASW: Fundamental to
    Defense," *USNIP* 83 (June 1957), pp. 583–589.
11. On the difficulties with existing ASW technology, see George P. Steele,
    "Killing Nuclear Submarines," *USNIP* 86 (November 1960), pp. 45–51, and
    "Navy Tells Why Soviet Subs Are So Difficult to Detect," *The Register*,
    19 July 1958. See also "Nuclear Submarines 'Hard Nut to Crack'," *The
    Guardian*, 8 December 1960.
12. JP(57)146(Final), SACLANT's Emergency Defence Plan for 1958,
    22 November 1958, DEFE 6/44, PRO.
13. Ibid.
14. James Elliot, "Sword Thrust," *Navy Magazine* 3 (November 1960),
    pp. 16–23; Press Release, Fall Exercises 60, "Digest of Press Conference
    with Admiral R.L. Dennison, SACLANT," 28 September 1960, and
    Brassey's Annual 1961 (London: William Clowes & Son, Ltd., 1961),
    pp. 326–327.

15. Vice Admiral John McNay Taylor, "The Striking Fleet Atlantic," *NATO's Fifteen Nations* (April 1962).

16. ONI, Typed Brief, "USSR submarine facilities attack on which would make a contribution towards reducing Soviet capabilities to conduct submarine warfare," 24 January 1951, File 3, Drawer 3, Ts no. 7869, ONI Ts Records, NHC.

17. Memorandum for CNO, 13 July 1955, Subject: Submarine Control of REGULUS (Enclosing Regulus Target List, Priority "B" [Atlantic]), A-5, Box 315, Strategic Plans Division Records, NHC.

18. "Vulnerability of Northern Fleet to Air Attack," *The ONI Review*, vol. 14, no. 4, 1959, NHC.

19. Ibid.

20. NEC Historical Report, 1 Jan. 1959–31 Dec. 1959, SECCOS, HQ AFNORTH. Also in 1957, the US Navy established an "Atomic Weapons Information Course" for allied officers serving under SACLANT. See *Semiannual Report of the Secretary of the Navy, 1 January 1957 to June 1957* (Washington, DC: USGPO, 1958).

21. "New Defence Force Established," *The Register*, 13 July 1957, and Admiral W. Cooper, "Meeting the Soviet Submarine Challenge in the Atlantic," in *Navy Magazine* 2 (April 1959).

22. "Admiral Wright Adds Two Anti-Sub Defence Groups to Atlantic Fleet," *Army–Navy–Air Force Journal*, 18 October 1958.

23. Vice Admiral Edmund B. Taylor, "A new Sense of Urgency," *Navy Magazine* 4 (February 1961). See also *Semiannual Report of the Secretary of the Navy, 1 January 1958 to June 1958* (Washington, DC: USGPO, 1959), pp. 214–16 and 218.

24. COS(58)99, Facilities in the UK for US Naval Forces, 9 April 1958, DEFE 5/83, PRO.

25. Admiral Denny to Lord Mountbatten, 20 December 1956, DEFE 205/110, PRO.

26. JP(57)124(Final), Allied Command Atlantic Minimum Forces Study, 1958–1962, 6 November 1957, DEFE 6/43, PRO.

27. Ibid.

28. COS(58)99, Facilities in the UK for US Naval Forces, 9 April 1959, DEFE 5/83, PRO.

29. JP(57)124(Final), Allied Command Atlantic Minimum Forces Study, 1958–1962, 6 November 1957, DEFE 6/43, PRO.

30. JP(58)45(Final), Facilities in the United Kingdom for United States Naval Forces, 18 April 1958, DEFE 6/50, PRO.

31. Lord Mountbatten to Sir Dermot A. Boyle, CAS, 1 January 1958, MB1/I311, Folder 2, Mountbatten Papers, Archives and Manuscripts, Southampton University Library.

32. Ibid.

33. Ibid.

34. Admiral Burke to Lord Mountbatten, 4 February 1958, PRO, ADM 205/173.

35. Vice-Admiral W.J.W. Woods to Lord Mountbatten, 11 April 1958, ADM 205/173, PRO.

36. JP(58)45(Final), Facilities in the UK for US Naval Forces, 18 April 1958, DEFE 6/50, PRO.
37. Ibid.
38. COS(58)99, Facilities in the UK for US Naval Forces, 9 April 1958, DEFE 5/83, PRO.
39. JP(58)45(Final), Facilities in the UK for US Naval Forces, 18 April 1958, DEFE 6/50, PRO. See also footnote 26.
40. Board Minutes, 8 May 1958, ADM 205/176, PRO.
41. Ibid.
42. Board Minutes, 2 October 1958, ADM 205/176, PRO.
43. It should be added here that Anglo-US defence relations at the time were going through a particularly good period with the repeal in July 1958 of the McMahon Act and the signature in its place of the Agreement for Co-operation on Uses of Atomic Energy for Mutual Defence Purposes. See Alistair Horne, "The Macmillan Years and Afterwards," in *The Special Relationship: Anglo-American Relations Since 1945*, ed. Wm. Roger Louis and Hedley Bull (Oxford: Clarendon Press, 1986), pp. 89–90.
44. COS(58)185, US/UK forces in the Atlantic, Note by the Admiralty and Air Ministry, 31 July 1958, DEFE 5/84, PRO.
45. Ibid.
46. JP(58)45(Final), Facilities in the United Kingdom for United States Naval Forces, 18 April 1958, DEFE 6/50, PRO.
47. Letter from DDE to The Hon. Sam Rayburn, 13 May 1958, OF 208, Box 883, Dwight D. Eisenhower: Records as President, White House Central Files, OF205(2), DDEL.
48. Admiral Jerauld Wright, "NATO's Naval Forces," *NATO's Fifteen Nations* (Spring 1959).
49. "Vulnerability of Northern Fleet to Air Attack," *The ONI Review* vol. 14, no. 4, 1959, NHC. In April 1960, the Lang Report on U.S. overseas bases also stressed the need for "intensified intelligence activities from posts situated around the communist bloc" and "more efficient visual, photographic or electronic observation of the enemy homeland." Review of US Overseas Military Bases (Lang Report), April 1960, Base-Rights (4), Box 2, NSC Series – Subject Subseries, WHO: Office of Special Assistant for National Security Affairs, DDEL.
50. This is one of several points that emerge from a Norwegian Foreign Ministry memorandum, Notat, Rekognoseringsflyvninger, 9 desember 1959, 33. 6/14b, Bd. I. UD.
51. Ibid. See also Tamnes, *Cold War in the High North,* pp. 122–124, and 177. For Admiral Wright's concern about the "submarine menace" and his emphasis on the need for continuous monitoring late in 1959, see also "NATO Chief's Warning on Submarine Threat – Daily US Plane Patrols," *Daily Telegraph*, 19 September 1959, and "West's Peril Seen By Atlantic Chief," *New York Times*, 14 November 1959.
52. These stations were manned by Norwegians, though technical equipment, assistance and training of personnel attached to radio intercept stations were provided by the CIA. See p. xix.
53. Memorandum, From: OP-03D3 To: AFOIN, 25 August 1952, EF-61, Subj: A Study of Potential Soviet Action against the US from Northern Areas, EF-61, Box 289, Strategic Plans Division Records, NHC.

54. "Svalbard," *The ONI Review*, vol. 9, no. 8, 1954, NHC. For Svalbard and Bear Island as areas appropriate for the location of radars to "assist commercial and military transpolar flights," see also "Meeting the Threat of Surprise Attack (Killian Report)," reprinted in Trachtenberg, ed., *The Development of American Strategic Thought*, p. 418.

55. "Svalbard," *The ONI Review*, vol. 9, no. 8, 1954, NHC.

56. Ibid.

57. See Memorandum, From: Ass. Director of Intelligence, To: Distribution List, Subject: Special Presentation on SVALBARD Expedition, 17 October 1955, A-5, Box 315, Strategic Plans Division Records, NHC; "Intelligence Brief," *The ONI Review*, vol. 11, no. 4, 1956, NHC; Memorandum, Franz Josef Land Electronic Reconnaissance Flight of 20 May 1953, 26 May 1953, Ts. No. 3-1900 to 3-2699 (1953), Entry 214, Rg. 341, NARA.

58. Memorandum to J. Lay, 10 November 1960, enclosing additions to NSC 6001/1, Box 28, NSC Series – Policy Papers Subseries, WHO: Office of the Special Assistant for National Security Affairs, DDEL.

59. Ibid.

60. Briefing Note for NSC Meeting, 1 April 1960, Attached to summary of 439th NSC Mtg., Box 12, NSC Series, Papers of Dwight D. Eisenhower as President, DDEL.

61. NEC Historical Report, 1 January–31 December 1959, SECCOS, HQ AFNORTH. In addition to these maritime air facilities, other airfields were also upgraded with infrastructure funds.

62. Lord Mountbatten to Sir Dermot A. Boyle, CAS, 1 January 1958, MB1/I311, Folder 2, Mountbatten Papers, Archives and Manuscripts, Southampton University Library. These squadrons were designated for operations in Norway.

63. NEC Historical Report, 1 Jan. 1958–31 Dec. 1958 (Tasks and Projects), SECCOS, HQ AFNORTH.

64. Ibid.

65. "Bodø Flyplass bygges ut for tunge jetfly," *Arbeiderbladet*, 21 March 1958, "Utbedring av flyplasser av infrastruktur-midler," *Arbeiderbladet*, 17 January 1959. See also discussion in the Norwegian Chiefs of Staff Committee, "Internt Referat fra møte I Den sentrale sjefsnemd,10 oktober 1958", FO. For the "important" role of maritime aircraft in Norway by 1960, see also SACLANT Press Release, "Maritime Patrol Aircraft Have Important Role in NATO Exercises," FALLEX 60, 28 September 1960.

66. NEC Historical Report (AIRNORTH), 31 Dec. 1957–31 Dec. 1958, SECCOS, HQ AFNORTH. SACLANT's failure on previous occasions to forward target information again suggests a high degree of planning autonomy as well as an absence of proper co-ordination in nuclear planning.

67. JP(57)146(Final) SACLANT's Emergency Defence Plan for 1958, 22 November 1958, DEFE 6/44, PRO.

68. Ibid.

69. Historical Report, 1 January–31 December 1958, SECCOS, HQ AFNORTH. Between 1958 and 1960, infrastructure funds were specifically allocated to upgrade communications between naval forces and NATOs Northern Command (2 "radio stations" were approved in 1958), St. prp. nr. 88, 1958, p. 3.

70. St. prp. nr. 88, 1958, p. 2–3, and St. prp. nr. 12, 1959, p. 2.
71. JP(57)146(Final), SACLANT's Emergency Defence Plan for 1958, 22 November 1958, DEFE 6/44, PRO.
72. Address by John Foster Dulles, "The Evolution of Foreign Policy", 12 January 1954, reprinted in US *Nuclear Strategy: A Reader*, ed. P. Bobbitt, L. Freedman, G.F. Treverton (London: The Macmillan Press Ltd., 1989), p. 124.
73. Stromseth, *The Origins of Flexible Response,* p. 19. A prominent critique of administration policy before this was produced by William Kaufmann, "The Requirements of Deterrence," in *Military Policy and National Security,* ed. W.W. Kaufmann (Princeton: Princeton University Press, 1956).
74. JIC 498/199, JIC on Joint Strategic Capabilities Plan, 1 July 1956–30 June 1957, 12 June 1956, JCS 1954-56, JIC Papers, ccs 334 JIC (12-28-55) sec. 10, Rg. 218, NARA.
75. JCS 2073/1555, Report by the JSPC to the JCS on Understanding of Certain Terms, JCS Geographic File 1958, ccs 092(3-12-48)(2),Rg. 218, NARA.
76. Forsvarsstaben til Det Kgl. Forsvarsdepartement, 17 Oktober 1958, "Pasvikutbyggingen – utvidelse, eventuelt omorganisering, av Grenseoppsynet i Sør-Varanger, Nsj. Hem. 893/010, FD. See also Lt. Gen. Bjarne Øen, "Aktuelle militære problemer i forbindelse med gjennomføringen av den nye forsvarsorganisasjon," (Speech 28 October 1957), *Norsk Militært Tidsskrift* 116 (1957), pp. 691–92.
77. The Norwegians wanted to know whether the Alliance would help with conventional forces or whether a full-scale nuclear war would follow. See "Brief for Macmillan's visit to Norway, 7–10 June 1960," ND, FO 371/151721, PRO. For nature of Norwegian military concerns see discussion in the Chiefs of Staff Committee, "Internt Referat fra møte I Den sentrale sjefsnemd, 19 juni 1959," FO.
78. For a highly representative "Navy" view of the problem of limited war, see Commander Malcolm W. Cagle, "Sea Power and Limited War," *USNIP* 84 (July 1958).
79. The Navy had also been opposed to aspects of the "New Look" in 1953 on the grounds that it was a "prepare-for-one-type-of-war-policy." See "Congress Takes a Look at "New Look" in Defence," US *News & World Report*, 26 February 1954. For a succinct internal critique along the same lines, see Enclosure To JCS 2101/112, Memorandum by CNO for JCS on Military Strategy and Posture, 7 December 1953, ccs 381(1-31-50) sec. 32, box 32, JCS Geographic File 1954-56, Rg. 218, NARA.
80. "Study of Attack Carrier Force Levels (Cold War)," 13 October 1953, A4, Box 280, Strategic Plans Division Records, NHC. For similar US Navy concerns before the creation of NATO, see "Quarterly Military Survey, Norway," 7 September 1948, EF-50 Norway, Box 245, Strategic Plans Division Records, NHC.
81. Interview with Admiral Arleigh Burke, 18 July 1990, Fairfax, Virginia.
82. Admiral Burke to Lord Mountbatten, 4 February, 1958, enclosing study of "The Carrier Task Force in the Missile Age," ADM 205/173, PRO.
83. Ibid.
84. Ibid. Burke reiterated his concern about going "too far down on the megaton road" and its implications for "small wars" in another letter to Mountbatten

in May, Admiral Burke to Lord Mountbatten, 10 May 1958, ADM 205/173, PRO.

85. Proposed Presentation to Congress by Admiral Jerauld Wright, CIN-CLANTFLT, 11 February 1959, JCS 1959, CJCS 092. 2 Rg. 218, NARA.

86. B. H. Liddell-Hart, "NATO's Weakest Spot–the Northern Flank," (MF) B/NATO/2J, IISS. The paper formed the basis for a subsequent article, "Danger on the Flanks of NATO," published in the US *Marine Corps Gazette* in January 1961.

87. NEC Historical Report, 1 July 1954–30 June 1955, SECCOS, HQ AFNORTH. These forces were in peacetime earmarked as SACEUR's strategic reserve.

88. NEC Historical Report, 1 July 1956–31 Dec. 1957, SECCOS, HQ AFNORTH.

89. NEC Historical Report, 1 Jan. 1960–31 Dec. 1960, SECCOS, HQ AFNORTH.

90. Ibid.

91. Office of the First Sea Lord, NATO, 4 November 1958, MB1/I311, Folder 2, Mountbatten Papers, Archives and Manuscripts, Southampton University.

92. Interview with Admiral Arleigh Burke, 18 July 1990, Fairfax, Virginia.

93. Ibid. With later generations of SSBNs, Poseidon and Trident, the need to operate far forward disappeared as both missile accuracy and range increased substantially.

94. Naval Warfare Analysis Group, Study No. 1, Introduction of the Fleet Ballistic Missile into Service, ND, Reference Collection of Misc. Declassified Documents, DDEL.

95. For an early assessment of the technical problems involved and possible solutions, see Frank C. Lynch, Jr., "The Role of Navigation in the Submarine Weapon System," *Navigation* 5 (September 1956), pp. 128–130, and Capt. E.P. Wilkinson, USN, "Nuclear Submarine Navigation," *Navigation* 5 (Autumn 1957), pp. 332–336.

96. Infrastructure redundancy was also intended to assure that the even after absorbing a pre-emptive strike, command systems would still be intact.

97. Basically, the SINS was designed to determine true north, speed and vertical ship position in order to allow for accurate missile launching. See Charles D. LaFond, "Special report: FBM Accuracy Starts with SINS," *Missiles & Rockets*, 25 July 1960, pp. 24–26. See also, B. McKelvie and H. Galt, Jr., "The Evolution of the Ship's Inertial Navigation System for the Fleet Ballistic Missile Program," *Navigation* 25 (Fall 1978), pp. 310–22.

98. Joseph F. Caligiuri, "The Navigation System for the Polaris Submarine," *Navigation* 7 (Spring 1960), p. 3.

99. G. Spinardi and D. MacKenzie, "The Shaping of Nuclear Weapons Technology: US Fleet Ballistic Guidance System and Navigation: From Polaris to Poseidon," *Social Studies of Science* 18 (August 1988), p. 431.

100. Memorandum, enclosure to, JCS 141/95, Report by the J-6 on Long Distance Ground Based Navigational Aids, 24 June 1959, JCS 1959, ccs 6700 (22 June 1959), Box 89, Rg. 218, NARA.

101. Spinardi and MacKenzie, "The Shaping of Nuclear Weapons Technology," p. 432.

102. Memorandum for the Administrator, Federal Aviation Agency, ND Subj: Long Range Ground-based Electronic Aids to Navigation, Enclosure "C" (Discussion), ccs 6700 (22 June 1959), JCS 218, Rg. 218. NARA.
103. Ibid.
104. Annex to COS(58)157, Admiralty View on Installation of Loran "C" Stations by the United States, 16 June 1958, DEFE 5/84, PRO.
105. On the military importance of ocean gravitational surveys, see Memorandum for Secretary for Defence, 16 October 1956, enclosing, Appendix "A", "DoD Requirements for Ocean Gravitational Surveys," and Appendix "B", "Application of Gravity Data to DoD Requirements," DDC (1981), 57b, 1981.
106. COS(59)147 (Annex), Strategic Implications of the Polaris Type Missile, 24 June 1959, DEFE 5/92, PRO.
107. Ibid.
108. Quoted in Wilkes and Gleditsch, *Loran-C and Omega*, p. 81.
109. Ibid.
110. *Loran og Omega: Innstilling fra utvalget til undersøkelse av saken om etablering av Loran C og Omega-stasjoner i Norge* (henceforth "Schei-rapporten") (Oslo: Pax Forlag, 1977), p. 22.
111. Ibid.
112. Memorandum for the Administrator, Federal Aviation Agency, ND Subj: Long Range Ground-based Electronic Aids to Navigation, Enclosure "C", ccs 6700 (22 June 1959), JCS 1959, Rg. 218, NARA. The other two stations in the chain *not* on Norwegian soil were located on the Faeros (Ejde) and in Iceland (Keflavik).
113. "Schei-rapporten," p. 46.
114. See Wilkes and Gleditsch, *Loran-C and Omega*, pp. 265–266.
115. *Jane's Fighting Ships, 1959–60* (London: Sampson Low, Marston & Co. Ltd., 1959), p. 448.
116. In the mid-1970s, when the Loran-C and Omega installations became the subject of a major domestic political controversy in Norway, the relationship between Polaris and Loran-C in Norway was derived from an analysis largely of open sources. See N.P. Gleditsch, "Hvordan og hvorfor Norge fikk Loran C," *Internasjonal Politikk,* No. 4 (1976), pp. 823–843.
117. Report by J-6 to JCS on Long Distance Ground Based Navigational Aids, 24 June 1959, ccs 6700 (22 June 1959), JCS 1959, Rg. 218, NARA.
118. Review of US Overseas Military Bases (Lang Report), April 1960, Base-Rights (4), Box 2, NSC Series – Subject Subseries, WHO: Office of Special Assistant for National Security Affairs, DDEL.
119. COS(58)157, 16 June 1958, United States Negotiations for the Installations of the LORAN "C" Navigation System, DEFE 5/84, PRO.
120. Memorandum for Secretary of State, enclosure to, JCS 141/95, Report by the J-6 on Long Distance Ground Based Navigational Aids, 24 June 1959, JCS 1959, ccs 6700 (22 June 1959), Box 89, Rg. 218, NARA.
121. JWPC 474/1, 13 May 1947, ccs 092 USSR (3-27-45), sec. 20, Geographic File, 1946–47, Rg. 218, NARA.

122. Richard Luckett, *The White Generals: An Account of the White Movement and the Russian Civil War* (New York: The Viking Press, 1971), pp. 196–208.

123. Among the important technological advances after the 1957 were development of new nuclear-powered attack submarines and the first nuclear-powered carrier (USS *Enterprise*). See Norman Polmar, "Building the United States Fleet, 1947–67," in *Brassey's Annual 1966*, pp. 72–77.

124. References to *Soviet Fleet* are taken from ONI translations. I am most grateful to Maxim Shashenkov of Nuffield College, Oxford, who kindly translated relevant articles in *Pravda* and *Red Star*.

125. *Soviet Fleet*, 26 August 1958, and "Soviet Propaganda on Missile Launching Submarines," *The ONI Review* 14 (February 1959).

126. Ye. Astrakov and M. Chuprikov, "On the occasion of the journey of the U.S. nuclear submarine *Nautilus*," *Red Star*, 15 August 1958.

127. *Soviet Fleet*, 4 November 1958. See also article in *Red Star* on 21 November 1958 by General A. Antonov.

128. Captain Iu. Nikonov, "The Arctic Strategy of the United States," *Soviet Fleet*, 25 October 1958. On Soviet concerns about the "special attention" given to the Arctic by the US, see also Admiral A.T. Chabanenko (Commander of the Northern Fleet), "Protecting the Soviet Arctic," *Red Star,* 23 March 1958, and "Soviet Comment on POLARIS," *The ONI Review*, vol. 15, no. 1, 1960, NHC.

129. See particularly "Now US has "Bases" North of Russia," U.S. *News & World Report*, 22 August 1958, and Hanson W. Baldwin, "Strategic Value of Arctic proved," *Daily Telegraph*, 9 August 1958. See also Cmd. G.W. Kittredge "Under the Polar Cap: A Voyage That Must Be Made," *USNIP* 84 (February 1958), pp. 61–65, and Rear Admiral I.J. Galantin, "The Future of Nuclear-Powered Submarine," *USNIP* (June 1958), pp. 34–35.

130. Marshal V.D. Sokolovsky, *Military Strategy: Soviet Doctrine and Concepts* (London: Pall Mall Press, 1959 and 1963).

131. Ibid., p. 299

132. Ibid.

133. Captain Iu. Nikonov, "The Arctic Strategy of the United States," *Soviet Fleet*, 25 October 1958.

134. Michael MccGwire, "The Soviet Navy and World War," in *The Sources of Soviet Naval Conduct,* ed. P.S. Gillette and W.C. Frank (Toronto: Lexington Books, 1990), p. 198.

135. As regards the rest of the submarine fleet: 15 per cent would be used for anti-submarine operations; 15 per cent for missile launching; 15 per cent for anti-shipping and 5 for mining. Appendix to Annex to JP(59)140(Final), "Likely Deployment of Soviet Submarines in the Atlantic Area," 20 November 1959, DEFE 6/58, PRO.

136. Sir F. Roberts to Sir E. Shuckburgh, 9 November 1960. FO 371/151733, PRO.

137. Ibid.

7 NORWAY AS A POLITICAL ALLY: THE US AND THE
NORDIC REGION

1. Frances E. Willis to Department of State, Despatch no. 900, 18 June 1958, 757. 5 MSP/6-1888, Rg. 59, NARA.
2. George F. Kennan, *Memoirs: 1950–1963* (Boston: Little, Brown and Company, 1972), p. 143.
3. NSC 6006/1, 6 April 1960, Box 28, NSC Series – Policy Papers Subseries, WHO: Office of Special Assistant for National Security Affairs, DDEL.
4. Memorandum, James Lay to NSC, 4 October 1960, Subject: US Policy Toward Scandinavia, Box 28, NSC Series – Policy Papers Subseries, WHO: Office of Special Assistant for National Security Affairs, DDEL.
5. "Scandinavia on the World Stage," *The Economist*, 9 October 1957.
6. US European Command Report, 12 January 1959, US European Command Report on NATO Area – Book 1, Box 18, Draper Committee, Records, 1958–59, DDEL.
7. NSC 6006/1, 6 April 1960, Box 28, NSC Series – Policy Papers Subseries, WHO: Office of Special Assistant for National Security Affairs, DDEL.
8. Briefing Note for NSC Meeting of 1 April 1960, Scandinavia (NSC 6006), 30 March 1960, NSC 6006/1 – Scandinavia, Box 28, NSC Series – Policy Papers Subseries, WHO: Office of Special Assistant for National Security Affairs, DDEL.
9. British Embassy, Oslo, to Selwyn Lloyd, Foreign Office, 9 November 1959, FO 371/143157, PRO.
10. "Instruction for the Dept. of State to Certain Diplomatic Missions," 3 August 1957 and 10 October 1957, *FRUS 1955–57 Vol. XI*, p. 209 and 506. See also T. Bergh and H. Pharo, eds., *Vekst og Velstand: Norsk Politisk Historie, 1945–65* (Oslo: Universitetsforlaget, 1989), p. 223.
11. British Embassy, Oslo, to Foreign Office, 20 January 1959, FO 371/143157, PRO.
12. Lodge(UN) to Secretary of State, 18 December 1956, Nuclear Weap. Tests, Sept.–Dec. 1956 (6), Box 6, WHO: Office of the Special Assistant for Disarmament, DDEL.
13. Ibid.
14. UNGA, Eleventh Session, First Committee, Report of the Disarmament Commission, 25 January 1957, Four Power Report [March–August 1957] (1), Box 9, WHO: Office of the Special Assistant for Disarmament, DDEL. According to Harold Stassen, the US government "consulted regularly" with the Norwegian government on disarmament issues.
15. This led Lange to vote in favour of NATO's Indo-China resolution in 1952, for which he was criticised by a majority of the Parliamentary Foreign Affairs Committee. See Briefing Paper: Norwegian Attitudes on Far Eastern Situation, ND, Norway (3), Box 37, International Series, Papers of Dwight D. Eisenhower as President, DDEL, and Bergh and Pharo, *Vekst og Velstand*, p. 290 and 294.
16. US European Command Report, 12 January 1959, US European Command Report on NATO Area – Book 1, Box 18, Draper Committee, Records, 1958–59, DDEL.

17. Memorandum for the President, 3 March 1953, Subj: Visit of Foreign Minister Halvard Lange of Norway, Dulles, J.F., March 1953, Box 1, Dulles-Herter Series, Dwight D. Eisenhower Papers as President, DDEL.
18. NSC 6006/1, 6 April 1960, Box 28, NSC Series – Policy Papers Subseries, WHO: Office of Special Assistant for National Security Affairs, DDEL.
19. On the strongly anti-communist orientation of the Norwegian trade union leadership and its ties to American labour and embassy representatives in Oslo, see Konrad Nordahl, *Dagbøker, vol. I–II* (Oslo: Tiden Norsk Forlag, 1991–92), pp. 26, 192–93 (vol. I), pp. 59 (vol. II).
20. Interview with Jens Boyesen, 15 April 1991.
21. Ibid.
22. Interview with Sivert Nielsen, 16 April 1991.
23. US understanding of Finland's position within the Nordic region is discussed in the final chapter.
24. For a detailed account of the relationship between Norwegian and Danish policies in the 1950s, see Rolf Tamnes, "Samspillet mellom Norge og Denmark i NATO i 1950-årene," in *Denmark, Norden og NATO, 1948–1962*, ed. C. Due-Nielsen, J.P. Noack and N. Petersen (København: Jurist-og Økonomforbundets Forlag, 1991), pp. 38–39. The relationship between Sweden, the US and Norway is discussed below.
25. Eriksen and Skodvin, "Storbritannia, NATO og et skandinavisk forbund," p. 502.
26. Lange, "Scandinavian Co-operation in International Affairs," p. 291.
27. Nikolaj Petersen, "Atlantpagten eller Norden? Den danske alliancebeslutning 1949," in *Denmark, Norden og NATO, 1948–1962*, ed. C. Due-Nielsen, J.P. Noack and N. Petersen (Copenhagen: Jurist- og Økonomforbundets Forlag, 1991), pp. 38–39.
28. Dean Acheson, *Present at the Creation: My Years in the State Department* (New York: Norton & Company, 1969), p. 279.
29. Summary of Discussion between Gen. Eisenhower and Norwegian Government Officials, 9 May 1952, Memos of Conversations (SHAPE) 1951–52, Box 136, Dwight D. Eisenhower: Pre-Presidential Papers, 1916–52, DDEL.
30. Ambassador in the UK (Aldrich) to the Secretary of State, 27 September 1955, *FRUS 1955–57, Vol. IV.*, p. 572.
31. Frances E. Willis to Department of State, Despatch no. 900, 18 June 1958, 757. 5 MSP/6–1888, Rg. 59, NARA.
32. Interview with Jens Boyesen, 15 April and 11 September 1991. This view also prevailed in NATO where references to Lange would typically be accompanied by the comment that "... it was largely on the initiative of Mr Lange that Norway joined NATO from its foundation." See *NATO Letter*, vol. 4, no. 6, 1956.
33. Interview with Jens Boyesen, 15 April 1991. This view was shared by Sir Frank Roberts, Britain's Permanent Representative to NATO from 1957 to 1960. Interview with Sir Frank Roberts, 14 March 1992, London.
34. Pharo and Eriksen, "De fire sirklene i norsk utenrikspolitikk," p. 196.
35. Interview with Jens Boyesen, 11 September 1991. This "developing tension" within the Labour Party leadership is discussed more fully in the following chapter.

36. See Halvard Lange, *Norsk Utenrikspolitikk siden 1945: foredrag og debattinnlegg* (Oslo: Johan Grundt Tanum, 1952), p. 9 and pp. 226–27.
37. Lange quoted in *NATO Letter*, vol. 4, no. 6, June 1956.
38. Lange, "Scandinavian Co-operation in International Affairs," p. 293.
39. See "Mr Lange on NATO," *NATO Letter*, vol. 5, no. 1, 1957.
40. Lord Ismay, NATO: *The First Five Years*, (Paris: NATO, 1954), p. 151.
41. Robert S. Jordan, *Political Leadership in NATO: A Study in Multinational Diplomacy*(Boulder, Colorado: Westview Press, 1979), p. 170.
42. Lie, ... *slik jeg ser det*, pp. 106–107.
43. NSC Summary of Discussion, 11 May 1956, 284th Mtg of the NSC, Box 7, NSC Series, Papers of Dwight D. Eisenhower as President, DDEL. See also Memorandum for Goodpaster, Subject: Norwegian Foreign Minister Lange's Speech, 25 August 1959, Norway, Box 11, International Series, WHO: Office of the Staff Secretary, DDEL.
44. See NSC 5819, Part 2, 8 September 1958, DoD to NSC Status of Military Assistance Programs (p. 27 "Norway"), NSC 5819(3), Box 8, NSC Series – Status of Project Series, WHO: Office of Special Assistant for National Security Affairs, DDEL. Even in this respect, however, US officials were more critical of Danish efforts. See Letter from Gen. Norstad (SACEUR) to Poul Hansen (Minister of Defence), 23 January 1960, Denmark (3), Box 47, The Papers of General L. Norstad, DDEL.
45. "Effects of a US Foreign Military Aid Programme," CIA, 24 February 1949, ASD FMA, numerical-subject file 1949, Entry 192, Rg. 330, NARA.
46. Ibid.
47. "Neutralism in Norway," ND, No. 9 Bandung (2), Box 2, Planning Co-ordination Group Series, WHO: NSC Staff Papers, DDEL.
48. Intelligence Report No. 7992 (Bureau of Intelligence and Research), "Western European Pressures for Disengagement," Rg. 59, NARA.
49. Much interesting material can be found in Paul M. Cole, "Neutralité du jour: The conduct of Swedish security policy since 1945," (Ph.D. diss., The Johns Hopkins University, 1990).
50. *Had There Been a War ...* (See chapter 2)
51. The telegram is reproduced *in extenso* in Cole, "Neutralité du jour," pp. 358–362.
52. Ibid.
53. See here JIC 558/392 Intelligence Estimate of Soviet Bloc Capabilities and Probable Courses of Action between Now and the End of 1960, 6 February 1956, J.C.S. 1954–56, 334 JIC (12-7-55), Rg. 218, NARA, and Remarks of General Hoyt S. Vandenberg (COS/USAF), 28 November 1952, General Papers – World Trips, Oct.–Nov. 52, Box 84, The Papers of Hoyt S. Vandenberg, Manuscript Division, Library of Congress.
54. Notat fra møte på Forsvarsministerens kontor, 13 fredag 1950, and J. Chr. Hauge til Den Norske Ambassade i Stockholm, 7 november 1950, 25. 2/72, UD. See also report of discussions between Halvard Lange and Lord Alexander, British Minister of Defence, in March 1954 in COMNAVNORTH (Oslo) to the First Sea Lord, 26 March 1954, ADM 205/102, PRO.
55. Interview with Sivert Nielsen, 16 April 1991, Oslo. ("... Norge som et kontakt-ledd til Sverige ...").
56. Pharo and Eriksen, "De fire sirklene i norsk utenrikspolitikk," p. 198.

57. Memorandum for Mr Dickinson, Deputy for Installations, ASFMA, 10 December 1951, Col. Bernt Balchen Collection, Miscellaneous documents on defense of Norway, Sweden and Denmark, 40/04/24-65/08/23, (MF) Roll no. 30926. Office of Air Force History, Bolling AFB.

58. "Discussions I have had pertaining to the Norwegian Base Policy," Col. Bernt Balchen Collection, Miscellaneous documents on defense of Norway, Sweden and Denmark, 40/04/24-65/08/23, (MF) Roll no. 30926. Office of Air Force History, Bolling AFB.

59. Interview with Jens Boyesen, 15 April 1991.

60. On exchanges of personnel and training, see report on visits to US by Mr Karl-Arvid Norlin and two officers from the Swedish Air Force, History of Air Technical Intelligence Center, 1 July 1954–31 December 1954, Ts. 5-531 to 5-1431 (1955), Box 81, Entry 214, Rg. 314, NARA.

61. Memorandum, Office of the Vice Chairman, National Security Resources Board, 29 May 1952, Military Matters, Box 18, The Papers of Bernt Balchen, Manuscript Division, Library of Congress.

62. "Towards the end of the 1950s, an exchange of intelligence occurred between the International Department of the Defence Staff and all military services of Norway, Denmark, the UK, and the United States". See *Had There Been a War ...* p. 133.

63. "Release of Guided Missile Information to Sweden," 14 July 1960, 6. Foreign Correspondence (Sweden), Box 37, Papers of Thomas D. White, Manuscript Division, Library of Congress.

64. General S.T. Wray, Commander, to General Thomas White, C/USAF, 10 February 1960, 6. Foreign Correspondence (Sweden), Box 37, Papers of Thomas D. White, Manuscript Division, Library of Congress.

65. *Had There Been a War ...*, p. 191. According to the report this direct "connection was tested weekly" and was "probably" still operational in the late 1960s.

66. NSC 6006/1, 6 April 1960, Box 28, NSC Series – Policy Papers Subseries, WHO: Office of Special Assistant for National Security Affairs, DDEL. (My emphasis)

67. Briefing Note for NSC Meeting of 1 April 1960, Scandinavia (NSC 6006), 30 March 1960, NSC 6006/1 – Scandinavia, Box 28, NSC Series – Policy Papers Subseries, WHO: Office of Special Assistant for National Security Affairs, DDEL.

68. NSC 6006 (DRAFT), 14 March 1960, NSC 6006/1 – Scandinavia, Box 28, NSC Series – Policy papers Subseries, WHO: Office of the Special Assistant for National Security Affairs, DDEL.

69. Memorandum to NSC, 10 November 1960, and addition to NSC 6006/1, Box 28, NSC Series – Policy Papers Subseries, WHO: Office of the Special Assistant for National Security Affairs, DDEL.

70. Summary of Discussion, 439th Mtg. of the NSC, 2 April 1960, NSC Series, Dwight D. Eisenhower Papers as President, DDEL.

71. As the JCS saw it, the question was not merely one of principle, that is, non-allied countries should not have the same benefits as NATO allies. It was also one of security since the US was not in a position to impose controls on Swedish use of US technology once it had been transferred. The US was extremely concerned about the issue of export controls.

72. "Doktordisputas – *The United States and the Cold War in the High North,*" *Historisk Tidsskrift 2* (1992), pp. 208–209.
73. Turner, "Britain, The United States and Scandinavian Security Problems," pp. 153–54. An American proposal in October 1945 for 99-year leases of military bases in the country, was rejected by the Icelandic government.
74. Archer, "US Defence Areas in Greenland," p. 127.
75. Lundestad, *America, Scandinavia and the Cold War*, p. 64, and pp. 340–341. In October 1946, an agreement was reached between the US and Iceland for the interim use of Keflavik airport by US aircraft.
76. *The US Iceland Defence Agreement of 1951 and Supplementary Understandings of 1954*, Annex I. to NSC 5426, 12 July 1954, NSC 5426-Iceland, Box 12, WHO: Office of Special Assistant for National Security Affairs, DDEL.
77. NSC 5426, 12 July 1954, NSC 5426 – Iceland, Box 12, WHO: Office of Special Assistant for National Security Affairs, DDEL.
78. Ibid.
79. Robert Jackson, *Strike Force: The USAF in Britain Since 1948* (London: Robson Books, 1986), pp. 17–19, and J. Hopkins and S. Goldberg, *The Development of Strategic Air Command* (Nebraska: Office of the Historian HQ SAC, Offutt Air Force Base, 1986), p. 34, 55, and 84.
80. Memorandum for Members, OCB Working Group on Iceland, 16 December 1955, Iceland File No. 3(1), Box 35, OCB Central File, WHO: NSC Staff Papers, DDEL.
81. NSC 5712/1, 20 May 1957, NSC 5712/1-Iceland, Box 21, NSC Series – Policy Papers Subseries, WHO: Office of Special Assistant for National Security Affairs, DDEL.
82. See Review of US Overseas Military Bases (Lang Report), April 1960, Base-Rights (4), Box 2, NSC Series – Subject Subseries, WHO: Office of Special Assistant for National Security Affairs, DDEL, p. 15 and p. 18.
83. Officially this change was described as a natural consequence of the "increasing participation of the USN in the defence of the NATO North West defence areas." Enclosed "Announcement" to letter from British Embassy to FO, 29 Nov. 1960, FO 371/151655, PRO.
84. Hanson Baldwin, "Navy to Tighten Arctic Air Alert," *New York Times*, 19 December 1960.
85. Summary of NSC Discussion, 17 May 1957, 323rd Mtg of the NSC, Box 8, NSC Series, Papers of Dwight D. Eisenhower as President, DDEL.
86. Ibid.
87. Ibid. In the final version, the term chosen was "grave" rather than an "unacceptable" weakening of the North Atlantic Defence system.
88. Interview with Bjørn Egge, 9 April 1991. "Island, NATO og Norge," *Aftenposten*, 16 April 1956.
89. TS Memorandum No. 47, From: D/Logistics Plans Division, To: Distribution List, 13 April 1953, Subject: Acquisition of US Military Rights in Foreign Territory, A-14, Box 283, Strategic Plans Division Records, NHC. See also footnote 76.
90. P.M. Reykjavik 6 desember 1952, 33. 6/11, Bind I, UD.

91. TS Memorandum No. 47, From: D/Logistics Plans Division, To: Distribution List, 13 April 1953, Subject: Acquisition of US military Rights in Foreign Territory, A-14, Box 283, Strategic Plans Division Records, NHC. This report has not been declassified.

92. NSC 5426, 12 July 1954, NSC 5426 – Iceland, Box 12, WHO: Office of Special Assistant for National Security Affairs, DDEL.

93. Benedikt Grøndal, *Iceland from Neutrality to NATO Membership* (Oslo: Universitetsforlaget, 1971), pp. 43–44.

94. NSC 5426, 12 July 1954, NSC 5426 – Iceland, Box 12, WHO: Office of Special Assistant for National Security Affairs, DDEL.

95. Grøndal, *Iceland from Neutrality to NATO Membership*, pp. 52–57.

96. Mary S. Olmsted, "Communism in Iceland," *Foreign Affairs* 36 (January 1958), p. 345. See also Memorandum, From: D/CNO(P&P) To: D/NI, 6 December 1955, Subject: Communist Interference in Iceland, EF, Box 325, Strategic Plans Division Records, NHC.

97. NSC Progress Report on Iceland by OCB, 25 February 1955, NSC 5426 – Iceland, Box 12, NSC Series – Policy Papers Subseries, WHO: Office of Special Assistant for National Security Affairs, DDEL.

98. Clearly eager to find a simple solution to the problem of Soviet penetration of the Icelandic economy, Eisenhower in the summer of 1954 suggested that "we should find out precisely what the USSR is paying for Icelandic fish and thereafter see if we cannot buy up the entire catch and give it to some country as part of our aid program." Summary of Discussion, 23 July 1954, 207 Mtg. of the NSC, Box 5 NSC Series, Papers of Dwight D. Eisenhower as President, DDEL.

99. NSC 6025, US Policy Toward Iceland, 29 December 1960, NSC 6025, Box 16, NSC Series – Policy Papers Subseries, WHO: Office of Special Assistant for National Security Affairs, DDEL, and "Icelandic Crack in NATO," *The Economist*, 7 April 1956.

100. NATO Letter, vol. 4, no. 7, 1956.

101. OCB Minutes of Mtg, 20 April 1956, OCB Minutes of Mtgs. 1956 (2), Box 3, OCB Series – Administration Subseries, WHO: Office of Special Assistant for National Security Affairs, DDEL.

102. NSC 6025, US Policy Toward Iceland, 29 December 1960, NSC 6025, Box 16. NSC Series – Policy papers Subseries, WHO: Office of Special Assistant for National Security Affairs, DDEL.

103. Fortrolig Melding til Norges Delg. Paris, 9.4.56, 33. 6/11, Bind II., UD, and "Island, NATO og Norge," *Aftenposten*, 16 April 1956.

104. Iceland File No. 4 (3), Box 36, OCB Central File Series, WHO: NSC Staff Papers 1948–61, DDEL.

105. See "Dulles vil drøfte Island med Lange og H.C. Hansen," *Verdens Gang*, 4 April 1956

106. This is one of several points that emerge from a Norwegian Foreign Ministry memorandum, Fra Kgl. Ambassade Reykjavik, til Kgl UD, 29 mai 1956 Nr. 148, USA og Island, Samtale med ambassadør Muccio, 33. 6/11, Bind III, UD.

107. Ibid.

108. Ibid.

109. "US Reaction to Iceland Vote," *The Times*, 27 June 1956.
110. This is one of several points that emerge from a Norwegian Foreign Ministry memorandum, Fra UD til Delg. Paris, Fortrolig Melding, 27 juli 1956, 33. 6/11, Bind III, UD.
111. Notat, Samtale mellom utenriksminister Lange og ambassad¿r Corrin Strong, 4/8/1956, 33. 6/11, Bind III, UD.
112. Fra Norwegian Embassy, Washington, til Kgl UD, 27 juli 1956, Nr. 743, Situasjonen på Island, 33. 6/11, Bind III, UD.
113. This is one of several points that emerge from a Norwegian Foreign Ministry memorandum, Notat, Islands stilling i NATO, 24 August 1956, 33. 6/11, Bind IV, UD.
114. This is one of several points that emerge from a Norwegian Foreign Ministry memorandum, Notat, Amerikansk henvendelse vedrørende Islands stilling i NATO, 1 august 1956, 33. 6/11, Bind IV, UD.
115. Notat, Til Utenriksråd Skylstad fra Statsråd Skaug, Island og NATO, 6 August, 33. 6/11, Bind IV, UD. Norwegian views on these issues were reiterated to Haydon Raynor, the American Counsellor in Oslo.
116. This is one of several points found in a Norwegian Foreign Ministry memorandum, Notat, Island's stilling i NATO, 24 August 1956, 33. 6/11, Bind IV, UD.
117. The changing "world situation" was the principal argument used by the Icelandic government when it explained its decision not to press for a full US withdrawal from the island. Fra Kgl. Norsk Ambassade, Reykjavik til Det Kgl UD, 21 november 1956, Nr. 363, 33. 6/11, Bind V, and Fra Kgl. Norsk Ambassade, Reykjavik til Det Kgl UD, 8 desember 1956, Nr. 378, 33. 6/11, Bind V, UD. See also "An Icelandic Somersault," *The Economist*, 8 December 1956, and "Iceland Reconsiders," *New York Times*, 8 December 1956.
118. NSC 6025, 29 December 1960, NSC 6025, Box 16, NSC Series – Policy Papers Subseries, WHO: Office of Special Assistant for National Security Affairs, DDEL.
119. NSC Progress Report on Iceland by the OCB, 1 May 1957, NSC 5426 – Iceland, Box 21, NSC Series – Policy Papers Subseries, WHO: Office of Special Assistant for National Security Affairs, DDEL.
120. See Memorandum for Goodpaster, 19 September 1959, Subject: General Pritchard's transfer from Iceland, Iceland [September 59–June 61], Box 7, International Series, WHO: Office of the Staff Secretary, DDEL, and "US decision to cut garrison in Iceland," *Guardian,* 7 December 1959.
121. The Lang Report on US overseas bases in 1960 emphasised the future importance of Greenland as an early warning outpost for ICBM attack against North America. Scheduled for completion in mid-1960 was the extension of the DEW line eastward from Cape Dyer across the Greenland ice cap to meet up with the seaward extension of the line from the east coast of Greenland to Iceland, the Faeroes and the UK. Thule was also the site of one of the three Ballistic Missile Early Warning System (BMEWS) constructed by the US in the late 1950s and early 1960s. And, as we have seen earlier, it was revealed in 1995 that the US stationed nuclear warheads at Thule in the period between 1958 and 1965.

8   NORWAY, THE UNITED STATES AND THE MANAGEMENT
OF BILATERAL RELATIONS, 1954–60

1.   See Rolf Tamnes, "Integration and Screening: The Two Faces of Norwegian Alliance Policy, 1945–1986," in *Defence Studies VI 1987* (Oslo: Tano, 1987).
2.   J.J. Holst, "The Security Pattern in Northern Europe: A Norwegian View," in *Britain and NATO's Northern Flank*, ed. G. Till (London: Macmillan Press, 1988), p. 38.
3.   Summary of Discussion between Gen. Eisenhower and Norwegian Government Officials, 9 May 1952, Memos of Conversations (SHAPE) 1951–52, Box 136, Dwight D. Eisenhower: Pre-Presidential Papers, 1916–52, DDEL. See also "Norges Luftforsvar Meget Utilstrekkelig," *Morgenbladet*, September 1952 (Interview with Colonel Balchen).
4.   Ibid. The Longman Dictionary of Contemporary English defines "pressure" as "the action of putting force or weight onto something" or alternatively "forceful influence." In the context of this argument, American "actions" would amount to "pressure" if it involved an explicit linkage between conduct of Norwegian security policy and the provision or withholding of US benefits.
5.   Record of Meeting, 28 June 1952, FO 800/814, PRO.
6.   NSC, Geographical Area Policies, Part VI, Europe (Scandinavia), 1 November 1952, 001028, DDC, vol. XV, 1989.
7.   On 3 March, Halvard Lange told John Foster Dulles in Washington that he was "disturbed" by recent evidence of a downgrading of "Northern NATO defenses." See Memorandum of Conversation, 3 March 1953, *FRUS 1952–1954, Volume VI, Part 2*. Similarly, after a visit to Norway in early 1953, Selwyn Lloyd told Churchill that "the Norwegians have been upset by an idea that the Northern flank is not considered worth holding." See For Prime Minister, 14 April 1953, FO 800/814, PRO.
8.   Notat, Norske og sovjetiske uttalelser om Norges sikkerhets og basepolitikk, 1. 11. 61, 33. 6/14, Bd. III, UD.
9.   ("... avtalefeste norske utsagn om basepolitikken ...") Notat, Gerhardsen og Skaugs samtale med ambassadør Gribanov i Sovjetambassaden torsdag 2 Mai 1957, 34. 4/99, Bind X, UD.
10. Memorandum, From: Norwegian Minister of Defence, To: SACEUR and SACLANT, 11 December 1959, Hagy thru Hansen (4), Box 68, General L. Norstad Papers, DDEL. (my emphasis)
11. Ibid.
12. Memorandum, D/Strategic Plans Division, To: D/Logistic Plans Division, 10 October 1955, Subject: Base Rights for Support of US Forces Earmarked for Deployment to Norway, EF, Box 325, Strategic Plans Division Records, NHC.
13. Interview with Field Marshal Lord Carver, 16 October 1991, London. See also comments on bases in Norway by the British Commander of Allied Naval Forces, Northern Europe, Admiral Evans-Lombe, reported in "Norway May Ease Foreign Troop Ban," *New York Times*, 21 May 1953.

14. NEC Historical Reports, 1 Jan. 1954–30 June 1954, D/COS, O&T, SECCOS, HQ AFNORTH.
15. Ibid.
16. From: CNO, To: CINCLANT, 13 June 1955, Subj: Base Rights for Support of US Forces Earmarked for Deployment to Norway, EF, Box 325, Strategic Plans Division, Records, NHC.
17. This is one of several points that emerge from a Norwegian Foreign Ministry memorandum, Notat, Rekognoseringsflyvninger, 1 desember 1959, 33. 6/14b, Bd. I, UD. There is necessarily here a grey area between "peripheral reconnaissance," "patrol" and "intelligence" flights which will be discussed below.
18. Notat, Forenkling av fremgangsmåten for klarering av militærfly tilhørende NATO-land. 8/11-1956, 38. 15/7, Bind. III, UD.
19. Ibid.
20. Notat, 5 og 11 september 1956, 38. 15/7, Bind. III, UD.
21. Ibid.
22. *Aide-Mémoire*, 12 mai 1956, 38. 15/7, Bind. III, UD.
23. In my sources, I have not found specific references to restrictions on the carrying of tactical nuclear weapons onboard US Navy Neptune patrol bombers.
24. HQ, RNAF, To: Distribution List, 28 April 1959, Subject: Exercise Directive for USN Maritime Patrol Aircraft Navigation/Familiarisation Flights to Norway, (Exercise "Neptune Journey"), A/H 003623, FD.
25. J.J. Holst, *Norsk Sikkerhetspolitikk i Strategisk Perspektiv,* p. 89.
26. Annex IV, "USSR Note to Norway, 13 May," U-2 [Vol. III] (2), Box 25, Subject Series, Alpha, WHO: Office of the Staff Secretary, DDEL.
27. Notat, Samtale med viseutenriksminister Pusjkin under overlevering av norsk svarnote 22 juli 1960, 33. 1/7, Bind VI, UD.
28. See Michael R. Beschloss, *Mayday: Eisenhower, Khrushchev and the U-2 Affair* (New York: Harper and Row, 1986). On the U-2 incident and Norway, see Tamnes, *Cold War in the High North,* pp. 133–135 and 178–82. On the RB-47 episode, see Tamnes, Cold *War in the High North,* pp. 123–124. On the history of the U-2, see *Oral History Interview with Richard M. Bissell, Jr.* 9 November, 1976, DDEL. Jay Miller's book on the U-2 provides an excellent account of the operational history of the aircraft under both the CIA and the USAF.
29. Notat, Samtale med ambassadør Gundersen hos statssekretæren 4 august 1960, Ad-doss. 25/4/99, Bd. I, UD.
30. *Yearbook of the United Nations 1958* (New York: Columbia University Press, 1959) p. 16, and "Complaint of the Representative of the USSR," 18 April 1958, F0 371/151998, PRO.
31. Ibid.
32. NSC 5724/1, 16 December 1957, "Comments and Recommendations on the Report ... " NSC 5724 – Gaither Committee, Box 22, NSC Series, Policy Papers Subseries, WHO: Office of the Special Assistant for National Security Affairs, DDEL. SAC alert force operations began in October 1957. See Gen. T. S. Power (CC SAC) to Gen. T. White (COS/USAF), 22 October 1958, 1958-TS general file (4) Box 19, The Papers of T. D. White, Manuscript Division, Library of Congress.

33. Briefing for the President, SAC Ops. with Sealed Pit Weapons, ND, DoD Vol. II (9) [July 1958], Box 1, Subject Series, DoD Subseries, WHO: Office of the Staff Secretary, DDEL.

34. Discussion at 367th Mtg. of NSC, 29 May 1958, "1. Launching of SAC Alert Forces," Box 10, NSC Series, Dwight D. Eisenhower Papers as President, DDEL. In the autumn of 1958, the 42nd Bomber Wing based in Maine conducted the first B-52 airborne alert test, see Hopkins and Goldberg, *The Development of the Strategic Air Command,* p. 74. See also "B-52's Expanding Alert in Atlantic and Arctic Area," *New York Times,* 11 November 1961.

35. Interview with Erik Himle, 11 April 1991, Oslo.

36. Memorandum to Gen. Goodpaster, 22 April 1958, Subj: Soviet Note on Overflights, State Dept.-1958 (Feb.–April)(4), Box 2, State Department Subseries, WHO: Office of the Staff secretary, Records, DDEL. The note shows that the Soviet Union was fully aware of the type, mission and flight-path of each operation but unable to take effective countermeasures.

37. From Nolting (Paris) to Secretary of State, 1 July 1960, U-2 Incident [Vol. III](1), Subject Series, Alpha, WHO: Office of the Staff Secretary, DDEL.

38. Sir Patrick Reilly (Moscow) to FO, 22 January 1959, FO 371/143176, PRO. Discussing the incident in 1960, Norwegian Foreign Ministry officials observed that the "Russians were very well oriented about what was happening in Bodø and probably had direct connections there." Notat, Samtale med ambassadør Gundersen hos statssekretæren 4 august 1960, Ad-doss. 25/4/99, Bd. I. UD.

39. Ibid.

40. Notat, Norske og sovjetiske uttalelser om Norges sikkerhets og basepolitikk, 31 oktober 1960, 33. 6/14, Bd. III, UD, and "Ikke grunnlag for sovjethenvendelse om flyspeidingene," *Arbeiderbladet,* 31 January 1959.

41. Notat, Ambassadør Gundersen besøk hos statsminister Khrushchev 9. Februar 1959, 34. 4/99, Bd. XI, UD.

42. Ibid.

43. For a detailed study of the Svalbard issue see Rolf Tamnes, *Svalbard og den politiske avmakt: Striden om flyplass, olje og telemetri-stasjon, 1955–1970* (Oslo: Institutt for Forsvarsstudier, 1992).

44. "USSR and Norway Exchange Notes on Plans for Military Airfields on Spitzbergen," *Soviet News,* 15 November 1960, copy in FO 371/151733, PRO.

45. Ibid.

46. Notat, Samtale med ambassador Gundersen hos statssekretæren 4 august 1960, Ad-doss. 25/4/99, Bd. I, UD.

47. USSR National Affairs, 9 May 1960, U-2 Incident Vol. I (1), Box 25, Subject Series, Alpha, WHO: Office of the Staff Secretary, DDEL.

48. Moscow Telegram to Foreign Office No. 605, 9 May 1960, FO 371/151995, PRO.

49. Annex IV, "USSR Note to Norway, 13 May," U-2 [Vol. III] (2), Box 25, Subject Series, Alpha, WHO: Office of the Staff Secretary, DDEL.

50. Ibid. The most menacing and overt threats came from Marshal Malinovsky, the Soviet Defence Minister. See "Soviet Rocket Troops Ordered to Retaliate on Bases," *The Times,* 31 May 1960.

51. Mikoyan visited Norway from 23 to 29 June. Earlier in the month, Macmillan had visited Norway and was told by Lange that the Russians were "accusing the Norwegians of circumventing their own restrictions by permitting excessive use of their bases." Record of Conversation with Gerhardsen, Macmillan's trip to Norway 7–10 June 1960, FO 371/151723, PRO.

52. Statement By Mr. Gunneng, Acting Permanent Representative to Council, July 6, 1960, FO 371/151718, PRO. For US reporting on Mikoyan's visit, see Willis (Oslo) to Secretary of State, 28 and 29 June 1960, (Mikoyan visit), USSR Vol. II of II(4), International Series, WHO: Office of Staff Secretary, DDEL.

53. Norwegian involvement in the RB-47 incident was also generally assumed by the international press. See for example Hanson W. Baldwin, "Kremlin Cloud Over Our Bases," *New York Times Magazine*, 9 October 1960.

54. From Moscow to Sec. of State, 11 July 1960, USSR – Vol. II of II (5) July 1960, Box 15, International Series, WHO: Office of the Staff Secretary, DDEL.

55. "Tension-raising Soviet actions since June 27, 1960," ND, USSR – Vol. II of II(5), July 1960, Box 15, International Series, WHO: Office of the Staff Secretary, DDEL.

56. Embtel 940, to Secretary of State, 10 May 1960, U-2 Incident Vol. I (4), Box 25, Subject Series, Alpha, WHO: Office of the Staff Secretary, DDEL.

57. Ibid.

58. Tamnes, *Cold War in the High North*, pp. 178–179. Lt. Colonel Just Ebbesen, who was Norwegian Air Force liaison with U-2 personnel in Bodø, has later claimed that the Norwegian Defence minister, Nils Handal "must have known about the real purpose of the U-2 aircraft in Bodø." See "Bare sikkerheten gjelder," *Aftenposten*, 16 June 1991.

59. Tamnes, *Cold War in the High North*, p. 179. Chr. Christensen has argued earlier that Evang felt that he had been disinformed by the CIA over the operation and that he "never regained confidence" in the Americans after the incident. See Christensen, *Vår Hemmelige Beredskap*, pp. 98–99.

60. Sir Peter Scarlett to Foreign Office, 16 May 1960, FO 371/180353, PRO.

61. Notat, Norske og sovjetiske uttalelser om Norges sikkerhets og basepolitikk, 31 oktober 1960, 33. 6/14, Bd. III, UD.

62. Notat, Samtale med ambassadør Gundersen hos statssekretæren 4 august 1960, Ad-doss. 25/4/99, Bd. I. UD. The Loran-C transmitter station in Vesterålen was initially manned by one US officer and 18 enlisted men. In July 1960, the Loran monitor station in Vesterålen was manned by one Norwegian and five Americans, see Regjeringskonferanse 12 juli, 1960, RA.

63. Notat, møte med ambassadør Frances Willis 13 mai 1960, 31. 1/7, Bind II, UD.

64. Sir P. Scarlett to FO, 16 May 1960, FO 371/151997, PRO.

65. Gerhardsen told Macmillan that "while the Norwegians have been disappointed by the American action in sending the U-2 across Russia, they had reacted very strongly against Mr. Khrushchev's threats." Record of Conversation with Gerhardsen, Macmillan's trip to Norway 7–10 June 1960, FO 371/151723, PRO.

66. *Oral History Interview with Richard M. Bissell, Jr.* 9 November, 1976, DDEL, pp. 9–11.
67. Memorandum, 22 December 1958, Intelligence Material (7), [December 1958], Box 15, Subject Series, Alpha, WHO: Office of the Staff Secretary, DDEL.
68. Memorandum, 12 February 1959, Intelligence material (8), [Jan.–Feb. 1959], Box 12, Subject Series, Alpha, WHO: Office of the Staff Secretary, DDEL.
69. Memorandum, 12 May 1960, Staff Notes May 1960 (1), Box 50, DDE Diary Series, Dwight D. Eisenhower Papers as President, DDEL.
70. Sec. State, Herter, to Amembassy Oslo, 1086, 10 May 1960, U-2 Incident Vol. I (4), Box 25, Subject Series, Alpha, WHO: Office of the Staff Secretary, DDEL.
71. Ibid.
72. Ibid.
73. Notat, møte med ambassadør Frances Willis 13 mai 1960, 31. 1/7, Bind II, UD, and D. Dillon to Amembassy Paris, 15 May 1960, U-2 Incident Vol. I (5), Box 25, Subject Series, Alpha, WHO: Office of the Staff Secretary, DDEL.
74. By contrast, the Democrat Senator Mansfield, regretted the "embarrassment of allies providing bases on the Soviet periphery." See "Mansfield bitter over U-2 incident," *New York Times*, 24 June 1960.
75. Memorandum of Conversation with Senator Knowland, 10 June 1957, Memos of Conv. – General J through K (2), Box 1, General Correspondence and Memoranda Series, J.F. Dulles Papers, 1951–59, DDEL.
76. NEC Historical Report, 1 July 56–31 Dec. 57, SECCOS, HQ AFNORTH.
77. Memorandum of Conversation with Senator Knowland, 10 June 1957, Memos of Conv. – General J through K (2), Box 1, General Correspondence and Memoranda Series, J.F. Dulles Papers, 1951–59, DDEL.
78. Memorandum of Conference with Bipartisan Leaders, 26 May 1960, Staff Notes May 1960 (1), Box 50, DDE Diary Series, Dwight D. Eisenhower Papers as president, DDEL (parts of the document are still classified).
79. Ibid. This could only refer to Norway since neither Pakistan nor Turkey delivered a similar "protest" to the USA.
80. Ibid.
81. Ts Msg., From CG 7th Air Division, to CG SAC, 6 Dec. 1952, The Papers of Curtis LeMay, Manuscript Division, Library of Congress. (My emphasis).
82. Ibid.
83. D/Naval Intelligence to D/Intelligence, USAF, 25 May 1954, Ts. No. 1114–to 4–2146 (1954), Box 77, Entry 214, Rg. 341, NARA.
84. Tamnes, *Cold War in the High North*, p. 175.
85. Notat, Til Forsvarsministeren, 23 Oktober 1957, H-001012 28. 10. 57, FD.
86. Ransom, "Secret Intelligence in the United States," pp. 205–210. On the early problems of co-ordination and the fragmented nature of the intelligence community in the 1950s, see Scott D. Breckinridge, *The CIA and the US Intelligence System* (Boulder: Westview Press, 1986), pp. 41–43.

87. Official White House Transcript of President Eisenhower's Press and Radio Conference no. 185, 11 May 1960, Press and Radio Conference 5/11/60, Box 10, Press Conference Series, Papers of Dwight D. Eisenhower as President, DDEL.

88. "USSR and Norway Exchange Notes on Plans for Military Airfields on Spitzbergen," *Soviet News,* 15 November 1960, copy in FO 371/151733, PRO.

89. Ibid.

90. Tamnes, *Svalbard og den politiske avmakt*, p. 25, and British Emb. Oslo to FO, 16 November 1960, both in FO 371/151733, PRO.

91. From UK Delegation to NATO to FO, 9 November 1960, FO 371/151733, PRO.

92. Ibid.

93. Fra Norges ambassade i Washington til UD, 23 november 1960, Nr. 1403. Sak: Norsk Basepolitikk, 33. 6/14, Bd. III, UD.

94. NSC 6006/1, Scandinavia, 6 April 1960, Box 28, NSC Series – Policy Paper Subseries, WHO: Office of Special Assistant for National Security Affairs, DDEL.

95. "Neutralism in Europe, Summary Report," and "Neutralism in Europe," ND, No. 9 Bandung (2), Box 2, Planning Co-ordination Group Series, WHO: NSC Staff Papers, DDEL.

96. "US Policy Toward Finland," 12 January 1954, NSC 5403 (2), Box 8, NSC Series, Policy Papers Subseries, WHO: Office of Special Assistant for National Security Affairs, DDEL.

97. An important contribution in this respect is W.H. Brands, *The Specter of Neutralism: The United States and the Emergence of the Third World, 1947–60* (New York: Columbia University Press, 1989). For a critical appraisal of this book, see Dennis Merrill, "America Encounters the Third World," *Diplomatic History* 16 (Spring 1992), pp. 325–330.

98. Ibid. p. 308.

99. In 1956, John F. Dulles, in characteristic manner, described "neutrality" as both an "immoral and short-sighted conception," quoted in Gaddis, *Strategies of Containment,* p. 154. For an earlier assessment of Dulles's attitude, see Townsend Hoopes, *The Devil and John Foster Dulles* (Boston: Little & Brown, 1973), p. 316.

100. NSC 5501, Basic National Security Policy, 6 January 1955, reprinted in Trachtenberg, ed. *The Development of American Strategic Thought*, p. 102.

101. NSC 5602/1, Basic National Security Policy, 15 March 1956, reprinted in Trachtenberg, ed. *The Development of American Strategic Thought*, p. 154.

102. Neutralism in Europe, Summary Report, ND, No. 9 Bandung (2), Box 2, Planning Co-ordination Group Series, WHO: NSC Staff Papers DDEL.

103. Ibid.

104. Ibid.

105. Ibid.

106. Lester C. Strong (Oslo) to State Department, 17 July 1955, 757. 5 MSP/7–857, Rg. 59, NARA.

107. G. Hauge to the President, 11 September 1955, Hauge, Gabriel 1952–55 (1), Box 18, Administration Series, Papers of Dwight D. Eisenhower as President, DDEL.

108. Ibid.
109. Summaries of Mission Chief's Country Program Review, 4 December 1956, ICA (1), Fairless Committee, Records, 1956–57, DDEL.
110. Ibid.
111. For Soviet policy towards Norway, see two important articles by T.H. Hetland, "Da Moskva sa nei til Norge: Sovjets syn pa Norden og NATO 1948–1952," and "Atomrasling og avspenning: Sovjet og norsk tryggingspolitikk 1953–1958," both in *Defence Studies IV 1985,* ed. R. Tamnes (Oslo: Tano A/S,1985).
112. Hetland, "Atomrasling og avspenning," pp. 73–78, and Aleksander Kan, *Naboskap under kald krig og perestrojka: Forholdet Norge-Sovjet sett fra Moskva* (Oslo: Forsvarsstudier no. 6 1988), pp. 28–29.
113. For 1955 as a year of transition in Soviet foreign policy more generally, see A. Ulam, *Expansion and Coexistence: the History of Soviet Foreign Policy, 1917–67* (New York: Frederick A. Praeger, 1968), pp. 564–571, and, J.L. Nooge and R.H. Donaldson, *Soviet Foreign Policy since World War II, Second Edition* (Oxford: Pergamon Press, 1987), pp. 112–119.
114. Ingemar Lindahl, *The Soviet Union and the Nordic Nuclear-Weapons-Free-Zone Proposal* (London: Macmillan Press, 1988), p. 35.
115. Hetland, "atomrasling og avspenning," pp. 68–70. For the Soviet interest in "neutralism" as a "new movement in international politics" in the late 1950s, see P.H. Vigor, *The Soviet View of War, Peace and Neutrality* (London: Routledge & Kegan Paul Ltd., 1975), pp. 189–94.
116. "United Front in Iceland," *New York Times,* 24 July 1956, and "US Is Worried By Iceland Move to Oust Troops," *New York Herald Tribune,* 30 March 1956.
117. "The Crisis in NATO," *Washington Post,* 30 March 1956. For another contemporary view of NATO as "seriously threatened" in Scandinavia partly as a result of the "great change in Soviet tactics in 1955 and 1956," see Lyman B. Burbank, "Scandinavian Integration and Western Defence," *Foreign Affairs* 35 (October 1956), p. 144 and 150.
118. "US Is Worried By Iceland Move to Oust Troops," *New York Herald Tribune,* 30 March 1956.
119. "Soviet Attempts to Control the Baltic Sea," *The ONI Review,* vol. 13, no. 8 1958, NHC.
120. Neutralism in Europe, Summary Report, ND, No. 9 Bandung (2), Box 2, Planning Co-ordination Group Series, WHO: NSC Staff Papers 1948–61, DDEL.
121. For a detailed study of the opposition to the dominant line in Norwegian security policy during this period, see Johan Kr. Meyer, *NATOs Kritikere: Den sikkerhetspolitiske opposisjon, 1949–61* (Oslo: Institutt for Forsvarsstudier 1989).
122. Trond Bergh, *Arbeiderbevegelsens Historie i Norge, vol. 5: Storhetstid, 1945–1965* (Oslo: Tiden Norsk Forlag, 1987), pp. 441–446. See also Edvard Bull, *Norge i Den Rike Verden: Tiden etter 1945* (Oslo: J.W. Cappelens Forlag, 1979), pp. 391–392.
123. See diary entries for 16 November 1955 and 10 January and 22 June 1956, Nordahl, *Dagbøker* (vol. I), pp. 396–397, and (vol. II), p. 12 and 59.

124. On Gerhardsen's "mission to Moscow," see Lie, ... *slik jeg ser det*, pp. 112–119.
125. NATO Head of Government Meeting, Briefing Book, Dec. 1957 – NATO Briefing Papers (1), Box 27, Administration Series, Papers of Dwight D. Eisenhower as President of the US, DDEL.
126. Ibid.
127. Fully aware of the tensions within the Labour party leadership, Soviet diplomacy towards Norway after the Paris meeting aimed at exacerbating tensions between the Foreign Ministry and the Prime Minister's Office by almost completely ignoring the former. See Hetland, "Atomrasling og avspenning," pp. 97–98, and Nordahl, *Dagbøker vol. II*, p. 150.
128. Address is reprinted in K.E. Eriksen and G. Lundestad, eds. *Norsk Utenrikspolitikk* (Oslo: Universitetsforlaget, 1972), pp. 129–132.
129. Interview with Jens Boyesen 14 April 1991. Boyesen did the "redrafting" of the speech in Paris with Lange.
130. Summary of discussion, 348th Mtg of NSC, 13 December 1957, Box 9, NSC Series, Dwight D. Eisenhower Papers as President, DDEL.
131. Entry for Tuesday 21 January 1958, Nordahl, *Dagbøker* (vol. II), p. 148. See also Lie, ... *slik jeg ser det*, pp. 92–100.
132. "Neutralist Trend held Peril to Pact – US and British Delegates Disturbed by Stand of Norway and Denmark," *New York Times*, 18 December 1957. See also "New East-West Peace Effort is Urged as US Offers Arms to NATO Allies," *Washington Post and Times Herald*, 18 December 1957.
133. Ibid.
134. "Neutralism in Norway: A New Peril for NATO," *Philadelphia Inquirer*, 25 August 1959.
135. Those sections of the American press which occasionally did address themselves to Northern European issues were frequently ill-informed and usually tended to overemphasise the strength of neutralist sentiment in Norway and Scandinavia as a whole. See for example articles by Ludwell Denny, "Neutralist Sentiment Growing in Norway," and "Many Norwegians Blind to Red Threat," both in *San Francisco News*, 15 and 16 September 1954 respectively.
136. "Talking points for NSC discussion of December 1958 NATO Ministerial Meeting," (State Draft), ND, NATO Ministerial Mtg. 1958 and 1959, Box 7 Special Assistant Series – Subject Subseries, WHO: Office of Special Assistant for National Security Affairs, DDEL.
137. Letter from J.F. Dulles to Selwyn Lloyd, 29 January 1959, Dulles, January 58 (1), Box 7, Dulles-Herter Series, Papers of Dwight D. Eisenhower as President, DDEL. For the Gerhardsen-Bulganin exchange of letters in 1957–58, see Holst, *Norsk Sikkerhetspolitikk i Strategisk Perspektiv*.
138. Intelligence Report No. 7992 (Bureau of Intelligence and Research), "Western European Pressures for Disengagement," Rg. 59, NARA.
139. NSC 6006/1, Scandinavia, 6 April 1960, Box 28, NSC Series – Policy Paper Subseries, WHO: Office of Special Assistant for National Security Affairs, DDEL.
140. Nordahl's diaries show that an important source of knowledge about trends and attitudes within in the Norwegian labour movement came from the

extremely close relations that existed in the 1950s between the "labour attaché" at the American embassy in Oslo and the Trade Union leadership. See Nordahl, *Dagbøker vol. II*, p. 64, 81, 166. See also here an interesting report on discussion between the US Chargé d'Affairs in Oslo, Hayden Raynor, and Andreas Andersen in 1955, Foreign Service Despatch, Amembassy, Oslo, to Dept. of State, 14 October 1955, Subject: General Defence Questions, Prime Minister's Moscow Visit, EF-61, Box 327, Strategic Plans Division Records, NHC.

141. Memorandum of Information, From: Director, International Affairs To: Vice Chief of Naval Operations, 15 August 1952, Subj: Tactical Air Force Base Rights in Norway, A-14, Box 271, Strategic Plans Division Records, NHC.
142. Neutralism in Europe, Summary Report, ND, No. 9 Bandung (2), Box 2, Planning Co-ordination Group Series, WHO: NSC Staff Papers, DDEL.
143. Northern European Chiefs of Mission Conference, London September 19–21, 1957, Conclusions and recommendations, *FRUS 1955–57, Vol. IV*, p. 636.
144. Memorandum of Information, From: Director, International Affairs, To: Vice Chief of Naval Operations, 15 August 1952, Subj: Tactical Air Force Base Rights in Norway, A-14, Box 271, Strategic Plans Division Records, NHC.
145. Lange, "Scandinavian Co-operation in International Affairs," p. 292.
146. Ibid.
147. Ibid.
148. "US Policy Toward Finland," 12 January 1954, NSC 5403 (2), Box 8, NSC Series, Policy Papers Subseries, WHO: Office of Special Assistant for National Security Affairs, DDEL.
149. NSC 5914/1, 14 October 1959, NSC 5914/1, Box 27, NSC Series, Policy Papers Subseries, WHO: Office of the Special Assistant for National Security Affairs, DDEL.
150. Ibid.
151. NSC 6006/1, Scandinavia, 6 April 1960, Box 28, NSC Series – Policy Paper Subseries, WHO: Office of the Special Assistant for National Security Affairs, DDEL. See also footnote 68, Chapter 7.
152. See Memorandum of Conference with the President, 17 June 1959, DOD Vol. III (6), Box 1, Subject Series – DOD Subseries, WHO: Office of the Staff Secretary, DDEL.
153. See Den Sentrale Sjefsnemnd, "Notat: Atomvåpen i det norske forsvar...", 9 juni 1959, FO. Between 1957 and 1961, some preparations were made for the Norwegians to accept tactical nuclear weapons: infrastructure funds were allocated for Atomic Storage Sites and Norway accepted a US offer of the Honest John and Nike *Hercules* missile system (widely regarded as tactical nuclear-delivery systems). See Tamnes, *Cold War in the High North*, pp. 160–165.
154. Ibid.
155. Hetland, "Atomrasling og avspenning," p. 72.
156. For the "classic" exposition of the "theory of Nordic balance," see Arne O. Brundtland, "The Nordic Balance," *Cooperation and Conflict* II, (1966), pp. 30–63.

CONCLUSION: THE US–NORWEGIAN ALLIANCE, 1954–60

1. Robert E. Osgood, *Alliances and American Foreign Policy* (Baltimore: The Johns Hopkins Press, 1967), p. 18.
2. For the concept of "power consumers" and "suppliers," see Steven L. Spiegel, *Dominance and Diversity: The International Hierarchy* (Boston: Little and Brown, 1972), pp. 133 and 136.
3. Johan J. Holst, "Lilliputs and Gulliver: Small States in a Great Power Alliance," in *NATO's Northern Allies*, ed. G.Flynn (London: Croom Helm), p. 263.
4. Clive Archer, *Uncertain Trust: The British-Norwegian defence relationship* (Oslo: Institutt for Forsvarsstudier, 1989), p. 23.
5. For the problems of defining "small" and "weak" states, see Niels Amstrup, "The Perennial Problem of Small States: A Survey of the Research Effort," *Co-operation and Conflict* 11 (1976)Amstrup, pp. 167–168. For examples where "small" and "weak" are used interchangeably, see Arnold Wolfers, "Power and Influence: The Means of Foreign Policy," in *Discord and Collaboration* (Baltimore: The Johns Hopkins University Press), p. 112 and Erling Bjøl, "The Power of the Weak," *Cooperation and Conflict* no. 3 (1968), p. 158.
6. Jacob Bercovitch, "Alliances in International Relations: Aspects of Performance and Problems of Management," in *ANZUS in Crisis: Alliance Management in International Affairs,* ed. Jacob Bercovitch, (London: Macmillan Press, 1988), p. 14.
7. Holst, "Lilliputs and Gulliver," p. 260.
8. Robert O. Keohane, "The Big Influence of Small Allies," *Foreign Policy* no. 2 (Spring 1971), p. 167.
9. The other two levels of action open to a small power are: (1) formal diplomatic bargaining through diplomatic channels, and (2) "informal" attempts to influence domestic opinion and private interest groups in the US. This analytical framework is discussed with reference to the behaviour in the 1950s and 1960s of countries such as Pakistan, Israel, Spain, the Philippines, Nationalist China and Iran, all of which, according to Keohane, provide "illuminating examples" of how smaller allies can influence US policy, Ibid. pp. 161–67.
10. Ibid., p. 165.
11. Ibid.
12. Ibid.
13. Admiral Arleigh Burke, "The Soviet Threat: A CNO Appraisal," *Marine Corps Gazette*, August–September, 1961, p. 22.
14. Norway's role in US air strategy, albeit important, was principally indirect and has in this study been subsumed under the categories of intelligence and early warning.
15. Bjøl, "The Power of the Weak," p. 161.
16. Ibid.
17. As seen in the last chapter, however, this was also a consequence of stricter Norwegian control over allied operations following the U-2 and RB-47 incidents.

18. For this role of small allies in an alliance, see Nils Ørvik, "NATO: The Role of the Small Members," *International Journal (Canadian Institute of International Affairs)* 21 (Spring 1966).

19. For an interesting discussion of these issues, see comments by Helge Pharo in "Doktordisputas – *The United States and the Cold War in the High North*," *Historisk Tidsskrift* 2 (1992), pp. 208–209.

20. For an account of how "ideological orientation" may influence alliance formation and maintenance, see Holsti et al., *Unity and Disintegration in Alliances*, pp. 49–50, 52–54, 61–64, and Bercovitch, "Alliances in International Relations," pp. 10–11.

21. Commander, Allied Naval Forces Northern Europe to First Sea Lord, 26 March 1954, ADM 295/102, PRO. This impression of a Norwegian concern about maintaining close ties to Britain was also noted by Selwyn Lloyd when he visited the country in April 1953, see Selwyn Lloyd to Prime Minister, 14 April 1953, FO 800/814, PRO.

22. Memorandum, From: D/NI, To: D/Op-30, 2 November 1955, Subj: Briefing Memorandum for CNO regarding V. Adm. Jacobsen, CNO of Norway, EF, Box 325, Strategic Plans Division Records, NHC.

23. It interesting to note in this connection that Field Marshal Lord Carver could not "recall anything specific about Norway during the time [he] was Director of Plans at the War Office, and therefore a member of the Joint Planning Staff, in 1958 and 1959." Letter to author from Field Marshal Lord Carver, 23 September 1991.

24. NSC 6006/1, Scandinavia, 6 April 1960, Box 28, NSC Series – Policy Papers Subseries, WHO: Office of the Special Assistant for National Security Affairs, DDEL.

25. TS Memorandum, No. 45, From: Head, Foreign Military Rights Branch, 28 August 1952, Subj: Acquisition of US Military Rights in Foreign Territory, ND 1952, A14-1, Box 271, Strategic Plans Division Records, NHC.

26. Keohane, "Small States in International Politics," p. 301.

27. This study has examined the air and maritime perspective since these were of principal concern to Norway. The centrality of nuclear weapons in planning for land-battle operations was, of course, equally pervasive. See John P. Rose, *The Evolution of US Army Nuclear Doctrine, 1945–1980*, (Boulder, CO: Westview Press, 1980), pp. 55–76.

28. Bernard Brodie, *Strategy in the Missile Age* (Princeton: Princeton University Press, 1959), p. 249. For Eisenhower's continued commitment to the New Look after Sputnik, see Memorandum of Conference with the President, 27 July 1959, JCS (7), March–Aug. 1959, Box 4, WHO: Office of the Staff Secretary, DDEL.

29. Johan J. Holst, for example, speaks of Norway and Denmark as having "pursued a policy of distance and near virginity" with regard to nuclear weapons. Holst, "Lilliputs and Gulliver," p. 274.

30. Tamnes, Cold *War in the High North*, p. 103.

31. Although Norway's "nuclear ban" policy had first been adopted by the Labour Party conference in 1957 and then enunciated by Prime Minister Gerhardsen at the NATO summit later in the year, the question of storing

nuclear weapons at Special Ammunition Storage sites and of incorporating tactical nuclear weapons into Norwegian forces, continued to be discussed after 1957. Any alternative to the non-nuclear line was finally rejected in 1960–61. See Rolf Tamnes, "Handlefrihet og lojalitet: Norge og atompolitikken i 1950 årene," in *Historiker og Veileder: Festskrift til Jakob Sverdrup, ed.* H. Pharo and Trond Bergh (Oslo: Tiden Norsk Forlag, 1989).

32. Memorandum for President, 16 November 1954, NATO, Box 27, Administration Series, Dwight D. Eisenhower Papers as President, DDEL.

33. See Stromseth, *The Origins of Flexible Response*, pp. 14–15 and 21–22.

34. According to Rosenberg, of the 18,000 nuclear weapons in the US arsenal in 1960, only about 4000 were strategic weapons. "The rest were designed for air defence, or to be used directly or indirectly to affect the outcome of engagements on a conventional battlefield." See Rosenberg, "The Making of United States Nuclear Strategy," p. 42.

35. Bracken, *Command and Control of Nuclear Forces*, p. 7.

36. Nitze, "Atoms, Strategy and Policy," p. 187.

37. On the importance of preserving consensus in the making of post-war foreign policy-making in Norway, see Olav Riste, "The Foreign Policy-Making Process in Norway: An Historical Perspective," in *Defence Studies 1982* (Oslo: Tanum-Norli, 1983), ed. R. Tamnes, pp. 242–243.

38. A major research effort, spearheaded by Sven Holtsmark at the Institute for Defence Studies in Oslo, has been undertaken to collect and translate Soviet sources on the history of Soviet–Norwegian relations. A documentary collection covering the period 1917–55 was published in 1995. Sven G. Holtsmark, ed., *Norge og Sovjetunion: En utenrikspolitisk dokumentasjon* (Oslo: Cappelen, 1995).

Bibliography

PRIMARY SOURCES

I. ARCHIVE COLLECTIONS

UNITED STATES

The Dwight D. Eisenhower Library, Abilene, Kansas:

Dwight D. Eisenhower, Pre-Presidential Papers (SACEUR period), 1916–1952.
Dwight D. Eisenhower, Records as President, White House Central Files, 1953–61.
Dwight D. Eisenhower, Papers as President of the US, 1953–61 (Ann Whitman File):
- Administration Series.
- DDE Diary Series.
- Dulles-Herter Series.
- International Series.
- Miscellaneous Series.
- NSC Series.
- Name Series.
- Press Conference Series.

White House Office Files:
- Office of the Staff Secretary, Records, 1952–61.
- National Security Council staff (Paul T. Carroll, Andrew J. Goodpaster, L. Arthur Minnich and Christopher H. Russell), Papers, 1948–61.
- Office of the Special Assistant for National Security Affairs (Robert Cutler, Dillon Anderson and Gordon Gray), Records, 1952–61.
- Office of the Assistant for Disarmament (Harold Stassen), Records, 1955–58.
- Office of the Special Assistant for Science and Technology (James R. Killian and George B. Kistiakowsky), Records, 1957–61.

Aurand, Evan P., (Naval Aide to the President 1957–61), Papers, 1934–72.
Dulles, John Foster, (Secretary of State, 1953–59), Papers, 1951–59.
Gray, Gordon, (Special Assistant to the President for National Security Affairs, 1958–61), Papers, 1946–76.
Gruenther, Alfred M., (SACEUR, 1953–56), Papers, 1942–83.
Harlow, Bryce N., (Special Assistant to the President, 1953–61), Records, 1953–61.
Herter, Christian A., (Under Secretary and Secretary of State, 1957–61), Papers, 1957–61.
Jackson, C.D., (Special Assistant to the President for International Affairs, 1953–54), Papers, 1931–67.
Norstad, Lauris, (Air Deputy, SHAPE 1953–56; SACEUR 1956–63), Papers, 1930–87.

Quarles, Donald A., (Secretary of the Air Force, 1955–57, Deputy Secretary of Defense 1957–59), Papers, 1917–60.

US President's Committee to Study the US Military Assistance Programme (Draper Committee), Records, 1958–1959.

US President's Citizen Advisors on the Mutual Security Programme (Fairless Committee), Records, 1956–57.

National Archives and Records Administration, Washington DC:

Record Group 218, Joint Chiefs of Staff Records.

Record Group 341, Records of Headquarters of USAF.

• Entry 241 (Directorate of Air Force Intelligence).

Record Group 59, US Department of State.

Record Group 273, US National Security Council Records.

Operational Archives Branch of The US Navy, Naval Historical Center, Washington DC:

Strategic Plans Division, Records (OP–30).

Office of Naval Intelligence Review, 1945–62.

ONI Ts Records.

German Naval Records Collection.

The Office of Air Force History, Bolling Air Force Base, Washington, DC:

Colonel Bernt Balchen Collection (MF).

The Library of Congress, Manuscript Division, Washington, DC:

The Papers of Thomas D. White, Chief of Staff USAF, 1957–61.

The Papers of Curtis E. LeMay, Commanding General, SAC, 1947–57.

The Papers of Nathan F. Twining, Chief of Staff USAF, Chairman Joint Chiefs of Staff, 1957–61.

The Papers of Hoyt S. Vandenberg, Chief of Staff USAF, 1948–53.

The Papers of Colonel Bernt Balchen.

UNITED KINGDOM

Public Record Office:

ADM 1	Admiralty and Secretariat Papers
ADM 167	Board of Admiralty Minutes and Memoranda
ADM 205	First Sea Lord's Records
DEFE 4	Chiefs of Staff Committee Minutes
DEFE 5	Chiefs of Staff Committee Memoranda
DEFE 6	Joint Planning Committee
DEFE 7	Register Files: General Series
CAB 128	Cabinet Minutes
CAB 129	Cabinet Memoranda
CAB 130	Cabinet Committees
CAB 131	Cabinet Defence Committee
AIR 8	Chief of Air Staff Papers

FO 800   Ministerial Papers
FO 371   Foreign Office Records

Southampton University Library, Archives and Manuscript Collection:
The Papers of Lord Mountbatten (Broadland Archives).

Imperial War Museum Archives, London:
The Papers of Field Marshal Montgomery.

NORWAY

The Norwegian National Archives, (Riksarkivet):
Referat fra regjeringskonferanser (Record of Government Meetings, 1945–65).

Ministry of Defence Archives, Oslo:
Subject Files:
* Nasjonalt hemmelig arkiv.
* A-Pakt arkivet.

Ministry of Foreign Affairs Archives, Oslo:
Subject Files:
* 33.1/7   Ulovlige overflyvninger av Sovjet og andre Østblokklands territorier.
* 33.6/14   Spm. om baser i Norge.
* 34.4/99   Norge-Sovjet politikk.
* 25.4/99   Sovjet-samveldet, politikk.
* 33.6/11   Island og A-Pakten. Baser. Forsvar av Island.
* 38.15/7   Norske Regler for anløp av krigsskip og militære luftfartøyer.Spm. gjensidighet.
* 33.11/8. Flyplasser. Infrastruktur.
* 33.2/18   Atlantpakten, Nordkommandoen.
* 25.2/75   Nordisk militært samarbeid under Atlanterhavspakten.
* 33.2/86   LORAN-C

The Norwegian Defence High Command Archives, Oslo:
Miscellaneous Papers.

Office of The Secretary to the Chief of Staff, Headquarters Allied Forces Northern Europe (Nato), Kolsås
CINCNORTH's Historical Reports for the Northern European Command Area, 1951–1961.

II. GOVERNMENT PUBLICATIONS

UNITED STATES

* D.D. Eisenhower, *Public Papers of the Presidents of the United States: Dwight D. Eisenhower*, Vol. 1953–60. Washington, DC: US Government Printing Office, 1961.

• US Department of State, *Foreign Relations of the United States, 1952–54 Vol. V: Western European Security and Integration.* Washington, DC: US Government Printing Office, 1983.
• US Department of State, *Foreign Relations of the United States, 1952–54 Vol. II: National Security Affairs.* Washington, DC: US Government Printing Office, 1984.
• US Department of State, *Foreign Relations of the United States, 1952–54 Vol. VI: Western Europe and Canada, Part 2.* Washington, DC: US Government Printing Office, 1986.
• US Department of State, *Foreign Relations of the United States, 1955–57 Vol. IV: Western European Security and Integration.* Washington, DC: US Government Printing Office, 1986.
• US Department of State, *Foreign Relations of the United States, 1958–60 Vol. II: UN and General International Relations.* Washington, DC: US Government Printing Office, 1990.
• US Department of Defence, *Semiannual Reports of the Secretary of Defence and the Semiannual Reports of the Secretary of the Army, Secretary of the Navy and Secretary of the Air Force, 1953–60.* Washington, DC: US Government Printing Office, 1954–61.
• Department of the Navy, *Hearings before the Subcommittee of the Committee of Appropriations 1954, House of Representatives, 83rd Congress (Subcommittee on the Department of the Navy), Part 1.* Washington, DC: US Government Printing Office, 1953.
• Scott A. Koch, *CIA Cold War Records: Selected Estimates on the Soviet Union, 1950–1959,* CIA History Staff, Center for the Study of Intelligence, CIA, Washington, DC, 1993.
• Richard Wolf, *The United States Air Force: Basic Documents on Roles and Missions (Air Staff Historical Study).* Washington, DC: Office of Air Force History, 1987.

NORWAY

• *Forsvarskommisjonen av 1946, Del. I, Grunnleggende synspunkter og forslag,* October, 1949.
• *Forsvarskommisjonen av 1974,* NOU 1978: 9, Oslo: 1978.
• *Stortingsmeldinger* (Government White Papers).
• *Stortingstidende* (Parliamentary records).
• *Loran C og Omega, Instilling fra Utvalget til Undersøkelse av saken om etablering av Loran C og Omega – stasjoner i Norge.* Oslo: Pax Forlag, 1977.

SWEDEN

• *Om Kriget Kommit ... Förberedelser för mottagande av militärt bistånd 1949-1969* (Betänkande av Neutralitetspolitikkommissionen), Stockholm: Statens offentliga utredningar, 1994:11. Vol.I and II (documents).

III.   INTERVIEWS AND ORAL HISTORIES

Interviews:

Jens Boyesen, 15 April and 11 September 1991, Oslo.

Position: State Secretary, Norwegian Ministry of Foreign Affairs, February 1951–September 1954; State Secretary, MOD, September 1954–January 1955; Norwegian Ambassador to NATO and OEEC, August 1955–January 1964.

Vice-Admiral Sir Ronald Brockman, 18 March 1991, London.
Position: Admiral's Secretary to Admiral of the Fleet Lord Mountbatten in all appointments, 1943–1959.

Admiral Arleigh Burke, 18 July 1990, Fairfax, Virginia.
Position: Chief of Naval Operations, 17 August 1955–1 August 1961.

Field Marshal Lord Carver, 16 October 1991, London.
Position: Col. GS SHAPE 1952–54; Director of Plans, War Office, 1958–59.

Major General Bjørn Egge, 9 April and 9 September 1991, Oslo.
Position: Joined the Defence Intelligence Staff in April 1952; worked in SHAPE's Intelligence Division, Paris, 1955–1958; continued his career with the Defence Intelligence Staff after returning from SHAPE.

Jens Christian Hauge, 10 April 1991, Oslo.
Position: Minister of Defence, November 1945–January 1952; Minister of Justice, January 1955–November 1955.

Erik Himle, 11 April 1991, Oslo.
Position: Head of Division, Norwegian MOD, June 1952–January 1956; Director General, MOD, January 1956–June 1958; State Secretary, MOD, July 1958–February 1961.

Sivert A. Nielsen, 16 April 1991, Oslo.
Position: Head of Division, Norwegian MOD, March 1950–August 1951; Director General, MOD, March 1952–August 1955; State Secretary, MOD, August 1955–July 1958; Norwegian Ambassador to the UN, 1958–1966.

Sir Frank Roberts, 14 March 1992, London.
Position: Deputy Under-Secretary of State, Foreign Office, 1951–54; UK Permanent Representative on the North Atlantic Council, 1957–60; Ambassador to Moscow, 1960–62.

Sir Patrick Reilly, 1 May 1992, Oxford.
Position: Ambassador to Moscow, 1957–60; Deputy Under-Secretary of State, Foreign Office, 1960–64.

The Earl of Selkirk, 24 January 1991, London, and 23 October 1991 (telephone interview).
Position: First Lord of the Admiralty, 1957–59.

Oral Histories:

The Reminiscences of Admiral John S. Thach, USN (ret.), Oral History Office, US Naval Institute, Annapolis, Maryland, 1977, NHC.
The Reminiscences of Rear Admiral Charles E. Loughlin, US Navy (ret.), Oral History Office, US Naval Institute, Annapolis, Maryland, 1982, NHC.

The Reminiscences of Admiral Arleigh Burke, Vol. II Special Series, Oral History Office, US Naval Institute, Annapolis, Maryland, 1980, NHC.

Oral History Interview with Richard M. Bissell, Jr., 9 November 1976, OH 382, DDEL.

Oral History Interview with Charles Bohlen, 17 December 1970, OH 136, DDEL.

SECONDARY SOURCES

For a complete bibliography of secondary literature see the bibliographic details provided in the original dissertation on which this book is based.

BOOKS

Aliano, Richard A. *American Defence Policy from Eisenhower to Kennedy.* Athens, OH: Ohio University Press, 1975.

Ambrose, Stephen E. *Eisenhower: The President.* New York: Simon and Schuster, 1984.

Ambrose, Stephen E. and R. Immerman. *Ike's Spies: Eisenhower and the Espionage Establishment.* New York: Doubleday & Company, Inc. 1981.

Archer, Clive. *Uncertain Trust: The British-Norwegian Defence Relationship.* Oslo: Institutt for Forsvarsstudier, 1989.

Baylis, John. *Anglo-American Defence Relations, 1939–1980: The Special Relationship.* London: The Macmillan Press Ltd., 1981.

Barnett, R.W., and Colin Gray, eds. *Seapower and Strategy.* Annapolis, MD: US Naval Institute Press, 1989.

Bergh, Trond. *Arbeiderbevegelsens Historie i Norge, Vol. 5: Storhetstid, 1945–1965.* Oslo: Tiden Norsk Forlag, 1987.

Beschloss, Michael R. *Mayday: Eisenhower, Khrushchev and the U-2 Affair.* New York: Harper and Row, 1986.

Brands, H.W. *Cold Warriors: Eisenhower's Generation and American Foreign Policy.* New York: Columbia University Press, 1988.

Brands, H.W. *The Specter of Neutralism: The United States and the Emergence of the Third World, 1947–60.* New York: Columbia University Press, 1989.

Breyer, Siegfried. *Die Seerüstung der Sowjetunion.* Munich: J.F. Lehmanns Verlag München, 1964.

Brodie, Bernard. *Strategy in the Missile Age.* Princeton: Princeton University Press, 1959.

Brodie, Bernard. *A Guide to Naval Strategy.* Princeton: Princeton University Press, 1958.

Bulkeley, Rip. *The Sputniks Crisis and Early United States Space Policy.* London: Macmillan Academic and Professional Ltd., 1991.

Burrows, William E. *Deep Black: Space Espionage and National Security.* New York: Random House, 1986.

Cole, Wayne S. *Norway and the United States 1905–1955: Two Democracies in Peace and War.* Ames: Iowa State University Press, 1989.

Davies, M.E., and William R. Harris. *RAND's Role in the Evolution of Balloon and Satellite Observation Systems and Related US Space Technology (R-3692-RC).* Santa Monica: The RAND Corporation, 1988.

Divine, Robert A. *Eisenhower and the Cold War.* New York: Oxford University Press, 1981.

Divine, Robert A. *Foreign Policy and US Presidential Elections: 1952–1960*. New York: New Viewpoints, 1974.

Due-Nilsen, Carsten, Johan P. Noack and Nikolaj Petersen, eds. *Danmark, Norden og NATO, 1948–1962*. Copenhagen: Jurist- og Økonomforbundets Forlag, 1991.

Eisenhower, Dwight D. *The White House Years: Mandate for Change 1953–1956*. London: Heinemann, 1963.

Eisenhower, Dwight D. *The White House Years: Waging Peace*. London: Heinemann, 1966.

Eriksen, Knut Einar. *DNA og NATO: Striden om norsk NATO-medlemskap innen regjeringspartiet, 1948–1949*. Oslo: Gyldendal, 1972.

Freedman, Lawrence. *US Intelligence and the Soviet Strategic Threat*. London: The Macmillan Press Ltd., 1986.

Freedman, Lawrence. *The Evolution of Nuclear Strategy*. London: The Macmillan Press Ltd., 1983.

Friedman, Norman. *US Aircraft Carriers: An Illustrated Design History*. Annapolis, MD: Naval Institute Press, 1983.

Friedman, Norman. *The Postwar Naval Revolution*. London: Conway Maritime Press, 1986.

Gaddis, John L. *Strategies of Containment: A Critical Appraisal of Postwar American National Security Policy*. Oxford: Oxford University Press, 1982.

Gaddis, John L. *The Long Peace: Inquiries into the History of the Cold War*. Oxford: Oxford University Press, 1987.

Gaddis, John L. *Russia, The Soviet Union and The United States: An Interpretive History, Second Edition*. New York: McGraw Hill, 1990.

Galambos, Louis, ed. *The Papers of Dwight D. Eisenhower: NATO and the Campaign of 1952: XII*. Baltimore and London: The Johns Hopkins University Press, 1989.

Gillette, Philip S., and Willard C. Frank, *The Sources of Soviet Naval Conduct*. Toronto: Lexington Books, 1990.

Greenstein, Fred I. *The Hidden-Hand Presidency: Eisenhower as Leader*. New York: Basic Books, Inc., 1982.

Gretton, Sir Peter. *Maritime Strategy: A Study of British Defence Problems*. London: Cassell and Company Ltd., 1965.

Grove, Eric J. *Vanguard to Trident: British Naval Policy since World War II*. London: The Bodley Head, 1987.

Hattendorf, John B., and Robert S. Jordan, eds. *Maritime Strategy and the Balance of Power: Britain and America in the Twentieth Century*. London: Macmillan/St Antony's College, 1990.

Herrick, R.W. *Soviet Naval Strategy: Fifty Years of Theory and Practise*. Annapolis, MD: US Naval Institute, 1968.

Hewlett, Richard G., and Francis Duncan. *Nuclear Navy, 1946–1962*. Chicago and London: University of Chicago Press, 1974.

Holst, Johan J. *Norsk Sikkerhetspolitikk i Strategisk Perspektiv, Vol. I and II*. Oslo: Norsk Utenrikspolitisk Institutt, 1967.

Holsti, Ole R., P.T. Hopmann and J.D. Sullivan. *Unity and Disintegration in International Alliances: Comparative Studies*. Toronto: John Wiley & Sons, Inc., 1973.

Hoopes, Townsend. *The Devil and John Foster Dulles*. Boston: Little, Brown and Co., 1973.

Horensma, Pier. *The Soviet Arctic.* London and New York: Routledge, 1991.

Huston James A. *One For All: NATO Strategy and Logistics through the Formative Period, 1949–1969.* London and Toronto: Associated University Presses, 1984.

Immerman, Richard H., ed. *John Foster Dulles and the Diplomacy of the Cold War.* Princeton: Princeton University Press, 1990.

Jordan, Robert S., ed. *Generals in International Politics: NATO's Supreme Allied Commanders, Europe.* Lexington: The University Press of Kentucky, 1987.

Jordan, Robert S. Alliance *Strategy and Navies: The Evolution and Scope of NATO's Maritime Dimension.* London: Pinter Publishers, 1990.

Kaufmann, William, ed. *Military Policy and National Security.* Princeton: Princeton University Press, 1956.

Kent, Sherman. *Strategic Intelligence for American World Policy.* Princeton, NJ: Princeton University Press, 1949 (reprint, 1966).

Killian, James R. *Sputnik, Scientists and Eisenhower: A Memoir of the First Special Assistant to the President for Science and Technology.* Cambridge, MA: MIT Press, 1977.

Kinnard, Douglas. *President Eisenhower and Strategy Management.* Lexington, KY: University Press of Kentucky, 1977.

Kistiatowsky, George B. *A Scientist at the White House.* Cambridge, MA: Harvard University Press, 1976.

Liska, George. *Nations in Alliance: The Limits of Interdependence.* Baltimore: The Johns Hopkins Press, 1967

Loftsson, Elfar. *Island i NATO: Partierna och Førsvarsfragan.* Gøteborg: Førfattares Bokmaskin i Gøteborg, 1981.

Love, Robert William Jr., ed. *The Chiefs of Naval Operations.* Annapolis, MD: Naval Institute Press, 1980.

Lundestad, Geir. *Scandinavia, America and the Cold War, 1945–59.* New York: Columbia University Press, 1980.

Lundestad, Geir. *The American "Empire".* Oxford/Oslo: Oxford University Press/Oslo University Press, 1990.

Martin, Laurence W. *The Sea in Modern Strategy.* London: Chatto & Windus, 1967.

Miller, Jay. *Lockheed U-2.* Austin, Texas: Aerofax Inc., 1983.

Navias, Martin S. *Nuclear Weapons and British Strategic Planning 1955–1958.* Oxford: Clarendon Press, 1991.

Nordahl, Konrad. *Dagbøker: 1950–1955 (Bind I).* Oslo: Tiden Norsk Forlag, 1991.

Nordahl, Konrad. *Dagb¿ker: 1956–1975 (Bind II).* Oslo: Tiden Norsk Forlag, 1992.

Osgood, Robert E. *Alliances and American Foreign Policy.* Baltimore and London: The Johns Hopkins Press, 1968.

Palmer, Michael, A. *Origins of the Maritime Strategy: American Naval Strategy in the First Postwar Decade.* Washington DC: US Government Printing Office, 1988.

Pharo, Helge Ø., and G. Lundestad, eds. *Norsk Utenrikspolitikk: Kilder til moderne historie 1.* Oslo: Universitetsforlaget, 1972.

Pharo, Helge Ø., and Knut E. Eriksen, *Norsk sikkerhetspolitikk som etterkrigshistorisk forskningsfelt.* Bergen: LOS-senter Notat 92/13 (Norwegian Research Center in Organization and Management),1992.

Helge Pharo Ø., and Knut Einar Eriksen, *Kald Krig og internasjonalisering, Norsk utenrikspolitikks historie*. Oslo: Cappelen 1997.

Polmar, Norman. *Aircraft Carriers: A Graphic History of Carrier Aviation and its Influence on World Events*. London: Macdonald & Co. Ltd., 1963.

Polmar, Norman. *The Naval Institute Guide to the Soviet Navy (Fifth Edition)*. Annapolis, MD: Naval Institute Press, 1988.

Polmar, N., and J. Noot. *Submarines of the Russian and Soviet Navies, 1718–1990*. Annapolis, MD: Naval Institute Press, 1991.

Poole, Walter S. *History of the Joint Chiefs of Staff, Vol. IV: The Joint Chiefs and National Policy, 1950–52*. Washington, DC: JCS, Historical Division, 1979.

Prados, John. *The Soviet Estimate: US Intelligence Analysis and Russian Military Strength*. New York: The Dial Press, 1982.

Ranft, B., and Geoffrey Till. *The Sea in Soviet Strategy, Second Edition*. Annapolis, MD: Naval Institute Press, 1989.

Richelson, Jeffrey T. *American Espionage and the Soviet Target*. New York: William Morrow and Company, Inc., 1987.

Riste, Olav. *Isolasjonisme og stormaktsgarantiar*. Oslo: Institutt for Forsvarsstudier, 1991.

Riste, Olav, ed. *Western Security: The Formative Years – European and Atlantic Defence, 1947–1953*. Oslo: Norwegian University Press, 1985.

Ross, Steven T. *American War Plans, 1945–50*. New York and London: Garland Publishing, Inc., 1988.

Rothstein, Robert L. *Alliances and Small Powers*, New York and London: Columbia University Press, 1968.

Ryan, Paul B. *The First Line of Defence: The US Navy Since 1945*. Stanford: Hoover Institution Press, 1981.

Sapolsky, Harvey. *The Polaris System: Bureaucratic and Programmatic Success in Government*. Cambridge, MA: Harvard University Press, 1972.

Saunders, M.G., ed. *The Soviet Navy*. London: Weidenfeld and Nicolson, 1958.

Schoenebaum, E.W, ed. *Political Profiles: The Eisenhower Years*. New York: Facts On File, Inc., 1977.

Skodvin, Magne. *Norden eller NATO? Utenriksdepartementet og alliansespørsmålet, 1947–1949*. Oslo: Universitetsforlaget, 1971.

Sloan, G.R. *Geopolitics in United States Strategic Policy, 1890–1987*. London: Wheatsheaf Books Ltd. 1988.

Sokolsky, Joel J. *Seapower in the Nuclear Age: The United States Navy and NATO 1949–80*. London and New York: Routledge, 1991.

Stefanick, Tom. *Strategic Anti-submarine Warfare and Naval Strategy*. Toronto: Lexington Books, 1987.

Tamnes, Rolf. *The United States and the Cold War in the High North*. Oslo: Ad Notam Forlag, 1990.

Tamnes, Rolf. *Svalbard og den politiske avmakt: Striden om flyplass, olje og telemetri-stasjon, 1955–1970*. Oslo: Institutt for Forsvarsstudier, 1992.

Taylor, Maxwell. *The Uncertain Trumpet*. Westport, CT: Greenwood Press, 1959.

Till, Geoffrey, et al. *Maritime Strategy and the Nuclear Age*. London: The Macmillan Press, Ltd., 1984.

Trachtenberg, Marc, ed. *The Development of American Strategic Thought: Basic Documents from the Eisenhower and Kennedy Periods, Including the Basic*

National Security Papers from 1953 to 1959. New York & London: Garland Publishing, Inc., 1988.

Treverton, G.F., P. Bobbitt, and L. Freedman. *US Nuclear Strategy: A Reader.* London: The Macmillan Press, Ltd., 1989.

Vigor, P.H. *The Soviet View of War, Peace and Neutrality.* London: Routledge & Kegan Paul Ltd., 1975.

Villaume, Poul. Alliert med forbehold: *Danmark, NATO og den kolde krig. En studie i dansk sikkerhedspolitik 1949–1961.* Copenhagen: Eirene 1995.

Watson, Robert J. *History of the Joint Chiefs of Staff, Vol. V: The Joint Chiefs and National Policy, 1953–54.* Washington, DC: JCS, Historical Division, 1986.

Wilkes, Owen, and N.P. Gleditsch. *Loran-C and Omega: A Study of the Military Importance of Radio Navigation Aids.* Oslo: Norwegian University Press, 1987.

Wittkopf, E.R., and C.W. Kegley. *Perspectives on American Foreign Policy: Selected Readings.* New York: St. Martin's Press, 1983.

Wolfers, Arnold. *Discord and Collaboration: Essays in International Politics.* Baltimore and London: The Johns Hopkins Press, 1962.

Wolfers, Arnold, ed. *Alliance Policy in the Cold War.* Baltimore: The Johns Hopkins Press, 1959.

Yergin, Daniel. *Shattered Peace: The Origins of the Cold War and the National Security State.* London: Andre Deutsch Ltd., 1979.

Ørvik, Nils, ed. *Semialignment and Western Security.* London and Sydney: Croom Helm, 1986.

JOURNAL ARTICLES AND RESEARCH PAPERS

Amstrup, Niels. "The Perennial Problems of Small States: A Survey of Research Efforts." *Cooperation and Conflict,* No. 2 (1976).

Archer, Clive. "Greenland and the Atlantic Alliance." *Centrepiece* 7 (Summer 1985).

Archer, Clive. "The United States Defence Areas in Greenland." *Cooperation and Conflict,* No. 3 (September 1988).

Berg, Roald. "'Det land vi venter hjælp af..' England som Norges beskytter 1905–1908." In *Defence Studies IV,* edited by Rolf Tamnes. Oslo: Tano, 1985.

Betts, Richard K. "Analysis, War, and Decision: Why Intelligence Failures Are Inevitable." *World Politics* 31 (July 1979).

Bercovitch, Jacob. "Alliances in International Relations: Aspects of Performance and Problems of Management." In *ANZUS in Crisis: Alliance Management in International Affairs,* edited by J. Bercovitch. London: Macmillan Press, 1988.

Bjøl, Erling. "The Power of the Weak." *Cooperation and Conflict,* No. 3 (1968).

Buzzard, A.J. Slessor and R. Lowenthal. "The H-Bomb: Massive Retaliation or Graduated Deterrence?" *International Affairs* 32 (April 1956).

Cagle, Malcolm W. "A Philosophy for Naval Atomic Warfare." *United States Naval Institute Proceedings* 83 (March 1957).

Cagle, Malcolm W. "Sea Power and Limited War." *United States Naval Institute Proceedings* 84 (July 1957).

Caligiuri, Joseph F. "The Navigation System for the Polaris Submarine". *Navigation* 7 (Spring 1960).

Carney, Robert. "Principles of Sea Power." *United States Naval Institute Proceedings* 81 (September 1955).

Denny, Admiral Sir Michael. "The Atlantic in a World War: What Does it Mean?" *The Journal of the Royal United Services Institution, No.* 603 (August 1956).

Dinerstein, Herbert S. "The Transformation of Alliance Systems." *The American Political Science Review* 59 (September 1965).

Eriksen, Knut Einar. "Storbritannia og baseproblematikken i Norden 1945–1947." In *Defence Studies 1981,* edited by Rolf Tamnes. Oslo: Tanum-Norli, 1982.

Kohn, Richard H., and Joseph P. Harahan, ed. "US Strategic Air Power, 1948–1962: Excerpts from an Interview with Generals Curtis E. LeMay, Leon W. Johnson, David A. Burchinal, and Jack J. Catton." *International Security* 12 (Spring 1988).

Lange, Halvard. "Scandinavian Co-operation in International Affairs." *International Affairs* 30 (July 1954).

Lundestad, Geir. "Nasjonalisme og internasjonalisme i norsk utenrikspolitikk: Et faglig-provoserende essay." *Internasjonal Politikk* (1985).

Lynch, Frank C. Jr. "The Role of Navigation in the Submarine Weapon System." *Navigation* 5 (September 1956).

Galantin, I.J. "The Future of the Nuclear-Powered Submarines." *United States Naval Institute Proceedings* 84 (June 1958).

Garthoff, Raymond L. "Soviet Attitudes toward Modern Air Power." *Rand Corporation Report P-603* (November 1954).

Greenwood, John T. "The Emergence of the Postwar Strategic Air Force, 1945–1953." In *Air Power and Warfare: Proceedings of the Eight Military History Symposium, USAF Academy.* Washington DC: Office of Air Force History, 1979.

Grove, E. "British Naval Policy, 1945–57." In *Post-war Britain, 1945–64: Themes and Perspectives,* edited by A. Gorst, L. Johnman and W.S. Lucas. London: Pinter Publishers, 1989.

Grove, E., and Geoffrey Till, "Anglo-American Maritime Strategy in the Era of Massive Retaliation, 1945–60." In *Maritime Strategy and the Balance of Power,* edited by J. Hattendorf and R. Jordan. London: Macmillan/St. Antony's College, 1990.

Hetland, T.H. "Atomrasling og avspenning: Sovjet og norsk tryggingspolitikk 1953–1958." In *Defence Studies IV 1985,* edited by Rolf Tamnes. Oslo: Tano, 1985.

Holloway, David. "Research Note: Soviet Thermonuclear Development," *International Security* 4 (Winter 1979/80).

Hoopes, Townsend. "Overseas Bases in American Strategy." *Foreign Affairs* 37 (October 1958).

Holst, Johan. J. "The Security Pattern in Northern Europe: A Norwegian Perspective." In *Britain and NATO's Northern Flank,* edited by Geoffrey Till. London: Macmillan Press, 1988.

Horne, Alastair. "The Macmillan Years and Afterwards." In *The Special Relationship: Anglo-American Relations Since 1945,* edited by W. Roger Louis and Hedley Bull. Oxford: Clarendon Press, 1986.

Huntington, Samuel P. "National Policy and the Transoceanic Navy." *US Naval Institute Proceedings* 80 (May 1954).

Keohane, Robert O. "Lilliputians' Dilemmas: Small States in International Politics." *International Organization* 23 (Spring 1969).

Keohane, Robert O. "The Big Influence of Small Allies." *Foreign Policy* No. 2 (Spring 1971).

Nelson, Anna K. "The 'Top of Policy Hill': President Eisenhower and the National Security Council." *Diplomatic History* 7 (Fall 1983).

Nitze, Paul. "Atoms, Strategy and Foreign Policy." *Foreign Affairs* 34 (January 1956).

Nuechterlein, D.E. "Small States in Alliances: Iceland, Thailand, Australia." *Orbis* 13 (Summer 1969).

Petersen, Nikolaj. "Britain, Scandinavia, and the North Atlantic Treaty, 1948–49." *Review of International Studies* 8 (1982).

Quester, George H. "Was Eisenhower a Genius?" *International Security* 4 (Fall 1979).

Ransom, Harry H. "Secret Intelligence in the United States, 1947–1982: The CIA's Search for Legitimacy." In *The Missing Dimension: Governments and Intelligence Communities in the Twentieth Century*, edited by C. Andrew and D. Dilks. London: Macmillan Press, 1984.

Rees, Wyn G. "The 1957 Sandys Defence White Paper: New Priorities in British Defence Policy?" *The Journal of Strategic Studies* 12 (June 1989).

Rees, Wyn G. "Brothers In Arms: Anglo-American defence co-operation in 1957." In *Post-war Britain, 1945–64: Themes and Perspectives*, edited by A. Gorst, L. Johnman and W.S. Lucas. London: Pinter Publishers, 1989.

Riste, Olav. "Isolationism and Great Power Protection: The Historical Determinants of Norwegian Foreign Policy." *FHFS (Research Centre for Defence History) Notat* 2 (1984).

Riste, Olav. "Fra integritetstraktat til atompolitikk: det stormaktsgaranterte Norge, 1905–1983." In *Defence Studies 1983–4*, edited by Rolf Tamnes. Oslo: Tanum-Norli, 1984.

Riste, Olav. "The Genesis of North Atlantic Defence Co-operation: Norway's "Atlantic Policy", 1940–45." In *Defence Studies 1981*, edited by Rolf Tamnes. Oslo: Tanum-Norli, 1982.

Riste, Olav. "Functional Ties – a Semi-Alliance? Military Co-operation in North-West Europe, 1944–1947. In *Defence Studies 1981*, edited by Rolf Tamnes. Oslo: Tanum-Norli, 1982.

Riste, Olav. "The Foreign Policy-Making Process in Norway: An Historical Perspective." In *Defence Studies 1982*, edited by Rolf Tamnes. Oslo: Tanum-Norli, 1983.

Riste, O. and R. Tamnes. "The Soviet Naval Threat and Norway." *FHFS (Research Centre for Defence History) Notat* 3 (1986).

Rosenberg, David Alan." 'A Smoking Radiating Ruin at the End of Two Hours': Documents on American War Plans for Nuclear War with the Soviet Union, 1954–1955." *International Security* 6 (Winter 1981/82).

Rosenberg, David Alan. "The Origins of Overkill: Nuclear Weapons and American Strategy, 1945–1960." *International Security* 7 (Spring 1983).

Rosenberg, David Alan. "Reality and Responsibility: Power and Process in the Making of United States Nuclear Strategy, 1945–68." *Journal of Strategic Studies* 9 (March 1986).

Rosenberg, David A. "American Postwar Air Doctrine and Organization: the Navy Experience." In *Air Power and Warfare: Proceedings of the Eight Military*

History Symposium, USAF Academy. Washington DC: Office of Air Force History, 1979.

Rosenberg, David A. "Arleigh Albert Burke." In *The Chiefs of Naval Operations*, edited by R.W. Love Jr. Annapolis: Naval Institute Press, 1980.

Rowen, Henry S. "The Evolution of Strategic Nuclear Doctrine." In *Strategic Thought in the Nuclear Age*, edited by Laurence Martin. London: Heinemann, 1979.

Spinardi, G., and Donald MacKenzie. "The Shaping of Nuclear Weapons Technology: US Fleet Ballistic Guidance System and Navigation: I From Polaris to Poseidon." *Social Studies of Science* 18 (August 1988).

Slessor, John. "British Defence Policy." *International Affairs* 35 (July 1957).

Tamnes, Rolf. "Integration and Screening: the two faces of Norwegian alliance policy." *FHFS (Research Centre for Defence History) Notat* 5 (1986).

Tamnes, Rolf. "Norges hemmelige tjenester under den kalde krigen: Et sammen-lignende internasjonalt perspektiv." *IFS Info* 2 (1992).

Thies, Wallace J. "Alliances and Collective Goods: A Reappraisal." *Journal of Conflict Resolution* 31 (June 1987).

Trachtenberg, Marc. "A 'Wasting Asset': American Strategy and the Shifting Nuclear Balance, 1949–1954." *International Security* 13 (Winter 1988/89).

Watt, D.C. "Demythologizing the Eisenhower Era." In *The Special Relationship: Anglo–American Relations Since 1945*, edited by W. Roger Louis and Hedley Bull. Oxford: Clarendon Press, 1986.

Wilkinson, E.P. "Nuclear Submarine Navigation." *Navigation* 5 (Autumn 1957).

Wells, Samuel F. "Sounding the Tocsin: NSC 68 and the Soviet Threat." *International Security* 4 (Fall 1979).

Wells, Samuel F. "The Origins of Massive Retaliation." *Political Science Quarterly* 96 (Spring 1981).

Wohlstetter, A.J. "The Delicate Balance of Terror," *Foreign Affairs* 37 (January 1959).

Zaloga, Steven J. "The Soviet Nuclear Bomb Programme: the First Decade," *Jane's Soviet Intelligence Review* 3 (April 1991): 174–181.

Ørvik, Nils. "NATO: The Role of the Small Members." *International Journal (Canadian Institute of International Affairs)* 21 (Spring 1966).

THESES, REPORTS AND UNPUBLISHED PAPERS

Breemer, Jan S. "Estimating the Soviet Strategic Submarine Missile Threat: A Critical Examination of the Soviet Navy's SSBN Bastion Strategy." Ph.D. diss., University of Southern California, 1987.

Cole, Paul M. "Neutralité du jour: The conduct of Swedish security policy since 1945." Ph.D. diss., The Johns Hopkins University, 1990.

Crowe, William J. "The Policy Roots of the Modern Royal Navy, 1946–1962." Ph.D. diss., Princeton University, 1965.

Hellebust, Anders. "NATO-fellesfinansiert og bilateral infrastrukturbygging i Norge: en analyse av beslutningsprosseser og innflytelsesrelasjoner." Dissertation (Hovedfag), University of Oslo, 1974.

Pruessen, Ronald W. "Making the World Safe for 'Ike's America': Perceptions of 'Dangers' and 'Enemies' in Eisenhower's Foreign Policies." Paper presented at the "Ike's America" conference, University of Kansas, October 1990.

Tamnes, Rolf. "Defence of the Northern Flank, 1949–56." Paper presented at the conference on "The North Atlantic Alliance, 1949–56," Freiburg, 11–13 September, 1990.

Turner, Howard. "Britain, The United States and Scandinavian Security Problems, 1945–1949." Ph.D. diss., Aberdeen University, 1982.

Wilkes, O. and N.P. Gleditsch. "Intelligence Installations in Norway: Their Number, Location, Function and Legality." Oslo: International Peace Research Institute, 1979.

Wohlstetter, A.J., F.S. Hoffman, R.J. Lutz, and H.S. Rowen, "Selection and Use of Strategic Air Bases" – A report prepared for USAF Project RAND, The RAND Corporation, R-266, April 1954.

Index